Brandywine Valley

THE INFORMED TRAVELER'S GUIDE

Brandywine Valley

Sharon Hernes Silverman

THE INFORMED TRAVELER'S GUIDE

STACKPOLE
BOOKS

To Alan, Jason, and Steven,
who make the Brandywine Valley
the most special place of all–home.

Copyright © 2004 by Sharon Hernes Silverman

Published by
STACKPOLE BOOKS
5067 Ritter Road
Mechanicsburg, PA 17055
www.stackpolebooks.com

Printed in China

10 9 8 7 6 5 4 3 2 1

FIRST EDITION

Design by Beth Oberholtzer
Cover design by Wendy Reynolds

Cover: *Winterthur's reflecting pool in autumn.* PHOTOGRAPH BY GOTTLIEB HAMPFLER, COURTESY OF WINTERTHUR, AN AMERICAN COUNTRY ESTATE.

Library of Congress Cataloging-in-Publication Data

Silverman, Sharon Hernes.
    The Brandywine Valley / Sharon Hernes Silverman.–1st ed.
        p.   cm.
    Includes bibliographical references and index.
    ISBN 0-8117-2974-5 (pbk.)
    1. Brandywine Creek Valley (Pa. and Del.)–Guidebooks. I. Title.
F157.B77S55   2004
917.48'10444–dc21

                                                                2003008845

CONTENTS

Introduction to the Brandywine Valley

The heart of the Brandywine Valley is nestled where Pennsylvania and Delaware form a ball-and-socket joint. Rich in history, culture, and natural beauty, this ideal vacation destination is conveniently situated just thirty miles southwest of Philadelphia. Quaint villages, exquisite gardens and estates, Revolutionary War sites, and world-class museums are just some of the delights the Brandywine Valley has to offer. Add its fine complement of art galleries and antique shops, places to canoe and hike, lovely backcountry roads, performing arts to suit every taste, and a variety of accommodations and dining options, and you'll begin to understand the appeal.

The Brandywine River itself rises in the Welsh Mountains of Chester County, Pennsylvania, and flows southward to join the Christina River in Wilmington, Delaware, before emptying into the Delaware River. Officially, it's known as a creek above Chadds Ford and a river below, but as a practical matter, the terms are used interchangeably.

Lenni-Lenape natives were the area's original inhabitants. The Dutch began exploring the area in the 1620s. Swedes, Finns, Dutch, and other European pioneers established settlements starting in the 1630s. The settlers appreciated the area's excellent natural resources: rich soil, a wealth of building materials including the greenish stone known as serpentine, thick forests, bountiful hunting and fishing, and the power generated by the Brandywine River.

The biggest single-day conflict of the Revolutionary War, involving twenty-six thousand soldiers, was the 1777 Battle of Brandywine near Chadds Ford, in which British and Hessian forces advancing on Philadelphia defeated George Washington's troops. The cannon fire soon quieted, but gunpowder would play a major role in the Brandywine Valley's development, thanks to the 1802 arrival of Eleuthère Irénée du Pont de Nemours and family. Their successful black powder mills near Wilmington generated immense wealth and influence for the du Ponts.

Andrew Wyeth is one of the many artists who have had a strong connection to the Brandywine Valley. This painting is *Arthur Cleveland*, 1946, tempera on board, forty-two inches by thirty-and-three-quarters inches. DELAWARE ART MUSEUM

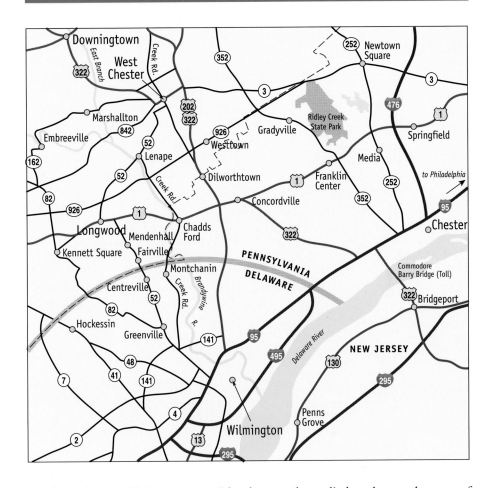

The nickname "château country" has been aptly applied to the area because of the du Pont mansions that dot the countryside. Today Winterthur and Nemours welcome visitors, as does Pierre S. du Pont's masterpiece, Longwood Gardens. Hagley Museum is on the site of the original powder mills. Many other local attractions owe their existence to *la famille* du Pont.

Wyeth is the other name forever intertwined with the Brandywine Valley. Patriarch N. C. Wyeth arrived in Chadds Ford in 1902 to study with illustrator and Wilmington native Howard Pyle. The collective style of Pyle and his many students came to be known as the Brandywine School.

N. C. Wyeth remained in the area for the rest of his life, working and raising a family. He trained his children in art while imparting his love of the land to them. This legacy is apparent in N. C.'s son Andrew Wyeth, for whom the landscape is a central character. Andrew's sisters Carolyn and Henriette were also painters, as were N. C.'s sons-in-law Peter Hurd and John McCoy. The artistic dynasty continues with Andrew's son Jamie, whose portraits of people and animals are particularly arresting.

Many works by the extended Wyeth family are displayed at the Brandywine River Museum, one of the area's top attractions. Other venues for art include the Delaware

The Conservatory at Longwood Gardens presents a spectacular display of blooms throughout the year.
LONGWOOD GARDENS/LARRY ALBEE

Art Museum and the Delaware Center for the Contemporary Arts, along with numerous galleries and public buildings.

The Brandywine Valley truly has something for everyone. History lovers will find plenty of places to visit, from Revolutionary War battlefields to Underground Railroad stations. Historic homes and museums are open for tours. For fans of antiques and decorative arts, Winterthur and Nemours are at the fore; shops throughout the area make it possible to purchase your own treasures. Prime shopping areas include downtown Wilmington, West Chester, Westtown, and Kennett Square, outlets along the Wilmington Riverfront (in Delaware, all shopping is tax-free), and the Olde Ridge Village Shoppes and the Chadds Ford Barn Shoppes, both in Chadds Ford. Sales of the electronic variety are showcased on the QVC Studio Tour.

Sports enthusiasts can visit the Delaware Sports Museum and Hall of Fame, take in a Wilmington Blue Rocks minor league baseball game, and perhaps attend an LPGA tournament or a professional tennis match. Families will enjoy local parks and playgrounds, as well as the American Helicopter Museum, Delaware Museum of Natural History, Hagley Museum, tall ship *Kalmar Nyckel,* and the Delaware Toy & Miniature Museum. If you like off-the-beaten-path spots, check out the Christian C. Sanderson Museum, Brinton 1704 House, and Baldwin's Book Barn. One-of-a-kind events like the annual Mushroom Festival, Chester County Day, Winterthur's Point-to-Point horserace, and the Great Pumpkin Carve are unique to the region.

And then there are the gardens. Longwood Gardens, Winterthur, the Nemours Mansion and Gardens, the wildflower garden at the Brandywine River Museum, and dozens of smaller horticultural gems bring a symphony of color to the Brandywine Valley. Major gardens have changing themes and events year-round. The countryside has its own casual floral charm, starting with daffodils, azaleas, cherry trees, and dogwoods in early spring, followed by blooming banks of daylilies throughout the summer, and then mellowing into the yellows, reds, and oranges of fall foliage before the first snow falls.

The Brandywine flows for sixty miles, far too large an area to cover thoroughly in one travel guide. For that reason, this book focuses on the core of the Brandywine Valley: Chadds Ford, Kennett Square, West Chester, and Wilmington.

A Word about Spelling

Careful readers will notice spelling and punctuation inconsistencies. These are

Much of the Brandywine Valley is known as horse country. You may spot an impeccably groomed horse and rider amidst the rolling hills. CHESTER COUNTY CONFERENCE AND VISITORS BUREAU

dictated by the preferences of the people and sites mentioned. For example, du Pont family members use a lowercase *d* and a space before *Pont,* except for Alfred I. duPont, who dispensed with the space. Then there's the DuPont Company, which prefers the capital *D* and no space, unless it's the complete company name, E. I. du Pont de Nemours and Company, Inc., in which case the rules are reversed.

Chadds Ford also has several variants. The ferryman's name was John Chad. His house, open as a historical site, is known as the John Chads House, *sans* apostrophe. The village calls itself Chadds Ford (two *d*s, no apostrophe); the winery is known as Chaddsford. Similarly, Marshallton appears with one *l* or two.

Spelling and punctuation appear as the individuals and institutions requested.

Getting to the Brandywine Valley

By Car

From the north, destination Pennsylvania: Take Interstate 95 south to U.S. Route 322 west to U.S. Route 1 south. Stay on Route 1 south for Chadds Ford and Kennett Square. If West Chester is your destination, turn off Route 1 to go north on U.S. Route 202.

From the north, destination Delaware: Take Interstate 95 south to Delaware Exit 7. Turn left at the top of the off-ramp to reach downtown Wilmington locations. (Note: Exits on I-95 are numbered separately by Pennsylvania and Delaware.)

From the south, destination Pennsylvania: Take Interstate 95 north to Delaware Exit 8, and follow U.S. Route 202 north into Pennsylvania. For West Chester, continue north on Route 202. For Chadds Ford and Kennett Square, turn left off Route 202 to go south on U.S. Route 1.

From the south, destination Delaware: Take Interstate 95 north to Delaware Exit 6. Follow Martin Luther King Boulevard east. Turn left on West Street or Walnut Street to reach the riverfront. For downtown Wilmington, get off I-95 at Delaware Exit 7. When the road comes to a **T** intersection at Delaware Avenue, turn right.

From the New Jersey Turnpike: Take the turnpike to its southern terminus, Exit 1. Take Interstate 295 (Delaware Memorial Bridge) west to Interstate 95 north. Follow directions for "From the south," above. Or take the turnpike to Exit 6, where it joins the Pennsylvania Turnpike. Follow the Pennsylvania Turnpike west to Exit 326, Valley Forge. Take U.S. Route 202 south toward West Chester. For West Chester, exit Route 202 onto High Street northbound. For Chadds Ford and Kennett Square, follow Route 202 south to U.S. Route 1 south. For Wilmington, follow Route 202 south to Interstate 95 south; get off at Delaware Exit 7B, and turn left at the top of the off-ramp to reach downtown Wilmington locations. Or, take the New Jersey Turnpike to Exit 2. Follow U.S. Route 322 west across the Commodore Barry Bridge. After a brief routing onto I-95 south, continue on Route 322 west to reach Pennsylvania, or remain on I-95 south to get to Wilmington.

From the west: Take the Pennsylvania Turnpike east to Exit 312, Downingtown. Follow PA Route 100 south to U.S. Route 202 south. For West Chester, exit Route 202 onto High Street northbound. For Chadds Ford and Kennett Square, follow Route 202 to U.S. Route 1 south. For Wilmington, follow Route 202 south to Interstate 95 south; get off at Delaware Exit 7B, and turn left at the top of the off-ramp to reach downtown Wilmington locations.

By Train

All north-south Amtrak trains (800-USA-RAIL, www.amtrak.com) stop in Wilmington, Delaware. The train station is centrally located at Martin Luther King Boulevard and French Street, just a few blocks from downtown hotels. In addition, SEPTA Commuter Rail Service (215-580-7800, www.septa.org) from Philadelphia has regular trains to and from Wilmington.

By Airplane

The closest major airport is Philadelphia International Airport (215-937-6937, www.phl.org), just a half-hour drive from the Brandywine Valley. The airport is served by US Airways (800-428-4322, www.usairways.com), American Airlines (800-433-7300, www.aa.com), and Delta Air Lines (800-221-1212, www.delta.com), among others.

An alternative entry point is Baltimore-Washington International Airport, about an hour-and-a-half drive from the Brandywine Valley (800-I-FLY-BWI, www.bwiairport.com).

Private and charter aircraft should contact New Castle County Airport just south of Wilmington (302-571-6474, www.newcastleairportilg.com).

Car Rental

For rental car information, contact Avis (800-230-4898, www.avis.com), Budget (800-527-0700, www.budget.com), Enterprise (800-Rent-a-Car, www.enterprise.com), or Hertz (800-654-3131, www.hertz.com).

Getting Around

Traveling on foot is easy in Chadds Ford, West Chester, Kennett Square, or Wilmington. SCCOOT (Southern Chester County Organization on Transportation, 877-612-1359, www.tmacc.org) buses run from West Chester south to Chadds Ford, Kennett Square, Avondale, West Grove, and Oxford. To go anywhere other than these destinations, or to see the more spread-out attractions, a car is essential.

The major arteries are U.S. Route 202, running north-south from West Chester to Wilmington; U.S. Route 1, running north-south at a different angle from Chadds Ford through Kennett Square; Creek Road (formerly PA/DE Route 100), running north-south from West Chester through Chadds Ford through Greenville, Delaware; and PA/DE Route 52, running southeast from Kennett Square through Mendenhall and Fairville, Pennsylvania, then through Centreville and Greenville, Delaware.

DART (800-652-DART, www.DartFirstState.com) is Wilmington's bus service. The number 32 rubber-tire trolley covers most of downtown Wilmington and the Christina Riverfront. Fare is just 25 cents for each ride.

Up-to-Date Information

Every effort has been made to ensure that all information is correct at press time; however, in a dynamic area like the Brandywine Valley, change does occur. Visit my *Brandywine Valley Guidebook* website, www.brandywineguide.com, for updated information. New information will be posted as soon as it is available. You may also contact me through that website with comments, suggestions, or corrections. It's a good idea to check directly with your destination, too.

Resources

You can learn more about the Brandywine Valley and get helpful trip-planning information from the following sources. Ask about getaway packages to get the most for your money, and mention any memberships, such as AAA or AARP, that may entitle you to additional discounts.

Borough of West Chester
401 E. Gay St.
West Chester, PA 19380
Telephone: 610-692-7574
Fax: 610-436-0009
Website: www.west-chester.com

The Brandywine Dot Com
www.thebrandywine.com
This website has good basic information. It accepts sponsored advertising. Double-check the information with the sites listed.

Brandywine Conference & Visitors Bureau
One Beaver Valley Rd.
Chadds Ford, PA 19317
Telephone: 610-565-3679 or 800-343-3983
Fax: 610-565-0833
Website: www.brandywinecvb.org

Brandywine Valley Guidebook website
www.brandywineguide.com
Service-oriented site maintained by the author. No advertising accepted.

Chamber of Commerce of Greater West Chester
40 E. Gay St.
West Chester, PA 19380
Telephone: 610-696-4046
Fax: 610-696-9110
Website: www.greaterwestchester.com

Chester County Conference & Visitors Bureau
400 Exton Square Parkway
Exton, PA 19341
Telephone: 610-280-6145 or 800-228-9933
Fax: 610-280-6179
Website: www.brandywinevalley.com

Chester County Conference & Visitors Bureau Visitors Center
300 Greenwood Rd.
(Off U.S. Route 1 near Longwood Gardens)
Kennett Square, PA 19348
Telephone: 610-388-2900 or 800-228-9933
Fax: 610-388-6241
Website: www.brandywinevalley.com

Chester County eConnection
www.ecountyinfo.com/pa/chester

City of Wilmington Office of Cultural Affairs
800 N. French St., 9th Floor
Wilmington, DE 19801
Telephone: 302-576-3095 (events hotline)
Website: www.ci.wilmington.de.us/
departments/cultural.htm

Delaware Division of the Arts
820 N. French St.
Wilmington, DE 19801
Telephone: 302-577-8278
Website: www.artsdel.org

Delaware State Parks
89 Kings Highway
Dover, DE 19901
Telephone: 302-739-4702
Website: www.destateparks.com

Delaware Tourism Office
99 Kings Highway
Dover, DE 19901
Telephone: 866-2-VISIT-DE
Fax: 302-739-5749
Website: www.VisitDelaware.com

Greater Wilmington Convention & Visitors Bureau
100 W. Tenth St., Suite 20
Wilmington, DE 19801-1661
Telephone: 302-652-4088 or 800-489-6664
Fax: 302-652-4726
E-mail: info@wilmcvb.org
Website: www.VisitWilmingtonDE.com

Kennett Square Borough
120 N. Broad St.
Kennett Square, PA 19348
Telephone: 610-444-6020
E-mail: ksboro@Kennett.net
Website: www.Kennett-square.pa.us

Kennett Square Revitalization Task Force
106 W. State St.
Kennett Square, PA 19348
Telephone: 610-444-8188
E-mail: ksrtf@Kennett.net
Website: www.historickennettsquare.com

Pennsbury Township
702 Baltimore Pike
Chadds Ford, PA 19317
Telephone: 610-388-7323
Fax: 610-388-6036
Website: www.pennsbury.pa.us

**Southern Chester County Chamber
of Commerce**
P.O. Box 395
206 E. State St.
Kennett Square, PA 19348
Telephone: 610-444-0774
Fax: 610-444-5105
E-mail: info@scccc.com
Website: www.scccc.com

Thornbury Township, Chester County
8 Township Dr.
Cheyney, PA 19319
Telephone: 610-399-1425
Fax: 610-399-6714
Website: www.thornburytwp.com

Thornbury Township, Delaware County
6 Township Dr.
Cheyney, PA 19319
Telephone: 610-399-8383
Fax: 610-399-3162
Website: www.thornbury.org

**West Chester Business Improvement
District and Welcome Center**
24 S. High St.
West Chester, PA 19382
Telephone: 610-738-3350
Fax: 610-692-9205
Website: www.westchesterbid.com

West Chester Recreation
401 E. Gay St.
West Chester, PA 19380
Telephone: 610-436-9010
Fax: 610-436-0009
Website: www.west-chester.com/recreation.htm

West Chester University
West Chester, PA 19383
Telephone: 610-436-1000
Website: www.wcupa.edu

West Goshen Township
1025 Paoli Pike
West Chester, PA 19380-4699
Telephone: 610-696-5266
Fax: 610-429-0616
Website: www.wgoshen.org

Westtown Township
1039 Wilmington Pike
Westtown, PA 19382
Telephone: 610-692-1930
Fax: 610-692-9651
Website: www.westtown.org

Keeping Informed

Newspapers

Daily Local News
250 N. Bradford Ave.
West Chester, PA 19382
Telephone: 610-696-1775
Fax: 610-430-1180
Website: www.dailylocal.com

Kennett Paper
112 E. State St.
Kennett Square, PA 19348
Telephone: 610-444-6590
Website: www.kennettpaper.com

News Journal
950 W. Basin Rd.
New Castle, DE 19720
Telephone: 302-324-2500 or 800-235-9100
Website: www.delawareonline.com

Philadelphia Inquirer
P.O. Box 8263
Philadelphia, PA 19101
Telephone: 215-854-2000
Website: www.philly.com

Magazines

Chester County Town & Country Living
510 B Durham Rd.
Newtown, PA 18940
Telephone: 215-968-0321
Fax: 215-968-0328
Website: www.buckscountymagazine.com

County Lines
ValleyDel Publications, Inc.
842 Street Rd., P.O. Box 31
Westtown, PA 19395
Telephone: 610-399-1720
Fax: 610-399-9738

Delaware Today
3301 Lancaster Ave., Suite 5-C
Wilmington, DE 19805
Telephone: 302-656-1809 or 800-285-0400
Fax: 302-656-5843
Website: www.delawaretoday.com

The Hunt
P.O. Box 336
Mendenhall, PA 19357
Telephone: 302-656-4868
E-mail: huntmag@mediatwo.com

Main Line Today
4699 West Chester Pike
Newtown Square, PA 19073
Telephone: 610-325-4630 or 888-217-6300
Website: www.mainlinetoday.com

Out & About Magazine
813 Tatnall St.
Wilmington, DE 19801
Telephone: 302-655-6483
Fax: 302-654-0569
Website: www.out-and-about.com

Philadelphia Magazine
1818 Market St.
Philadelphia, PA 19103
Telephone: 215-564-7700
Website: www.phillymag.com

Health and Safety

For emergencies, dial 911.

Hospitals

**Alfred I. duPont Institute/
DuPont Hospital for Children**
1600 Rockland Rd.
Wilmington, DE 19803
Telephone: 302-651-4186 (Emergency Services)
Website: www.nemours.org

Chester County Hospital
701 E. Marshall St.
West Chester, PA 19380
Telephone: 610-431-5000
Website: www.cchosp.com

St. Francis Hospital
Seventh and Clayton Sts.
Wilmington, DE 19805
Telephone: 302-421-4100
Website: www.stfrancishealthcare.org

Wilmington Hospital
501 W. Fourteenth St.
Wilmington, DE 19801
Telephone: 302-733-1000
Website: www.christianacare.org

Driving

It's a great pleasure to drive along country lanes in the Brandywine Valley. These backroads are often winding, hilly, and narrow. You may find yourself sharing the road with bicyclists or the occasional Amish buggy. Do not pass on hills or curves, or where passing is prohibited.

In towns like West Chester and Kennett Square, many intersections have all-way stop signs. At some intersections, however, traffic only stops in one direction. Do not assume that opposing traffic has a stop sign.

The traffic lights in Delaware aren't stuck, it just seems that way. You may have to wait several minutes for a light to turn green, especially on major highways like Concord Pike (U.S. Route 202) in Delaware.

Deer can be a serious road hazard, especially at dusk. Do not fixate on the deer that already ran across the road; the animals following it are the ones you have to worry about.

Pennsylvania requires all children under eight years old to ride in a child restraint seat (booster seat). Delaware requires the use of child safety seats for children under age four.

Lyme Disease

Where there are grass and trees, there may be ticks. A few simple precautions can help you avoid tick-borne health problems like Lyme disease, caused by the bacterium *Borrelia burgdorferi.* Here's what you should know.

Lyme disease is transmitted by black-legged ticks, also known as deer ticks. These ticks are so small—in their larval and nymphal stages the size of a tiny freckle—that many people do not even know they have been bitten.

To prevent Lyme disease, avoid tick habitats like wooded areas and tall grass when possible, especially in spring and summer; ticks can even be found on closely mown lawns. Wear light-colored clothes so it's easier to see ticks. Wear long sleeves, and tuck pant legs into your socks. DEET insect repellent reduces the risk of tick attachment. Use according to package directions.

A tick has to be attached for about thirty-six hours before infection occurs. Therefore, a nightly tick check, and removal of any attached ticks, can help prevent infection. Check all areas of skin, including the scalp, between the toes, and under the arms. Taking a vigorous shower in the evening may also wash off any unattached ticks. Be especially vigilant in checking children.

If you find an attached tick, don't panic. Remove it with tweezers positioned as close to the skin as possible. When you return home, consult your physician. Not all deer ticks carry Lyme. Be alert for a bull's-eye rash, achy joints, flulike symptoms, or malaise.

It can take up to a month for the early symptoms of Lyme disease to appear; in many cases, no symptoms are noticed, especially if the infected person is not aware of having been bitten. If you become ill sometime later, tell your physician you had been in an area where Lyme disease is known to exist.

Getting the Most for Your Money

Contact tourist boards to inquire about package deals.

Rates for accommodations vary widely depending on time of year, day of week, and method of reservation. Online reservation services are worth checking. In addition, contact hotels directly and ask for their best deals and any packages. Mention any memberships to organizations such as AAA, AARP, public radio, or frequent visitor clubs to see if a discount applies.

Chadds Ford

The village of Chadds Ford–fondly known as "Wyethville, U.S.A."–is the heart of the Brandywine Valley. Named for ferryman, farmer, and tavernkeeper John Chad, the village became a household word after the Battle of Brandywine on September 11, 1777, the biggest conflict of the Revolutionary War.

In more peaceful times, artists gravitated toward the sylvan landscape with its hills, forests, and the Brandywine River. Howard Pyle and his students, collectively known as the Brandywine School, put Chadds Ford at the forefront of early-twentieth-century illustration.

Pyle's most famous disciple was N. C. Wyeth, who settled in Chadds Ford and raised his family here. N. C.'s son Andrew is intimately identified with the area. In Andrew's paintings, the landscape takes on the role of a character, sometimes benign, sometimes vaguely disturbing. Andrew's son James completes the "Wyeth cubed" equation. Jamie's portraits of people and animals have detail and strength that make them absolutely mesmerizing.

The Wyeth dynasty extends to in-laws and cousins, including Peter Hurd, John McCoy, and others. Works from N. C., Andrew, James, and extended family members comprise the core of the collection at the renowned Brandywine River Museum.

Colonial transportation seems appropriate outside Brandywine Battlefield Park's historic buildings.
BRANDYWINE BATTLEFIELD PARK

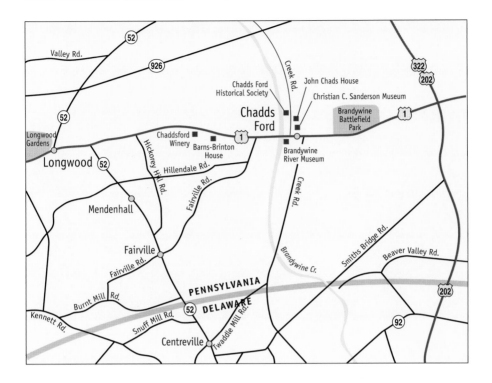

Getting Around

Although Chadds Ford is a village, there are no sidewalks. If you like to walk around, your best bet is to park the car at the Chadds Ford Barn Shoppes, located with the Brandywine River Hotel and the Chadds Ford Inn. Along with easy access to the dozen or so shops, boutiques, and an art gallery in the complex, you can easily reach the Christian C. Sanderson Museum, Chadds Ford Historical Society Headquarters, John Chads House, and Hank's Place on foot if you don't mind walking a few yards on the side of the road. Be careful, though, when crossing Creek Road.

A half-mile trail behind the Chadds Ford Historical Society barn leads to the Brandywine River Museum. If the weather has been wet recently, you may want to forgo this path, which can get muddy, and drive instead.

North on U.S. Route 1 is Brandywine Battlefield Park. South on Route 1 you'll find Chaddsford Winery and the Barns-Brinton House. Antique shops are located in both directions.

Several picturesque roads turn south off U.S. 1, including Creek Road, Ring Road, and Heyburn Road. If you enjoy taking a ride through the country, driving along the winding lanes over rolling hills is particularly rewarding.

Pennsylvania Route 52 from U.S. Route 1 south to the Delaware state line is a pretty drive lined with homes, estates, villages, and antique shops.

U.S. Route 202 marks the eastern edge of Chadds Ford. A mile or so south on 202 is the quaint Olde Ridge Shopping Village, with the more contemporary Glen Eagle Shopping Center on the other side of the highway.

The "balloon glow" at Pennsbury Township's annual event lights up the evening sky. SHARON HERNES SILVERMAN

SCCOOT (Southern Chester County Organization on Transportation) buses run from Chadds Ford north to West Chester and south to Kennett Square, Avondale, West Grove, and Oxford. For information on routes, fares, and schedules, call 877-612-1359, or visit www.tmacc.org.

Calendar of Events

Most local events are sponsored by the attractions featured in this chapter. Consult those listings for details.

Pennsbury Township sponsors an annual Pennsbury Land Trust Hot Air Balloon Festival one weekend in mid-September. About two dozen tethered hot-air balloons are lit Friday evening in a "balloon glow." The balloons look like giant colorful candles when the heaters are turned on. Festivities continue throughout the weekend, with balloons lifting off at sunrise and sunset. Admission is charged. Contact the township at 610-388-7323 or visit www.pennsbury.pa.us.

FEATURED ATTRACTIONS

Brandywine Battlefield Park

September 11 was a somber day in American history long before the terrorist attacks of 2001. On that date in 1777, the Battle of Brandywine between the British and Americans was fought. It was the largest single-day battle of the Revolutionary War, with twenty-six thousand soldiers involved, and proved to be a devastating defeat for George Washington's forces at the hands of Sir William Howe's army.

Visiting Brandywine Battlefield Park

1491 Baltimore Pike
U.S. Route 1 between U.S. Route 202 and Creek Rd.
(Mailing Address: Box 202), Chadds Ford, PA 19317
Telephone: 610-459-3342 • Website: www.ushistory.org/brandywine

Hours: March through November, Tuesday through Saturday, 9 A.M. to 5 P.M.; Sunday, noon to 5 P.M. Closed Mondays. In December, January, and February, Thursday through Saturday, 9 A.M. to 5 P.M.; Sunday, noon to 5 P.M. There are no house tours in winter, just the Visitor Center exhibits and video. House tours resume weekends in March.

Admission for house tours: Adults $5, seniors $3.50, ages six to seventeen $2.50. Ticket package includes exhibit, video, and house tours. Special reduced pricing during winter hours when house tours are closed.

Credit cards: Visa and MasterCard accepted for shop purchases and admission fees.

Personal checks: Checks accepted for shop purchases and admission fees.

Group tours: Available by advance arrangement. Call 610-459-3342, ext. 3003, or e-mail hmahnke@state.pa.us.

School programs: Programs geared to specific age groups are presented by Brandywine Battlefield Park staff in period garb. Topics include musket drills, colonial toys, a comparison of modern-day items with their colonial counterparts, and early American medicine. Available Monday through Friday. For details and reservations, call 610-459-3342, ext. 3003, or e-mail hmahnke@state.pa.us.

Special considerations: The Visitor Center is wheelchair accessible. The Benjamin Ring House and the Gideon Gilpin House are not accessible. Vans for tours are not wheelchair accessible, but arrangements are possible. Call 610-459-3342.

Shop: The museum shop sells books, maps, and other items relevant to the Battle of Brandywine. The shop closes at 4:30 P.M.

The fighting took place over a ten-square-mile area. Brandywine Battlefield Park preserves fifty-two acres of this land. Visitors can take guided tours of the Benjamin Ring House, which served as Washington's Headquarters, and the Gideon Gilpin House, where Lafayette stayed. The Visitor Center has an eighteen-minute video that gives a good summary of the battle—and what came before and after—along with exhibits and a museum shop.

The hilly park is part meadow and part forest and is a fine spot to walk, picnic, and ponder the events that took place here. If you visit during a reenactment, you won't have to imagine cannon fire and commotion, you'll experience it yourself.

The larger area of Brandywine Battlefield National Historic Landmark was dedicated as the first Commonwealth Treasure, to recognize its importance in the American Revolution.

The Battle

By late summer 1776, the flood of passion for independence that had begun with resistance to the Stamp Act of 1775, grown during flash points such as the Boston

Massacre and maintained its momentum from the opening battles at Lexington and Concord through the signing of the Declaration of Independence, had dwindled. The reality of war's carnage was sinking in. New York City fell to the British in the summer of 1776, leaving the Continental Army in tatters. Desertion and disobedience were common. Congress had failed to provide adequate artillery, uniforms, and basic supplies. Only Washington's Christmas night 1776 crossing of the ice-choked Delaware River on his way to success at Trenton and Princeton stopped the British from crushing the American Revolution completely.

These victories bought the Continentals some time, but the British weren't about to turn tail and go home. By spring 1777, Sir William Howe was making preparations for an assault on Philadelphia. In late August, Howe's army landed in Maryland, sixty miles away from the Continental capital. To achieve his goal, Howe would have to navigate at least one of the two obstacles in his way: the Schuylkill River and the Brandywine Creek.

As Howe's strategy became clear, Washington responded by moving his troops to protect the east bank of the Brandywine. His army was in place on September 9. The following day, Howe positioned his fighters six miles away in Kennett Square. His plan was to come around one or both of Washington's flanks.

Washington knew that Howe would have to cross the Brandywine at one of the various fords along the creek. From south to north, he stationed the majority of his troops at Pyle's Ford, Chads' Ferry, Chads' Ford (the spelling was changed later), Brinton's Ford, Jones' Ford, Wistar's Ford, and Buffington's Ford. The next ford north, Jefferies', was incorrectly reported to be impassable due to high water. The Continentals left it unprotected and vulnerable. Generals John Armstrong, Nathanael Greene, Anthony Wayne, and John Sullivan were the commanders in the field.

The Revolution's biggest battle comes to life at Brandywine Battlefield Park's annual reenactment.
BRANDYWINE BATTLEFIELD PARK

The British had two divisions. The main one, nearly eight thousand strong, was commanded by Gen. Charles Cornwallis; Hessian lieutenant general Wilhelm von Knyphausen led the other group of seven thousand men. Along with British Army regulars and Hessian troops were Americans who were loyal to the king.

The weather on September 11, 1777, was typical for late summer in the Brandywine Valley: hazy, hot, and humid, with morning fog. Knyphausen's task was to make a lot of noise and smoke, misleading Washington into thinking that the main attack would occur at Chads' Ford. This would give Cornwallis's column cover to cross the Brandywine to the north and descend on the right flank of Washington's army.

The Brandywine splits above Buffington's Ford. Cornwallis and his men crossed the west branch at Trimble's Ford around 9 A.M. Knyphausen marched from Kennett Square and ran into Washington's forces halfway to Chads' Ford. The Continentals retreated toward Kennett Meetinghouse.

As the infantry under American general William Maxwell moved back across the Brandywine, the artillery began to exchange fire. This peaceful hillside country had never seen anything like it. Cannons could be heard as far away as Philadelphia, more than twenty miles distant. Thick, white smoke clogged the humid air.

Then things got even more confusing. Washington first ordered Sullivan to attack Knyphausen, then changed his mind and called him back. Cornwallis's forces hadn't been spotted, so Washington considered the possibility that the British were trying to get the Americans to cross the Brandywine only to hit them from the rear. As several hours went by with no intelligence reports from the right flank, a frustrated Washington was indecisive on how to proceed.

Meanwhile, Cornwallis's men marched toward the east fork of the Brandywine and found Jeffries' Ford undefended. Unbelievably, the steep gorge the troops had to climb from the ford the half mile to Sconneltown, a perfect spot for the Americans to ambush the Brits, was also unguarded.

Finally, Washington received the news that Cornwallis's troops had been seen. He dispatched two divisions to head them off at Birmingham Meeting. Combat was intense. Muskets, rifles, and cannons fired continuously, and men fought hand-to-hand with bayonets. The Marquis de Lafayette, fighting in support of the Americans, was shot in the calf. The British advanced, and Sullivan had to retreat from Birmingham. Washington ordered troops from Chads' Ferry to Dilworthtown as backup for Sullivan. Adding to the Continentals' woes, one Maryland brigade mistakenly fired on another.

Late in the afternoon, Knyphausen's British and Hessians advanced toward Chads' Ford and Chads' Ferry, while American artillery on nearby hilltops tried to repel them. The Brandywine Creek ran red with British blood, yet the British continued to advance, gaining the crucial high ground.

As the day drew to a close, George Washington ordered a general retreat. In a valiant effort, Polish volunteer count Casimir Pulaski led a cavalry charge that may have averted more American casualties. The American toll was some three hundred dead, six hundred wounded, and three hundred captured. The British suffered at least ninety killed and four hundred wounded, most likely underestimates, plus an unknown number missing.

It was a terrible defeat for the Continentals. On September 26, Cornwallis and his men occupied Philadelphia. Washington was again defeated at the Battle of Germantown on October 4. The general and his troops would settle in for the long winter in Valley Forge. The battle may have been lost, but the war was far from over.

The Park

It is no small irony that the biggest battle of the Revolutionary War took place in the midst of a Quaker stronghold. Members of the Society of Friends were known for their pacifism; many today would be classified as conscientious objectors.

These principles meant that battles—and battle sites—were left largely unmemorialized. Interest in the area was kindled, however, when the Marquis de Lafayette toured the battlefield in 1824, pointing out the spot where he had been wounded. After the Civil War, some markers were installed in the Birmingham cemetery. In 1876, cannons were placed around the Sandy Hollow battlefield site near Dilworthtown. These cannons are still visible, as is the 1893 monument nearby on Birmingham Road that commemorates Lafayette's injury.

In 1947, Pennsylvania had the foresight to set aside fifty-two acres to honor what took place at the Battle of Brandywine and to interpret it for the public. Today the Pennsylvania Historical and Museum Commission, supported by the volunteer group Brandywine Battlefield Park Associates, offers exhibits and programs to interest and educate visitors.

After watching the video in the Visitor Center, take a look at the artifacts. A Ferguson rifle got its first real test in the Battle of Brandywine, proving its worth as a breech-loading weapon that had a rifle's accuracy but could be loaded more quickly than a musket. Bayonets and cannons were used extensively in the Battle of Brandywine. War and pageantry were closely allied at the time, as illustrated by the Scottish Highlanders' tartan kilts and the fifteen-inch-tall bearskin caps of the elite British grenadiers.

The guided tour of the Benjamin Ring House, rebuilt after it burned down in the 1930s, and the original Gideon Gilpin House takes about an hour. Washington made the Ring House his headquarters during the battle, and it's set up to look like it might have in 1777. Benjamin Ring was a Quaker miller who owned 160 acres of land.

Lafayette stayed in the nearby home of Gideon Gilpin. The main part of the stone building was constructed around 1745. It's arranged like a typical workman's home of the time. The Gilpins,

Youngsters learn how to handle wooden muskets at Brandywine Battlefield Park's reenactment.
SHARON HERNES SILVERMAN

also Quakers, had a 193-acre farm. The furnishings allow the tour guide to interpret the life of a prosperous farmer of that period.

Calendar of Events

Occasionally: "Meet a Hero from History." First-person interpreters portray people involved in the Battle of Brandywine and the Revolutionary War. Past subjects have included the Marquis de Lafayette, Sir William Howe, Gen. George Washington, Edward "Ned" Hector (a free black teamster and artilleryman), and Maj. Benjamin Tallmadge, Washington's chief intelligence officer.

February, usually the Sunday before Washington's Birthday, noon to 4 P.M.: Birthday celebration with musket drills, birthday cake, refreshments.

March, second Sunday, noon to 4 P.M.: Charter Day, commemorating William Penn's charter for Pennsylvania. Special program featuring colonial and military demonstrations. Free admission, including tours of historic houses.

April through October, second Sunday of the month, 1 to 4 P.M.: Living-history demonstrations, highlighting different aspects of colonial life, such as the life of a soldier and his family, the gruesome experiences of a physician, or eighteenth-century toys and games.

April and November, Saturdays, 10 A.M. to 12:30 P.M.: Narrated two-and-a-half-hour van tours of the ten-square-mile Brandywine Battlefield National Historic Landmark, revealing the full scope of this large battle. A guide explains sites, troop movements, and battle tactics along the seventeen-mile tour, which includes Old Kennett Meeting House, Osborne's Hill, Birmingham Meeting House, and Birmingham-Lafayette Cemetery. Admission fee. Reservations required.

June through August: Summer History Camp. Weeklong sessions geared to subsets of ages six to fourteen. Tuition fee. Advance registration required.

September, one Sunday late in the month, 10 A.M. to 4:30 P.M.: Revolutionary times battle reenactment, with hundreds of reenactors commemorating the battle and colonial life. Features two big battle reenactments complete with artillery and muskets, military encampments, music, entertainment, and eighteenth-century crafts. Admission: adults $10, ages twelve and under $2. Call 610-459-3342 for exact date.

November: Van tours. (See April.)

December, first Saturday, 2 to 7 P.M.: Candlelight Christmas in conjunction with the Chadds Ford Historical Society. A drive-yourself tour of several historic houses in the area. Colonial festivities, entertainment, and refreshments in the Visitor Center. One of the site's historic houses is often part of the park festivities. Admission charged. Reservations recommended.

Brandywine River Museum

It makes perfect sense for Chadds Ford to be the site of a world-class art museum. After all, it's at the heart of the Brandywine Valley, an area that has inspired artists for centuries. The restored mill that houses the Brandywine River Museum is so striking, and in such harmony with the environment, that it's worth a visit just to see the building itself. An internationally famous art collection, a wildflower garden, a tour of the N. C. Wyeth house and studio, and special exhibits and events make this a don't-miss destination.

Visiting the Brandywine River Museum

U.S. Route 1 just south of Creek Rd.
(Mailing address: P.O. Box 141), Chadds Ford, PA 19317
Telephone: 610-388-2700 • Fax: 610-388-1197
E-mail: inquiries@brandywine.org • Website: www.brandywinemuseum.org

Hours: Daily, 9:30 A.M. to 4:30 P.M. Closed Christmas. Wildflower and Native Plant Garden are open 8 A.M. to dusk.

Admission: Adults $6; seniors, students with identification, and children six to twelve $3; free for members and children under six. Audio tours $3. Studio tours $3 plus regular admission. Group rates available with advance reservations. Gardens free.

Credit cards: MasterCard and Visa.

Personal checks: Accepted with proper identification.

Group tours: Guided tours for groups of fifteen or more can be scheduled Monday through Friday. Self-guided tours can be scheduled on weekends. Contact the group tours office at 610-388-8366 for reservations and information, or e-mail grouptours@brandywine.org.

School programs: School programs can be arranged. Call the education office, 610-388-8382, or e-mail education@brandywine.org.

Special considerations: The museum, N. C. Wyeth House and Studio, and the shuttle bus to the studio tour are wheelchair accessible. Strollers are prohibited during certain exhibitions, notably at Christmastime. Children may be carried in backpacks. Call ahead for details and restrictions.

Shop: The museum shop offers art, environmental, and children's books; art reproduction; and arts and crafts collectibles. Phone 610-388-8326 to reach the shop directly.

Restaurant: A restaurant overlooking the Brandywine serves sandwiches, hot entrees, and soups. Beer and wine are available. Hours: 10 A.M. to 3 P.M. Closed Mondays and Tuesdays in January, February, and March.

In 1967, local residents got wind of a plan to develop the area around Hoffman's Mill, a nineteenth-century gristmill. They mobilized quickly and bought the land at auction before it could be snapped up for industrialization. That group, the Brandywine Conservancy, is still passionately dedicated to preserving the Brandywine environment and heritage through its Brandywine River Museum and Environmental Management Center.

"We started as an environmental organization," explains Halsey Spruance, public relations director at the Brandywine Conservancy, "protecting water quality and quantity. Preserving open space also preserves the natural and cultural resources that have inspired the artists and lets visitors see what inspired them." So far, the Conservancy has been responsible for protecting more than thirty-eight thousand acres, including scenic views.

Baltimore architect James R. Grieves accepted the Conservancy's challenge to transform Hoffman's mill, and in 1971, the Brandywine River Museum opened. The building radiates from a brick-floored circular stairway. Pine floors, original

The Brandywine River Museum is housed in a restored mill surrounded by beautiful wildflower gardens.
BRANDYWINE RIVER MUSEUM

John W. McCoy: Defining Himself through Art

Artist is the last profession anyone would have predicted for Delaware native John McCoy, born in 1910. McCoy's father, Jack, was a business executive for DuPont and had a rigid career path in mind for his son. Jack McCoy insisted that his son get a traditional education, despite John's obvious artistic talent.

McCoy went off to Cornell University, but instead of majoring in business or engineering, he pursued a bachelor's degree in fine arts, graduating in 1933. From this quiet young man, an emotional intensity was emerging, expressed through his paintings. McCoy's training continued at the Beaux Arts School in Fontainebleau, France, and at the Pennsylvania Academy of Fine Arts in Philadelphia.

The seminal time in McCoy's life and work began in 1933, when he was dating Andrew Wyeth's sister, Ann, whom he subsequently married. N. C. Wyeth, the family patriarch, invited McCoy to study with him as partner and foil for seventeen-year-old Andrew. The two painted together for about two years in the studio, then outdoors until the early 1950s.

McCoy's inclusion in the Wyeth family was good for him and for them. The Wyeths' warmth melted McCoy's stiffness a little. At the same time, his discipline, steadiness, and dignity brought calmness to a sometimes zany bunch.

John McCoy taught for a quarter century at the Pennsylvania Academy of Fine Arts. He continued to paint, with a hiatus to work for DuPont during World War II. His technique evolved from oil, tempera, and watercolor to mixed media inspired in part by Abstract Expressionism and in part by his own desire for experimentation.

One painting may have been an attempt to resolve a heartbreaking event from McCoy's childhood. "When my father was about eight, he had some pigeons in cages that were his pets," says his daughter, called Anna B. "He was taking care of them and he would feed them and he loved them. I believe he had gotten sick, and maybe the doctor said that the birds could have been making him sick. My grandfather let them out and shot them." Anna B. speculates that Jack McCoy was motivated by a philosophy that boys should be tough and unsentimental.

In 1948, John McCoy painted *Craige's Meadow,* a view of a field as seen from between two pillars of a barn. Nestled in the rafters are two pigeons, safe and sound. In this painting, John McCoy sheltered the birds he had been unable to protect as a boy.

Alzheimer's disease stopped McCoy from painting in the early 1980s. The 1982 dark and brooding mixed media *Thunderclouds* was an omen of the approaching storm. John McCoy died in 1989.

"I believe he painted for all the right reasons," says Anna B. McCoy—a painter herself—with fondness and respect. "He loved it. He wanted to paint. He had to."

Forest Light, mixed media on paper, was painted by John McCoy c. 1970. ANNA B. MCCOY; PRIVATE COLLECTION

beams, and pristine white plaster walls evoke the feeling of the old mill without being a cliché. Huge glass walls offer spectacular views of the Brandywine River.

The museum focuses on American art with emphasis on landscapes, still lifes and genre paintings, illustration, and Wyeth family art. A recently added fifteen-thousand-square-foot wing has provided two new galleries, a library, storage space, and a children's classroom. Future plans include tours of the nearby Kuerner Farm, which inspired many of Andrew Wyeth's paintings and is now owned by the museum.

Changing exhibitions highlight important aspects of American art and regional accomplishments. Past shows include *A Brush with Conflict: The Battle of Brandywine in Art* and *Elegant Etiquette: 19th-Century Figural Napkin Rings.*

If you bring children with you, the $1.95 *Family Guide: A Museum Activity Book* may make the visit more interesting and enjoyable. It can be used during or after the visit to encourage youngsters to interact with and appreciate the art.

The Collections

The Brandywine Valley has long influenced landscape painters. In fact, the country's first published lithograph, by Bass Otis in 1819, was a Chester County scene, *House and Tree at Waterside.*

Artists interested in observing nature and drawing from real life continued to come here to explore the relationship between man and nature. Hudson River School painters like William Trost Richards, Thomas Doughty, Thomas Cole, and Jasper Cropsey extended the tradition of landscape painting in this region, followed by painters as diverse as George Cope, Clifford Ashley, Peter Hurd, and George Weymouth.

Still life painting also has strong roots here. This style was especially popular in the late nineteenth century. Many *trompe l'oeil* ("fool the eye") works were done for gentlemen's clubs, hence the preponderance of posthunt tableaux and other heavy masculine subjects. William Michael Harnett and George Cope are two of the artists whose works are displayed.

The interior scenes known as American genre painting give a wonderfully intimate look into people's everyday lives. Horace Pippin, born in West Chester, painted captivating scenes of family and community.

The Brandywine River Museum is a major repository of American illustration and interprets that art form's influence on our artistic and social heritage. A veritable parade of illustrators marched to the Brandywine Valley, beginning with F. O. C. Darley, who settled just north of Wilmington in 1859. Howard Pyle, who revolutionized illustration by bringing drama and dimensionality to it, ran art schools in Wilmington and Chadds Ford. The generation of illustrators he trained—Frank Schoonover, Violet Oakey, Jessie Willcox Smith, N. C. Wyeth, and others—carried his principles forward and created skillful, imaginative pictures. Books containing illustrations by Pyle and his students are periodically reissued and are still loved today. Other illustrators and cartoonists whose works are in the museum's collections are Winslow Homer, Charles Dana Gibson, Maxfield Parrish, Al Hirschfeld, Charles Addams, Charles Schulz, and Theodor Geisel, a.k.a. Dr. Seuss.

Wyeth family art is the backbone of the museum, with illustrations and paintings by N. C.; watercolor, dry brush, and tempera paintings by Andrew in the

White walls and wooden support beams house the art galleries in the Brandywine River Museum.
BRANDYWINE RIVER MUSEUM

gallery named for him; and precise portraits and landscapes by Jamie. Henriette Wyeth Hurd and Carolyn Wyeth, two of Andrew's sisters, also have works on display, as do Peter Hurd and John W. McCoy, two of Andrew's brothers-in-law, and other members of the extended Wyeth family.

The Grounds

Take some time to stroll through the Wildflower and Native Plant Garden. The staff of the Brandywine Conservancy selects plants to provide a succession of bloom from early spring through the first hard frost. Plants are set in their preferred habitat: woodland, wetland, flood plain, or meadow.

The path between the museum and the river is a favorite among visitors, especially children. Two lifesize sculptures, a cow named *Miss Gratz* by J. Clayton Bright and a pig named *Helen* by André Harvey, create a bronze petting zoo. Kids are welcome to hug the sculptures, climb on them, and pretend to feed them. The river is only a few steps away, though, so keep an eye on the wee ones.

Ambitious walkers with sturdy shoes may want to follow the path along the Brandywine, under U.S. Route 1, and on to the Chadds Ford Historical Society headquarters. The short part of the path that goes under the road bridge isn't very scenic, though the rest is, and sometimes the boardwalk that runs to the Historical Society is damaged by severe weather, but it's still a pleasant walk on a nice day. It's best to walk back on the same path, making a mile round-trip.

The N. C. Wyeth House and Studio

In 1911, flush with the proceeds from his illustrations of *Treasure Island*, N. C. Wyeth bought eighteen acres on Rocky Hill, about a half mile from the village of Chadds Ford. Its northern exposure and scenic view were just what N. C. had been looking for. Today visitors can tour Wyeth's house and studio to get some insight into how the illustrator lived and worked until his death in 1945. His widow remained in the house until 1973. Their daughter, Carolyn, lived in the house and painted in the studio until she died in 1994.

The shuttle bus from the museum first stops at the house, a brick structure with white-painted wood accents and balcony. Indoors, the Big Room is set up to look like it would have in the 1930s. This is where the action was for the Wyeth family. The large, brick fireplace warmed the room, from the oriental rugs over wood floors to the white-painted ceiling with deep white beams. N. C., wife Carolyn (usually called Carol), and their brood of five listened to the radio here and gathered near the Christmas tree. The children did their lessons, read, discussed their paintings, and worked on their music in this room. The tour guide may point out a bust of N. C.'s favorite composer, Ludwig von Beethoven, on the windowsill, reminding visitors that daughter Ann was nicknamed "Beethoven" because of her precocious interest in music—and because an occasional facial expression made her resemble the composer.

Artwork in the Big Room includes a 1982 painting Andrew Wyeth did of his sister Carolyn sitting on the porch. One of N. C.'s originals also hangs here. *Henriette in the Orchard* was painted around 1910 in an Impressionist style very different from N. C.'s illustrations, evidence of his periodic experimentation with styles other than illustration. A study for a mural is surrounded with nails, guides that helped the artist move from the smaller piece to a wall-size work.

The other room on the house tour is the dining room. On the way there from the Big Room, peek into the pantry to see some of the linens and dishes collected by Mrs. Wyeth.

The dining room was originally a kitchen. A 1926 extension added the pantry and a new kitchen, plus two bedrooms on the second floor; the previous kitchen became the dining room. The appointments in the snug room are rich but tasteful. Oak paneling covers the walls and the side of the stairway. Spode dinnerware is displayed on the hutch. Four silver candlesticks from the Philadelphia jewelry store Bailey, Banks, & Biddle were a gift from N. C. to his wife. They are engraved with the couple's initials and the date 1925.

The paintings in the dining room belonged to the Wyeths but were not done by family members. Some are portraits of their ancestors. There are also two unsigned paintings of the USS *Constitution* in battle during the War of 1812.

After about ten to twelve minutes in the house, visitors reboard the shuttle bus for a sixty-second ride farther up the hill past the springhouse and the 1912 barn to the studio, made a National Historic Landmark in 1997.

A stone path leads to the studio entryway. Here some relevant artifacts are displayed, including a famous photo of N. C. in his cowboy gear, complete with buffalo-hide chaps. At the suggestion of Howard Pyle, Wyeth journeyed west to Colorado, Arizona, and New Mexico in 1904 to immerse himself in cowboy culture, the better to paint it on his return. The woolly chaps are stored in the huge wooden trunk under the photo.

The next room is the main studio, designed largely by the artist, where visitors feel the presence of N. C. Wyeth most keenly. On the north side of the room is a large Palladian window that lets in the light the painter craved. N. C.'s last painting, a picture of George Washington, remains unfinished on his easel. The palette and brushes he was using on that painting are also on display. The palette is huge, about eighteen inches from end to end. It's symbolic of the artist himself: slightly bigger than life.

The reflection of the studio's Palladian window can be seen in the reproduction of *Dusty Bottle,* painted in this room. Wyeth sometimes boasted how fast he could complete a picture. He triumphantly marked this still life "3 HRS" in the upper right corner.

The studio also houses several busts, including one of George Washington that N. C. was using for his final painting, and life masks of Beethoven and Abraham Lincoln. The most memorable prop is the birch bark canoe that hangs from the ceiling. You're welcome to sit on a bench and soak up the atmosphere while the guide talks.

The next room is the mural studio. The building's open plan has the rooms flowing into one another, so it's easy to see into the mural studio even though visi-

N. C. Wyeth stored props, like this birch bark canoe, in his studio. The building is open to visitors seasonally. BRANDYWINE RIVER MUSEUM

tors are not permitted to enter that area. It was added in 1923 to replace a smaller section. One wall is almost completely windows, but these are greenhouse-style rather than Palladian.

N. C. Wyeth painted thirteen murals in his career. One is displayed here. It was done in 1932 for the Penn Mutual Life Insurance Company in Philadelphia. The pictorial history of William Penn is eleven feet wide and fourteen feet high. Wyeth used the canvas like a chronology: seventeenth-century England with King Charles II appears on the right, then a picture of the ship Penn came over on, followed by a depiction of Quaker Pennsylvania. To create something this large, N. C. sometimes used a projector to enlarge pictures of his studies to mural size. Finished panels were removed from their frames, rolled up, and transported to their destination, where N. C. supervised the final installation.

The Wyeths used the studio space for more than painting. Birthday celebrations, Halloween parties, plays, even Ann Wyeth's wedding to John W. McCoy took place here.

In the prop room on the way out, every artifact evokes one of N. C.'s beloved illustrations. From a saddle to snowshoes, farm implements to moccasins, Wyeth got the details just right.

Calendar of Events

April through mid-November, Wednesday through Sunday: N. C. Wyeth House and Studio tours. Shuttle buses leave the museum for forty-five-minute tours at timed intervals beginning at 10 A.M. Tour and van are wheelchair accessible. No children under six. No indoor photography. No restrooms at house or studio. $3 per person, in addition to museum admission. Reservations recommended. Pick up tickets and check in at the museum shop.

May, Mother's Day weekend, 9:30 A.M. to 4:30 P.M.: Wildflower, plant, and seed sale. Admission free to the sale in the courtyard.

May, Memorial Day weekend, 10 A.M. to 5 P.M.: Antiques show, featuring furniture, porcelain, glass, silver, rugs, prints, and other objects. $7 fee includes museum admission.

July, Thursday mornings: Educational workshops for children ages three to eleven accompanied by an adult. Each program includes a thematic guided museum tour followed by a hands-on art project. Free with museum admission. Preregistration required; call the education office at 610-388-8382 or e-mail education @brandwine.org.

September and October, most weekends: Fall harvest market. Regional artisans showcase their crafts in the courtyard. Free with museum admission.

November and December, most weekends: Holiday shops. Regional artisans exhibit and sell their work on a rotating basis, with seven featured each weekend. Free with museum admission.

The day after Thanksgiving through early January, daily except Christmas, 9:30 A.M. to 4:30 P.M., and until 6 P.M. between Christmas Day and New Year's Day: A Brandywine Christmas. Holiday displays include an O-gauge model railroad on more than two thousand feet of track, an elaborate Victorian dollhouse, and thousands of "critter" ornaments.

December, first weekend: Critter Sale. Ornaments of natural materials handmade by museum volunteers are on sale to the public. These exquisite, whimsical pieces have adorned trees at the White House and the Smithsonian Institution. Admission free to the sale in the basement lecture room.

Chadds Ford Historical Society

"Necessity is the mother of invention," the saying goes, and such is the case with the Chadds Ford Historical Society. When the John Chads House was on the market in 1968, a group of local citizens feared that its sale could result in the historic property's destruction. To prevent this, they formed the nonprofit Chadds Ford Historical Society and acquired the house themselves. The following year, the group also purchased the Barns-Brinton House, a few miles away.

Thanks to these dedicated individuals, both of these early-eighteenth-century structures have been returned to their original luster. Nationally known restoration architect John Milner oversaw the restoration process. The John Chads House and the Barns-Brinton House were added to the National Register of Historic Places in 1971 and are designated as "contributing resources" of the Brandywine Battlefield National Historic Landmark.

To better fulfill its mission to preserve, interpret, and educate the public about life in Chadds Ford, especially during the eighteenth century, the Society built a headquarters in 1991. Designed to look like a Pennsylvania bank barn, the building, known as the Barn, is across the street from the John Chads House on the site of a former dairy barn. The Barn houses a small museum, a library, offices, and a meeting room. A retail display offers items for sale. An original springhouse on the grounds is open to visitors during the summer tour season.

The John Chads House has a beehive oven visible at left. CHADDS FORD HISTORICAL SOCIETY

Visiting the Chadds Ford Historical Society

1736 Creek Rd., .25 mile north of U.S. Route 1
(Mailing address: P.O. Box 27), Chadds Ford, PA 19317
Note: The John Chads House is directly opposite from the Barn,
and the springhouse is at the same site. The Barns-Brinton House is on
U.S. Route 1 at Pond's Edge Drive near Chaddsford Winery, 1.5 miles south
of the Brandywine River Museum.
Telephone: 610-388-7376 • Fax: 610-388-7480
E-mail: info@chaddsfordhistory.org • Website: www.chaddsfordhistory.org

Hours: The Barn, including the museum room and small shop, is open Monday through Friday, 9 A.M. to 2 P.M. From May through September, also open on Saturday and Sunday, noon to 5 P.M. The Barns-Brinton House, John Chads House, and springhouse are open from May through September, noon to 5 P.M.

Admission: Free to the Barn; $5 for adults to enter all three other sites; $3 for children.

Group tours: Year-round by appointment.

Food: Not available on-site. Several restaurants are nearby, including Hank's Place, the Chadds Ford Inn, and the café located inside the Brandywine River Museum. There are other restaurants located both north and south on U.S. 1.

Special considerations: The Barn is wheelchair accessible; the historic properties are not.

Parking: Free on-site parking is available at the Barn (for the Barn, John Chads House, and springhouse) and at the Barns-Brinton House. For some special events, parking is extended onto the meadow next to the Barn on Creek Road.

The Society maintains a collection of objects and photographs significant to the history of Chadds Ford. Some of these artifacts are used to furnish the John Chads House and the Barns-Brinton House, while others are displayed on a rotating basis in the museum room. A short video explains some local history.

Education is a key component of the Chadds Ford Historical Society's activities. In spring, a lecture series presents free talks by area historians. From May through September, visitors can tour the Society's two historic houses, led by a guide in colonial dress, and can explore the springhouse on their own. Hearth cooking is demonstrated regularly. Other living-history programs acquaint twenty-first-century folks with things like medicinal herbs, dairying, and colonial family life.

Major events are held throughout the year. An antique car show with gleaming automobiles takes place in July. At the Chadds Ford Days Colonial Fair in September, artists and artisans display and sell their wares. Some eighteenth-century crafts are demonstrated.

A one-of-a-kind festival is the Great Pumpkin Carve, held annually before Halloween. Dozens of huge pumpkins are delivered to the field behind the Barn for the carving competition. The incredible results are lit and displayed for several evenings. Past creations have included Cinderella's carriage, a pumpkin marionette theater where large pumpkins manipulated smaller ones on strings, a turtle, a fire-breathing dragon, and, in homage to Andrew Wyeth's best-known model, a Helga pumpkin complete with braids.

The self-drive Candlelight Christmas program is held in conjunction with Brandywine Battlefield. Several local homes of historical significance open their doors to visitors. The Chadds Ford Historical Society's properties and the Battlefield also welcome visitors.

For walkers, a trail maintained by the Brandywine Conservancy starts behind the Barn, goes under U.S. Route 1, and leads to the Brandywine River Museum. Most of the path is scenic (though the part under the road bridge isn't), and sometimes the boardwalk that covers part of the trail is damaged by severe weather, but it's a fine walk on a nice day. It's best to return on the same path, making a mile round-trip. Other worthwhile stops nearby include the Christian C. Sanderson Museum and the Chadds Ford Barn Shoppes behind that museum. If you choose to walk along Creek Road to get from one site to another, be careful on the busy road.

John Chads House

The village of Chadds Ford is named for John Chad (he used only one *d*), a well-known local ferryman and farmer. Chad was well off, having inherited five hundred acres of land along the Brandywine from his father, but he lived unostentatiously, in keeping with his Quaker upbringing. The bluestone building where he made his home was constructed circa 1725 on a hillside above the water, giving it a commanding view and some protection against flooding. It was built into the hill bank-style and is a fine example of early-eighteenth-century Pennsylvania architecture. The exterior of the well-proportioned house has a continuous cornice; inside, wood paneling and trim are indicators of the owner's social status.

Chad married Elizabeth Richardson in 1729. By 1736, the enterprising Chad had received a tavern license and had begun a ferry service. He leased both businesses to a relative in the 1740s.

Elizabeth Chad continued to live in the house from the time John Chad died in 1760 until her death thirty years later. She was at home during the Battle of Brandywine on September 11, 1777, when smoke from cannon and musket fire hung heavy in the humid air. Elizabeth reportedly hid her silver spoons in her pocket in case of looting. She watched the movements of Hessian and Continental forces from the attic window, but her property and her person remained safe.

Today the building has been authentically restored and furnished. Many of its features, including the wide plank floors, are original. Touring the house gives visitors insight into the lifestyle of the home's eighteenth-century occupants. The beehive oven is often used. If you're lucky, you'll get to sample some fresh-baked goods.

Springhouse

A springhouse near the Barn is open for self-guided tours. It may well have been completed before the John Chads House so that Chad, a stonemason, and the mason's apprentices had a roof over their heads while the house was being built. After Chad moved into his new home, the springhouse was occupied by a tenant who worked on Chad's land. Tradition has it that during the Battle of Brandywine, the northwest corner of the structure was damaged by British and Hessian artillery fire.

From 1837 to 1839, the building served as a one-room school, and it is interpreted as such today. When there is sufficient water, you can still see the spring running through the lower level.

Barns-Brinton House

Just two miles from the John Chads House is the Barns-Brinton House. Originally the home and business of tavernkeeper and blacksmith William Barns, the structure was built in 1714. Ideally situated on what was at the time the major highway between Philadelphia and Baltimore, the spacious brick building had a private side for the family and an inn side, complete with bar, to accommodate guests. The house is recognized for its Flemish bond brickwork with black headers.

Barns operated the tavern from 1722 until his death in 1731. After that, the house was sold several times. It was purchased by James Brinton (grandson of one of the area's earliest settlers, William Brinton) in 1753 and remained in the Brinton family for more than a century.

The part of the house now visible from U.S. Route 1 is actually the back. Before the road was relocated in 1938, it ran right in front of what is now the kitchen garden outside the home's true front entrance.

Visitors will appreciate the fine woodwork and paneling in the interior of the house. Much of the original hardware, probably wrought by Barns himself, is still intact. The cage bar on the first floor, where the tavern owner could lock up his spirits, was installed in 1982 with guidance from architect John Milner as to the position of the original bar.

The Barns-Brinton House on U.S. Route 1 next to the Chaddsford Winery has a thriving herb garden out front. CHADDS FORD HISTORICAL SOCIETY

No boring jack-o-lanterns here: the annual Great Pumpkin Carve inspires amazing creations. CHADDS FORD HISTORICAL SOCIETY

Hearth cooking is demonstrated on summer Saturdays. Guides provide information about herbs, baking, and other aspects of eighteenth-century life and are happy to give out recipe cards. If you're inspired by the idea of a tavern, it's a short walk up a footpath to Chaddsford Winery.

Calendar of Events

February and March: Kids' art exhibit. Local school students enter an art show with a historical theme. Contact the society for requirements, prizes, and exhibit times.

April, Tuesday evenings at 7:30 P.M. Lecture series. Area historians give talks on a variety of topics. Advance registration required. Admission is free.

May: Golf outing fund-raiser at the Wyncote Golf Club in Oxford, Pennsylvania. Open to all: entry fee is $150 per person. Contact the Society for details.

May through September, weekends, noon to 5 P.M. John Chads House, Barns-Brinton House, and the Barn. Guided tours of eighteenth-century restorations and "domestick" arts demonstrations, including cooking. In the Barn, see the video *Sharing the Spirit* and current exhibits. Admission fee of $5 covers the John Chads House, springhouse (self-guided), and Barns-Brinton House; admission to the Barn is free.

July, one Saturday late in the month, from 9 A.M. to 3 P.M. Antique car show featuring pre-1982 vehicles: antique, street rod, and classic, as well as motorcycles. Adults $2, under twelve free. Food is available. A flea market is also on site.

September, the weekend after Labor Day: Chadds Ford Days open-air colonial fair. Colonial crafts are demonstrated and sold. Live music, country rides, games, and food. Held in the meadow on the Society grounds. Adults $5, ages seven to twelve $1, ages six and under free.

October, the Thursday through Saturday before Halloween: The Great Pumpkin Carve. On Thursday from 5 to 9 P.M., local artists, families, and business representatives carve dozens of huge pumpkins on the grounds of the Chadds Ford Historical Society. Friday and Saturday from 5 to 9 P.M., candle-lit carved pumpkins, with winners identified in several categories, are displayed on the grounds. All three nights offer music, hayrides, and food. Ages seven and up $2, ages six and under free.

Late November through the Sunday after Christmas, Monday through Friday, 9 A.M. to 2 P.M.; Saturday and Sunday, noon to 4 P.M. Holiday tree exhibit in the Historical Society Barn.

December, first Saturday, 1 to 6 P.M. Candlelight Christmas, jointly sponsored by the Chadds Ford Historical Society and Brandywine Battlefield Park Associates. This drive-yourself tour ushers in the holiday season with a festive tour of several of the Brandywine Valley's finest private homes and historical sites. All are candlelit and dressed in their holiday finery. Advance tickets for adults are $14; tour-day tickets cost $17. Tickets are $5 for children twelve and under. Wear low-heeled, comfortable shoes. Group tours cannot be accommodated.

Chaddsford Winery

Chaddsford Winery proves once and for all that there doesn't have to be anything snobby about great wine and the people who make it. Since 1982, owners Eric and Lee Miller have developed a high-tech winemaking operation of the first order, garnering a magnum of awards along the way. At the same time, the couple has remained accessible, enthusiastic, friendly, and committed to educating people about wine.

"What I want to get across," says Lee, "is that it's easy to learn about wine and to be comfortable with wine. By coming to a place like this, you get a lot of education. We can help you figure out what you like and why. Then you can use that knowledge when you order wine in a restaurant or serve it at home."

Tours begin in the renovated seventeenth-century barn that now houses the winery. "Our goal is to give people an understanding of what a wine really is by showing how it's made," says Lee. "Wines are just like a food, pretty simple, with minimal processing."

In the small vineyard out front, the tour guide explains the different tastes of different types of grapes. The group then moves back inside to the aging tanks and barrels for a discussion of how aging determines flavor. "We tell them that some wines are aged in stainless steel tanks to preserve the light, fruity smells and flavors, while others are aged in oak barrels to produce more

Wine aged in wooden barrels takes on a rich, earthy taste. CHADDSFORD WINERY

Visiting Chaddsford Winery

632 Baltimore Pike (U.S. Route 1), Chadds Ford, PA 19317
Telephone: 610-388-6221 • Fax: 610-388-0360
E-mail: cfwine@chaddsford.com • Website: www.chaddsford.com

Hours: Open daily noon to 6 P.M. for tours, tasting, and sales. Closed New Year's Day, Easter, Thanksgiving, Christmas. Tours last about a half hour.
Bus groups: By reservation only.
Shop: Store on site sells wine and related items.
Special considerations: Not wheelchair accessible. Children may take the tour, but tasting is limited to age twenty-one and over.

earthy, woody wines," Lee explains. "People will say, 'Oh, that's why I like some wines.' One simple thing can really open the world to them."

The guide discusses sweet wines versus dry ones and tells visitors about the fermentation process that converts sugars to alcohol. Several wines are available for tasting to bring all of this theory to life.

The atmosphere at the winery is casual, but the Millers are serious about the wines they produce. Eric spent some of his formative years in Europe, then returned with his family to New York, where they started the first farm winery in the Hudson Valley. As grape grower and winemaker for Benmarl Vineyards, Eric pioneered wine types that figure prominently in today's premium eastern wine industry and conducted extensive barrel aging experiments with woods from different regions. The column Eric writes for the winery's newsletter attests to the depth of his knowledge and interest.

Lee got involved in the wine business as a journalist, when an assignment led her to interview Eric. The Millers chose to open their joint venture in the Brandywine Valley because they believed its climate, soils, and growing conditions were ideal for producing world-class European-style wines. Apparently they were right. As their wine production has increased to thirty-five thousand cases annually, their clientele and recognition have grown steadily.

Chaddsford Winery produces varietal wines, including Chardonnay, Pinot Grigio, Cabernet Franc, Cabernet Sauvignon, Merlot, Pinot Noir, and Chambourcin. Regional wines include Proprietor's Reserve (white and red) and Sunset Blush. Chaddsford also bottles some seasonal and sweet wines, including Spring Wine, Niagara, Sangri-La Sangria, Spiced Apple, and Riesling.

Chaddsford Winery's products have garnered national and international praise. CHADDSFORD WINERY

Chaddsford wines have been featured and rated highly in prestigious publications like *Bon Appetit, Saveur, Wine Spectator, Cooking Light, Wine Enthusiast,* and *Santé.* American wine guru Robert Parker gives Chaddsford high marks. And the Millers consistently receive medals and awards from top international competitions including Intervin International, the New World International Competition, the *Dallas Morning News* Competition, the Los Angeles County Fair, and the San Francisco International Wine Competition.

These affirmations from their wine-savvy peers are gratifying to the Millers, but the recognition hasn't distracted them from their day-to-day life at the winery. "We still live here and work here," says Lee. "We give a lot of classes and are both involved in the industry. We have several major events every year, and that's always fun for us."

Chaddsford Winery has quality without pretense. *Salut!*

Calendar of Events

Note: You must be twenty-one or older to participate in wine tastings at any Chaddsford event. Chilled wines are available, but no alcoholic beverages may be brought onto the property.

Memorial Day weekend, noon to 6 P.M. each day. Brandywine River Blues Fest. $16 per person includes wine tasting, concerts, and a souvenir Chaddsford logo wine glass. Guests may purchase picnic foods at the festival from a local restaurant or bring their own. Several bands play each day. No reservations.

Late May through mid-September, Fridays and occasional Saturdays, 7 to 9:30 P.M. Summer Nights Under the Stars Outdoor Concert Series. $16 per person (opera night $20). Gates open 6 P.M., wine tasting begins at 6:30. Reservations recommended, as many concerts sell out.

Labor Day weekend, noon to 6 P.M. each day. Jazz Festival. $16 per person includes wine tasting, concerts, and a souvenir Chaddsford logo wine glass. Guests may purchase picnic foods at the festival from a local restaurant or bring their own. Several bands play each day. No reservations.

Christian C. Sanderson Museum

Calling the late Christian Carmack Sanderson a collector is like saying Mozart was good at music. Over his eighty-four years, Sanderson accumulated memorabilia and relics related to his interest in, well, just about everything. He was especially passionate about American history, and about history in the making. Many of his most prized items relate to the nation's significant events.

After Sanderson died in 1966, his friends sifted through truckloads of mementos, unearthing everything from cannonballs to presidential signatures to century-old dyed Easter eggs. These dedicated individuals accomplished what Sanderson had always been too busy to do, organizing a lifetime of accumulated objects into some semblance of order.

In 1968, the first floor of the Christian C. Sanderson Museum was opened in the Chadds Ford house Sanderson had shared with his widowed mother; the second floor was opened to the public three years later. A visit to the museum is like a trip in a time machine: fascinating, memorable, educational, and a little disorienting.

Visiting the Christian C. Sanderson Museum

1755 Creek Rd. just north of U.S. Route 1
(Mailing address: Box 153), Chadds Ford, PA 19317
Telephone: 610-388-6545 • Website: www.sandersonmuseum.org

Hours: Saturday and Sunday, 1 to 4:30 P.M.; Memorial Day, July 4, and Labor Day,
1 to 4 P.M. Open weekdays by appointment. Closed in January and February.
Admission: Free; donations appreciated.
Parking: Limited parking is available directly across the street from the museum
on Creek Road, but it can be difficult to back out afterward if traffic is brisk.
Parking is also available in the Chadds Ford Barn Shoppes lot on U.S. Route 1
just north of Creek Road. From there, you can walk alongside the museum
from the back to get to the front entrance.
Special considerations: Not wheelchair accessible. The museum is best suited to
school-age children through adults. For food, the Chadds Ford Inn is located
behind the museum, and Hank's Place is at the intersection of U.S. 1 and
Creek Road.
Other nearby attractions: The Chadds Ford Barn Shoppes are fun for shoppers.
The Chadds Ford Historical Society Headquarters is a short distance north
on Creek Road. The Brandywine River Museum is on the other side of U.S. 1,
just south of Creek Road.

The Collector's Life

Christian Carmack Sanderson was born in Port Providence, Pennsylvania, on January 7, 1882. Both of his grandfathers had served in the Civil War. Sanderson's father, Robert, was employed at a nearby ironworks. Mother Hanna took care of "Christie" and his younger brother, Robbie. She also managed the house and garden and the occasional home-based business project.

Even at a young age, Sanderson stood out from the crowd. He became a recognized figure toting his violin back and forth to lessons. His intelligence, inquiring mind, and writing ability led the editor of a local newspaper to give him regular assignments starting when Sanderson was eleven.

Robert Sanderson died while his eldest son was in high school. The loss was emotionally devastating, especially to Hanna, and it also darkened the family's economic prospects considerably. Nonetheless, Sanderson was able to enroll in West Chester Normal School, now West Chester University, in pursuit of a three-year teaching degree.

Sanderson participated enthusiastically in college life. He joined friends on trips to Philadelphia, walking miles up and down the streets after they disembarked from the train. He took part in dormitory high jinks. He found ways to communicate with Stella Bolton, a special friend, even though male and female students weren't supposed to talk. He became friendly with some faculty members, including one professor who brought Sanderson a piece of holly back from Charles Dickens's home in England.

After graduating from West Chester State Normal School in June 1901, Sanderson got a teaching position at Garwood School in Montgomery County. He was esteemed by the students but on the outs with the board, whose members apparently thought his teaching methods were too liberal and unconventional. In the pattern that would typify his career, he had trouble with the administration and stayed only a short time at the school, yet he kept in touch with the pupils for the rest of his life.

A succession of teaching jobs followed over the next twenty-eight years. Sanderson's final position was at the Oak Grove School in Elsmere, Delaware, in 1929. The board there received a letter from the board at Sanderson's previous school, discrediting him and urging that he be fired. After some time, he was. Nevertheless, the students at Oak Grove thought so much of their outgoing teacher that they named their alumni association in his honor.

Sanderson and his mother had moved several times during his teaching years. In 1906, they rented the east portion of the Benjamin Ring House in Chadds Ford, which had served as George Washington's Headquarters during the Battle of Brandywine. The battle occurred on September 11, 1777, when the Continentals were protecting the Brandywine Creek, hoping to prevent the British from coming across and marching on Philadelphia. The British and Hessians outflanked the Americans and dealt them a bitter defeat. Washington was forced to retreat, ultimately to Valley Forge for the winter of 1777–78.

It was appropriate that history lover Christian Sanderson should live in Washington's Headquarters. When he wasn't teaching, Sanderson immersed himself in battle history and troop movements, showed people around the battlefield, and set up a little museum in one room of the house. His mother was an eager partner in this endeavor, often offering hearth-baked treats to visitors. The pair never charged a cent for their hospitality.

After sixteen years renting Washington's Headquarters, the Sandersons were forced to move out in 1922, when the building's owners decided that they needed it for family members.

In 1927, the Brandywine Memorial Association was formed to plan the commemoration of the 150th anniversary of the Battle of Brandywine. Christian Sanderson, the "Sage of the Brandywine," who had lived and breathed the atmosphere of the site, wasn't asked to be part of the committee. It was a bitter blow.

Money was a problem, too. After Sanderson lost his teaching job in 1930, he had to find a way to make ends meet. He was an accomplished fiddle player, so he founded an orchestra, the Delmarvans. When that group petered out, he started up the Pocopson Valley Boys, who were popular at dances and folk festivals and on the radio. Sanderson also had his own weekly radio show, in which he shared music, local history, and folklore with the listeners. His encyclopedic knowledge kept him in demand as an after-dinner speaker. He was a square dance caller and taught square dancing in adult evening school.

Sanderson got to these various engagements by walking or hitchhiking, no matter what the weather. He didn't own a car. Yet in ten straight years of weekly radio broadcasts, he never missed one. He was never even late.

In 1937, the Sandersons were able to return to Chadds Ford. The front of a house in the village was rented to the blacksmith, but the rear was available. They moved into the Little Gray House.

Hanna died at home on Christmas Day 1943. Christian Sanderson continued his active, eccentric life. He had many loyal friends, yet there were those who obviously had something against him. In 1947, he was not appointed to the new Brandywine Battlefield Park Commission. Five years later, Sanderson was again overlooked at the dedication of the rebuilt Washington's Headquarters, which had burned down. Though he and his mother had lived there for sixteen years, sharing their knowledge with any and all comers, Sanderson's name was omitted from the list of people invited to the main platform. In response, he arranged to give a speech that night at a local elementary school. Every seat was taken.

When the front two rooms of the Little Gray House became available, Sanderson took advantage of that space. At the urging of friends, he put a small portion of his collection on display in September 1959.

Late in his life, Sanderson finally got some of the recognition he deserved. He received awards from the Freedoms Foundation and from West Chester State College (now West Chester University). The Delaware Valley Industrial Editors named him Man of the Year in 1957. More than seven hundred people attended his eightieth birthday celebration in 1962. A year later, Henderson High School in West Chester honored Sanderson during the halftime festivities of a football game. The eighty-one-year-old took the field and gave a vigorous demonstration swinging his Indian clubs. His efforts to establish Brandywine Battlefield Park were posthumously recognized in 1977, when a plaque was installed at Washington's Headquarters.

Christian Sanderson died at age eighty-four on November 19, 1966. He probably would have known immediately that the date was the anniversary of Lincoln's Gettysburg Address. Like the events he commemorated in his collection, Christian C. Sanderson is gone but not forgotten.

The Museum

Christian Sanderson never met an artifact he didn't like. The museum reflects that eclecticism. It also demonstrates the hard work of the people who spearheaded the museum's creation, including artist Andrew Wyeth and Thomas R. Thompson, author of *Chris: A Biography of Christian C. Sanderson.*

On the first day of 1967, cleanup of the home's eight rooms began. It took more than a year and a half to go through the treasures and detritus that were Sanderson's legacy. Blessed with a strong sense of mission and a lot of intestinal fortitude, Sanderson's friends were able to open three rooms on the first floor to the public in August 1968. The upstairs rooms were added to the museum in 1971.

Entering from the front porch is like a trip back in time. Music from the early to mid-twentieth century reminds visitors that Sanderson was a fiddler and bandleader. There's something to see no matter which way you turn. Experienced docents explain the items' origins and answer questions about Sanderson's life.

The long relationship between the Sandersons and the Wyeths is evident in the artwork that appears throughout the museum by many members of the Wyeth family: N. C., Andrew, and Jamie Wyeth, as well as Peter Hurd, Henriette Wyeth Hurd, and John McCoy. Christian Sanderson and N. C. Wyeth arrived at Chadds Ford at about the same time and became lifelong friends. The Sandersons spent Christmas Day 1920 with N. C. and family. N. C. generously offered to help the Sandersons financially if necessary; he even guaranteed that he'd pay the rent on the Little Gray House if the Sandersons couldn't. Sanderson posed for Andrew Wyeth and appears in several of his paintings.

Christian C. Sanderson collected memorabilia for his entire life. Much of his collection is on display in the museum that bears his name. THOMAS R. THOMPSON

When Hanna Sanderson died, Andrew Wyeth was one of the first people Sanderson called. The artist came right over. Hanna's body inspired Wyeth's tempera *Death on Christmas Morning*. Andrew's son Jamie drew the cover art for the brochure given out to guests at Sanderson's eightieth birthday party in 1962.

One room contains items relevant to American history, including a piece of William Penn's treaty elm and a papier-mâché shoe from the Revolutionary War. Another room is full of military memorabilia, including an impressive display of cannonballs and grapeshot.

Other artifacts you're not likely to find anywhere else, at least not under one roof, include a leaf from the wreath Woodrow Wilson placed on Lafayette's tomb in Paris, sand from an atomic bomb blast, a picture made from butterfly wings, strands of George Washington's hair, and two bottles of water from melted South Pole ice.

Sanderson's interest in music is shown by his extensive collection of violins. His fondness for practical jokes is also obvious: Ask a docent to show you the "lung tester" designed to blow soot in the face of the unsuspecting testee.

Sanderson made an effort to see history makers in person wherever possible. He attended presidential inaugurations from Theodore Roosevelt through Lyndon Johnson. He saw Japan's crown prince one day in Philadelphia and Nikita Khrushchev in Washington the next. When Charles Lindbergh came to Wilmington, Sanderson was there. He collected autographs from many luminaries, including such diverse individuals as Patrick Henry, Gen. Anthony Wayne, Queen Victoria, Rudyard Kipling, Shirley Temple, and Roger Staubach.

Christian Sanderson would undoubtedly be pleased that his collection is now accessible to all. Through the items he left behind, he continues to educate and entertain.

ART, ANTIQUES, AND SELECTIVE SHOPPING

**Brandywine River Antiques Market
at the "White Barn"**
878 Baltimore Pike (U.S. Route 1) at Hickory
Hill Road
Chadds Ford, PA 19317
Telephone: 610-388-2000
Fax: 610-388-2720
Hours: Wednesday through Sunday, 10 A.M.
to 5 P.M. Closed Monday and Tuesday.
Limited wheelchair access.

Chadds Ford Barn Shoppes
U.S. Route 1 at Creek Rd.
Chadds Ford, PA 19317
Specialty shops here include the Tin Whistle
for cards, gifts, and stationery (610-388-9300);
Whiskazz and Pawzz pet boutique (610-388-
7010); the antique shops Ancient of Days
(610-388-7012) and the Wooden Knob (610-
388-3861); and Ye Olde Jewelry Exchange
(610-388-1766). The Brandywine River Hotel
and Chadds Ford Inn are also located here.
Hank's Place, the Christian C. Sanderson
Museum, Chadds Ford Historical Society, and
Brandywine River Museum are close by.

Chadds Ford Gallery, Inc.
U.S. Route 1 and Creek Road at Chadds Ford
Village and Barn Shoppes
Chadds Ford, PA 19317-0179
Telephone: 610-459-5510
Fax: 610-388-3482
E-mail: chaddsford@awyethgallery.com
Website: www.awyethgallery.com
Hours: Monday through Saturday,
10 A.M. to 5 P.M.; Sunday, noon to 5 P.M.
Full-service gallery specializing in Wyeth, and
also featuring regional, national, international,
and award-winning artists. Annual Christmas
in Miniature show features original framed art
created in miniature by about fifty artists. With
prices ranging from $50 to $400, they make
excellent gifts. Partially wheelchair accessible.
Call for details on which driveway to use.

Critter Run Antiques
Smithbridge Rd. (South of U.S. Route 1
and just east of U.S. Route 202)
Glen Mills, PA 19342
Telephone: 610-558-3260
Hours: Wednesday through Sunday,
10 A.M. to 5 P.M.
Country primitive furniture and accessories.
Not wheelchair accessible.

Elizabeth L. Matlat Antiques
134 Wilmington Pike (U.S. Route 202)
Brandywine Summit Center
Chadds Ford, PA 19317
Telephone: 610-358-0359
Hours: Monday through Saturday,
10 A.M. to 5 P.M. Call ahead.
Period items, books, some furniture.
Not wheelchair accessible.

Frances Lantz Country Antiques
U.S. Route 202 at Pennsylvania-Delaware State
Line (southbound side of 202)
Chadds Ford, PA 19317
Telephone: 610-459-4080
Hours: By appointment. Limited hours.
Eighteenth- and nineteenth-century country
furniture and accessories. Not wheelchair
accessible.

J&L West Antiques
Fairville Road at PA Route 52
Chadds Ford, PA 19317
Telephone: 610-388-2014
Fax: 610-388-2016
Hours: Monday through Friday, 10 A.M.
to 4 P.M.; Saturday, 11 A.M. to 4:30 P.M.;
Sunday, by chance or by appointment.
Fine collection of period American and English
furniture, accessories, and paintings. Not
wheelchair accessible.

Mykonos
Glen Eagle Square
(Mailing address: P.O. Box 355)
U.S. Route 202 at Springhill Drive
Chadds Ford, PA 19317
Telephone: 610-558-8000

Holly Peters Oriental Rugs

The contemporary handmade carpets at Holly Peters Oriental Rugs are a triumph of traditional materials and techniques. "The productions we carry are one-of-a-kind," says Peters. "They're completely handmade, with vegetal-dyed hand-spun wool. Most of our rugs are made in cottage workshop settings, small ateliers in villages, or dwellings of nomadic tribes."

Long ago and far away, Eastern artisans wove hand-spun yarn into fabulous carpets. The names of the plants they used to dye their wool—madder root, pomegranate, indigo, chamomile—are as exotic and beautiful as the rugs themselves. Natural variations in the dyes created soft, striated colors. These carpets, sometimes 100 to 150 years old, are still prized by collectors; rugs older than that are museum pieces.

Then came the industrial revolution, and with it, the invention of synthetic dyes and fibers. Rugs could be made more cheaply, but the uniform, harsh colors lacked splendor and character. Because of economic pressures, weavers preferred the less expensive methods. It seemed as though the ancient techniques would disappear for good.

But progressive companies stepped in, removing the economic burden from the crafters by providing vegetal dyes, rejuvenating the process of hand-spinning wool, setting up a creative workshop environment, and especially by paying a fair wage for carpets created the old-fashioned way. "It's kind of a revival," says Peters, "and my store reflects that. We sell rugs that most likely will be the antiques of the future."

There's no need to sift through stacks of rugs here. The forty-five-hundred-square-foot shop offers plenty of floor space for Peters to spread out beautiful carpets, from scatter size to palace size. Other rugs hang on the walls, an inspiration to anyone looking for a unique wall treatment. The colors and abstract forms are drawn from the landscapes that surround the weavers in places like Turkey, Nepal, and the area once called Persia.

Peters, who studied design at Drexel University in Philadelphia, clearly has an eye for style. Along with carpets, she carries handcrafted furniture and eclectic accessories. Peruvian mahogany and leather chairs are complemented by Moroccan tile-top tables and Turkish earthenware. Candleholders and oil lamps add a touch of enchantment. Updated American classics from tavern chairs to punched-tin jelly cupboards fit right in, too. These reproductions, inspired by American primitive furniture, coexist beautifully with antiques.

The successful meshing of styles has beautiful results and should motivate timid decora-

(continued on page 46)

Holly Peters Oriental Rugs carries furniture and handmade carpeting that could well be tomorrow's prized antiques. HOLLY PETERS ORIENTAL RUGS/GARY MCKINNIS

(continued from page 45)

tors to try something a little different. "We encourage people to exercise their individuality, to personalize their choices," says Peters. "Mixing and matching rugs with similar colors is a great way to bring a room together, to add color, texture, warmth, and charm. Choosing a few key pieces of furniture can complete the effect. I want people to be comfortable, so I choose items very carefully. Everything in the store is something I'd be happy to live with."

VISITING HOLLY PETERS ORIENTAL RUGS

In the White Barn Shops, 884 Baltimore Pike (U.S. Route 1), between PA Route 52 (Kennett Pike) and Creek Road. The shop is located at the intersection of Hickory Hill Road and Baltimore Pike, Chadds Ford, PA 19317. Telephone: 610-388-6150 • Website: www.hollypeters.com

Hours: Tuesday through Saturday, 10:30 A.M. to 5:30 P.M.; Sunday, noon to 4 P.M. Closed Sundays in summer.
Special considerations: Wheelchair accessible.

Hours: Monday through Saturday, 10 A.M. to 8 P.M.; Sunday, noon to 5 P.M.
Mykonos features an extensive kaleidoscope collection; original jewelry, glass, and pottery; gift items; and unique art clothing. Wheelchair accessible.

Olde Ridge Village Shoppes
U.S. Route 202 at Ridge Road, 1.5 miles south of U.S. Route 1
Chadds Ford, PA 19317
Telephone: 610-558-0466
Website: www.olderidgevillage.com
Boutiques, specialty stores, restaurants, and craft shops fill this picturesque shopping area. Some of the shops are the Book Fair (610-358-1954), a children's bookstore; Christopher Fine Foods for premium chocolates (610-358-1838); Paper Pickins for stationery (610-459-4841); and Wolfe's Baldwin Brass Center (610-358-3013).

Pennsbury–Chadds Ford Antique Mall
640 E. Baltimore Pike (U.S. Route 1 between Brandywine River Museum and Longwood Gardens)
Chadds Ford, PA 19317
Telephone: 610-388-1620
Hours: Upper level, Thursday through Monday, 10 A.M. to 5 P.M.; lower level, Saturday and Sunday, 10 A.M. to 5 P.M.

Multidealer mall with furniture, jewelry, china, sterling, books, dolls, oriental rugs, clocks, and military items. Wheelchair access through lower level.

P-R Antiques
3911 Pyle Rd. at U.S. Route 202 northbound side (Pennsylvania-Delaware state line)
Chadds Ford, PA 19317
Telephone: 610-459-7890
Hours: Thursday through Sunday, 10 A.M. to 5 P.M.
A 1900s farmhouse full of antique furniture, collectibles, and reproduction furniture made by local craftspersons. Not wheelchair accessible.

R. M. Worth Antiques, Inc.
810 Baltimore Pike (U.S. Route 1)
Chadds Ford, PA 19317
Telephone: 610-388-4040
Fax: 610-388-3392
Hours: Tuesday through Saturday, 10 A.M. to 5:30 P.M., closed Sunday and Monday.
Eighteenth- and nineteenth-century American furniture, paintings, and related decorative arts. Limited wheelchair access.

RECREATION AND LEISURE

Bicycling

Delaware Valley Bicycle Club
P.O. Box 156
Woodlyn, PA 19094-0156
Website: www.dvbc.org
Visit the website for information on road and trail biking. Meetings and rides are open to the public.

Mountain Bike Pennsylvania
Website: www.mountainbikepa.com

Smithbridge Cellars Winery
159 Beaver Valley Rd., .5 mile west of
   U.S. Route 202
Chadds Ford, PA 19317
Telephone: 610-558-4703
Website: www.smithbridge.com
Nature trails suitable for mountain biking. Can be accessed from the winery.

Hiking and Walking

Brandywine Battlefield
U.S. Route 1 between U.S. Route 202 and
   Creek Road
Chadds Ford, PA 19317
Telephone: 610-459-3342
Website: www.ushistory.org/brandywine
Grounds open Tuesday through Saturday,
   9 A.M. to 5 P.M.; Sunday, noon to 5 P.M.

Brandywine River Museum
U.S. Route 1 just south of Creek Road
Chadds Ford, PA 19317
Telephone: 610-388-2700
Website: www.brandywinemuseum.org
Hours: Dawn to dusk.
Half-mile trail along the Brandywine goes under U.S. 1 to the Chadds Ford Historical Society headquarters. Wildflower gardens.

Smithbridge Cellars Winery
159 Beaver Valley Rd., .5 mile west of
   U.S. Route 202
Chadds Ford, PA 19317
Telephone: 610-558-4703
Website: www.smithbridge.com
Nature trails suitable for hiking. Can be accessed from the winery.

Winery

Smithbridge Cellars Winery
159 Beaver Valley Rd., .5 mile west of
   U.S. Route 202
Chadds Ford, PA 19317
Telephone: 610-558-4703
Website: www.smithbridge.com
Hours: Labor Day to Memorial Day, open
   Saturday and Sunday only, noon to 6 P.M.;
   in summer, open Tuesday through Sunday,
   noon to 6 P.M.
Also has picnic area and nature trails. Concert series. One step down to tasting area.

ACCOMMODATIONS

Brandywine River Hotel

It's nice to find the best of both worlds in accommodations, a place that combines the character of a bed-and-breakfast with the amenities of a full-service hotel. One such hybrid is the Brandywine River Hotel, a forty-room facility that blends the two styles seamlessly.

Set back from U.S. Route 1 in the center of Chadds Ford, the hotel is located with the Chadds Ford Barn Shoppes. The boutiques, specialty stores, and an art gallery in a restored colonial homestead offer items representative of the Brandywine Valley. For lunch and dinner, Chadds Ford Inn is just steps away. Hank's Place, on the other side of Creek Road, serves informal breakfast, lunch, and dinner.

The Brandywine River Hotel is centrally located in Chadds Ford. Rooms are comfortable and cozy; some have fireplaces. BRANDYWINE RIVER HOTEL

From the hotel, you can easily walk to the Christian C. Sanderson Museum without crossing any streets; the Chadds Ford Historical Society, John Chads House, and the Brandywine River Museum are also close by. Route 1 and Creek Road aren't the safest for pedestrians, though, so you may want to drive to these attractions or take advantage of the hotel's van service.

Charm and congeniality are apparent as soon as you enter the lobby, which has the feel of an English drawing room with its fireplace, cozy furniture, and fresh flower arrangements. Plum wall-to-wall carpeting is topped with oriental rugs. Complimentary afternoon tea is served here every afternoon from 4 to 6 P.M.

The reception staff is friendly and helpful. A curio cabinet at the desk highlights local attractions and events. Wheelchair users will appreciate the low counter on the side of the check-in area, easily reachable from a sitting position.

Room sizes and layouts accommodate different needs and budgets. A deluxe double with two double beds is a great choice for a family of four. Executive suites have a sofa in a roomy seating area. Fireside Jacuzzi suites come with a fireplace and king or queen bed. The top-of-the-line premium suite, a favorite of honeymooners, has a four-poster king bed, Jacuzzi, refrigerator, and fireplace.

Owners Jeffrey T. and Lori Yamas have paid attention to detail in the accommodations. Upgraded bedding and linens, contour neck pillows, and Queen Anne reproduction furniture are featured in every room. Subtly patterned wallpaper and floral draperies create a solid, traditional atmosphere. Menus from local restaurants are available to help guests make their dining decisions. Despite its proximity to U.S. Route 1, the hotel rooms are nice and quiet.

For corporate travelers, the Brandywine River Hotel has meeting and seminar rooms, with audiovisual equipment and other meeting supplies. The hotel's twelve-passenger van is available to shuttle to nearby businesses. Public transportation is available via SCCOOT (Southern Chester County Organization on Transportation) vehicles all along U.S. Route 1 and north on U.S. Route 202 from Oxford to West Chester.

Guests are welcome to use the fitness center and the complimentary business center. The latter has two workstations, a copier, and a fax machine.

The room rate includes a "European-plus" breakfast, served each morning in the cheery Ashley Dining Room. Coffee, tea, and juices, fresh fruit, cereals, and waffles are available. Muffins and other sweet breakfast breads are baked on the premises.

The hotel offers packages tailored to different interests. Some include tickets to local attractions; others feature meals at top local restaurants. The staff is happy to create custom packages and to help plan meetings and events. This kind of personal service in a homey atmosphere is another indication of how well the Brandywine River Hotel fills its niche.

Visiting the Brandywine River Hotel

U.S. Route 1 about 100 yards north of PA Route 100
(Mailing address: P.O. Box 1058), Chadds Ford, PA 19317
Telephone: 610-388-1200 or 800-274-9644
E-mail: brhdos@aol.com • Website: www.brandywineriverhotel.com
Rates: $125 to $169, including European-plus breakfast.
Credit cards: Visa, MasterCard, American Express, Discover, and Diner's Club.
Personal checks: Accepted for deposits only, at least one week in advance.
Check-in: 3 P.M.
Check-out: 11 A.M.
Smoking policy: Hotel is completely nonsmoking.
Wheelchair accessible: Yes.
Children: Well-mannered children welcome.
Pets: Pets up to twenty pounds can be accommodated for $20 per night. Owner must have a crate
    for the animal. Preapproved reservation required.
Food: Breakfast and afternoon tea are served. No on-site restaurant. The Chadds Ford Inn is a
    minute walk away. Several other restaurants are within a five-minute drive. The Brandywine
    River Hotel shuttle can take guests to Simon Pearce on the Brandywine.
Parking: Free on-site.
Other: Public transportation is available via SCCOOT (Southern Chester County Organization
    on Transportation) vehicles all along U.S. Route 1 and north on U.S. Route 202 from Oxford to
    West Chester. SCCOOT's closest stop to the hotel is at the intersection of U.S. Route 1 and PA
    Route 100, just yards from the hotel entrance. Longwood Gardens is one of the many stops the
    bus makes, as are the centers of West Chester and Kennett Square. For more information, call
    877-612-1359 or visit www.sccoot.org.

Fairville Inn Bed and Breakfast

Noel and Jane McStay are untiring ambassadors for the Brandywine Valley. The owners/innkeepers of the Fairville Inn Bed and Breakfast offer fifteen charming guest rooms and suites, and they also provide a wealth of information about area attractions, shopping, and dining. The McStays have brochures, maps, and menus for their guests to use, and the couple is available to answer questions about things to see and do. So deep is their commitment to giving their visitors complete information and to helping people make the most of their stay in the Brandywine Valley that the McStays even maintain an extensive list of previous guests' comments about local restaurants.

"The Fairville Inn provides a unique, homelike experience," says Noel, "and we're just three miles from Winterthur, Longwood Gardens, or the Brandywine River Museum. We want people to enjoy all that this area has to offer. We're surrounded by magnificent estates, antique shops, and miles of backroads for hiking and biking."

"At the same time," Jane says, "we provide an environment where people can relax. It's not like they're staying in a bedroom in our house. Guests have as much privacy or as little as they want."

The five-acre property is open for guests who care to stroll the grounds or simply sit and take in the pastoral setting. Bigger than most bed-and-breakfasts yet smaller than most hotels, the Fairville Inn is the ideal size for a gathering like a family reunion or a small wedding.

The inn has three buildings: the Main House, the Carriage House, and the Springhouse. All three have guest rooms; the reception area, a living room, and the dining room are in the Main House.

Upon arrival, guests are welcomed in the reception area, which was recently added but blends seamlessly with the rest of the building's 1857 construction. Rescued planks were used for the floor; the beadboard paneling keeps the walls neat and streamlined.

Adjoining the reception room is the living room, where guests may gather anytime. Newspapers are put out daily, there's a toasty fire in chilly weather, and quiet classical music is piped in. Local artwork graces the walls. If you see something that appeals to you, check with the innkeepers to see whether it is for sale.

Afternoon tea is served daily in the dining room, with a good selection of home-baked cookies and coffee cakes, plus cheese and crackers and a selection of teas. Noel's collection of presidential letters is showcased here.

The Fairville Inn has several types of accommodations, including suites. FAIRVILLE INN

Guests at Fairville Inn are welcome to relax in front of the fireplace in the living room. FAIRVILLE INN

This is also the setting for breakfast. Jane provides guests with several choices, including at least two egg dishes and one "bready" dish like waffles, pancakes, or French toast, plus a side dish like bacon or hash-brown potatoes. Cereals, oatmeal, yogurt, fresh fruit, toast, and coffee cake are also available.

Light colors, flowers, and elegant country furnishings create a warm, cheerful atmosphere in Fairville's guest quarters. The decor differs from room to room. Well-chosen accessories like cut-paper lampshades add a homey feel. Ten part-time employees keep everything shipshape.

The rooms are classified as standard, deluxe, and suites. All rooms have a private bathroom *en suite*, wall-to-wall carpeting, satellite television, individually controlled heating and air-conditioning, hair dryers, telephones, and modem plug-ins. Wireless connections are available in the main building. Irons and ironing boards are also provided. Many of the rooms have fireplaces for use in season. Bathrobes are provided in the deluxe rooms and suites; in addition, the suites have separate sitting areas.

Five guest rooms are available in the Main House. Main House 1 is on the first floor, right off the living room. If easy access to the living room and dining room is important to you, this is the room you want. It has a queen-size bed with a partial canopy, beadboard ceiling, white bedspread, and floral wallpaper. Outside, there's a private deck.

The four other guest accommodations in the Main House are on the second floor. Main House 2 feels almost like a tree house with its view of the outdoors. Main House 3 is in the front of the building and is the only room at Fairville Inn with twin beds. Room 4 has a queen-size canopy bed, and Room 5 has a queen-size four-poster.

A few steps away is the Carriage House. This building has two suites, one on the first floor and one on the second, plus two standard and two deluxe rooms. Suite 1 has a private sitting room with a second television and love seat. The bedroom has a king-size canopy bed, fireplace, sitting area with love seat and wingback chair, and French doors opening onto a deck.

The second-floor suite is decorated with blue and white toile wallpaper and has a sitting room with a secretary desk and love seat. There's a fireplace, a huge closet, and a lovely view of the property from the private deck. The bathroom has two sinks.

Carriage House 1, on the first floor, is a deluxe room notable for its vaulted ceiling. The "Z" on the door is a nod to the old barn-style doors that would have graced a carriage house in the 1800s.

A Palladian window and cathedral ceiling are notable in Carriage House 3, a deluxe room with a fireplace, king-size canopy bed, and private deck. Two standard rooms, Carriage House 2 and 4, also have private decks. Those rooms have queen-size canopy beds.

Fairville Inn's remaining four rooms are in the Springhouse. All rooms here have fireplaces. Springhouse 3 and Springhouse 4 are on the second floor and have queen-size canopy beds. Springhouse 1 and 2 have king canopies. These room pairs make good choices for couples traveling together, since their decks connect.

Noel and Jane McStay relocated to Chadds Ford from the Hamptons in 2003, and they couldn't be happier. Their enthusiasm for this area ensures that their guests will always have fond memories of the hospitality they received in the Brandywine Valley and at the Fairville Inn Bed and Breakfast.

Visiting Fairville Inn Bed and Breakfast

506 Kennett Pike (PA Route 52), Chadds Ford, PA 19317
Telephone: 610-388-5900 or 877-285-7772 • Fax: 610-388-5902
E-mail: info@fairvilleinn.com • Website: www.fairvilleinn.com
Rates: $150 to $250.
Credit cards: Visa, MasterCard, American Express, and Discover.
Personal checks: Accepted.
Check-in: 3 P.M.
Check-out: 11 A.M.
Air-conditioned: Yes.
Smoking Policy: Nonsmoking.
Wheelchair accessible: Main House 1 is on the first floor of the Main House, just off the living room. A wheelchair could access this room, but the bathroom facilities are not accessible.
Children: At least fifteen years old.
Pets: No.
Noise: Although Fairville Inn is on PA Route 52, the walls of the 1857 Main House are thick, and guests have not experienced noise problems. Rooms in the Carriage House and the Springhouse at the back of the property facing the meadow offer the most quiet and privacy.
Parking: Free on-site.
Other: Guests must walk outside to get from the Main House to the Carriage House and the Springhouse. The longest distance is about sixty yards. Some rooms have bathtubs and showers, others have large showers only. Most, but not all, rooms have fireplaces. Ask about these amenities when you reserve your room.

Harlan Log House

If your definition of the perfect vacation accommodations is spelled q-u-i-e-t, the Harlan Log House is the place you're looking for. This eighteenth-century Quaker homestead nestled on five acres off a very quiet road has a serenity that extends from its water garden to its comfortable kitchen to its two spacious guest suites.

The conduit of calm is innkeeper Beverly McCausland, who maintains the property in top condition yet manages to have a relaxed attitude. "I want people to be happy when they come," she says. "The grounds are peaceful and inspiring. People like to sit on the porch or by the water garden." Beverly's flexibility takes the pressure off her guests. For example, check-in time can be prearranged to suit visitors.

"There's also a continuity of history," she says. "I think of the mood here as 'the real thing.'" That history extends back almost three hundred years. The original acreage where the Harlan Log House now stands was purchased by Quaker George Harlan in 1710. He deeded the property to his son Joshua "in consideration of natural affection and fatherly love." The oldest part of the house, made of hewn (straight-sided) logs, was built by Joshua Harlan sometime between 1715 and 1720. The middle section was added by the Cloud family in 1814, and the newest portion was constructed in 1990. Harlan Log House is listed on the National Register of Historic Places.

"The Harlan family must have been fairly well off," speculates the innkeeper, "because the original building is almost four stories tall if you include the basement section that's aboveground." Wide plank floors are a reminder of the home's origins.

Inside, guests enjoy the "old kitchen" with its huge hearth. A full breakfast is served here daily. In keeping with the bed-and-breakfast's laid-back feeling, there's no set menu. Beverly serves "whatever you want, as long as the ingredients are on hand." It's a treat to sit in the cozy room trying to figure out what the fireplace

Harlan Log House is a quiet spot far from any noise or distractions. HARLAN LOG HOUSE

cooking implements were used for; if you're stumped, the innkeeper will explain their function.

As for the accommodations, there are two suites on separate floors. Part of each suite is in the home's oldest section—although you won't see rustic log walls, as the interior is plastered smooth and painted white—and part is in the nineteenth-century addition. Each features a bedroom with wood-burning fireplace, a private bath with tub and tile shower, and a sitting room.

The downstairs suite is decorated in crisp blue and white. A crocheted white canopy tops the wooden four-poster bed. The sitting room faces the garden and is a wonderful spot to enjoy the morning sun. Pianists are welcome to use the instrument here.

In the upstairs suite, a pewter-painted four-poster has a rose toile canopy. Beverly was a trendsetter in this regard. "I liked toile even before it became popular!" she says with a smile. The woodwork is painted a gray-green and deep rose. Both the bedroom and sitting room have plenty of furniture. The spool cabinet was constructed with many drawers to keep thread and other sewing accessories neatly sorted. An extra bedroom here is just right for a family or for traveling companions who want their own bedroom space.

Beverly doesn't claim to be an expert in American antiques, but she has assembled a very appropriate and comfortable assortment of furniture for the Harlan Log House. "I learned by going to auctions," she says. "I collected a lot of old furniture that seems to have found its home. When I came here, it was as if all the furniture was in the right place."

Harlan Log House is ideally situated for Brandywine Valley excursions: It's only three miles to Winterthur, Longwood Gardens, or the Brandywine River Museum. When you return from sight-seeing, take time to rock on the porch or explore the garden with its springhouse, fountain, and fish. It's an idyllic setting much like it must have been three centuries ago.

"I always dreamed of living in Chester County and having a farmhouse," says Beverly McCausland. "When I found this place, it was like coming home." For a tranquil stay in the Brandywine Valley, Harlan Log House is your home, too.

Visiting the Harlan Log House

205 Fairville Rd., Chadds Ford, PA 19317
Telephone: 610-388-1114
Website: www.bbonline.com/pa/harlan/suites.html
Rates: $110 to $155, including full breakfast. Premium added for Saturday night only stay.
Credit cards: Not accepted.
Personal checks: Accepted.
Check-in: Flexible; make arrangements with innkeeper.
Check-out: 11 A.M.
Air-conditioned: Yes.
Smoking policy: Nonsmoking.
Wheelchair accessible: No.
Children: Welcome.
Pets: No. There is a resident dog.
Noise: Almost none.
Parking: Free on-site.

Hedgerow Bed & Breakfast Suites

When Barbara and John Haedrich commissioned a local blacksmith to craft a wrought-iron banister for their bed-and-breakfast, they were looking for more than just a handrail. They also wanted something to symbolize the care and hospitality guests experience at Hedgerow. Ultimately they chose a blooming pineapple, a symbol of welcome, as the theme for the newel post.

This feeling—that you'll be comfortable and taken care of here—permeates everything at Hedgerow. Three spacious suites in a beautifully restored building called the Carriage House are luxuriously appointed. Guests are welcome to use the gathering room with fireplace, the terrace off the dining room, and a gazebo. The dining room has snacks for guests, and the cookie jar is always full.

"We pamper our guests," says Barbara. "When people make an inquiry, we ask them whether they're coming for business or pleasure. A lot of guests have spent their wedding night or an anniversary here, and they want to return on the same date. We also get many corporate guests who are tired of hotels and love staying here for their business trips." Longwood Gardens is just one mile north, while Winterthur is four miles south, and downtown Wilmington is just nine miles south.

"Whatever the reason for their visit," she adds, "we try to read their needs and to put everything in place that will keep them comfortable. Once they're here, we give them as much privacy as they want. We are always available to answer questions. As natives, we can help guests with information about attractions and restaurants."

Barbara grew up in Wilmington and John right here at Hedgerow, so they are great resources for directions and unique things to do. If they know where their

John and Barbara Haedrich at Hedgerow Bed & Breakfast Suites pamper their guests. The gathering room is charming and cozy. HEDGEROW BED & BREAKFAST SUITES

guests' interests lie, the Haedrichs can direct them to special local sites like covered bridges, country drives, champion trees, and du Pont estate properties.

John Haedrich has lived in the big 1905 Victorian main house since 1949, when he moved here with his family at age six. The separate building that houses the bed-and-breakfast was actually the barn for the Mendenhall Farm next door, built circa 1865. When Pierre S. du Pont, founder of Longwood Gardens, started an employee-housing program in the 1930s, the top part of the barn was converted into a residence.

"We bought both houses and the three acres from my parents in 1986," says John. "Since we had always enjoyed staying at B&Bs in our travels, we started the B&B in 1992. At that time, the building had the 1930s living quarters upstairs and a workshop and garage downstairs. In 1996, we began a major renovation that took about a year and a half to complete."

The Haedrichs approached the project with clear goals in mind for guests' comfort. "We took the building right down to the 1865 post-and-beam construction," Barbara says. "We tried to make it as allergen-free as possible. No fiberglass was used. The heat is gas. We installed HEPA filters." The Haedrichs also took pains to make the interior as quiet as possible by putting in soundproofing and special windows.

One look at the floors is a clear indication of the care that went into the design and construction of the Carriage House: a tumbled marble mosaic floor in the entry, maple in the kitchen, slate in the Longwood Suite entry, and cherrywood parquet elsewhere in that suite. The Haedrichs paid attention to details from the ground up.

Each suite is unique, yet all three share common elements. No matter which one you choose, your accommodations will include designer linens with down comforters and pillows, fresh flowers, turndown service, *en suite* private bathrooms, bathrobes, clock radios, a desk with telephone and data port, cable television and VCR, a hair dryer, iron and ironing board, plus a separate sitting room. Barbara has compiled menus and brochures into a regularly updated directory she places in each room.

The Winterthur Suite on the second floor has a colonial atmosphere and four rooms, for one to four guests. There are two bedrooms here: a large one with a cathedral ceiling and pineapple-topped queen-size four-poster bed, and a second one with two twin brass beds. The pale yellow and white sitting room is accented with blue and white porcelain and has a sofa and love seat. The bath has a tub with a shower and skylight overhead.

Also on the second floor is the Brandywine Suite, with three rooms that can accommodate up to three guests. Here a country-style atmosphere is created in muted tones of pink, cranberry, and white, offset by warm pine floors and appointed with handcrafted local ironwork and tinwork. The bright sitting room, furnished with Chester County oak pieces, has Wyeth prints and cozy striped wing chairs. The bedroom in the Brandywine Suite has a cathedral ceiling and queen-size canopy bed, and there's a twin bed in the alcove. The well-lit, spacious bathroom has a tub with shower and a large vanity table. The suite also offers a work area with desk, phone, and data port.

The Winterthur and Brandywine Suites share a thoroughly stocked kitchenette with microwave, refrigerator, coffeemaker, electric kettle, toaster, and plenty of snacks and beverages. This setup is much like the self-catering option common in British bed-and-breakfasts. The beautiful iron handrail ornaments the stairway from

The Brandywine Suite at Hedgerow Bed & Breakfast has a country atmosphere. HEDGEROW BED & BREAKFAST SUITES

the first floor to the suites and kitchenette. Over the steps is a lovely nightlight—a large piece of stained glass lit from behind.

The Longwood Suite is on the ground floor, accessed through a private entrance. The atmosphere is Victorian, with antique walnut and white marble furniture set against a soft green palette. Oriental rugs abound. This four-room suite includes an inviting sitting room with gas fireplace (in season) and a spacious bathroom with two-person Jacuzzi and seating area. The Longwood Suite does not share the kitchenette with the other two suites, so it has its own facilities, including a microwave, sink, and refrigerator, and is stocked with complimentary tea, coffee, soft drinks, and snacks. The bedroom has a king-size brass and enameled iron bed with a spacious dresser and a pedestal sink, plus a desk area with phone and data port. A pull-out sofa in the living room means that up to three people can be accommodated.

A full breakfast is served each morning. The Haedrichs will adjust breakfast time to meet your schedule, a refreshing change from the preset time often found at B&Bs. The menu can be customized depending on your preferences. "We ask if our guests have any special wants or needs," says Barbara. "Usually I serve an egg dish and a meat dish, plus toast, baked goods, cereals, fresh fruit, and yogurt. I'll adjust this depending on what guests want. I can make vegetarian meals. We have had several guests on the Atkins Diet, so all they wanted was eggs and sausage." Guests are served in the dining room, with its charming collection of teapots on display, or out on the terrace when the weather is nice. The grounds also feature fishponds and a screened-in gazebo.

No matter how you decide to spend your time at Hedgerow Bed and Breakfast Suites, you will receive individualized service to make sure your stay is perfect for you. If that's not hospitality, what is?

Visiting Hedgerow Bed & Breakfast Suites

268 Kennett Pike (PA Route 52), .25 mile south of U.S. Route 1, Chadds Ford, PA 19317
Telephone: 610-388-6080 • Fax: 610-388-0194
E-mail: info@brandywine-valley.com
Website: www.brandywine-valley.com/
Rates: $135 to $195, double occupancy; added charge for each extra person in suite. Two-night minimum stay; surcharge for single night, when available. Long-term and business rates available. Credit card required to hold reservation. Check website for specials.
Credit cards: Visa, MasterCard, Discover, and American Express accepted, but a surcharge is applied. Cash, personal checks, or traveler's checks are preferred.
Personal checks: Accepted.
Check-in: 4 to 10 P.M., unless other arrangements have been made.
Check-out: 11 A.M.
Air-conditioned: Yes.
Smoking policy: Nonsmoking.
Wheelchair accessible: No.
Children: Must be fifteen or older.
Pets: No. There are cats in the main house, but not in the carriage house where the accommodations are. Guests do not come into contact with the cats.
Noise: Mild road noise outside, none inside. The accommodations are set back from the road, and the innkeepers have installed special windows and soundproofing.
Parking: On-site paved area close to Carriage House.
Other: Candles not permitted.

Mendenhall Inn, Hotel and Conference Center

PA Route 52, about 1.5 miles south of U.S. Route 1, Mendenhall, PA 19357
Telephone: 610-388-2100 • Fax: 610-388-2460
E-mail: hionis@aol.com
Website: www.mendenhallinn.com
Rooms: 70 guest rooms, with either a king-size bed or two double beds. Suites have a Jacuzzi and a parlor that can be converted into a boardroom. All accommodations have data ports, high-speed Internet access, voice mail, cable television, minibars, clock radios, coffeemakers, and hair dryers.
Rates: $98 to $199, including full breakfast Monday through Friday and Continental breakfast buffet Saturday and Sunday. Contact the hotel or consult the website for details on packages.
Credit cards: Visa, MasterCard, American Express, and Discover.
Personal checks: Accepted with proper identification.
Check-in: 3 P.M.
Check-out: Noon.
Smoking policy: Entire hotel is nonsmoking.
Wheelchair accessible: Yes.
Children: Cribs and cots available.
Pets: No.
Food: The Mendenhall Inn is on-site, serving dinner daily, lunch Monday through Saturday, and Sunday champagne brunch.
Parking: Free on-site.
Other: Complimentary reception Monday through Thursday, 5 to 6:30 P.M., with wine, beer, and hors d'oeuvres. Same-day laundry valet service Monday through Friday. Twenty-four-hour Business Center has computers with Microsoft Office, high-speed Internet access, copier, laser printer, typewriter, and fax service. Fitness center. Extensive banquet and meeting facilities.

Pennsbury Inn

The Pennsbury Inn, picturesquely situated on eight acres, is a unique blend of historic architecture, designer interiors, and a relaxed innkeeper. "It's a historic setting, but it's also warm and cozy," says Cheryl Grono. "When people come here the first time, it's often because they have sight-seeing plans in the area. When they come back again, it's to stay here with us."

The inn is located between Chadds Ford and Kennett Square on land purchased from William Penn's commissioners in 1681. The original dwelling was erected in 1714 of Brandywine blue granite. A large addition expanded the house in 1759 and added a beehive oven; the front facade was clad in hand-molded Flemish bond brick. In the nineteenth century, a clapboard addition attached the kitchen to the rest of the house and included quarters for servants and coachmen. A twentieth-century addition on the garden side of the building created a spacious area with a garden view.

For Cheryl, it was love at first sight. Throughout her years of raising two sons and teaching, she had always wanted to run a bed-and-breakfast. The Pennsbury Inn had already been extensively renovated and decorated by the previous owners, and the building's spaciousness and historical character appealed to her. She and her husband purchased the property and reopened the inn in March 2001.

The Gronos brought in some "new" old furniture to add their personal touch. "I have collected lots of stuff," says Cheryl, who favors sturdy items like the nine-foot dining table made from solid heart pine rescued from a Philadelphia warehouse. "It doesn't bother me to have people touch the antiques. I like it when they use the furniture."

Cheryl discovered a terrific piece at a flea market, a huge Chinese walnut armoire with carved doors. "From what we've been able to find out, it's probably late Ming," she says. "We use it as a pantry between the kitchen and the dining room." The tall cabinet fits perfectly under the beamed ceiling and makes a creative room divider.

The Pennsbury Inn has six rooms with private baths, plus a seventh bedroom that can be added on to another bedroom to form a shared-bath suite. The accommodations are named for famous people and local places. Each room has a luxurious featherbed, telephone, modem hookup, CD player, and cable television. Fresh water, ice, and a home-baked snack arrive before bedtime.

The Pennsbury Inn is picturesque no matter what time of year. PENNSBURY INN

The oldest portion of the house is where you'll find the General Lafayette Room. To get there, climb the wooden winder stair. This room has a fireplace with electric firestove insert. The original wide floorboards add to the charm. There's a seating area, small refrigerator, king-size bed, and private bathroom with shower.

Daniel Webster, the statesman, lawyer, and orator, has a room named for him. There's a chance Webster may have recuperated here after a carriage accident. "We know he stayed in an inn along Baltimore Pike," says Cheryl, "and we think this was the only one in the area near the accident. It made sense to name a room after him." The Webster Room has an original 1759 paneled mantel and fireplace, Pierre Deux drapery panels, a queen-size antique brass four-poster bed, and a private bath with shower.

The John Marshall Room is the inn's smallest, but it's very cozy and quite popular. "Lawyers love staying here," says Cheryl. Perhaps they hope to pick up the aura of the Supreme Court's fourth chief justice, for whom the room is named. With dark furniture and gray-and-ivory-striped wallpaper, the John Marshall Room has a dignified air. There's an antique spool double bed and an electric firestove, with a full bath (tub and shower) accessed through the hallway.

A coachman's quarters no longer, the Longwood Room pays homage to the famous gardens nearby. The carpeting is green, the wallpaper is a Nina Campbell topiary print, and the headboard resembles a picket fence. The two twin beds here can be reconfigured into a king and secured so that the beds don't separate. A private bathroom with shower completes the room.

Also done in green is the Four Seasons Room. Pierre Deux green toile wallpaper portrays seasonal scenes, but it can't do justice to the garden view out the window. There's an antique headboard on the king-size bed; the bathroom with shower only is small, but the closet is ample. A refrigerator and microwave come with this room.

Once you see the Palladian window in the Winterthur Suite, it might be hard to consider staying anywhere else. The glass, with casements on either side, is a lovely echo of what you'll see at Longwood Gardens and in the N. C. Wyeth Studio. The view overlooks the garden. If you can tear your eyes away from the sight long enough to look inside, you'll notice the incredible rose toile wallpaper done in Chinese scenes. The Winterthur Suite has a private entrance hallway, electric firestove, and a queen-size bed. The private bath has a big soaking tub with Jacuzzi attachment and a shower.

The Guest Room has no bath, but it can be combined into a shared-bath suite with the Winterthur Suite, the Longwood Room, or the Four Seasons Room. It's a nice option for families or for friends traveling together who don't mind sharing a bathroom but prefer separate sleeping quarters.

Extensive gardens—some landscaped, some left natural—extend from the back of the Pennsbury Inn. PENNSBURY INN

Back downstairs in this comfortable country house, you can enjoy the stone fireplace in the 1714 section or the baby grand piano in the 1759 addition. The dining room and parlor make good meeting rooms.

Facing the back of the property is the Garden Room, kind of a combination dining room and family room. On chilly mornings, there's a fire in the stone fireplace; on warm days, guests are welcome to have breakfast on the terrace. Four acres of landscaped gardens beckon you through walls of glass; the grounds are an ideal place to walk after breakfast.

And speaking of breakfast, Cheryl offers a full cooked meal every morning. Her most requested dish is her own creation, a soft flour tortilla topped with creamy scrambled eggs, caramelized onions and peppers, sautéed local mushrooms, and a grated cheese mixture, with fruit salsa on the side. A close second is the peaches and cream French toast layered with caramel, topped with a cinnamony yogurt and cream mixture and toasted pecans. Coffee, assorted teas, juices, home-baked goods, and fruit are available daily.

The building materials for the Garden Room, where breakfast is served, were scavenged from elsewhere on the property. The beams and stone from a ruined icehouse were used here. The floor came from the home's attic.

Cheryl appreciates the fact that some guests are more private than others. "At breakfast, guests can sit at the table, or they can have their meal in a more secluded area near the fireplace, or even in their room."

The house is situated near the front of the property. Behind it are eight acres of sculpted grounds bordered by woodland trails. About half of the space is landscaped, and the rest is left in a more natural state. The arbor, porch swing, reflecting pool, and fish pond are classic and elegant. The inn hosts events ranging from corporate meetings to wedding receptions in the lovely garden.

Whether you visit the Pennsbury Inn for an event or on vacation, you'll enjoy the combination of historical importance and laid-back attitude. "I really do consider staying here an experience," says Cheryl. "When people pull into our driveway, it's like pulling into a different world."

Visiting the Pennsbury Inn

883 Baltimore Pike (U.S. Route 1), between PA Route 1 and PA Route 52,
  just opposite Hickory Hill Road and the White Barn, Chadds Ford, PA 19317
Telephone: 610-388-1435 • Fax: 610-388-1436 • Website: www.pennsburyinn.com
Rooms: 6 with private bath; 1 with no bath can be combined with another.
Rates: $72 to $225, including full or Continental-plus breakfast.
Credit cards: Visa, MasterCard, American Express, and Discover.
Personal checks: Accepted.
Check-in: 3 to 6 P.M. Guests may drop their luggage off earlier or arrive later by prior arrangement.
Check-out: Noon.
Smoking policy: Nonsmoking.
Wheelchair accessible: No.
Children: Well-mannered children welcome.
Pets: Accepted on a limited basis, with prior arrangement and with an extra charge. There is a
  miniature poodle in residence.
Noise: Road noise in the front. Quieter rooms are in the back, facing away from U.S. Route 1.
Parking: Free on-site.

FOOD

Best of Italy
1410 Baltimore Pike
Chadds Ford, PA 19317
Telephone: 610-459-9311
Fax: 610-459-9313
Hours: Tuesday through Thursday, 11 A.M. to
9 P.M.; Friday, 11 A.M. to 9:30 P.M.; Saturday,
8 A.M. to 9:30 P.M.; Sunday, brunch 8 A.M. to
3 P.M. and dinner 4 to 8 P.M. Closed Monday.
Prices: Breakfast $2.95 to $13.95, lunch $2.95
to $14.95, dinner $12.95 to $22.95.
Take-out: Yes.
Wheelchair accessible: Yes, through side door.
Restroom is accessible.
Smoking policy: All nonsmoking.
Dress: Casual.
Credit cards: Visa, MasterCard, American
Express, Discover, and Diner's Club.
Personal checks: Accepted with proper
identification.
Other: Full-service deli and bakery. Hand-
painted murals.

Brass Ladle Bistro
31 Old Ridge Village
U.S. Route 202 and Ridge Rd., one mile
south of U.S. Route 1
Chadds Ford, PA 19317
Telephone: 610-358-1422
Website: www.brassladle.com
Restaurant hours: Lunch Monday through
Saturday, 11 A.M. to 3 P.M. Dinner Tuesday
through Thursday, 4:30 to 9 P.M.; Friday and
Saturday, 4:30 to 10 P.M. Sunday brunch,
9 A.M. to 2 P.M.
Pub hours: Dinner Tuesday through Friday,
4 to 9 P.M.; Saturday, 4 to 10 P.M. Late-night
menu available until 11 P.M.
Prices: Lunch and brunch $5 to $10, dinner
$13 to $24.
Take-out: Yes.
Wheelchair accessible: Yes, including restrooms.
Smoking policy: Permitted in the pub area.
Dress: Casual.
Credit cards: Visa, MasterCard, American
Express, and Discover.

Personal checks: Not accepted.
Other: Vegetarian dishes available. Cake mixes
for sale. Located in quaint shopping center.

Chadds Ford Inn
U.S. Route 1 a few yards north of Creek Road
Chadds Ford, PA 19317
Telephone: 610-388-7361
Fax: 610-388-3960
Website: www.chaddsfordinn.com
Hours: Lunch Monday through Friday, 11:30
A.M. to 2:30 P.M.; Saturday, 11:30 A.M. to 4
P.M. Dinner Monday through Thursday, 5:30
to 9 P.M.; Friday and Saturday, 5 to 9:30 P.M.;
Sunday, 2:30 to 8:30 P.M. Sunday brunch,
11 A.M. to 2 P.M. Bartender serves food after
2:30 until dinner on weekdays.
Prices: Lunch averages $12, dinner averages
from $18 to $22.
Take-out: Yes.
Wheelchair accessible: Yes, including restrooms.
Smoking policy: Permitted only in tavern area.
Dress: Dressy casual.
Credit cards: Visa, MasterCard, American
Express, Diner's Club.
Personal checks: Not accepted.
Other: Historic inn in heart of Chadds Ford,
established 1736.

Chadds Ford Tavern & Restaurant
96A Baltimore Pike, Chadds Ford, PA 19317
Telephone: 610-459-8453
Fax: 610-459-9485
Website: www.chaddsfordtavern.com
Hours: Monday through Saturday, 11 A.M. to
11 P.M.; Sunday, noon to 10 P.M. Lunch and
light fare served in afternoons. Dinner
served Monday through Saturday starting
at 5 P.M., Sunday starting at 4 P.M.
Prices: Lunch averages $6, dinner averages $19.
Take-out: Yes.
Wheelchair accessible: Yes, including
restrooms.
Smoking policy: Nonsmoking restaurant.
Smoking permitted in tavern.
Dress: Casual.
Credit cards: Visa and MasterCard.
Personal checks: Accepted with proper
identification.

specialTeas Tea Room

Granted, the British tax on tea was a bad idea, but throwing chests of the valuable leaves into Boston harbor wasn't very nice, either. One of the most unfortunate ramifications of that nasty business (besides the Revolutionary War, of course) was that it soured Americans on the delightful tradition of afternoon tea. Now, more than two centuries later, we are finally rediscovering why our trans-Atlantic cousins have such an allegiance to the ritual.

specialTeas Tea Room in Olde Ridge Shopping Village is the perfect spot to become reacquainted with the culinary art of tea. Two dining rooms accommodate about sixty guests total. The larger room has burgundy beadboard wainscoting with white walls above. A little stenciled vine climbs near the ceiling. The smaller room is painted and stenciled to resemble an English garden with a wrought-iron fence, a birdbath, and morning glories drifting from above. A cardboard Beefeater guards the tables.

The proprietors, sisters Carole Bradley and Judith Finnigan, grew up with tea. "Our grandparents came from England," says Carole, "so we were familiar with the tradition. Then, when Judy went to California to visit her daughter, she saw how popular tea rooms were. When she got back, she said, 'We have to do it now!' Judy worked at Riddle Hospital and I was a bookkeeper. We both quit our jobs. We were in such a frenzy we didn't have time to be afraid."

The pair found the ideal location in Olde Ridge Shopping Village, a collection of specialty shops and restaurants. Judith does the baking, and Carole does food

Take a break from a busy day of touring and shopping to have tea at specialTeas Tea Room.
ALAN B. SILVERMAN

(continued on page 64)

(continued from page 63)

preparation and handles the finances. The atmosphere they've created is quite fetching; the food, scrumptious.

Your server may acquaint you with some of tea's history. The world's first cup of tea is said to have been drunk by Chinese emperor Shen Nung in 2737 B.C. when some *Camellia sinensis* leaves blew into his boiling water. Over the centuries, tea was cultivated in China, India, and Ceylon. The brew gradually became popular in Europe through the efforts of Dutch and British traders.

But it wasn't until Queen Victoria's reign that Anna, the seventh duchess of Bedford, invented what we know today as afternoon tea. The customary dinner hour of eight o'clock left the duchess with a "sinking feeling" in the afternoon, so she had her servants bring tea and cakes. This habit was soon adopted in court circles, and afternoon tea became an important social occasion. Sandwiches were refined into thin, crustless slivers; potters outdid themselves with decorative vessels and cups; hostesses displayed their tea services on acres of fine linen.

Today teatime provides a welcome intermission in a busy day. The predictable progression of dishes—sandwiches, then scones, then pastries—lends an air of regularity and serenity. Gracious service is the norm, and lingering is encouraged. Getting together with a friend for tea is the ideal way to practice the lost art of conversation.

specialTeas serves a traditional English tea menu, including delicate sandwiches, scones with Devonshire cream, lemon curd, and preserves, then sweet items for dessert. Sandwiches, salads, and quiches are also available, as is a children's tea with cookies.

specialTeas sells a wide variety of teas and tea-related items. ALAN B. SILVERMAN

The centerpiece of the meal is the tea itself. You can select from exotic names like Darjeeling, Empress of Japan, Formosa Oolong, and China Jasmine. There are about three dozen teas from which you may choose, including decaffeinated and herbal selections. Your pot will have loose tea leaves steeping inside, so position the little strainer over your cup before you pour.

Along with the dining rooms, specialTeas has a retail area. The store carries all manner of tea-related objects and accessories such as trays, plates, and pots. Fortnum & Mason and Taylors of Harrowgate teas, along with English biscuits, lemon curd, clotted cream, and other goodies, are for sale if you care to re-create the tea experience at home.

Meanwhile, enjoy the candle-scented air, fresh flowers, and quiet music at specialTeas while you relax with friends over some afternoon tea. As the Duchess of Bedford herself might have said, "Capital!"

VISITING SPECIALTEAS TEA ROOM
Olde Ridge Village Shoppes #37
Ridge Road & U.S. Route 202, Chadds Ford, PA 19317
Telephone: 610-358-2320 • Website: www.olderidgevillage.com

Hours: Tuesday through Saturday, 11 A.M. to 4 P.M. Open Monday for afternoon tea only (no lunch), noon to 3 P.M., with reservations. Tea is served on Sundays only for prearranged group events like birthday parties or bridal showers. The shop is open seven days a week; Sunday hours are noon to 5 P.M.

Reservations: Highly recommended; required for Monday afternoon tea.

Price range: Full afternoon tea is $12.50 per person; children's tea is half that. Lunch selections $4.50 to $6.50.

Credit cards: Visa, MasterCard, and Discover.

Children: Welcome.

Wheelchair accessible: There is one small step to enter the tea room. Restroom entrance cannot accommodate a wheelchair, but public restrooms in village can.

Other: Occasional tea parties are held with a fairy theme, the storybook character Angelina Ballerina, and Santa Claus. The tea room also holds periodic classes on tea traditions and the charm of English tea.

Other: Located across U.S. Route 1 from Brandywine Battlefield. Part of building constructed in 1830s. Fireplace in tavern area. Original paintings by local artists. Reservations recommended.

Cuisines Restaurant
200 Wilmington-West Chester Pike
(U.S. Route 202)
Chadds Ford, PA 19317
Telephone: 610-459-3390
Fax: 610-558-2767
Hours: Tuesday through Saturday, 5:30 to 10 P.M.; Sunday, 4 to 8 P.M. Closed Monday.

Prices: Dinner entrees $14 to $22.

Take-out: Yes.

Wheelchair accessible: Yes. The ladies' room is accessible; men's room is not.

Smoking policy: Smoking and nonsmoking sections. Cigarettes and cigars are permitted in lounge.

Dress: Upscale casual.

Credit cards: Visa, MasterCard, American Express, Discover, and Diner's Club.

Personal checks: Accepted with proper identification.

Ebenezer's Cafe

331 Wilmington Pike (U.S. Route 202),
Suite 3 in the Shoppes at Smithbridge
Glen Mills, PA 19342
Telephone: 610-459-3770
Fax: 610-459-3687
Website: www.ebscafe.com
Hours: Monday through Saturday, 6:30 A.M.
to 4:30 P.M.; Sunday, 6:30 A.M. to 3:30 P.M.
Prices: Sandwiches $5.99 to $6.99, breakfast
entrees average $5.75.
Take-out: Yes. Delivery available.
Wheelchair accessible: Yes, including
restrooms.
Smoking policy: Nonsmoking.
Dress: Casual.
Credit cards: Visa, MasterCard, American
Express, Discover, and Diner's Club.
Personal checks: Accepted with proper
identification.
Other: Creative and delicious sandwiches,
wraps, specialty coffee, bagels, and pastry.
Cozy upscale coffee-shop atmosphere.
Newspapers and magazines for patrons' use.
Local art for sale. It's a franchise but feels
like part of the neighborhood.

The Gables at Chadds Ford

423 Baltimore Pike
Chadds Ford, PA 19317
Telephone: 610-388-7700
Fax: 610-388-7264
Hours: Lunch Monday through Friday, 11:30
A.M. to 2:30 P.M. Dinner Monday, 5:30 to
9 P.M.; Tuesday through Thursday, 5:30 to
10 P.M.; Friday and Saturday, 5:30 to 11 P.M.;
Sunday, 5 to 9 P.M.
Prices: Lunch $7 to $11, dinner entrees
$16 to $25.
Take-out: Limited.
Wheelchair accessible: Yes, including
restrooms.
Smoking policy: In bar only, though even
seats far from the bar sometimes receive
secondhand smoke.
Dress: Upscale casual.
Credit cards: Visa, MasterCard, American
Express, and Discover.

Personal checks: Accepted with proper
identification.
Other: Structure originally constructed in 1700
on part of a William Penn land grant. Updated
to Victorian style in 1897. Live jazz Friday and
Saturday. Outdoor patio in warm weather.

Hank's Place

U.S. Route 1 and Creek Road
Chadds Ford, PA 19317
Telephone: 610-388-7061
Hours: Monday, 6 A.M. to 4 P.M.; Tuesday
through Saturday, 6 A.M. to 7 P.M.; Sunday, 7
A.M. to 3 P.M. Breakfast served all day Sunday.
Prices: Breakfast entrees $4.95 to $5.95, sand-
wiches $3.50 to $5.50, dinner platters $5.95
to $11.95, desserts no more than $3.50.
Take-out: Yes.
Wheelchair accessible: Yes, including restrooms.
Smoking policy: All nonsmoking.
Dress: Casual.
Credit cards: Not accepted.
Personal checks: Not accepted.
Other: About thirty-five seats plus counter;
crowded at breakfast on weekends. A
local institution.

McKenzie Brew House

451 Wilmington–West Chester Pike, on U.S.
Route 202 one mile south of U.S. Route 1
Glen Mills, PA 19342
Telephone: 610-361-9800
Fax: 610-361-0409
Website: www.mckenziebrewhouse.com
Hours: Lunch daily, 11:30 to 4 P.M. Dinner
Sunday, 4 to 10 P.M.; Monday through
Thursday, 4 to 11 P.M.; Friday and Saturday,
4 to midnight.
Prices: Lunch averages $7, dinner $11 to $16.
Take-out: Yes.
Wheelchair accessible: Yes, including
restrooms.
Credit cards: Visa, MasterCard, American
Express, Discover, and Diner's Club.
Personal checks: Not accepted.

Smoking policy: Restaurant is nonsmoking. Smoking permitted in bar and downstairs in the billiard area. The restaurant entrance and the tables closest to the bar area are subject to secondhand smoke.

Dress: Smart casual.

Other: Billiards and game room downstairs, 5 P.M. to 2 A.M. Karaoke Thursday starting at 9 P.M. Live entertainment Friday from 9 P.M. and Saturday, 10 P.M. to 1:30 A.M. Selection of microbrews.

Mendenhall Inn

PA Route 52 about 1.5 miles south of U.S. Route 1
Mendenhall, PA 19357
Telephone: 610-388-1181
Fax: 610-388-1184
Website: www.mendenhallinn.com

Hours: Lunch Monday through Saturday, 11:30 A.M. to 2:30 P.M. Dinner Monday through Saturday, 5 to 10 P.M. Sunday champagne brunch 10 A.M. to 2 P.M., dinner 4 to 8 P.M.

Prices: Lunch $9 to $16 (soups and salads $4.25 to $7), dinner $19 to $45.

Take-out: No.

Wheelchair accessible: Yes to restaurant, but must use restrooms in hotel area.

Smoking policy: Nonsmoking dining rooms. Smoking permitted in tavern.

Dress: Upscale casual, jackets preferred.

Credit cards: Visa, MasterCard, American Express, Discover, and Diner's Club.

Personal checks: Accepted with proper identification.

Other: Live piano or harp music at dinner.

West Chester

West Chester's contrasts make it special. It's big enough to be interesting, yet small enough to be walkable; rich in history, yet with a thriving contemporary arts scene; intent on preserving its physical environment, while also nurturing its cultural climate. There's an energy in town that makes West Chester fun, lively, and welcoming for residents and visitors alike. No wonder the July 26, 2001, *Philadelphia Inquirer* called West Chester "one of the world's most perfect small towns."

Chester County, established by William Penn in 1682, is one of the three original Pennsylvania counties. The county seat was moved from Chester, in what is now Delaware County, to West Chester in 1786. This was due in part to West Chester's location at the crossroads of Lancaster Pike, which connected Philadelphia and Lancaster, and the north-south Pottstown Pike.

At that time, the burg was called Turk's Head, for the sign at the tavern opened by Phineas Eachus in 1762. When it was made a borough by the legislature in 1799, the more decorous name West Chester was made official.

The many Greek Revival structures earned the borough the nickname "the Athens of Pennsylvania." The most impressive edifice of this type is Thomas U. Walter's 1848 courthouse, with its Corinthian columns and wide front stairs. Walter later went on to design the capitol dome in Washington, D.C.

Greek Revival is just the tip of the architectural iceberg, though. The borough has

a happy mélange of Federal, Italianate, Romanesque Revival, Queen Anne, Victorian, and Art Deco style buildings, more than four hundred of which are listed on the National Register of Historic Places. The entire downtown area is also on this list.

West Chester University is a vital part of town. The main campus covers several blocks in the southwestern quadrant. In recognition of its significant architecture, the Quadrangle Historic District was awarded a spot on the National Register.

West Chester has had its share of important people and events. Horace Pippin, the noted painter especially of primitive scenes, was from West Chester,

West Chester's shops and art galleries welcome visitors. BUSINESS IMPROVEMENT DISTRICT/RICK DAVIS

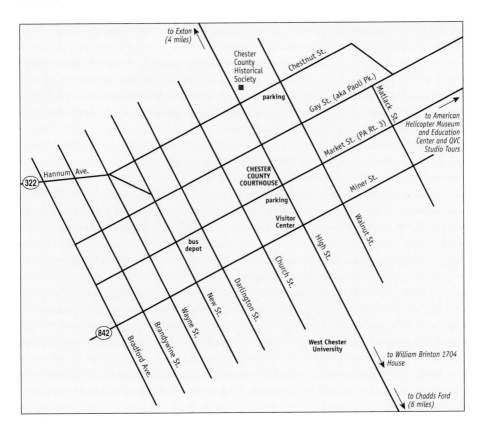

as was the composer Samuel Barber. Claude Rains of *Casablanca* fame retired here with his family. Abraham Lincoln kicked off his first presidential campaign in West Chester; the first biography of the Great Emancipator was published here in a series of editorials. Civil rights activist Bayard Rustin called West Chester home.

Today about eighteen thousand people have that privilege. For those who live here and those who visit, West Chester offers everything that's best in America's small towns. In addition, nearby attractions like the American Helicopter Museum and Education Center and the studio tour at television shopping colossus QVC are worthwhile excursions.

Getting Around

The best way to explore West Chester is on foot. There are parking garages on High Street just south of Market and on Chestnut Street east of High Street. There are also many metered spaces. If you park on the street, read the signs; some areas are designated for resident parking only.

To get oriented, it helps to understand West Chester's grid layout. High Street is the main north-south street through town; Gay Street runs east and west, though traffic is one-way westbound; Market Street parallels Gay, with one-way traffic going east. The intersection of High and Market, site of the county courthouse, marks the center of the quadrants that make up the 1.8-square-mile borough.

West Chester has a variety of architectural styles. This ornate ironwork looks like it would be at home in New Orleans. BUSINESS IMPROVEMENT DISTRICT/RICK DAVIS

You may want to make your first stop the Business Improvement District office (24 S. High St.) or the Chester County Historical Society (225 N. High St.). At either location, you can pick up a booklet for a self-guided walking tour and get answers to your questions. The BID stocks a selection of brochures about local attractions, events, restaurants, retail establishments, and accommodations.

Shopping, restaurants, and galleries are located mostly on High Street, Gay Street, and Market Street. Many restaurants offer outdoor dining in summer. If you have time, stroll along the tree-lined side streets as well.

Leaving West Chester by car, you'll find quaint country lanes along New Street and Creek Road. U.S. Route 202 is a major highway to Wilmington. Westtown, west of U.S. Route 202 on PA Route 926, has its own leafy charm.

The first Saturday in October presents a unique opportunity to see some of West Chester's historical and architectural gems, as well as special spots throughout Chester County. Known as Chester County Day, this event opens approximately fifty properties to ticket holders. An amazing array of beautifully restored homes and spectacular gardens makes this event a don't-miss.

As for public transportation, SCCOOT (Southern Chester County Organization on Transportation) buses run from West Chester to Chadds Ford, Kennett Square, Avondale, West Grove, and Oxford. For information on routes, fares, and schedules, call 877-612-1359, or visit www.tmacc.org.

Calendar of Events

Many local events are sponsored by the attractions featured in this chapter. Consult those listings for details.

May through August, one Thursday per month 6:30 to 9:30 P.M.: Swingin' Summer Thursdays, Gay Street. Call 610-738-3350 or visit www.westchesterbid.com.

May to October, Saturday mornings: Growers Market, Church and Chestnut Streets.

May, first Sunday, 11 A.M. to 5 P.M.: May Day festival, Everhart Park, West Union Street and South Bradford Avenue. Crafts, family entertainment, food, and amusements. Call 610-436-9010.

May, one weekend midmonth: May Festival. Chester County Hospital, 701 E. Marshall St. Amusement rides, games, and entertainment. Visit www.cchosp.com.

June, first Friday, 5 to 9 P.M.: Gallery Walk, downtown West Chester. Call 610-696-4046 or visit www.greaterwestchester.com.

June, first or second Sunday, 11 A.M. to 5 P.M.: Super Sunday street fair along Gay Street between Matlack and Darlington Streets. Food, crafts, antique cars, kids' rides, clowns, jugglers, live bands, and more. Call 610-436-9010 or e-mail wcrec@aol.com.

July, date varies, noon to 8 P.M.: Turk's Head Music Festival, Everhart Park. Call 610-436-9010 or e-mail wcrec@aol.com.

September, third Sunday: Downtown Restaurant Festival, Gay Street. Call 610-436-9010 or e-mail wcrec@aol.com.

Brick sidewalks and old-fashioned street lamps give West Chester a cozy feel as evening begins.
BUSINESS IMPROVEMENT DISTRICT/RICK DAVIS

Tidy, well-kept homes like this one are part of West Chester's appeal. BUSINESS IMPROVEMENT DISTRICT/RICK DAVIS

October, first Friday, 5 to 9 P.M.: Gallery Walk, downtown West Chester. Call 610-696-4046 or visit www.greater westchester.com.

October, first Saturday: Chester County Day. This self-drive annual event opens some fifty historic homes and properties. Tickets are required; contact the organizers for cost. Preview slide shows are given Friday evening at the Chester County Courthouse and at Longwood Gardens. No children under twelve years old, including babes-in-arms or kids in backpacks, are permitted. Indoor photography is prohibited. No high heels. Call 610-431-5301 or visit www.greaterwest chester.com.

October, Thursday before Halloween: Halloween Parade, downtown West Chester.

December, a Friday through Monday early in the month: Old-fashioned Christmas, downtown West Chester. Starts with a parade at 6:45 P.M. Friday evening. Activities and concerts continue throughout the weekend. Call 610-696-4046 or visit www.greaterwestchester.com.

December, first Saturday, 10 A.M. to 5 P.M.: YWCA Holiday House Tour. About a dozen historic and contemporary homes in the borough are on this walking tour. Donation $20. Call 610-692-3737, fax 610-692-5014, or e-mail ywca_gwc @netzero.net.

FEATURED ATTRACTIONS

American Helicopter Museum & Education Center

Most of us probably take helicopters for granted, maybe glancing upward when we hear one, but that's pretty much it. It's time we gave more appreciation to these complex flying machines. Today more than forty thousand helicopters are in service around the world. Civilian uses include ambulance and rescue service, police surveillance, traffic monitoring, firefighting, corporate transport, and construction. Helicopters are used by the military to move troops, to sweep for mines, in surveillance, and for combat missions.

The best place to learn more is at the American Helicopter Museum & Education Center, dedicated to helicopters and the people who design and build them. Thirty-five rotorcraft—including eight you can climb into and handle the controls—

Visiting the American Helicopter Museum & Education Center

1220 American Boulevard, off Airport Road at Brandywine Airport
West Chester, PA 19380
Telephone: 610-436-9600 • Fax: 610-436-8642
Website: www.helicoptermuseum.org

Hours: Wednesday through Saturday, 10 A.M. to 5 P.M.; Sunday, noon to 5 P.M. Open Monday and Tuesday by appointment only. Closed New Year's Day, Easter, Thanksgiving Day, and Christmas.

Admission: Adults $6, seniors sixty-five and older $5, children three through eighteen and college students with valid identification $4, ages two and under free.

Group tours: Tours at discounted rates are available with at least two weeks' notice. Call for information and reservations.

Educational programs: Available for school groups. Call for field trip information and cost. Reservations must be made at least three weeks in advance.

Credit cards: MasterCard, Visa, and Discover accepted for admissions, gift shop sales, and helicopter rides.

Personal checks: Accepted with proper identification for admissions, gift shop sales, and helicopter rides.

Special considerations: The museum is wheelchair accessible, including hands-on exhibits.

Food service: Vending machines. Other food available at special events. Food is available nearby on Gay Street in West Chester.

Other: If you are interested in touring QVC, Studio Park is located in the same industrial park as the American Helicopter Museum & Education Center.

are on display, supplemented by models, videos, written material, and photographs in a fun and fascinating atmosphere suitable for all ages. Regular festivals and demonstrations show helicopters in action. And yes, rides are available.

The History of Rotorcraft

The idea of a flying rotor is nothing new. The word *helicopter* comes from the Greek *heliko*, meaning spiral or winding, and *pteron*, meaning feather or wing. An ancient Chinese toy was exactly that: feathers on the end of a stick, spun by rapidly pushing one hand forward and pulling the other back. The rotor would rise upward and then spin gently to the ground.

In the mid-1500s, Leonardo da Vinci drew a machine very similar to modern helicopters, which he called the "aerial-screw." Other inventors over the years modified Leonardo's design or came up with their own, but technical problems prevented putting theory into practice. Even inventor Thomas Edison experimented with models. Although his experiments never resulted in a working machine, they were useful in proving that two conditions had to be met for success: an aerodynamically efficient rotor and sufficient power.

Steam engines in the 1800s were too heavy for the rotors of the time to lift off the ground. The late-nineteenth-century development of the internal combustion

This V-22 Osprey tilt-rotor is on display at the American Helicopter Museum & Education Center.
AMERICAN HELICOPTER MUSEUM & EDUCATION CENTER

engine gave rotorcraft pioneers a way to develop adequate power with much less weight.

In 1907, French bicycle maker Paul Cornu's twin-rotor helicopter lifted into the air for a few seconds. A breakthrough, certainly, but one that revealed as many problems as it solved. One was torque, which caused the fuselage to rotate in the opposite direction from the rotor. Another was the unequal lift on the rotor's advancing and retreating blades. This had the undesirable effect of causing the helicopter to flip over.

Scientists, engineers, and inventors around the world tried to conquer these obstacles. In 1909, Igor Sikorsky gave it a shot in Russia. After a while, he abandoned the idea, only to return to it decades later in the United States. In Denmark, Austria, Britain, the United States, and elsewhere, great minds attacked the questions of rotary-wing flight and came up with a variety of solutions. Some of these look absurd to us today, like the machine where four rotors were baffled with five biplane wings apiece.

Spanish engineer Juan de la Cierva built a hybrid rotary-wing vehicle, with the wings and tail of a conventional aircraft, plus an unpowered rotor mounted above the fuselage. The first successful model lifted off in 1923. The Autogiro was not a true helicopter, but it was close.

De la Cierva's contribution was very important. In the United States, the Kellett and Pitcairn companies obtained manufacturing licenses from de la Cierva's company. The first American autogyro flew in 1928.

In Germany, Heinrich Focke of the Focke-Wulf Company worked on rotating-wing aircraft starting in 1933. He and a partner built the first successful machine with two rotors side by side, the Fw61. It was unprecedented in two ways: It could be controlled completely, and it permitted successful autorotation—the ability to keep the rotor spinning and make a safe landing in the event of engine failure.

Philadelphia aeronautical engineer Laurence LePage saw the Fw61 at the Focke-Achgelis factory near Bremen, Germany, in 1938 and filmed the helicopter in action. Driven by two three-bladed rotors, the craft rose straight up and could attain speeds of ninety miles per hour. It flew forward, backward, and sideways and could hover. Even if the motor quit, the Fw61 came down more slowly than a parachute. A practical helicopter was finally a reality. The pictures created a sensation in the United States, spurring the U.S. government to authorize $2 million for rotary-wing research.

Igor Sikorsky, having emigrated from Russia, again worked on helicopters. One of his creations was nicknamed "Igor's nightmare." The VS-300 flew in 1939. It could hover and go sideways and backward, but it balked at going forward. Sikorsky's subsequent models refined the configuration. Several of the R-5/S-51 series were produced by Sikorsky Aircraft.

Southeastern Pennsylvania was the center of the burgeoning American helicopter industry. In fact, several of the major U.S. helicopter manufacturers in business today can trace their roots back to the Philadelphia area. Arthur Young's work led to the design of the Bell Helicopter Company's Model 47, the first helicopter in the world to be certified for commercial use. Frank Piasecki's company, Piasecki Helicopter Corporation, developed the overlapping tandem rotor configuration.

One of aviation's most famous people, Amelia Earhart, also made a mark in this region. In April 1931, she set an altitude record of 18,415 feet in a Pitcairn-Cierva autogiro at Willow Grove's Pitcairn Field.

In the last half of the twentieth century and into the twenty-first, developments on helicopters continue to improve performance, reliability, efficiency, and lifting capability. These safe and versatile flying machines play an important role in modern aviation.

Visitors may get into many of the rotorcraft on display. AMERICAN HELICOPTER MUSEUM & EDUCATION CENTER

Museum History

In 1993, the American Helicopter Society's Philadelphia Chapter was preparing to celebrate its fiftieth anniversary. As part of this milestone, the society assigned a committee to establish "a lasting tribute to those men and women who pioneered the development of rotary-wing aircraft in the Delaware Valley." The endeavor garnered immediate and enthusiastic support from individuals and industry. Under the leadership of founder and board chairman Peter Wright Jr. and a dedicated team of volunteers, the American Helicopter Museum & Education Center opened in October 1996 in the former MBB helicopter assembly plant next to Brandywine Airport. It's the nation's premier museum dedicated solely to helicopters.

Frank Robinson, founder and president of Robinson Helicopter Company, gave the museum $1 million in 2002. With this generous donation, the museum was able to purchase the building it had been leasing half of, doubling its square footage. This expanded space will enable the museum to present new collections and displays, emphasizing interactive exhibits. The new section is scheduled to open in 2006.

Exhibits

The American Helicopter Museum & Education Center is a fun place to learn about the country's rotorcraft heritage, whether you're seriously involved in aviation or just have a casual interest.

The most exciting part of the museum is the whirlybirds themselves. Over thirty-five aircraft are on display, and visitors are allowed to get in eight of them to "be the pilot" and work the controls. There's nothing like a hands-on experience to make a museum visit memorable.

Featured aircraft include Pitcairn's PCA-1 1929 autogiro; the Sikorsky XR-4, the prototype for the world's first mass-produced helicopter; the Piasecki PV-2, the second successful helicopter to fly in the United States; the Bell Model 30-1A from 1943, the earliest surviving Bell helicopter; and the Bell 47B, the first commercially certified helicopter. Also on display are a Bell H-13 (47D-1) in its "MASH" configuration from Korea, used for transporting injured from the battlefield, and a Bell TH-1L "Huey," familiar from the Vietnam War.

A real showstopper sits outdoors: the only V-22 tilt-rotor Osprey on public exhibition, on loan from the U.S. Marine Corps. The Osprey is partially stripped so visitors can see the cockpit and wiring.

Back inside, information panels present information about early rotary-wing design. Videos explain the beginnings of the helicopter industry and examine helicopter use in the Korean War and the Vietnam War. Scale models of futuristic designs theorize about upcoming innovations.

Helicopters have enabled people to do some pretty incredible things, and the museum's exhibits present these feats. Don't miss the displays of people performing power line maintenance on a platform suspended from the struts of a hovering chopper, with 230,000 to 500,000 volts going through those lines. Helicopters have also helped people extinguish fires, maintain oil rigs, and position man-made nests for eagles.

This helicopter is familiar to visitors as the MASH-type used in Korea. AMERICAN HELICOPTER MUSEUM & EDUCATION CENTER

For more in-depth information, the library and archives contain original photographs, documents, and manuscripts, plus technical manuals for helicopter manufacture and operation.

It's easy to see why the American Helicopter Museum has won accolades including "Best Educational Outing for Kids" from *Main Line Today* and "Best Scientific Outing for Kids" from *Philadelphia Magazine*. Little kids can pull up a rug square near a play table and use paper, clipboards, and crayons to draw their own helicopter designs. School-age children are intrigued by the working model of a wind tunnel, where they can see how air affects rotors. Children—and adults, too—love to climb into the helicopters and work the controls.

Festivals are held several times a year. The biggest event is the All-Helicopter Airshow—Rotorfest, one weekend in mid-October, featuring static and flight demonstrations by military helicopters like the Cobra and Apache, Coast Guard rescue demonstrations, police aircraft, medical evacuation helicopters, and news choppers. Helicopter rides, flight simulators, food, and kiddie rides round out the program.

A visit to the American Helicopter Museum & Education Center will deepen your appreciation for rotorcraft and will inspire you to let your own imagination take flight.

Calendar of Events

Ongoing: Liberty Aviation Services, Inc., in cooperation with the museum, offers helicopter rides Wednesday through Saturday, 1 to 1:30 P.M. No appointment necessary. First-come, first-served. $35 per person. These are one-person rides for six to eight minutes. Children must be at least twelve years old.

By appointment: Half-hour and one-hour sight-seeing tours over the Brandywine Valley. Half-hour rides for up to three passengers cost $275; a one-hour ride for up to three passengers costs $535. Call the museum for information, reservations, or gift certificates.

Third Saturday of every month, 11 A.M. to 3 P.M.: Family helicopter rides. $35 per person. First-come, first-served.

February, Presidents' Day, 11 A.M. to 5 P.M.: Open house. Kids twelve and under admitted free when accompanied by an adult. Refreshments served. Family helicopter rides available for $35 per person.

Father's Day, noon to 4 P.M.: Fatherfest. Admission $5. Antique cars and motorcycles are on display. Food is sold. Helicopter rides available.

July through mid-August, Mondays and Tuesdays, 10 A.M. to 3 P.M.: Aerocamp. Two-day sessions of hands-on experience for ages eight to fourteen. Campers learn fundamentals of flight while designing, building, and flying their own gliders. Tuition $50 for members, $60 for nonmembers. Lunch and snacks included.

October, one weekend midmonth, 10 A.M. to 4:30 P.M.: All-Helicopter Air Show—Rotorfest, the only all-helicopter air show in America. Adults $10, children $5. Flight demonstrations, helicopter rides, amusement rides, food.

Late November and early December, two Saturdays, 10:30 A.M. to noon, and 1 to 2:30 P.M.: Visit with Santa Claus. Adults $6, seniors $5, ages three to twelve $10, ages two and under $5. Santa arrives via helicopter to greet children. Includes photo with Santa, refreshments, Christmas activities. Family helicopter rides available 11 A.M. to 3 P.M.

The William Brinton 1704 House

The Brinton 1704 House is an example of the importance of documentation and family ties. Thanks to meticulous records that have been kept for centuries and interest on the part of the builder's descendants, this historic Quaker home has been restored to its original straightforward elegance. The building, with its pent eaves and twenty-seven leaded casement windows, has been called one of the most authentic restorations in Pennsylvania.

William the Elder was the first Brinton to arrive in Pennsylvania. In 1684, this English Quaker and his wife and son weathered their first colonial winter in a cave. Soon after, the family built a wood cabin and began to farm 450 acres, a William Penn land grant.

By 1704, the younger William, called "William the Builder," had his own wife and children. He built a stone home in medieval English style. According to the Historic American Buildings Survey, the house originally had a basement kitchen, two rooms on the first floor, and a large unfinished attic. Walnut was used for door and window frames and for interior partitions. The walls, from stone quarried nearby, are twenty-two inches thick.

William died in 1751. His son, grandson, and great-grandson occupied the house in succession. Then things got complicated. The house passed to Joseph Brinton, who was from a different branch of the family. Joseph passed the property on to his children. In 1829, the house was bought by Ziba Darlington, a direct descendant of "William the Builder." It changed hands several times through the rest of the nine-

Visiting the William Brinton 1704 House

1435 Oakland Rd. just west of U.S. 202, .25 mile south of Brinton's Bridge Road
Dilworthtown (West Chester), PA 19382
Telephone: 610-399-0913 • Website: www.brintonfamily.org

Hours: May through October, Monday through Friday, 10 A.M. to 2 P.M.; Saturday and Sunday, 11A.M. to 6 P.M. Closed holidays.
Admission: $3.
Groups: By appointment only.
Special considerations: Not wheelchair accessible.

teenth century and halfway through the twentieth. Various additions and wings were put on over the years. Finally, the house returned to the Brinton family when Francis D. and Deborah Brinton, historians and antiquarians, bought it in 1947.

Restoration commenced in 1954, with money raised by the Brinton Family Association, now called the Brinton Association of America. An extensive inventory of the furnishings at the time William the Builder died has proven priceless in restoring the house. Also useful was the diary West Chester lawyer John Hill Brinton kept between 1830 and 1892, which included extensive descriptions of the house as told

The William Brinton 1704 House is a fine example of a large colonial home. Stone for the structure was quarried nearby. WILLIAM BRINTON 1704 HOUSE

to him by older members of the family. A Thomas Eakins oil painting of the property was helpful in knowing what the exterior looked like.

During the restoration, the placement and size of the indoor bake oven were revealed, as were the locations of the seats by the front door and the stairways and closets. Furnishings match the 1751 inventory as closely as possible. Most of the flooring is original. The house was designated a National Historic Landmark in 1968.

Today the Brinton Association of America exercises careful stewardship over this fine Quaker home. The house is open for tours from late spring to early fall.

Calendar of Events

September, Saturday after Labor Day: Carriage House Attic Sale. $3 parking fee includes house tour.

Chester County Historical Society

The Chester County Historical Society (CCHS) does everything one would expect from an organization with that name: keeps records, maintains the archives, and preserves artifacts.

It also does so much more. In well-planned, beautifully executed displays worthy of any fine museum, the CCHS exhibits items that represent more than three hundred years of life in this part of Pennsylvania. The Society's collection comprises sixty-five thousand objects that were made or used locally, a fascinating array of items from agricultural equipment to fine furniture, political memorabilia to dollhouses, and everything in between. These permanent and changing exhibits are an important resource for understanding and appreciating the region. A hands-on area encourages children to interact with history in a fun way. A library, auditorium, classroom, museum store, and ongoing lecture series help the CCHS achieve its goals of preservation and education.

The Chester County Historical Society's headquarters has grown to include several structures in the center of West Chester. CHESTER COUNTY HISTORICAL SOCIETY

Visiting Chester County Historical Society

225 N. High St., West Chester, PA 19380-2691
Telephone: 610-692-4800 • Fax: 610-692-4357
E-mail: cchs@chestercohistorical.org • Website: www.chestercohistorical.org

Hours: Monday through Saturday, 9:30 A.M. to 4:30 P.M.; open Wednesday evenings until 8 P.M. Closed Sundays and holidays except for occasional special events. Library hours are the same, except on Wednesdays, when library hours are 1 to 8 P.M.

Admission: Adults $5, seniors and students with identification $4, children six through seventeen $2.50, ages five and under admitted free.

Credit cards: Visa and MasterCard.

Personal checks: Accepted.

Tours: Guided tours are available at no extra charge from volunteer guides Monday through Friday. If you're interested in a guided tour, tell the admissions clerk when you check in.

Special considerations: Completely wheelchair accessible.

Parking: There is a public garage on Chestnut Street across from the Chester County Historical Society. Metered on-street parking is available on High Street.

Group and special-interest tours: Special rates are available for groups of fifteen or more. Reservations required. Special-interest tours can also be arranged. Call for information and reservations.

Chester County Archives: The Archives are located in the Government Services Center about 1.5 miles from downtown West Chester at 610 Westtown Rd., Suite 80, P.O. Box 2747, West Chester, PA 19380-0990. For hours and information, call 610-344-6760.

The Historical Society's location in the heart of West Chester makes it the perfect spot to spend an hour or two before starting a tour of the town. Appreciate the past, then experience the present.

History

The Chester County Historical Society was formed on April 11, 1893, by an extraordinary group of forty community leaders. They offered membership to men and women: initiation fee $2, annual dues $1. Meetings were held at the West Chester Public Library on North Church Street.

As soon as word got out, artifacts started to come in. This presented a pressing need for storage space. The Society asked for room in the county courthouse, but the request was denied. By October 1898, the Society had 317 books, 615 pamphlets, 72 magazines, years' worth of county newspapers, and artifacts ranging from photographs to the sign from the old Turk's Head Inn.

The problem was temporarily alleviated when the State Normal School (now West Chester University) built a library in the southern part of West Chester borough. It didn't hurt that George Morris Philips was president of the Society and principal of the Normal School. In 1903, Philips got permission for the Society to house its collections in a room on the library's second floor.

To help educate the citizenry about the area's history, the Society issued pamphlets and erected markers to commemorate significant people, places, and events. Beginning in 1907, a formal banquet was held annually as a fund-raiser and a way to increase awareness about the CCHS and the things it was trying to preserve.

The Society continued to hope for a home of its own. Horticultural Hall in West Chester had been designed by Thomas Ustick Walter, who also designed the U.S. capitol's dome and wings. The building was erected in 1848 and used by the county Horticultural Society for meetings and exhibits. Uriah Hunt Painter, a local businessman and former Civil War correspondent, purchased the property in 1880 and turned it into an Opera House. He died in 1900, and in 1904 Painter's widow gave the property to a Civil War veterans' organization, with the proviso that it be conveyed to the CCHS when the Grand Army of the Republic group no longer needed it. The Society members paid the insurance premiums on the building, now renamed Memorial Hall, since they hoped to occupy it eventually.

Space problems recurred. The CCHS needed a building in good condition, large enough to house and preserve its collections, ideally in the center of town. The Society also needed a way to pay for it.

By November 1936, the GAR post was inactive, and the CCHS could use Memorial Hall, with a fireproof addition. It took four years to raise the necessary funds, but finally the collection was transferred. Twenty volunteers made over five hundred trips up and down the Normal School Library stairs during the move.

In the 1940s and 1950s, the press and public started to sit up and take notice of the collections. Exhibits were rotated to showcase pewter, majolica, election ban-

Furniture, needlework, and changing exhibits put historical events and early Chester County daily life into context. CHESTER COUNTY HISTORICAL SOCIETY

ners, and clocks, among other things. Craft and display rooms were set up: a bank, country store with post office, blacksmith shop, weaving area, and schoolroom.

A breakthrough exhibit in the 1960s brought additional positive attention to the CCHS. "Delaware Valley Dining" showed four dining rooms in different styles: William and Mary, Queen Anne, Chippendale, and Classical. The authenticity and beauty of the displays wowed critics and visitors alike.

Once again, the Society was cramped for space. A program of deaccessioning was begun so that inappropriate or duplicate items could be shed. Rather than move, the CCHS renovated and expanded Memorial Hall. The "new" building opened in October 1979.

Successful exhibitions continued in the 1980s and 1990s, including shows on wedding dresses, spice boxes, chairs, pewter, and Quaker clothing. In the midst of this, the Central Chester County YMCA, Memorial Hall's next-door neighbor, asked the Society whether there was interest in buying the YMCA's old building just across the alley. The board voted yes, adding thirty-five thousand square feet of welcome space. Renovations were made, and the buildings were linked by a second-floor bridge. With the additional space, the CCHS now has a total of nine galleries, collectively renamed "The History Center." The grand opening was in April 1995.

If the attendance record-breaking 2002–04 exhibit "Just Over the Line: Chester County and the Underground Railroad" is any indication, the Chester County Historical Society is fulfilling its mission to bring the past to the people more fully than ever.

Permanent Exhibits

A good place to start your tour is with "Chester County, A View of the Past." This introductory exhibit provides an overview of Chester County's natural resources, the people who settled here, and their customs and traditions.

Always a favorite, "Chester County Craftsmanship" explores the material culture of the area's European settlers from the 1680s to the 1820s. The more you learn about the decorative arts, the more you can see relationships between the objects and the traditions of the people who used them. For example, English Quakers favored chests of drawers for storage, while the Pennsylvania Germans preferred blanket chests that opened with a hinged lid. Examining the way items changed over time also offers a window into technological innovations.

The Society's collections of items like spice boxes, wainscot furniture, and tall-case clocks are attractively housed in alcoves of architectural woodwork from area homes.

The "History Lab" provides the kind of space families love: a place where kids (and adults) can touch things. This hands-on gallery encourages tactile exploration. Visitors can assemble a Chippendale chair, churn pretend butter, and don nineteenth-century-style clothing. These experiences make a visit to the CCHS fun and memorable for the younger set.

For browsers and serious researchers alike, the CCHS library has an extensive collection of personal, family, business, and organizational records. Along with books, maps, and newspapers, the library houses diaries, letters, postcards, and other relevant items. The collection is particularly strong in daguerreotypes and photographs, with approximately eighty thousand images from the 1850s on.

Hoop skirts and parasols are some of yesteryear's formal clothing. CHESTER COUNTY HISTORICAL SOCIETY

The museum shop sells Chester County–related items, including books and crafts. Elementary- and middle-school-age children may enjoy the "Passport to Historic West Chester," which serves as a guide to a West Chester walking tour. The passport teaches visitors to look for datestones, markers, and monuments; to identify "leftover" objects that once served a purpose but no longer do; and to identify architectural styles found in town.

Calendar of Events

March: Antiques Show. Date and location vary. Admission charged. More than fifty dealers participate. Lectures, appraisals, and more.

Spring and Fall, one day a month: Lunchtime programs, including book discussions, concerts, special exhibition tours, and lectures.

Spring: History Day. Students from across the region and the country participate in the annual History Day competition. Projects are on display. Held at West Chester University.

September through May, Wednesday evenings: Lectures, living-history performances, special programs. Admission fee charged.

October, one day: African-American art exhibit.

November: Fall conference. Chester County Historical Society and West Chester University team up for a full-day conference featuring prominent scholars discussing an issue pertinent to the region, in the past and today.

December: Holiday events include an open house as part of West Chester's Old-Fashioned Christmas; children's entertainment, greens sale, holiday concerts, specials at the museum shop, and more. Dates and times vary.

QVC Studio Tour

West Chester has its own slice of Hollywood at QVC Studio Park. A one-hour guided walking tour gives a behind-the-scenes look at what goes into the television retailer's polished shows, from product selection to on-air presentation. The guide also explains the origins and philosophy of QVC. The tour is lively and fun, and visitors even get to stand on an observation deck overlooking a live broadcast in progress. Whether you're new to QVC or have been a regular shopper for years, the tour will deepen your appreciation for what the company does and how well it's done.

The Company

QVC is the result of one man's idea for a "better mousetrap." Joseph Segel, founder of the Franklin Mint (known for its plates, coins, and collectibles), saw a televised shopping show in the mid-1980s and was appalled by the hard-sell approach. Segel saw an opportunity for a technology-based retail business, but one that was true to the principles of quality, value, and convenience, hence the name QVC.

QVC's first broadcast on November 24, 1986, was a modest but respectable debut carried by fifty-eight cable systems in twenty states. Sales that day were $7,400. In its first fiscal year, the company set a record for sales by a new public company. Fast-forward fifteen years to December 2, 2001, when QVC achieved $80 million worth of orders in a single day. The network now reaches eighty-five million homes in all fifty states, and also broadcasts in the United Kingdom, Germany, and Japan.

Other statistics are equally staggering. Studio Park is an eighty-four-acre campus with thirty-three hundred employees. Off-site storage capacity is equivalent to sixty-six football fields. QVC provides more live programming than any other network except ones that are all news.

Everyone from soup lovers to sports nuts will find something to like in QVC's product mix. Each hour has a theme and is specially choreographed to target a distinct demographic profile. Homey-looking sets and friendly, calm hosts draw people in and make them comfortable with the products being sold. As the company has grown and been successful, it has remained faithful to its goal to create long-term relationships with its customers.

The Tour

Your tour begins in the Milestone Room, where your guide will share background information and show a short film about

Studio tours at QVC give visitors a sneak peek behind the scenes of the world's largest electronic retailer. QVC

QVC Studio Tour

1200 Wilson Dr. (in the Brandywine Industrial Park), West Chester, PA 19380
Telephone: 800-600-9900 • Website: www.qvctours.com

Hours: Tours daily on the hour 10 A.M. to 4 P.M. The store is open 9:30 A.M. to 6 P.M. Closed Thanksgiving Day, Christmas, and New Year's.

Admission: Adults $7.50, ages six to twelve $5. Group rates available. Reservations required for groups of ten or more.

Parking: Free on-site.

Photography: Not permitted.

Food: Vending machines only. Numerous restaurants nearby on West Chester Pike (PA Route 3), on Gay Street between QVC and downtown West Chester, and in West Chester itself.

Special considerations: Completely wheelchair accessible.

Other: To join the audience for a live broadcast, reservations are required. Admission is free. Anyone under eighteen must be accompanied by an adult. Audience guests are required to show identification. "Meet and Greet" sessions, in which QVC hosts mingle with visitors, are scheduled periodically. Call QVC or check the website for information.

QVC. Next, it's a walk through the QVC Scrapbook. This wide hallway has 150 photographs that immortalize memorable moments and guests at QVC. You'll see pictures of luminaries from Judy Collins to Cal Ripken Jr. and everyone in between. A similar display is in the Hall of Records, where standout products and sales records are touted.

The sets at QVC are truly amazing. Big windows afford views of some of the more than twenty thousand square feet of studio space. At least a dozen sets are updated and redecorated constantly, giving the overall impression of an ongoing construction site.

The home set is a favorite of visitors. This eight-thousand-square-foot area includes zones for a living room, dining room, family room, kitchen, two bedrooms, home office, and garage. Some of the beams and other interior elements came from a seventeenth-century Chester County farmhouse.

It takes a lot of work and tons of supplies to keep the sets looking fresh and to change them regularly. Everything from lamps to lawn furniture is stored on-site, available to the set designers. Because of the high quality of the props, nothing looks temporary or faked; the sets really do look like the inside of a beautiful home.

It's fascinating to hear how a product makes it into the QVC line. A video explains the three-part process: selection, inspection, and preparation. Vendors must submit a product description and picture first, and be able to show proof of inventory and insurance. If an item survives this initial assessment, the vendor is asked to send samples.

Next, the team in the Quality Assurance Laboratory takes over, subjecting each item to minute scrutiny. Lab-coated workers use microscopes to check for flaws in jewelry. Gold is weighed to make sure it's as valuable as the vendor claims. Craft kits are tried out, cookware is used and cleaned, appliances are tested. Then there's the infamous "drop test," in which packaged products are dropped eleven different ways from waist height. If the product gets damaged, it's back to the drawing board for the vendor. Of the more than 250 new products that are evaluated every week, only 15 percent pass on the first try.

On-air hosts go through a selection process that's equally rigorous (although fortunately, it doesn't include the "drop test"). They're an amazingly accomplished group of people whose on-screen presence is the culmination of extensive education, talent, and experience. Once candidates pass the audition, they spend six months in training. Among other tasks, the hosts meet with buyers, vendors, and producers to immerse themselves in the products they'll be presenting and the format they'll use to do so. Hosts go to great lengths to become familiar with a product so they can educate buyers on its features and benefits. It's not unusual for a presenter to tour a mine to see how gems are extracted, or to go to a factory and watch a product being made. This focus on the "product as the star" is a hallmark of QVC.

If you think you don't have enough closet space, just be glad you don't have to deal with QVC's inventory. The company keeps at least two of each product backstage, one to be worn or demonstrated by the host, the other to be shown in an on-camera "beauty shot." Personnel from Product Central pull the products twenty-four hours before airtime, then clean and prepare them as necessary.

A walk through the broadcasting hallway gives a close look at the technical side of QVC. Everything is done in-house, from graphics to video production to dubbing. Watching the action in the control room gives you a feel for what a carefully orchestrated operation this is.

The highlight of the tour is a step out onto the observation deck overlooking a live broadcast, maybe with one of your favorite hosts or guests. You'll have to be quiet here, because the only thing standing between you and the microphone is fifty feet of air. Look to your right, and you'll see the producer calling the shots. He or she has a video monitor that displays sales statistics. The producer keeps an eye on this in real time and passes instructions to control room and set.

Before your tour is over, you'll see the working kitchen and other sets and will pass the 150-seat theater where audiences are sometimes invited to broadcasts. If you're interested in participating

The Visitors' Lobby, auditorium, and sets at QVC are designed to be comfortable and welcoming.
QVC

in this, or in one of the informal "Meet and Greet" sessions with QVC hosts, ask for information before you leave.

To take home a souvenir, shop in the Studio Store. This is not an outlet, but a retail shop where a selection of QVC's popular products are for sale. You can also place an on-line order using one of the kiosks in the lobby.

QVC has managed to enjoy huge success without losing sight of its principles. This dedication extends to the community. The network has been an active partner in local events and fund-raisers. It may have big-city style, but QVC has wonderfully small-town sensibilities.

Calendar of Events

For the most up-to-date information on events, live audiences, or group tours, visit QVC's tour website, www.qvctours.com.

ART, ANTIQUES, AND SELECTIVE SHOPPING

West Chester's shopping opportunities start in the center of town. Gay Street, High Street, Market Street, and the side streets are lively with galleries and boutiques. A map and directory of retail stores is available free in many shops.

The first Friday in June and October, West Chester hosts a gallery walk in the evening. It's a great chance to experience the burgeoning art scene in the borough and enjoy this eminently walkable town. Artwork runs the gamut from traditional to contemporary. Stores stay open late the first Friday of each month from May through December.

Other worthwhile stores and antique shops are just a short drive away. From wearable art to rare books, you're sure to find what you're looking for.

The Home Works Gallery on Gay Street carries everything the well-appointed home needs, from sculpture to furniture to art. BUSINESS IMPROVEMENT DISTRICT/RICK DAVIS

Baldwin's Book Barn

For book lovers, a visit to Baldwin's Book Barn feels like a homecoming. The 1822 five-story building exudes bookish charm with its cozy nooks, stone walls, friendly Jack Russell terrier, wood-burning stove, and shelf upon shelf of books, maps, and prints.

Set on six acres of grassy hillside just south of West Chester, the structure was built as a dairy barn. When William C. and Lilla H. Baldwin discovered the property in 1946, the site was used for grazing. The Baldwins thought the barn would be perfect for the bookselling business they had run in West Chester and Wilmington since 1934, so they purchased it and converted it into living quarters and a bookshop.

Current owner Tom Baldwin, the founders' son, explains that the structure had to be reinforced to withstand the weight of the books. Baldwin had the run of the barn as a child and earned 50 cents an hour after school hauling and stacking books. Little by little, more sections of the barn were opened; today the building is fully utilized. Tom Baldwin's office and the art gallery occupy the former milking house, and the front room used to be a wagon shed.

It's a complete sensory pleasure to browse through this antiquarian bookshop. The woodsy smell from the antique stove, the angle of the sun through the windows, the sounds of creaky floors, a softly ticking clock, the feel of a big old book held in one's hands . . . no wonder visitors lose track of time as they wander up and down the stacks.

As for selection, the ever-changing inventory—three hundred thousand volumes on-site—covers any topic one could imagine. "We're generalists," explains Tom Doherty, manager, "although we're choosy about fiction because there's so much of it published." Baldwin's Book Barn has new and used books, rare and out-

Book lovers could spend an entire day at Baldwin's Book Barn. BALDWIN'S BOOK BARN

(continued on page 90)

(continued from page 89)

of-print titles, and special editions. It also sells antique maps and prints, and the occasional piece of antique furniture.

Tom Baldwin and his full-time staff of seven, plus fifteen to twenty part-time employees, amass their stock from estate sales, auctions, and individuals far and wide. "We travel," says Doherty. "We'll look at someone's library and purchase it if it's worthwhile." Baldwin's Book Barn will gather a customized set of volumes for researchers, scholars, or anyone with a specific area of interest.

Visiting the barn is like taking a step back two hundred years, but behind the scenes is a high-tech operation that's distinctly twenty-first century. The Internet connects the Book Barn with bibliophiles all over the world. The business has its own website and also trades on-line at eBay, amazon.com, and Sotheby's website, as well as at auction.

This technology provides a useful tool the dedicated staff can use to find exactly what customers are looking for. There's nothing Baldwin's employees like better than tracking down a book someone has been desperately searching for.

Some customers are more interested in the book covers than the contents. For them, Baldwin's offers designer bookbindings: leather and cloth books to fit any interior design need. Choose the color, style, and how much space you want the books to take up, and voilà—instant tasteful library. Corporations, stores, and homeowners have availed themselves of this unique decorating service.

It's easy—and fun—to get slightly lost in the Book Barn. Two separate staircases reach different parts of the upper floors. As you explore, keep in mind that the building is a real barn. Stairways are steep and narrow, with uneven treads and low overhangs, so watch your step and watch your head! The bank barn is built into a hillside, and the large double doors on the third floor are opened on summer days to admit a cooling breeze. There's also an air conditioner on the fifth floor, but it can be stuffy when it's hot out. Consider visiting first thing in the morning if it's going to be a scorcher. Chairs are thoughtfully situated throughout the stacks.

Don't miss the children's book room. It's like a cozy trip down Memory Lane, complete with little seats where kids can look through old books that will soon be new favorites. Grown-ups appreciate the selection, too. "Oh, I loved this book!" may be the most frequently heard exclamation in the room.

It's lovely to page through old volumes, soaking up the ambience and enjoying the camaraderie of other readers. For book lovers, the welcoming atmosphere at Baldwin's Book Barn speaks volumes.

VISITING BALDWIN'S BOOK BARN

865 Lenape Rd., West Chester, PA 19382
Telephone: 610-696-0816 • Fax: 610-696-0672
E-mail: info@bookbarn.com • Website: www.bookbarn.com

Hours: Monday through Friday, 9 A.M. to 9 P.M.; Saturday and Sunday, 10 A.M. to 6 P.M. Closed Thanksgiving Day and Christmas.

Special considerations: Partially accessible to wheelchairs. Call ahead for specifics and to make arrangements.

Chester County Art Association
100 N. Bradford Ave.
West Chester, PA 19382
Telephone: 610-696-5600
Website: www.chescoart.org
Hours: Monday through Saturday, 9:30 A.M.
    to 4 P.M; Sunday, 1 to 4 P.M.
Wheelchair accessible.

debottis Gallery Fine Art and Framing
113 N. High St.
West Chester, PA 19380
Telephone: 610-696-8887
Website: www.debottisgallery.com
Hours: Monday through Friday, 10 A.M.
    to 6 P.M.; Saturday, 10 A.M. to 5 P.M.
    Closed Sunday.
Dedicated to the work of local and regional
artists. Emphasis is on diversity, medium,
and content. Wheelchair accessible.

DragonFly Gallery
29 S. High St.
West Chester, PA 19382
Telephone: 610-692-2560
Website: www.thedragonflygallery.com
Hours: Monday through Thursday, 10 A.M.
    to 6 P.M.; Friday, 10 A.M. to 7 P.M.; Saturday,
    10 A.M. to 5 P.M. Closed Sunday.
DragonFly is a progressive gallery that
presents exceptional new talent. Jewelry,
accessories, and items for home and garden
are stunning and beautiful. New items come
in frequently. Glass and multimedia pieces
join pearls, gems, and ironwork in Kathleen
Cole's funky, friendly gallery. Not wheelchair
accessible.

Garrubbo Bazán Gallery
16 W. Market St.
West Chester, PA 19382
Telephone: 610-696-1266
Fax: 610-696-1667
Website: www.gbgfineart.com
Hours: Tuesday through Saturday, 11 A.M.
    to 5 P.M. Closed Sunday and Monday.
Contemporary painting, sculpture, and pho-
tography from around the world for first-time
buyers, seasoned collectors, and corporations.

A dynamic exhibition schedule brings a select
group of international artists to the gallery every
four to six weeks. One step up to entrance.

Home Works
117 E. Gay St.
West Chester, PA 19380
Telephone: 610-430-7337
Website: www.homeworks.com
Hours: Tuesday through Saturday, 10 A.M.
    to 5 P.M. Closed Sunday and Monday.
West Chester's largest gallery, offering a broad
selection of fine art, photography, sculpture,
Italian furniture, antiques, oriental rugs, gifts,
and accessories. Wheelchair accessible through
the back door.

Joya
846 E. Street Rd. (PA Route 926), 1.5 miles east
    of U.S. Route 202
Westtown, PA 19395
Telephone: 610-399-5188

Unique jewelry, accessories, and fashions for the
home are creatively displayed at DragonFly
Gallery. DRAGONFLY GALLERY

Holland Art House

Ben Gall was tired of traveling from Chile to Alaska for his telecommunications business. This native of the Netherlands had been living in southeastern Pennsylvania for almost a decade, but he was hardly ever home long enough to enjoy the area or his family. Gall, who had always enjoyed collecting art, decided to make a radical career and lifestyle change: He'd open a gallery featuring Dutch contemporary art.

Next came the search for the perfect space. During this voyage of discovery, Gall's positive feelings for this part of the world in general, and for West Chester in particular, were cemented.

"We love it here," he says. "We were used to living below sea level in Holland. Everything is flat. Here, there are beautiful hills. An enormous number of trees. You see deer and foxes. Living in Malvern, I was more oriented toward the Main Line and wasn't very familiar with West Chester. An architect told me I should see this empty store downtown. It was a dump! Built in 1942. But the space was great, so here we are. When I was looking for a place and when renovations were going on, I walked all over West Chester and saw how special it is. There's something happening here."

After extensive renovations to the building, Holland Art House opened in April 2002. A colorful, Mondriaan-like facade hints at the contemporary art inside. The environment is clean and welcoming, with hardwood floors, excellent lighting, cozy seating where guests can read art books or watch art-related videotapes, and a backroom café where the coffee's hot and the conversation is interesting. Movable walls are set at angles throughout the three-thousand-square-foot space, creating intimate areas in which to view the art.

The overwhelming impression in the gallery is one of color. "I like colorful and contemporary art," says the owner. "Happy art." Many of the Dutch modern mas-

The warm and colorful Holland Art House exhibits works from modern Dutch masters. HOLLAND ART HOUSE

ters whose works are on display use vivid, intense palettes. For example, Clemens Briels favors bright colors in his acrylic-on-resin objects; Hayo Riemersma's large paintings on industrial sheet aluminum look as sleek as a freshly washed sports car; Susan Schildkamp's paintings are warm, homey images of daily life.

Holland Art House also shows paintings, sculpture, stained glass, and other objects by Peter Bol, Wim Heesakkers, Johanna Inden Haak Petropoulos, Peter Philippus, René Rietmeyer, and Herman Krikhaar. Black-and-white photographs of Cuban life by photojournalist Nico Koster are a welcome counterpoint to the brightness of the other art. Fans of industrial design will get a kick out of Maarten Kraanen's clocks made from bicycle parts. Although some of the artists may be unfamiliar to Americans, they are well known and highly successful in Europe.

Ben Gall is excited about the West Chester gallery scene and eager to acquaint people with new and interesting artwork in a pressure-free, comfortable atmosphere. "Art doesn't have to be colorless and stuffy," he says. "It can be fun."

VISITING HOLLAND ART HOUSE

113 W. Market St., West Chester, PA 19382
Telephone: 610-701-9330 • Fax: 610-701-9322
E-mail: BGall@HollandArtHouse.com • Website: www.hollandarthouse.com

Hours: Tuesday through Saturday, 11 A.M. to 5 P.M.; first Friday of each month, 11 A.M. to 9 P.M.; other times by appointment. Closed Sunday and Monday. Wheelchair accessible.

Hours: Tuesday through Thursday, 10 A.M. to 5 P.M.; Friday, 10 A.M. to 6 P.M.; Saturday, 9 A.M. to 4 P.M. Closed Sunday and Monday. Joya is located next to the Westtown Post Office, in the same parking lot as Goose Creek Grill and Westtown Station Pottery. Owners Suzann Jaagus and Paulette Yost carry women's clothing (easily classified as "wearable art"), accessories, and small items for the home. Their scarf collection is wonderful. Eclectic items include foot-shaped pumice stones, floating candles, and unusual handbags. The friendly atmosphere has made Joya a favorite among locals. Wheelchair accessible; aisles may be a tight squeeze, but the proprietors are very helpful and will "make it work."

J. Palma Antiques
U.S. Route 202, just north of PA Route 926
West Chester, PA 19382
Telephone: 610-399-1210
Hours: Friday through Monday, 10 A.M. to 6 P.M., or by chance or by appointment.

Eighteenth- and nineteenth-century American country furniture and accessories. Wheelchair accessible.

Mercury Arts
129 E. Gay St.
West Chester, PA 19380
Telephone: 610-692-6929
Fax: 610-918-2565
Website: www.mercuryarts.com
Hours: Monday through Friday, 10 A.M. to 6 P.M.; Saturday, 10 A.M. to 3 P.M.; other times by appointment.
Featuring contemporary impressionist and realist works by artists from around the world. One small step up from sidewalk; otherwise, wheelchair accessible.

Monroe Coldren & Son
723 E. Virginia Ave.
West Chester, PA 19380-4410
Telephone: 610-692-5651
Fax: 610-918-1722
Website: www.monroecoldren.com

Dennis K. Park: Painting His Roots

Dennis K. Park's watercolors are all about feelings: warm memories, comfort, nostalgia. Park's paintings depict local landscapes that, alas, are sometimes disappearing. These poignant sights, painted with meticulous brushwork in a soothing color palette, keep viewers lingering over Park's slices of Brandywine Valley life.

The artist's Chester County roots run deep. "My great-grandfather was the Marshallton blacksmith," Park says. "I grew up in Lenape Heights, one of the first developments in the area, and I graduated from Unionville High School." Park learned graphic and fine arts at the York Academy of Arts in York, Pennsylvania, then studied privately with local artist Dennis T. Minch.

Park speaks fondly about the subjects he preserves on canvas. Jamison's Dairy Bar was a popular place for ice cream and sandwiches when Park was growing up. "I heard that it might be torn down, so I wanted to paint it before it was too late," Park explains. "I had a lot of happy memories. You could get a black-and-white milkshake there, pre–Dairy Queen."

When West Chester Borough's Recreation Department commissioned Park to paint scenes for its bicentennial in 1999, Park looked for views that really said "West Chester." Rather than focus on something monumental like the Chester County Courthouse, Park created three paintings that are slices of borough life, collectively titled *Little Bits of West Chester.*

"For the downtown painting, I chose the old [1912] Municipal Building and the ones that surround it on High Street," Park says. "The architecture is typical of West Chester, familiar to anyone who walks around there."

The second in the series is *Everhart Path* at Everhart Park. "Everyone knows that path," Park explains. "The big sycamore tree, the mansion across the street . . . people can feel like they're almost part of the piece.

"West Chester's alleys are part of its charm and character, so I chose the alley between Miner and Barnard Streets for the third picture, *Quiet Alley.* I never realized how many schools and churches walk their kids down that path to play in the park," he says with a laugh. The painting gives viewers a comfortable feeling, as though they are heading home just as a light snow begins to fall.

Park's signature piece is *The Last Look,* a watercolor of the Carousel House at Lenape Park. Now a private picnic area, Lenape Park used to be a public amusement facility. "I'd spent a lot of time there as a kid," Park remembers. "There was something very special about that scene." The closed carousel makes it seem that the horses are inside resting after the season ends

Quiet Alley by Dennis K. Park captures the sweetness and homey feel of a West Chester residential area.
DENNIS K. PARK

and riders have bade them a fond farewell. It was a sadly prophetic title, because the horses were since sold and the carousel dismantled.

Park's work appears in many local galleries, including the Sunset Hill Fine Arts Gallery in West Chester and the Chadds Ford Gallery, where his detailed miniatures are featured annually in the "Christmas in Miniature" show. He also exhibits at regional festivals, including Chadds Ford Days in September.

Dennis Park's originals have attracted collectors nationwide, but he keeps his artwork accessible to a wide audience. "I sell prints and small pieces that are more affordable," he says. "I got a lot of support from all kinds of people when I was starting out, and I don't forget that."

Inquiries about Dennis Park's work can be directed to dpark1730@aol.com or 610-344-7350. You may also find Dennis at local festivals.

Hours: Monday through Friday, 8:30 A.M. to 5 P.M.; Saturday, 9 A.M. to 4 P.M. Closed Sunday.

Brass, copper, and ironwork. One of the leading suppliers of eighteenth- and nineteenth-century hardware, lighting, architectural elements, mantels, and fireplace equipment. Not wheelchair accessible.

Simple Pleasures Gallery
22 S. High St.
West Chester, PA 19382
Telephone: 610-344-9711
Website: www.simplepleasuresgallery.com
Hours: Monday through Thursday, 10 A.M. to 6 P.M.; Friday, 10 A.M. to 7 P.M.; Saturday, 10 A.M. to 5 P.M. Closed Sunday.
Beautifully crafted American-styled artworks, one-of-a-kind collectibles, and whimsical

Simple Pleasures Gallery showcases furniture and other well-crafted items in wood, ceramics, glass, and other media. SIMPLE PLEASURES GALLERY

Antique Needlework: A Sampling of Samplers

Antique needlework is striking for its visual appeal and the fine stitches with which it was wrought. Look a little deeper, though, and the letters, motifs, and overall style start to reveal information about the stitcher's background—including when she probably made the sampler, her school, and her heritage. Verses sewn into the fabric expand the story by hinting at love or loss, or by affirming the stitcher's piety and high moral standards. The samplers also offer a window into the history of female education in colonial and post-Revolutionary America.

Westtown School in Chester County was an important center for stitchery. Opened by the Philadelphia Yearly Meeting of the Religious Society of Friends in 1799, Westtown reflected the Quaker emphasis on equality, education, and morality. Needlework training started with a darning sampler, in which girls learned to mend holes and tears almost invisibly. Next, more complex projects were undertaken. Students who exhibited special proficiency were permitted to stitch more pictorial work, although elaborate samplers were discouraged because excessive ornamentation was at odds with the Quaker principle of simplicity.

Ruth J. Van Tassel, of Van Tassel/Baumann American Antiques, specializes in early schoolgirl needlework and needlework conservation. She explains that learning about samplers can help us understand the cultural roots of the crafter. "The

Samplers like this one, crafted by Mary Thompson in 1821, speak volumes about the education and status of the person who sewed them. MATTEO L. MOBILE

kind of lettering used, the motifs, the pictorial elements all give a very strong indication of where a sampler is from."

Van Tassel sees a lot of samplers bearing the Westtown influence. "The graduates were always in great demand as teachers when outlying regions began to found schools. Because Westtown's needlework designs were so specific, you can readily track how they began to appear in regions as far off as Ohio and Virginia. The school had an exponential geographic impact on needlework design from then on."

By the first quarter of the 1800s, samplers had become squarer, larger, and more decorative. The national interest in botany is evident in the plethora of flowers. Architectural portrayals, biblical themes, and genealogy were also popular.

"Many of the best samplers were worked by girls from the ages of fourteen to sixteen," says Ruth Van Tassel. "This must have been the usual age for completion of a young lady's education. An elaborate needlework was like her final exam and was doubtless the piece most prominently displayed in the family parlor. She was entering the time in life when her parents would be looking for a suitable marriage to encourage. The display of a densely patterned, beautifully executed sampler was a social statement that spoke volumes about the family's economic circumstances."

exhibits. Items range from glassware to furniture to jewelry. Some of the detailed work on the wooden items, such as cutting boards, is magnificent. Proprietor Joanne Sterlacci has assembled top-quality, interesting items that make wonderful gifts for others or for yourself. Wheelchair accessible.

Sunset Hill Jewelers and Fine Arts Gallery
23 N. High St.
West Chester, PA 19380
Telephone: 610-692-0374
Hours: Monday through Friday, 9:30 A.M.
    to 5:30 P.M. (until 7 P.M. on Wednesday);
    Saturday, 10 A.M. to 5 P.M. Closed Sunday.
Specializing in original paintings by more than thirty Chester County and area artists. Exclusive gallery for Harry Dunn. Not wheelchair accessible.

Van Tassel/Baumann American Antiques and Girlhood Embroidery
690 Sugartown Rd.
Malvern, PA 19355
Telephone: 610-647-3339
Website: www.antiquesandfineart.com/
    tasselbaumann

Hours: Tuesday through Saturday, 10:30 A.M.
    to 5 P.M., but a call ahead is suggested.
Early schoolgirl needlework and needlework conservation. Eighteenth- and nineteenth-century antiques and accessories. Not wheelchair accessible.

Visual Expansion Gallery
126 N. High St.
West Chester, PA 19381
Telephone: 610-436-8697
Hours: Monday through Saturday, 9:30 A.M.
    to 5:30 P.M. Closed Sunday.
Chester County's oldest existing gallery specializing in the Brandywine School of artists. Showcases original works and limited edition prints by Richard Bollinger, Bill Ewing, Daniel Gerhardtz, Rob Gonsalves, Keith Gunderson, Ray Hendershot, Lou Messa, Buckley Moss, John Powell, Peter Sculthorpe, Sara Simboli, R. B. Stine, Ineke Van Werkhoven, and Andrew Wyeth. Wheelchair accessible.

Viva
Parkway Center
929 S. High St.
West Chester, PA 19382
Telephone: 610-430-8044

Westtown Station Gallery

When potter Ken Kazanjian saw the decrepit Westtown Train Station in the early 1980s, he could tell it had potential. "It was all boarded up and slated for demolition," says Kazanjian. "I had just returned from the Peace Corps in New Guinea and was looking for a home and studio. There was no doubt in my mind that this was the place."

The 1858 station had formerly been a focal point in the community, housing the post and telegraph offices, and offering transportation to and from Philadelphia. By the time Kazanjian came along, it had long been abandoned and neglected.

Blessed with vision and patience, Kazanjian treated what had once been known as Street Road Station like a big sculpture, lovingly renovating it little by little in a lease/maintenance agreement with the owner, SEPTA (Southeastern Pennsylvania Transportation Authority). "It was eighteen months before I could move in," he remembers. "Then it took me a couple of years to get the studio going, and a couple more before I could open the gallery." Today Kazanjian and his wife, painter Shelley Shultis, occupy the restored station master's residence.

The ceramics gallery is on the first floor, complete with the old ticket window. Kazanjian sells his one-of-a-kind pottery items here, along with the bronze wind-bells, Mayan hammocks, South American Indian textiles, and primitive art he collects on annual buying trips.

The artist makes high-fire porcelain and stoneware on-site using a technique that comes from an Asian tradition. "In high-fire ceramics, colors tend to mute out," he explains. "The temperature is 2200 to 2300 degrees Fahrenheit. Low fire is more Mexican and Mediterranean style, with the temperature around 1800 degrees. All of my pieces are food safe and can go in the microwave and dishwasher."

When flicked with a fingernail, high-fire pieces give a distinctive ringing sound.

"The glaze and the clay begin to fuse almost into glass," says Kazanjian. "That's why it makes that distinctive ping." His blues, almost-black, ecru, and various shades of brown are equally at home in a contemporary or traditional setting. Interesting geometrics, leaf-shaped platters, and architectural pieces achieve Kazanjian's goal of creating functional art.

"Every piece is handmade," says the artist, who trained at Philadelphia College of Art (now University of the Arts). "I may do an edition—a series—of leaf platters, but no two are exactly the same. I'm not a dinnerware potter, but I do want people to use my pieces." When the pottery isn't being used, it adds a beautiful decorative accent to any room. Shoppers can expect to pay about $30 for an item from the previous year's line, to several hundred dollars for the

Ken Kazanjian's high-fire ceramics are functional and beautiful. KEN KAZANJIAN

larger sculptural pieces. There's a wide selection of pieces available in the $70 to $150 range.

Kazanjian and Shultis haven't just transformed the building, they've also created a sculpture garden around the station, and even incorporated the bridge that carries Route 926 over the tracks. "We were getting graffiti," Kazanjian says. "I was tired of scrubbing the walls with muriatic acid. We noticed when Shelley painted under the bridge nobody bothered her things, so we decided to start decorating the bridge. It just sort of evolved." The metal sculpture and "found objects" the couple affixed to the structure do double duty keeping vandals at bay and attracting potential customers. At Westtown Station Gallery, preservation and creation merge.

VISITING WESTTOWN STATION GALLERY

The Old Westtown Train Station on PA Route 926
1.5 miles east of U.S. Route 202
Westtown, PA 19395 • Telephone: 610-399-6986

Hours: May through December, daily, 10 A.M. to 6 P.M. Closed rest of year.
Credit cards: Not accepted.
Personal checks: Accepted.
Special considerations: Studio not wheelchair accessible but sculpture garden is. The gallery is adjacent to Joya, a chic boutique with women's clothing, home accessories, and unusual items; and with Goose Creek Grill, a top-notch gourmet pizzeria/restaurant with an eclectic menu of well-prepared food. Thornbury Township Park is right behind the buildings, with a walking trail, pavilion, and playground equipment.

Hours: Tuesday through Thursday, 10 A.M. to 5 P.M.; Friday, 10 A.M. to 6 P.M.; Saturday, 9 A.M. to 4 P.M.

The proprietors of Joya in Westtown opened this second store and added business partner Martha Philpott. The three have chosen clothing (starting at size 12), gifts, and accessories of the same quality you'd find at Joya. This store is a little roomier, but the friendly help is the same. The gift wrapping is creative: Jewelry goes in a tiny Styrofoam cup stuffed with shreds of crinkled paper and topped with a fabric bow. Wheelchair accessible.

RECREATION, LEISURE, AND PERFORMING ARTS

Bicycling

Bike Line of West Chester
909 Paoli Pike (West Goshen Shopping Center, just west of U.S. Route 202)
West Chester, PA 19380
Telephone: 610-436-8984

Website: www.bikelinewc.forabike.com
Bike Line is a full-service shop for bicycles and related equipment. The staff has information and literature about local places to ride and club events.

Delaware Valley Bicycle Club
P.O. Box 156
Woodlyn, PA 19094-0156
Website: www.dvbc.org
Check the website for information on road
and trail biking.

Mountain Bike Pennsylvania
Website: www.mountainbikepa.com

Canoeing, Kayaking, Tubing

Northbrook Canoe Company
1810 Beagle Rd.
West Chester, PA 19382-6799
Telephone: 610-793-2279 or 800-898-2279
Website: www.northbrookcanoe@aol.com,
then search for Northbrook Canoe
Season: April through October
Trips: Trips along the Brandywine depart
hourly beginning at 9 A.M. Canoe and
single-person kayak trips range from 1 to
6.5 hours. Splash boat trips in single-person
kayak-like boats with double-bladed paddles
range from 1.5 to 3.5 hours. Inner-tube trips
are 2 or 3 hours.
Prices: From $10 for a single tube for 2 hours
to $60 for a canoe for 6.5 hours. Equipment
deposit required. $1 per-person fee for
canoes. Nonholiday weekday discounts for
canoes and kayaks.
Other: Reservations required. Splash boats and
kayaks not recommended for children under
10. Tubers should be at least 4 feet tall.
Northbrook Canoe Company can haul your
privately owned canoe or kayak to any of
their access points for $20 plus $1 per person. Alcohol prohibited in parking lot, picnic
areas, and watercraft. Large coolers prohibited; one 6-quart cooler per person is allowed
in canoes. Changing rooms on-site. Food
available on-site.
*If you have your own canoe or kayak, you
may enter the Brandywine at Shaw's Bridge
on South Creek Road between PA Route 842
and Lenape Road (PA Route 52). Do not
use Brandywine Picnic Park or other private
property.

Golf

Tattersall Golf Club
1520 Tattersall Way
West Chester, PA 19380
Telephone: 610-738-4410
Website: www.tattersallgolfclub.com
Daily fee golf course.

Tee It Up Golf
21 Hagerty Boulevard (just east of U.S. Route
202 off Matlack Street)
West Chester, PA 19382
Telephone: 610-436-4469
Website: www.teeitupgolf.net
Driving range with fifty-four hitting stalls on
two levels, sixteen heated in winter, par three
course, miniature golf, pro shop, lessons.

Horseback Riding

**Viking Horses, Iceland Horses
of Chester County**
P.O. Box 3151
West Chester, PA 19381
Telephone: 610-517-7980
E-mail: lynne@vikinghorse.com
Website: www.vikinghorse.com
One-hour to all-day trail rides. Can include
chauffeur service to and from accommodations.

Ice Skating

Ice Line
700 Lawrence Dr.
West Chester, PA 19380
Telephone: 610-436-9670
Website: www.iceline3rinks.com

Musical and Theatrical Performances

West Chester University
West Chester, PA 19383
Telephone: 610-436-1000
Website: www.wcupa.edu
Contact the university for information
about plays, concerts, and student and
faculty recitals.

Parks and Playgrounds

Everhart Park
West Miner Street and South Bradford Avenue
West Chester, PA 19382
Telephone: 610-436-9010
Fax: 610-436-0009
Website: www.west-chester.com/recreation.htm
Shady playground.

Marshall Square Park
North Matlack and East Marshall Streets
West Chester, PA 19380
Telephone: 610-436-9010
Fax: 610-436-0009
Website: www.west-chester.com/recreation.htm
Shady playground.

Oakbourne Park
1014 S. Concord Rd.
West Chester, PA 19382
Telephone: 610-692-1930 (Westtown
    Township office)
Website: www.westtown.org
Tennis and basketball courts, roller hockey
area, fields, playground, trails.

Thornbury Township Park
(Goose Creek Park)
PA Route 926 west of U.S. Route 202
Telephone: 610-399-1425 (township office)
Website: www.thornburytwp.com
Behind Goose Creek Grill. Small amount of
playground equipment. Paved trail circles the
park. The trail is mostly flat, ideal for begin-
ning bicyclists.

West Goshen Community Park
At the intersection of Fern Hill Road and
    North Five Points Road
West Chester, PA 19380
Telephone: 610-696-5266 (township office)
Website: www.wgoshen.org
Tennis and basketball courts, fields, volleyball
courts, playground. A .8-mile paved trail surrounds the park. If you brought the kids' bikes,
this is a good place for them to ride. The trail
has some hills and long grades, so beginning
riders should stick to the paved flat area near
the playground.

Spa

Calista Grand Salon and Spa
The Commons at Thornbury, Building 300,
    Suite 301 (at the intersection of U.S. Route
    202 and PA Route 926)
Telephone: 610-399-6677
Website: www.calistagrand.com
Full-service day spa featuring facial therapies,
body-rejuvenating therapies, muscle therapies,
hydrotherapy, body wraps, and hand and foot
treatments, plus hair, nail, and cosmetic services. Gardenlike spa rooms and a two-story
stone waterfall set the stage for pampering
and stress reduction.

Spectator Sports

West Chester University
West Chester, PA 19383
Telephone: 610-436-1000
Website: www.wcupa.edu
Contact the university for a schedule of athletic
events you can watch, from football games to
swim meets to baseball games.

Tennis

Oakbourne Park
1014 S. Concord Rd.
West Chester, PA 19382
Telephone: 610-692-1930 (Westtown
    Township office)
Website: www.westtown.org

Penn Oaks Racquet and Fitness Club
52 Penn Oaks Dr. (off U.S. Route 202 between
    PA Route 926 and U.S. Route 1)
West Chester, PA 19382
Telephone: 610-399-0827
Call to reserve court time. Fee charged.

West Chester University
West Chester, PA 19383
Telephone: 610-436-1000
Website: www.wcupa.edu
Tennis courts on New Street, about .75 mile
south of Rosedale Avenue. May not be avail-
able if being used by WCU tennis team or
physical education department.

West Goshen Community Park
At the intersection of Fern Hill Road and
  North Five Points Road
West Chester, PA 19380
Telephone: 610-696-5266 (township office)
Website: www.wgoshen.org
Four tennis courts.

Train Excursions

West Chester Railroad
Market Street between Matlack and
  Franklin Streets
West Chester, PA 19380
Telephone: 610-430-2233
Website: www.westchesterrr.net
One of five diesel locomotives pulls an assort-
ment of vintage Reading Railroad passenger
cars on a short trip from West Chester to Glen
Mills. Operates Sundays, June through August.
Contact the railroad for schedule, fares, depar-
ture stations, and special events.

ACCOMMODATIONS

Broadlawns Bed and Breakfast

Gracious living is at the heart of Broadlawns Bed and Breakfast, a fully restored
1881 mansion in a quiet corner of West Chester. The spacious public rooms, plus
two guest rooms and one suite, offer a respite from twenty-first-century stresses in
an atmosphere that's both elegant and comfortable. And the large swimming pool
set amidst formal landscaping makes it hard to think about staying anywhere else.

Hosts Bill and Dorene Winters are the fifth family to reside at Broadlawns. The
home was built in 1881 by Stephen Paxson Darlington, a member of a prominent local

family. Darlington was a partner in the
thriving manufacturing firm of Hoopes
Brothers and Darlington, which made
wheels for Conestoga wagons. The house
was written up at the time of its construction as "a grand house and one of the
most expensive and beautiful in the Borough." The original oak, cherry, and walnut woodwork remains in top condition.

The next owner was Judge McElree,
from another eminent West Chester
family. He purchased the property from
Darlington in 1915 and later named it
Broadlawns.

The mansion is part Arts and Crafts
and part Victorian. The styles work well

The outdoor pool at Broadlawns Bed and Breakfast is the perfect spot to while away a summer
afternoon. BROADLAWNS BED AND BREAKFAST

together, with the solid architectural elements and linear quality of the former tempered by the curvy effusiveness of the latter. You'll notice the combination immediately in the imposing foyer. Solid oak wainscoting and trim are firmly rooted in the Arts and Crafts tradition, while the furniture is classic Victorian. A huge stone fireplace—one of ten in the home—warms the large space, which is decorated on the walls and ceiling with William Morris patterned wallpaper. The high ceiling establishes a marvelous sense of grandeur. Pocket doors can slide to close off the foyer.

Guests are welcome to use the library and parlor on the first floor. The library is an intimate room with a wooden fireplace mantel, oversize furniture, and lots of books visitors may borrow. The Victorian parlor is decorated with faux finishing, lit by a drop crystal chandelier, and furnished with period pieces as well as a piano, which guests may use. The parlor also gives access to the wraparound veranda, where comfortable furniture tempts visitors to tarry; from there, it's just a few steps down to the colorful garden and pool.

The master stairway leads from the entry hall to Broadlawns' three guest accommodations. The landing is graced by one of the home's signature features, a wall of stained glass anchored by wooden molding. Light pouring through the rectangles, squares, and half-circle of blues and pinks illuminates the first and second floors, as well as the stairway itself.

Upstairs, the second-floor hallway boasts an intricately coffered ceiling. All three guest rooms are on this floor. The General Howe Room has a queen-size sleigh bed, floral wallpaper, a seating area in front of the working fireplace, and a large private bathroom (shower only) accessed through the hall. The General Washington Room has a queen-size Victorian bed, private balcony, and a private hall bathroom with tub and shower.

The most romantic room at Broadlawns is the Brandywine Suite. The bedroom and seating area offer plenty of room, with a queen-size bed and a working fireplace. Faux painting around the room creates a whimsical atmosphere. The combination bathroom and sitting room has a second fireplace, shower, two sinks, whirlpool tub, and a comfortable seating area. The lingering scent of candles, along with plants and other homey touches, adds to the suite's appeal.

Bill and Dorene have gone out of their way to make their guests comfortable. A wine bar awaits visitors when they arrive. They're welcome to stow their leftovers in the refrigerator. Along with a working fireplace, each room has a television, VCR, private phone, and terrycloth bathrobes. Lots of books are waiting to be borrowed, and there are many good reading nooks in which to enjoy them.

Full breakfasts are served in the large dining room or out on the porch. Dorene likes to cook mushroom omelets, eggs Benedict, or perhaps baked pears with rum cream. Fruit, cereals, and breads round out the meal.

Broadlawns is an easy walk up tree-lined streets to West Chester's restaurants, shops, and art galleries, though those few blocks are far enough that the B&B is unaffected by downtown noise.

When you return to Broadlawns, the large swimming pool is a refreshing summer treat. How lovely to float on your back and gaze at the lush trees, landscaped gardens, and beautiful mansion whose presence has graced West Chester for almost 125 years.

Visiting Broadlawns Bed and Breakfast
629 N. Church St., West Chester, PA 19380
Telephone: 610-692-5477 • Fax: 610-692-5672
E-mail: broadlwn@erols.com
Website: www.bbonline.com/pa/broadlawns or www.broadlawnsbnb.com
Rates: $125 to $195, including full cooked breakfast.
Credit cards: MasterCard, Visa, and American Express.
Personal checks: Accepted for deposits only; must clear before arrival.
Check-in: 3 to 6 P.M.
Check-out: 11 A.M.
Air-conditioned: Yes.
Smoking policy: Nonsmoking.
Wheelchair accessible: No.
Children: Age twelve and over welcome.
Pets: No.
Noise: Occasional mild road noise.
Parking: Free on-street.

Faunbrook Bed and Breakfast

There's something very comforting about the chime of an antique clock. The melodic sound reminds us of days gone by and reassures us that the hours and minutes will continue to pass.

This unhurried elegance is at the heart of Faunbrook, a seven-room bed-and-breakfast set amidst lush gardens near West Chester University. The three-story Italianate mansion is decorated in Victorian style, with abundant cozy corners and elaborate woodwork. Among the furnishings is innkeeper Pat Phillips's collection of old clocks; the timepieces look and sound as if they were made for this location.

Pat made the decision to become an innkeeper in a thoughtful way that career counselors would certainly endorse. "I was a nurse for ten years, then I worked in the data communications industry for twenty," she says. "I wanted to get out of that competitive atmosphere and pull together all the things that I had most loved doing in my life: being a mom, entertaining, cooking, and gardening. I think old houses are beautiful." Running an inn seemed like the perfect way to combine these interests.

Next came the search for a property. "It took a long time," Pat recalls. "I had looked at fifty B&Bs. When I walked in here, I said, 'This is the house.'" She and business partners Gil and Liz Blankespoor bought it; Pat took the helm as Faunbrook's owner-innkeeper in October 2002 and immediately commenced making improvements. The most significant changes from guests' point of view are the installation of central air-conditioning and the addition of private baths for all guest rooms.

Faunbrook was built in 1860 by William Baldwin and is believed to have been designed by Samuel Sloan, a noted Philadelphia architect. Local tycoon Smedley Darlington purchased the home in 1867, using some of the proceeds from the fortune he had amassed in oil, real estate, and banking. Later, he served two terms as a U.S. congressman. Faunbrook's guest rooms are named for Darlington's children.

The mansion looks quite imposing from the street. There's none of the bright colors or gingerbread trim that characterize later Victorian structures, just a stately brick facade with black shutters. Trees, flowering plants, and shrubs—including huge rhododendrons transplanted from Longwood Gardens—add color and interest no matter where you look. As you get closer, the iron filigree trim becomes apparent.

The wraparound veranda is made of Honduran mahogany and looks like a cutting board, with every plank a different color wood. The porch is the perfect spot to relax in nice weather.

Inside, Faunbrook boasts twelve-foot ceilings and fabulous woodwork. To the left of the great stair hall is the parlor. It's surrounded on three sides by floor-to-ceiling windows. Two are Monticello style, opening all the way to the floor to permit access to the veranda. One of Pat's finds for the room is a carved chest from pre-Occupied Japan. The parlor also has a game table, a piano, and ample seating around the marble-surrounded fireplace.

To the right of the entry is the library. There's another fireplace here, this one with a wooden mantel and surround. Pat has stocked the shelves with books and tapes that guests are welcome to use.

The winter porch at the front of the house wins the award for "most extreme woodwork." The floor, walls, shutters, window mullions, and even the ceiling are made of rich, dark wood. Plants, bright red upholstered furniture, and the sunlight streaming in the window keep the room from feeling ponderous. Guests are welcome to have a glass of sherry here in late afternoon.

Upstairs, a queen-size four-poster bed is the centerpiece of the Darlington Room. The walls are the color of crushed violets, and an ivory rug tops the wooden floor. Elizabeth's Room has a double-size Lincoln bed. This style bed was installed in the White House during Lincoln's era and is characterized by its construction: The center portion of the headboard hangs from hooks on the sideposts so the whole thing can be disassembled and moved easily.

May's Room is a creamy concoction with a painted metal headboard and footboard. A mirrored cedar cabinet makes the perfect wardrobe in this room. The Percy Suite, more Arts and Crafts style than Victorian, includes a sitting room.

You'll find the Rose Room on the third floor, with pink walls to match its name. The double bed has a lovely wraparound footboard. There's also a daybed for an extra person. Isabel's Room comes with an exquisitely tiled bathroom. The pastel flowers in relief are charming.

Edith's Room is a favorite with guests. With windows on two sides and crisp blue and white accents, it's fresh and airy. The bathroom has double sinks and a soaking tub big enough for two.

Downstairs in the formal dining room, Pat puts out coffee and tea at 6:30 A.M. for early risers. Breakfast is served at 8 or 9, depending on the guests' pref-

This queen-size four-poster bed is the centerpiece of the Darlington Room at Faunbrook Bed and Breakfast. FAUNBROOK BED AND BREAKFAST

erence. The three-course meal is quite a feast. Pat's signature dish is pears poached in raspberry jam, cinnamon, cloves, and vanilla. She also makes either an egg dish, waffles, or pancakes, plus bacon or sausage. Homemade granola and other cereals are always available.

If you need some exercise after your meal, stroll through Faunbrook's secluded garden. You'll find a gazebo, two antique fountains, and the original icehouse. When you return to the house, listen for the gentle ticking of the clocks, symbolic of Faunbrook's timeless presence and style.

Visiting Faunbrook Bed and Breakfast

699 W. Rosedale Ave., West Chester, PA 19382
Telephone: 610-436-5788 or 800-505-3233 • Fax: 610-436-6371
E-mail: Innkeeper@faunbrook.com • Website: www.faunbrook.com
Rates: $85 to $135, including full cooked breakfast.
Credit cards: MasterCard and Visa.
Personal checks: Accepted.
Check-in: 3 P.M. or as agreed with innkeeper.
Check-out: 11 A.M.
Air-conditioned: Yes.
Smoking policy: Nonsmoking.
Wheelchair accessible: No.
Children: Well-mannered children welcome.
Pets: No. Resident dog and cat, but they do not come into contact with guests.
Noise: Occasional moderate road noise.
Parking: Free on-site.
Other: Can host special events like bridal showers, small weddings and receptions, and corporate meetings.

Other Recommended Accommodations

Best Western Concordville Hotel and Conference Center
U.S. Routes 1 and 322
Concordville, PA 19331
Telephone: 610-358-9400 or 800-522-0070
Fax: 610-358-9381
Website: www.concordville.com
Rooms: 115 rooms. Standard rooms have two double beds or one king bed. King suites have a small refrigerator and separate living room. Jacuzzi suites have a deep tub and two bathrobes.
Rates: $119 to $189; Presidential Suite $200, including a hot breakfast buffet Monday through Friday and deluxe Continental breakfast on weekends. Contact the hotel or consult the website for details on packages, some with discount tickets to local attractions.
Credit cards: Visa, MasterCard, American Express, Discover, and Diner's Club.
Personal checks: Not accepted.
Check-in: 3 P.M.
Check-out: noon.
Smoking policy: 85 percent of the guest rooms are nonsmoking.
Wheelchair accessible: Yes.
Children: Under seventeen stay free in parents' room.
Pets: No.
Food: Breakfast on-site. Lunch and dinner served at the Concordville Inn, in a separate building that shares the same parking lot.
Parking: Free on-site.
Other: Fitness center, sauna, indoor pool, game room, business center, laundry facilities, and room service. Corporate shuttle available Monday through Friday to businesses within a ten-mile radius. From 5 to 6:30 P.M. Monday through Thursday, guests are invited to the manager's cocktail party.

Comfort Inn & Suites of Brandywine Valley
1310 Wilmington Pike (U.S. Route 202)
West Chester, PA 19382
Telephone: 610-399-4600 or 800-228-5150
Fax: 610-399-6171
Website: www.comfortatbrandywine.com
Rooms: 75 rooms and suites. Rooms have one king bed or two queens. Suites have a data port, two phone lines, voice mail, sofabed, microwave, refrigerator, wet bar, and free HBO/CNN/ESPN. Some suites have whirlpool baths.
Rates: $70 to $160, including deluxe Continental breakfast. Contact the hotel or consult the website for details on packages.
Credit cards: Visa, MasterCard, American Express, Discover, and Diner's Club.
Personal checks: Not accepted.
Check-in: 3 P.M.
Check-out: 11 A.M.
Smoking policy: 70 percent of guest rooms are designated nonsmoking.
Wheelchair accessible: Yes. One room has a roll-in shower.
Children: Under eighteen stay free with parents. Cribs available.
Pets: No.
Food: No on-site restaurant, but a deluxe Continental breakfast with waffles is served. Dozens of restaurants nearby in both directions on U.S. Route 202, and a convenience store about fifty yards away.
Parking: Free on-site.
Other: Fitness center and indoor pool. One room set up for hearing-impaired guests. Business center and meeting facilities. Limo service to and from airport. Dry-cleaning services. High-speed internet access. Four-time Gold Hospitality Award winner.

1732 Folke Stone Bed & Breakfast
777 Copeland School Rd.
West Chester, PA 19380
Telephone: 610-429-0310 or 800-884-4666
Fax: 610-918-9228
E-mail: FolkBandB@aol.com
Website: www.bbonline.com/pa/folkestone/
Innkeepers: Marcy and Walter Schmoll

Rooms: Betsy Ross Room houses a refinished king brass bed adorned with a quilted patriotic comforter. Twin available. Pond view. King Louis Room has a king-size bed and French Provincial furniture. Jenny Lind Room has an open beam ceiling and antique spool queen-size bed. All rooms are air-conditioned and have a private bath and cable television. Two-night minimum stay on holiday weekends.
Rates: $75 to $100, including full gourmet breakfast served on the family's Wedgwood china in the great room or on the veranda.
Credit cards: MasterCard and Visa.
Personal checks: Accepted.
Check-in: After 2 P.M.
Check-out: 11 A.M.
Air-conditioned: Yes.
Smoking policy: Nonsmoking.
Wheelchair accessible: No.
Children: Must be at least twelve years old.
Pets: No. Cat in residence (only in kitchen).
Food: Many restaurants nearby in West Chester.
Other: Set on 1.5 acres with pond. Beautifully restored home on 1732 William Penn land grant. Read by the fireplace, play the Steinway piano, or just enjoy the surroundings from the patio, porch, or nearby walking trail.

Holiday Inn
943 S. High St. at the U.S. Route 202 bypass
West Chester, PA 19382-5418
Telephone: 610-692-1900 or 888-664-6665
Fax: 610-436-0159
Website: www.ichotelsgroup.com
Rooms: 142 rooms and 41 suites. Standard rooms have two double beds, two queen-size beds, or one king-size bed. Suites have a king-size bed plus a sitting area with pull-out sofa. All rooms have iron and ironing board, coffeemaker, data ports, voice mail, and hair dryer. Rates start at $89.
Credit cards: Visa, MasterCard, American Express, and Discover.
Personal checks: Not accepted.
Check-in: 3 P.M.
Check-out: Noon.

Packages: Yes. Check the website for details.
Children: No extra charge for children in
  parents' room.
Pets: Not accepted.
Smoking policy: Smoking and nonsmoking
  rooms available.
Wheelchair accessible rooms.
Food: On-site restaurant. Kids eat free.
Parking: Free on-site.
Other: Fitness center and outdoor pool. Room
  service. Ballroom and banquet space. Dry
  cleaning, laundry, and coin laundry avail-
  able. Copier, fax, personal computer, and
  printer available. Trucks and buses welcome.

Microtel Inn and Suites

500 Willowbrook Lane
West Chester, PA 19382
Telephone: 610-738-9111 or 888-619-9292
Fax: 610-738-9192
Website: www.fieldhotels.com/miswc.htm
Rooms: 102 guest rooms and suites with one
  or two queen-size beds, desk, and window
  seat sitting area. One-room suites also
  include sleeper sofa, dining table, and kitch-
  enette with sink, microwave, coffeemaker,
  and refrigerator.
Rates: $69 to $84, including Continental
  breakfast. Check the website for details
  on packages.
Credit cards: Visa, MasterCard, American
  Express, Discover, and Diner's Club.
Personal checks: Not accepted.
Check-in: 3 P.M.
Check-out: 11 A.M.
Smoking policy: Smoking and nonsmoking
  guest rooms.
Wheelchair accessible: Yes.
Children: Cribs available.
Pets: Additional cost; by advance arrangement
  only.
Food: Continental breakfast daily. Vending
  machines and twenty-four-hour complimen-
  tary coffee. Many restaurants nearby on PA
  Route 3 and in West Chester; several will
  deliver to hotel.
Parking: Free on-site.

Other: Fitness center. Valet service and on-site
  car rental available. Meeting room holds up
  to forty. Telephones have data ports and
  voice mail. Coin laundry.

The Park Inn & Suites
(soon to be Brandywine Valley Suites Hotel)

1110 Baltimore Pike (intersection of U.S.
  Routes 1 and 202)
(Mailing address: P.O. Box 607)
Concordville, PA 19331
Telephone: 610-358-1700 or 800-670-7275
Fax: 610-558-0842
Website: www.brandywinevalleysuiteshotel.com
Rooms: 143 rooms and suites, including rooms
  with two double beds up to two-room suites
  with Jacuzzi. All rooms have coffeemakers,
  iron and ironing board, cable television
  including CNN, ESPN, HBO, and CNBC,
  voice mail, and data ports. Extended-stay
  rooms with a full kitchen, two bathrooms,
  living room, and dining room, and extended-
  stay business suites available.
Rates: $85 to $189, including Continental
  breakfast. Many special rates available.
  Contact the hotel for details on packages.
Credit cards: Visa, MasterCard, American
  Express, Discover, and Diner's Club.
Personal checks: Not accepted.
Check-in: 3 P.M.
Check-out: noon.
Smoking policy: One floor of guest rooms set
  aside for smoking.
Wheelchair accessible: No.
Children: Cribs available.
Pets: No.
Food: Hooters restaurant shares the parking
  lot with the hotel, as does a Beer Cellar and
  a Dunkin' Donuts. Several other restaurants
  are in the Painter's Crossing Shopping
  Center, diagonally across from the hotel,
  with dozens of other restaurants located
  north and south on U.S. Route 202.
Parking: Free on-site.
Other: Fitness center, outdoor pool, and laundry. Meeting facilities and a twenty-four-
  hour business center with copier, PC, laser
  printer, typewriter, fax service, and high-
  speed Internet access.

FOOD

Avalon Restaurant
312 S. High St.
West Chester, PA 19382
Telephone: 610-436-4100
Fax: 610-436-1858
Website: www.avalonrestaurant.org
Hours: Lunch Tuesday through Friday, 11 A.M. to 2 P.M.; dinner Tuesday through Saturday, 5 to 10:30 P.M. Sunday, 4 to 9 P.M.; Sunday brunch, including "create your own bloody Mary bar," 10 A.M. to 2 P.M.
Prices: Lunch ranges from $6 to $18; dinner entrees average $25.
Take-out: Yes.
Wheelchair accessible: Yes, including restrooms.
Smoking policy: Indoor dining all nonsmoking. Smoking permitted on patio, which is open in the spring and summer.
Dress: Casual to dressy.
Credit cards: Visa, MasterCard, and American Express.
Other: American-Continental cuisine with Cajun, southwestern, Asian, and European influences. Wood-burning fireplace inside. Outdoor dining open in spring and summer with a raw bar. Available for private parties. Bistro menu on Sunday, Tuesday, Wednesday, and Thursday. BYOB.

Baxter's
40 E. Market St.
West Chester, PA 19380
Telephone: Not available at press time. Visit www.brandywineguide.com for update.
Website: www.baxtersgv.com
Hours: Monday through Thursday, 11 A.M. to 10 P.M.; Friday, 11 A.M. to 11 P.M.; Saturday, 11 A.M. to 10 P.M.
Prices: Lunch $4.99 to $8.99, dinner $6.50 to $23.
Take-out: Yes.
Wheelchair accessible: Yes, including restrooms.
Smoking policy: Smoking and non-smoking sections.
Dress: Casual.
Credit cards: All major credit cards.

Personal checks: Not accepted.
Other: Live entertainment Wednesday through Saturday starting about 7 P.M. Banquet room available for private parties.

Coyote Crossing
102 West Market St.
West Chester, PA 19380
Telephone: 610-429-8900
Website: www.coyotecrossing.com
Hours: Lunch, Monday through Friday, 11:30 A.M. to 2:30 P.M.; dinner, Sunday through Thursday, 5 to 9:30 P.M.; Friday and Saturday, 5 to 10:30 P.M.
Prices: Lunch averages $12, dinner averages $19.
Take-out: Yes.
Wheelchair accessible: Yes, including restrooms.
Smoking policy: Smoking permitted in bar.
Dress: Casual.
Credit cards: Visa, MasterCard, and American Express.
Personal checks: Not accepted.
Other: Authentic Mexican cuisine in casually elegant atmosphere.

The Four Dogs Tavern
1300 W. Strasburg Rd., PA Route 162
West Chester, PA 19380
Telephone: 610-692-4367
Fax: 610-738-1206
Website: www.fourdogstavern.com
Hours: Monday through Wednesday, 11:30 A.M. to 10 P.M.; Thursday through Saturday, 11 A.M. to 11 P.M.; Sunday brunch, 11 A.M. to 2 P.M., overlapping lunch, 11 A.M. to 4 P.M., dinner, 4 to 10 P.M.
Prices: Lunch $6 to $15, dinner $7 to $20.
Take-out: Yes.
Wheelchair accessible: Yes, including restrooms.
Smoking policy: Permitted in bar.
Dress: Casual.
Credit cards: Visa, MasterCard, American Express, Diner's Club, and Carte Blanche.

Personal checks: Not accepted.

Other: Upbeat, casual watering hole in restored barn. In operation since 1814. Outdoor patio. Entertainment Thursday and Sunday, 8 P.M. to midnight.

Gilmore's French Cuisine
133 E. Gay St.
West Chester, PA 19380
Telephone: 610-431-2800
Fax: 610-431-9464
Website: www.gilmoresrestaurant.com
Hours: Tuesday through Thursday, two dinner seatings: 6 P.M. and 8:15 P.M.; Friday and Saturday, seatings at 6 P.M. and 8:30 P.M.
Prices: Entrees average $26. Three-course meal about $45.
Take-out: No.
Wheelchair accessible: No.
Smoking policy: All nonsmoking.
Dress: Smart casual.
Credit cards: Visa and MasterCard.
Personal checks: Not accepted.
Other: BYOB. Many specials. Sophisticated atmosphere. Seafood bisque a signature dish. Ask to sit in the larger dining room, not in the small one next to the kitchen.

Goose Creek Grill
PA Route 926 next to Westtown Post Office
West Chester, PA 19382
Telephone: 610-399-9800
Fax: 610-399-7023
Hours: Winter hours Wednesday and Thursday, 11:30 A.M. to 8:30 P.M.; Friday and Saturday, 11:30 to 10:30 P.M.; Sunday, 11:30 to 8 P.M.; closed Monday and Tuesday. Summer hours Monday through Thursday, 11:30 A.M. to 9:30 P.M.; Friday and Saturday, 11:30 A.M. to 10 P.M.; Sunday, 11:30 A.M. to 9 P.M.
Prices: Basic 8-inch pizza $5.50, luncheon wraps average $7.95, pasta dishes and entrees $9.25 to $18.95.
Take-out: Yes.
Wheelchair accessible: Yes, including restrooms.
Smoking policy: All nonsmoking indoors. Smoking permitted outdoors.
Dress: Casual.
Credit cards: Visa, MasterCard, and American Express.
Personal checks: Not accepted.

Other: Gourmet brick-oven pizzas, creative appetizers, salads, burgers, sandwiches, wraps, and full range of entrees including Italian dishes, meat, chicken, and seafood. Wide selection of beer. Soothing faux-finish decor. A favorite with locals, especially for Sunday dinner; come early, especially if there are more than four people in your party. Township park with walking trail and pavilion behind restaurant; you can get take-out from Goose Creek Grill and eat in the park. Joya, a popular boutique for gifts and wearable art, shares the parking lot with the restaurant, as does Westtown Station Gallery, a pottery shop.

High Street Caffe
322 S. High St.
West Chester, PA 19382
Telephone: 610-696-7435
Fax: 610-696-4441
Website: www.highstreetcaffe.com
Hours: Lunch Tuesday through Friday, 11:30 A.M. to 2:30 P.M. Dinner Tuesday through Saturday, 5:30 to 10 P.M.; Sunday, jazz dinner, 5 to 9 P.M. Closed Monday.
Prices: Lunch entrees average $9, dinner appetizers $5.95 to $10.95, entrees $13.95 to $25.95.
Take-out: Yes.
Wheelchair accessible: Yes, including restrooms.
Smoking policy: All nonsmoking.
Dress: Casual.
Credit cards: Visa, MasterCard, and American Express.
Other: Reservations recommended. New Orleans Cajun-Creole cuisine. Mardi Gras atmosphere, very purple. Cajun music piped in. Highly rated by *ZAGAT Survey;* numerous awards from local magazines. BYOB. Live entertainment Friday, Saturday, and Sunday starting at 7:30 P.M.

Ice Cream Co.
11 N. Five Points Rd.
West Chester, PA 19380
Telephone: 610-696-8883
Hours: Monday through Friday, 8:30 A.M. to 9 P.M.; Saturday, 11:30 A.M. to 9 P.M. Closed Sunday.

The Dilworthtown Inn

Just a stone's throw away from busy U.S. Route 202, a five-way intersection marks the quiet village of Dilworthtown. The centerpiece of the small cluster of buildings is the Dilworthtown Inn, where colonial elegance and exceptional cuisine offer guests a distinctive dining experience.

From the mid-1700s until the twentieth-century relocation of the main road, Dilworthtown was a thriving community at an important crossroads. Old Wilmington Pike saw heavy traffic as a main thoroughfare from West Chester to Wilmington. There was even an attempt to improve the highway with a wooden plank toll road in the mid-1800s. (This experiment failed; almost as many wagons ended up under the boardwalk as atop it.) Wood gave way to stone in 1859, then asphalt in 1907.

It was the relocation of the main road to present-day Route 202 that changed Dilworthtown from bustling to backwater, but nobody there is complaining. The Dilworthtown Inn and the two other businesses it runs here—the Inn Keeper's Kitchen and a soon-to-open country store—are embraced by an aura of history and tranquility that would be impossible to duplicate alongside a modern four-lane.

The restaurant operates on the site where James Dilworth built his family home in the mid-1750s. Son Charles inherited the property in 1769 and obtained a tavern license in 1770. Business was good for the strategically placed public house, which served locals, travelers, teamsters, and drovers.

Charles Dilworth was the owner during the Battle of Brandywine on September 11, 1777. As the Americans were pushed back, they made one last stand near Dilworthtown. Historians think patriots may have been held prisoner in the tavern's

For an elegant meal in a colonial setting, the Dilworthtown Inn is unsurpassed. THE DILWORTHTOWN INN

(continued on page 112)

(continued from page 111)

cellar, while British casualties were tended to in a nearby building. The inn was plundered and damaged to the tune of £820.

More than two centuries later, on October 5, 1987, the inn faced an even graver threat when its roof caught fire. Friends and neighbors rushed to save the inn's priceless art collection and wine inventory. Fire damage was largely confined to storage areas, the business office, and caretaker's residence, but water and smoke damage were extensive. Proprietors Jim Barnes and Bob Rafetto pledged to rebuild.

The inn underwent a multimillion-dollar restoration to exacting standards. Skilled artisans using period materials returned the fine dining establishment to its authentic colonial luster, down to the handmade nails, hand-hewn flooring, and authentic panes of rippled antique glass. Once again, evocative paintings of the Brandywine Valley by local artists including Andrew Wyeth, C. Phillip Wikoff, and Peter Sculthorpe grace the walls of the restaurant's fifteen candlelit dining rooms.

It's a satisfying and memorable experience to dine here. Menu items, preparation, and presentation are exquisite. No wonder the *ZAGAT Survey* compared the Dilworthtown Inn to Philadelphia's top French restaurant, Le Bec-Fin. The restaurant has received awards from *Gourmet* magazine ("Readers' Top Table"), *Delaware Today* ("Best Chester County Restaurant"), and *Main Line Today* ("Best of the Main Line"), among others. *Wine Spectator* gave the Dilworthtown Inn, which has more than 900 wines and 250 spirits available, its "Best Award of Excellence."

The menu changes seasonally to feature the freshest ingredients. A first course might be a ginger crisp lobster with baby spinach and apricot Thai sauce. Fans of Caesar salad get to enjoy watching it being prepared tableside. Entrees include duck, venison, seafood, and meat; the Chef's Duet of a six-ounce filet mignon and four-ounce broiled lobster tail is a popular choice.

Along with the fifteen indoor dining rooms, in warm weather the restaurant offers outdoor dining for about forty-five people in the Stables. Live entertainment is provided on weekends in this rebuilt area where the Dilworth family's original stables stood.

The Dilworthtown Inn has been slowly branching out to the other buildings at this historic intersection. Across the street from the restaurant is the Inn Keeper's Kitchen, a state-of-the-art demonstration kitchen where classes are taught by

renowned chefs. Students get to see the latest in cooking technology as well as eat the food prepared during class. The same setting can be used for private parties or meetings. The Dilworthtown Inn's line of condiments, spices, and salad dressings is available for purchase and can be packaged in a gift basket on request.

Cooking classes are given by top chefs at the Inn Keeper's Kitchen, run by the Dilworthtown Inn. THE DILWORTHTOWN INN

Plans include the opening of the country store building as a purveyor of fine gourmet food and retail items.

VISITING THE DILWORTHTOWN INN

1390 Old Wilmington Pike at Birmingham Road and Brinton's Bridge Road, .25 mile west of U.S. Route 202, West Chester, PA 19382
Telephone: 610-399-1390 • Fax: 610-399-1504
E-mail: info@dilworthtown.com • Website: www.dilworthtown.com

Hours: Dinner only. Monday through Friday, 5:30 to 9 P.M.; Saturday, 5 to 9:30 P.M.; Sunday, 3 to 8:30 P.M. Closed Christmas Day, New Year's Day, Super Bowl Sunday, Memorial Day, July Fourth, and the week that includes Labor Day.
Prices: First courses average $11; main courses average $30.
Reservations: Required.
Dress: Gentlemen should wear jackets; tie is optional.
Smoking: Bar only.
Wheelchair accessible: Yes. Mention need when making a reservation.
Credit cards: All major credit cards accepted.
Personal checks: Not accepted.
Parking: Free on-site.
Take-out: Not available.
Banquets: The Dilworthtown Inn can host special events for six to sixty people, by advance reservation only. For business meetings, phone, fax, sketch pads, and audiovisual aids are available.
Other: Atmosphere is elegant. Not suitable for young children; no high chairs or booster seats available. Guests are asked to turn off audible pagers and cell phones. No flash photography permitted, except in private rooms. For a schedule of classes at the Inn Keeper's Kitchen, call or consult the website.

Prices: Sandwiches average $7, ice cream concoctions average $3.50.
Take-out: Yes.
Wheelchair accessible: Yes, including restrooms.
Smoking policy: All nonsmoking.
Dress: Casual.
Credit cards: Not accepted.
Personal checks: Accepted with proper identification.
Other: Ice cream parlor atmosphere with wonderful soups and hot and cold sandwiches. Generous portions. Sundaes, shakes, and floats available. Frozen yogurt and dietetic ice cream available.

Iron Hill Brewery & Restaurant
3 W. Gay St. (at High and Gay)
West Chester, PA 19380
Telephone: 610-738-9600
Fax: 610-738-7240
Website: www.ironhillbrewery.com
Hours: Monday and Tuesday, 11:30 A.M. to 12:30 A.M.; Wednesday through Saturday, 11:30 A.M. to 1:30 A.M.; Sunday, 10:30 A.M. to 11:30 P.M.
Prices: Sandwiches average $7.50, wood oven pizza around $9.50, dinner appetizers $5.95 to $9.95, entrees $12.95 to $19.95.
Take-out: Yes.
Wheelchair accessible: Yes, including restrooms.
Smoking policy: Main dining room nonsmoking. There is a smoking section. Smoking permitted at bar.
Dress: Casual.

Credit cards: Visa, MasterCard, American Express, and Discover.
Personal checks: Not accepted.
Other: Microbrewery. Voted "Best Brewpub" by *Main Line Today.* DJ on Thursdays, DJ or band on Fridays. Outdoor dining in warm weather. New American cuisine.

Jimmy John's Pipin' Hot Sandwiches
1507 Wilmington Pike (U.S. Route 202), 1 mile north of U.S. Route 1
West Chester, PA 19382
Telephone: 610-459-3083
Hours: Daily, 10 A.M. to 8 P.M.
Prices: Hot dogs $1.50 to $3.
Take-out: Yes.
Wheelchair accessible: Yes, including restrooms.
Smoking policy: Smoking permitted in certain areas; depending on clientele, secondhand smoke may or may not be a problem.
Dress: Casual.
Credit cards: Not accepted.
Personal checks: Not accepted.
Other: Known for hot dogs. Miniature trains on display. Lots of the late Jimmy John's personal memorabilia also on display.

Kildare's
18–22 W. Gay St.
West Chester, PA 19380
Telephone: 610-431-0770
Fax: 610-431-2697
Website: www.kildarespub.com
Hours: Monday through Saturday, 10 A.M. to 2 A.M.; Sunday, 9 A.M. to midnight.
Prices: Appetizers $5 to $10, lunch salads $4 to $8, dinner salads up to $13, sandwiches $7 to $9, entrees $8 to $18.
Take-out: Yes.
Wheelchair accessible: Yes, including restrooms.
Smoking policy: Designated smoking and nonsmoking areas.
Dress: Casual.
Credit cards: Visa, MasterCard, American Express, and Discover.
Personal checks: Not accepted.
Other: Outdoor sidewalk dining and rear covered patio dining in season. Music: Monday, Irish jam session; Tuesday, open mike; Wednesday, DJ; Thursday through Saturday, live music with various performers.

Kooma Japanese Restaurant
151 W. Gay St.
West Chester, PA 19380
Telephone: Not available at press time. Visit www.brandywineguide.com for update.
Fax: Not available at press time. Visit www.brandywineguide.com for update.
Hours: Lunch Monday through Saturday, 11 A.M. to 2:30 P.M. Dinner Monday through Thursday, 5 to 10:30 P.M.; Friday and Saturday, 5 P.M. to 2 A.M.; Sunday, 5 to 9:30 P.M.
Prices: Lunch $5 to $10, dinner $10 to $20.
Take-out: Yes.
Wheelchair accessible: Yes, including restrooms.
Smoking policy: All nonsmoking.
Dress: Casual.
Credit cards: Visa and MasterCard.
Personal checks: Not accepted.
Other: Pan-Asian food served in dramatic modern setting. Sushi a specialty.

La Petite Bakery
106 W. Gay St.
West Chester, PA 19380
Telephone: 610-719-6440
Fax: 610-719-6441
Hours: Monday through Friday, 6:30 A.M. to 5 P.M.; Saturday, 7 A.M. to 3 P.M.; Sunday, 7 A.M. to 2 P.M.
Prices: Breakfast averages $3.50, lunch $6.25.
Take-out: Yes.
Wheelchair accessible: Yes, including restrooms.
Smoking policy: All nonsmoking.
Dress: Casual.
Credit cards: Visa, MasterCard, American Express, and Discover.
Personal checks: Accepted with proper identification.
Other: Delicious pastries including pies and sticky buns. Bread for sandwiches is baked fresh.

The Marshalton Inn
1300 W. Strasburg Rd., Route 162
West Chester, PA 19380
Telephone: 610-692-4367
Fax: 610-738-1206
Website: www.marshaltoninn.net
Meals and hours: Dinner Wednesday through
   Saturday, 5 to 10 P.M.; Sunday, 5 to 9 P.M.
Prices: $20 to $30.
Take-out: Yes.
Wheelchair accessible: Yes, including rest-
   rooms.
Smoking policy: Permitted in bar only.
Dress: Casual
Credit cards: Visa, MasterCard, and American
   Express.
Personal checks: Not accepted.
Other: Candlelit, rustic country inn operating
   since 1814. Outdoor dining in season.

The Mediterranean
150 W. Gay St.
West Chester, PA 19380
Telephone: 610-431-7074
Fax: 610-431-9020
Hours: Monday through Thursday, 11 A.M. to
   9 P.M.; Friday, 11 A.M. to 10 P.M.; Saturday,
   noon to 10 P.M.; Closed Sunday.
Prices: Lunch averages $7, dinner $15.
Take-out: Yes.
Wheelchair accessible: Yes, including restrooms.
Smoking policy: All nonsmoking.
Dress: Casual.
Credit cards: Visa, MasterCard, American
   Express, Discover, and Diner's Club.
Personal checks: Not accepted.
Other: Family-run restaurant. Food prepared
   fresh. Tablecloths and tea lights. BYOB.

New York Sandwiches and Eatery
39 W. Gay St.
West Chester, PA 19380
Telephone: 610-692-9777
Fax: 610-692-2475
Hours: Monday through Saturday, 11 A.M. to
   9 P.M.; Sunday, noon to 4 P.M.
Prices: Lunch with beverage about $6 or $7,
   dinner $10 to $12.
Take-out: Yes.

Wheelchair accessible: Historical building with
   a step. Staff is happy to help wheelchairs in.
   Restrooms accessible.
Smoking policy: All nonsmoking.
Dress: Casual.
Credit cards: Visa, Master Card, American
   Express, and Discover.
Personal checks: Not accepted.
Other: Exceptionally delicious sandwiches.

Ryan's Pub
124 W. Gay St.
West Chester, PA 19380
Telephone: 610-344-3934
Fax: 610-344-7461
Hours: Daily, 11:30 A.M. to 2 A.M.
Prices: Lunch averages $6.95, dinner $10.95
   to $20.
Take-out: Yes.
Wheelchair accessible: Downstairs and in
   restrooms on that level; no access to
   second floor.
Smoking policy: Permitted downstairs.
   Upstairs, the dining room is nonsmoking
   during the hours food is served (until 10
   P.M.). After 10 P.M., the room is used for
   an open bar and smoking is permitted.
Dress: Upscale casual.
Credit cards: Visa, MasterCard, American
   Express, and Discover.
Personal checks: Not accepted.
Other: Irish fare, steaks, seafood, and specials.
   Cozy pub atmosphere. Children's menu.
   Billiard room. Six large televisions. Reserva-
   tions required for parties of six or more.
   Live entertainment Sunday and Wednesday
   evenings; DJ on Thursday, Friday, and Satur-
   day. Karaoke and quiz nights; call for details.

Señora's Authentic Mexican Cuisine
505 E. Gay St.
West Chester, PA 19380
Telephone: 610-344-4950
Fax: 610-344-4837
Hours: Monday through Thursday, 11 A.M. to
   9 P.M.; Friday and Saturday, 11 A.M. to 10 P.M.
   Closed Sunday.
Prices: About $3.50 for appetizers to $7.50 for
   most expensive entree.
Take-out: Yes.
Wheelchair accessible: Yes

Smoking policy: All nonsmoking.
Dress: Casual.
Credit cards: Visa, MasterCard, American Express, and Discover.
Personal checks: Not accepted.
Other: Genuine Mexican food prepared exquisitely. Extensive menu. Homemade salsas. BYOB. Mexican items for sale. The restaurant has won numerous awards.

Spence Café
29–31 E. Gay St.
West Chester, PA 19382
Telephone: 610-738-8844
Fax: 610-738-8845
Website: www.cafespence.com
Hours: Lunch Monday through Friday, 11 A.M. to 2:30 P.M. Dinner Monday through Saturday, 5 to 10 P.M.; Sunday, 5 to 9 P.M.
Prices: Lunch average $8, dinner entrees $17 to $23.
Take-out: Yes.
Wheelchair accessible: Yes, including restrooms.
Smoking policy: Smoking and nonsmoking sections.
Dress: Upscale casual.
Credit cards: Visa, MasterCard, American Express, and Diner's Club.
Personal checks: Accepted with proper identification.
Other: Live entertainment Tuesday through Saturday, 10:30 P.M. to 2 A.M. Full bar and wine list.

The Three Little Pigs
131 N. High St.
West Chester, PA 19380
Telephone: 610-918-1272
Hours: Monday through Friday, 10 A.M. to 3 P.M.
Prices: Sandwiches average $5.95.
Take-out: Yes.
Wheelchair accessible: Yes, including restroom.
Smoking policy: All nonsmoking.
Dress: Casual.
Credit cards: Not accepted.
Personal checks: Accepted.
Other: Gourmet food in charming café atmosphere. Extensive variety of sandwiches. Baked goods, desserts, and soups made

daily on-site. Located near county courthouse in West Chester. Tables fill quickly at lunchtime; go early if possible.

Trattoria Enoteca Alberto
116 E. Gay St.
West Chester, PA 19380
Telephone: 610-430-0203
Fax: 610-430-0403
Website: www.trattorialberto.com
Hours: Lunch Monday through Friday, 11:30 A.M. to 2:30 P.M. Dinner Monday through Thursday, 5 to 10 P.M.; Friday and Saturday, 5 to 11 P.M. Closed Sunday.
Prices: Lunch averages $10, dinner $22.
Take-out: Yes.
Wheelchair accessible: Yes, including restrooms.
Smoking policy: Mostly nonsmoking. There is a designated smoking area.
Dress: Casual.
Credit cards: Visa, MasterCard, American Express, Discover, and Diner's Club.
Personal checks: Accepted with proper identification.
Other: Live piano music Wednesday, Friday, and Saturday evenings. Focacce and pannini excellent.

Turks Head Inn
15 S. High St.
West Chester, PA 19382
Telephone: 610-696-1400
Fax: 610-696-8809
Hours: Lunch Monday through Friday, starting at 11:30 A.M., open straight through until dinner. Dinner Monday through Thursday, 5:30 to 10 P.M.; Friday and Saturday, 5:30 to 11 P.M.; Sunday, 4:30 to 10 P.M.
Prices: Lunch entrees average $8.95, dinner entrees average $19.
Take-out: Yes.
Wheelchair accessible: No.
Smoking policy: Dining room nonsmoking. Smoking permitted in bar.
Dress: Upscale casual.
Credit cards: Visa, MasterCard, American Express, Discover, and Diner's Club.
Other: Historic building. Was West Chester borough's original Town Hall, which also

Simon Pearce on the Brandywine

Yes, there really is a Simon Pearce. He exists as certainly as the Brandywine Valley restaurant, glassblowing studio, and retail shop that bear his name.

Simon Pearce is a designer and glassblower brought up in Ireland. He trained under a master potter in New Zealand, then turned his talents to glassmaking. Pearce studied at the Royal College of Art in London, then worked at some of Europe's top glass firms. In Scandinavia, he apprenticed at Orrefors. The clean lines and simplicity of Scandinavian glass codified Pearce's own artistic convictions. He ran a glass workshop in Kilkenny, Ireland, for a decade and came to the United States in 1981.

That year, the artist opened a workshop in a restored woolen mill in bucolic Quechee, Vermont, using the Ottauquechee River to power the glass furnace. The mill was open to visitors, who watched the crafters in action and purchased the finished products. The inevitable question people asked was, "Where can we have lunch?" Along with his creative genius and entrepreneurial skills, Pearce is also food-savvy, having grown up as part of the household at a renowned Irish inn. It was a logical next step to open the Glassblower's Cafe at Quechee in 1985.

Pearce's business grew to include a dozen retail shops. All along, he kept his eyes open for a special spot like the one in Vermont. His search was rewarded when the building that housed the old Lenape Inn right alongside the Brandywine River became available. The structure was gutted and a tripartite space created: a semi-industrial glassblowing studio open to the public, a retail shop, and a restaurant.

Simon Pearce on the Brandywine opened in November 2000 and achieved immediate and well-deserved popularity. The interior design—like the glass made, sold, and used here—is a study in simplicity and elegance. The 125-seat restaurant defines clean lines with a Danish parquet floor, white walls, and expansive windows. Two-tiered seating gives every table a view of the Brandywine.

The lunch and dinner menus also follow this philosophy. Fresh, top-quality ingredients are chosen, and the dishes are prepared simply but with great care. Like the founder himself, the cuisine is American with an Irish accent.

Meals start with a selection of warm breads. A variety of soups and salads are available. Entrees may include cod encrusted with horseradish or crisp roast duckling with mango chutney. The lunch menu offers sandwiches and pastas; the dinner menu is a little more elaborate but just as faithful to using fresh, seasonal ingredients. The restaurant has an extensive wine list and also offers twenty-five wines by the glass. Service is friendly and knowledgeable. The gently curved wooden bar is a welcoming spot for a drink or a bite to eat.

Simon Pearce on the Brandywine serves lunch and dinner in a sleek, contemporary dining room overlooking the river. SIMON PEARCE ON THE BRANDYWINE

(continued on page 118)

Items like this one are made in the workshop on the lower level of Simon Pearce on the Brandywine, and sold upstairs in the retail store. SIMON PEARCE ON THE BRANDYWINE

(continued from page 117)

Lunch and dinner are served here during regular meal hours, with a bar menu in between.

Part of the restaurant's appeal is the tactile experience of using Simon Pearce glass and pottery. Each piece of glass has been hand-blown and hand-finished using traditional techniques. The aesthetic is simple and streamlined; no adornment is necessary. What a wonderful marriage of beauty and function.

During the day, you may look out over the sweeping lawn to see geese or a heron enjoying the river while you enjoy your meal. In the evening, outdoor lighting adds drama and romance to the view. Dinner is more formal than lunch, but the dress code is flexible. Jackets and ties are fine at dinner, but neat, more casual dress is just as acceptable.

The retail shop is quite lovely in itself. It features original Simon Pearce glass and pottery, along with wood items, fine linens, and accessories. The well-lit space has large, wooden display stands and great lighting with Simon Pearce chandeliers. A huge, clear glass bowl filled with colorful fruit is an eye-catching inspiration to home decorators.

Before you leave the premises, head downstairs to watch glassblowers in action. Wall charts explain the glassmaking process and display sample tools. The workers are happy to answer questions about their techniques or products. It's quite a fulfilling experience to see the origins of the items in the restaurant and shop, and to watch blobs of molten material become works of art.

SIMON PEARCE ON THE BRANDYWINE

1333 Lenape Rd. at PA Route 52, West Chester, PA 19382
Telephone: 610-793-0948 • Retail store: 610-793-0949
Fax: 610-793-0991 • Website: www.simonpearce.com

Restaurant hours: Lunch 11:30 A.M. to 2:45 P.M. Dinner 5:30 to 9 P.M. Bar menu available between lunch and dinner.
Workshop hours: 10 A.M. to 9 P.M.
Retail store hours: Daily, 10 A.M. to 9 P.M.
Smoking policy: Nonsmoking.
Wheelchair accessible: Yes.
Children welcome: Yes; high chairs available.
Credit cards: All major cards accepted.
Personal checks: Not accepted.
Take-out: No.
Other: A private dining room is available. Contact the restaurant for details.

housed police station, jail, and mayor's office. Outdoor dining in courtyard in warm weather. Name refers to the original name of West Chester, Turk's Head.

Vincent's
10 E. Gay St.
West Chester, PA 19380
Telephone: 610-696-4262
Fax: 610-696-4238
Hours: Lunch Monday through Friday, 11:30 A.M. to 2 P.M. Dinner Monday through Saturday, 5:30 to 10 P.M. Closed Sunday.
Price: Lunch $7 to $11, dinner $16 to $25.
Take-out: No.
Wheelchair accessible: No.
Smoking policy: Smoking and nonsmoking sections.
Dress: Casual.
Credit cards: Visa, MasterCard, and American Express.
Other: Piano player on Friday and Saturday starting at 6 P.M. Club upstairs has jazz on Thursday, blues on Friday, and jazz and blues on Saturday from 9:30 P.M. to 1 A.M. Bar only, no food upstairs.

West Chester Fish Market and Eatery
9 N. Walnut St.
West Chester, PA 19380
Telephone: 610-696-4180
Fax: 610-696-4028
Hours: Monday through Wednesday, 11 A.M. to 9 P.M.; Thursday through Saturday, 11 A.M. to 10 P.M.; Sunday, noon to 6 P.M.
Prices: Sandwiches average $6; salads average $7; entrees range from $9.50 to $13.50.
Take-out: Yes.
Wheelchair accessible: Yes, including restrooms.
Smoking policy: Nonsmoking.
Dress: Casual.
Credit cards: Visa and MasterCard.
Personal checks: Not accepted.
Other: Small storefront restaurant with a few tables. Fresh fish for sale. BYOB. Dinner specials nightly, fish 'n' chips on Fridays. Outdoor dining in season.

Kennett Square

Flowers and fungi aren't usually allies, but when "flowers" means Longwood Gardens and "fungi" refers to the mushroom capital of the world, it's a winning combination. Add an attractive historic district, plenty of shops and restaurants, a symphony orchestra, parkland, and abundant special events, including a Mushroom Festival, and you'll have even more reasons to visit Kennett Square.

The town is strategically located at an important crossroads. Hessian baron Wilhelm van Knyphausen and British general Sir William Howe stayed here the night before they defeated Washington's troops at the Battle of Brandywine on September 11, 1777. Kennett's central location was also partly responsible for Kennett Square's importance in the Underground Railroad. This aspect of the area's history is celebrated at the Kennett Underground Railroad Center's History Station.

Thanks to Pierre S. du Pont, Kennett Square is known worldwide for its spectacular horticultural jewel, Longwood Gardens. Events and displays take place all year round at Longwood, outdoors and under glass.

North and west of Longwood Gardens is Unionville, known as horse country. Large farms and open spaces present scenic vistas.

The borough itself is just one mile square, graced with historic homes, tree-lined streets, and a vibrant downtown. It's the smallest town in America that has its own

symphony. Self-guided walking tours are a good way to get to know Kennett Square. Pick up a brochure at any of the information kiosks around town. Anson B. Nixon Park on North Walnut Street is the place to go for outdoor play.

The Fungus among Us

From the small button mushroom to the plate-size portabella, Americans adore mushrooms: sliced and sautéed, breaded and fried, in sauces and salads. Kennett Square celebrates mushrooms with a two-day festival in early September, National Mushroom Month.

It was here in Kennett Square that nurserymen Harry Hicks and William

In late April and early May, the Flower Garden Walk at Longwood Gardens has thousands of blooming tulips. LONGWOOD GARDENS/LARRY ALBEE

Swayne started growing mushrooms under their greenhouse flowerbeds in the 1890s. Once they perfected temperature control and ventilation, the industry expanded quickly. Today Pennsylvania accounts for more than 40 percent of total U.S. mushroom production.

The festival has food, music, farm tours, and cooking demonstrations. There are presentations of how to grow mushrooms, from compost through cutting. An art show, microbrew festival, and soup and wine tasting are always big draws. Children's rides keep the little ones entertained. Most of the events are free, but a few charge admission.

Some years, you can even get mushroom ice cream.

The Mushroom Festival

P.O. Box 1000
Kennett Square, PA 19348
Telephone: 888-440-9920
E-mail: info@mushroomfest.com
Website: www.mushroomfestival.org

The Microbrew Festival held in conjunction with the Mushroom Festival is a popular event in Kennett Square. BOROUGH OF KENNETT SQUARE/SAM MELDRUM

Getting Around

Longwood Gardens is about three miles from the borough, so you'll want to drive if you're heading there. Back in town, there's plenty of on-street parking, plus a garage at Union and Linden. Kennett Square is a delightful place to walk around, whether you're shopping, gallery hopping, or just seeing the sights.

SCCOOT (Southern Chester County Organization on Transportation) buses run north to Chadds Ford and West Chester, and south to Avondale, West Grove, and Oxford. For information on routes, fares, and schedules, call 877-612-1359, or consult the website www.tmacc.org.

Calendar of Events

Many local events are sponsored by the attractions featured in this chapter. Consult those listings for details. Unless otherwise noted, call 610-444-8188 or visit www.historickennettsquare.com for information on events listed.

Monthly, first Friday, 6 to 9 P.M.: Art Stroll.

May, the Sunday closest to May 5, 1 to 4 P.M.: Cinco de Mayo. Held on State Street.

Mid-May through October, 2 to 6 P.M.: Kennett Square Farmers Market, walkway between State Street and parking garage. Market vendors sell a range of seasonal produce that includes fruits, berries, vegetables, cheese, baked goods, handmade soaps, jams and jellies, cut flowers, plants, fresh bread, corn, and potatoes. Free garage or street parking. Call 610-444-8188 or visit www.historickennettsquare.com.

May, Mother's Day: Willowdale Steeplechase. Intersection of PA Routes 82 and 926 (Office: 101 E. Street Rd., Kennett Square, PA 19348). $15 per person in advance or $20 on race day. A day full of fun including tailgate competition, restaurant booths, Jack Russell terrier races, and police canine demonstrations, culminating in a steeplechase race sanctioned by the National Steeplechase Association. Call 610-444-1582 or visit www.willowdale.org.

June, a Saturday early in the month: Blues & Brews on Broad Street, and Cruise Night on State Street. Barbeque, microbrewed beer, local wine, and live entertainment.

Fee charged. Call 610-444-1818 or visit www.historickennettsquare.com or www.kennettbrewfest.com.

June through August, usually Saturday: Summer concerts. Anson B. Nixon Park, North Walnut Street off State Street. For concert information, call 610-444-6443 or visit www.kennettsquare.pa.us/KAPA/.

Santa and Mrs. Claus herald the holiday season during the traditional tree lighting. BOROUGH OF KENNETT SQUARE/SAM MELDRUM

September, weekend after Labor Day: Mushroom Festival (see p. 121), and the Kennett Brewfest. Visit www.historickennettsquare.com or www.mushroom festival.org.

September, one Saturday midmonth: Antique festival. Dealers line downtown streets. Call 610-444-1818 or visit www.historickennettsquare.com.

October, one Sunday late in month: Pennsylvania Hunt Cup Races. Office: P.O. Box 100, Unionville, PA 19375, telephone 610-869-0557.

November, Friday after Thanksgiving, 6 P.M.: Tree lighting, holiday parade, and open house. Visit www.historickennettsquare.com.

December, Sundays: Horse-drawn carriage rides on State Street. Visit www.historic kennettsquare.com.

December, second Sunday, 4 to 7 P.M.: Old Home Candlelight Tour. Tickets are required; admission is charged. Visit www.historickennettsquare.com.

FEATURED ATTRACTIONS

Kennett Underground Railroad Center/Kennett History Station

The Underground Railroad was a secret network that helped slaves escape to freedom, especially between 1831 and 1863. Chester County in general, and Kennett Square in particular, played a vital role in this effort. One reason was location: Kennett Square was at the crossroads of main arteries between plantations in Maryland and Virginia to the south and escape routes to the north. The Quaker presence also contributed to the strength of the movement in and around Kennett.

In 1780, Pennsylvania passed a law abolishing slavery over a period of time, but not freeing existing slaves. Abolitionists banded together and held "indignation meetings" to promote the cause of freedom. In 1842, the U.S. Supreme Court ruled that states did not have to aid in the return of runaway slaves.

However, to appease the South, Congress passed the Compromise of 1850, which included a revised Fugitive Slave Bill. The new law gave slaveowners "the right to organize a posse at any point in the United States to aid in recapturing runaway slaves." Courts, police, and private citizens were obligated to assist in recapturing runaways. People who were caught helping slaves were fined and went to jail. This essentially meant that escaped slaves would have to go all the way to Canada to find safety.

Despite the chilling language of the bill and the serious risks it imposed on people trying to help slaves escape, the Underground Railroad continued its work. Publicly, people spoke out against the law and against the institution of slavery. The Longwood Meeting hosted many famous speakers, Sojourner Truth among them.

Privately, "conductors" and "station masters" worked clandestinely to spirit slaves northward. Escapees including Harriet Tubman went back and forth leading others out of bondage. Locals like John and Hannah Cox, who founded Longwood Meeting along with other like-minded folks, protected those who were fleeing.

An elaborate signal system, including the positioning of weather vanes, the singing of certain spirituals, and other private communications, got messages from

Visiting the Kennett Underground Railroad Center/ Kennett History Station

505 S. Broad St., (Mailing address: P.O. Box 202)
Kennett Square, PA 19348 • Telephone: 610-347-2237
E-mail: UndergroundRR@Kennett.net
Website: www.UndergroundRR.Kennett.net

Admission: Free.
Special consideration: Wheelchair accessible, including restroom.
Other: Trolleybus tours in summer. Contact the KURC for details.

one station to the next. Escaped slaves hid in attics and cellars, under stairs and behind false walls, in woodsheds and haymows, and sometimes in caves.

For obvious reasons, written records from the time are scarce. Nonetheless, the Kennett Underground Railroad Center (KURC) has identified more than two dozen local stations, possibly the largest concentration in the country.

The KURC was founded in 1998 by Frances Cloud Taylor, author of *The Trackless Trail* and *The Trackless Trail Leads On.* The organization's mission is to educate the public about what abolitionists and escaped slaves did to change the course of our nation's history. The KURC identifies and documents buildings that served as Underground Railroad stations and helps the owners get the sites listed on the National Register of Historic Places.

Longwood Progressive Meeting of Friends (circa 1855). Many people, including Sojourner Truth, spoke out against slavery at this Quaker Meeting House. Today the building houses the Chester County Visitors Center. KENNETT UNDERGROUND RAILROAD CENTER

Harriet Tubman, a "conductor" on the Underground Railroad, was nicknamed "Moses." The escaped slave led many others to freedom, sometimes through Kennett Square. John and Hannah Cox were local "station masters," aiding escapees and championing the cause of freedom. KENNETT UNDERGROUND RAILROAD CENTER

For visitors, the History Station is a place to learn in depth about the area's importance in the Underground Railroad. The building is a former freight train station that began operating in 1859 and was a vital part of local life for almost a century. The Kennett Square Historical Commission, in cooperation with Kennett Square Borough, the West Chester Railroad Heritage Association, and the Kennett High School Alumni Association Historic Committee, renovated the space into a local history museum. The KURC has two exhibit rooms plus a small shop; the Alumni Association displays its items in another room. There are also changing exhibits and information about local history and architecture.

Photographs and drawings of faces remind us that the people involved were real human beings. Interpretive signs tell us about these individuals and their lives.

An early-nineteenth-century period room—kind of a composite of a bedroom and kitchen—contains reproductions of original local hiding places. Visitors, especially children, are challenged to locate these and figure out how they worked, while a docent tells stories about escaped slaves and the people who helped them. A minute or two in a small space under some floorboards or in the back of a closet brings home the pain and discomfort the escapees were willing to suffer in order to gain their freedom. Period items like a sampler, cooking accessories, spindle bed, and chamber pot evoke the era of the Underground Railroad. A particularly poignant article is a dress, much worn and skillfully mended, in the style worn by slave girls.

The General Store offers an extensive selection of books and items about the Underground Railroad.

In summer, the KURC hosts trolleybus tours to local Underground Railroad sites. The guided rides last about an hour and are a wonderful way to experience a vital part of the area's history.

Longwood Gardens

National Geographic Traveler got it right when the magazine named Longwood Gardens one of America's "50 Places of a Lifetime." Longwood is known for its horticulture, with more than eleven thousand types of plants growing on the 1,050-acre property, including 4 acres under glass in the Conservatory, but that's only part of what it offers visitors. Add fountain displays, performing arts events, forest paths, meadows, a waterfall, themed festivals, educational programs, children's activities, top-notch food, and meticulous upkeep—the complete package is a jewel that surprises and delights newcomers and regular visitors alike.

Set aside at least half a day to spend here. Tickets are good for a whole day, so you can even break up your visit. Consider that option in summer, when you may want to explore the gardens, take a midday break, then come back for the evening fountain show. It's also a good choice during the very popular Christmas display: Visit the indoor areas early in the day, then return after 5 P.M. to enjoy the outdoor spectacular. Since you'll already have a ticket, you won't have to wait in line to purchase one. (Be aware, though, that parking can be very scarce, especially the week after Christmas.)

History of the Property

The land on which Longwood Gardens is located was once the home to the Lenni-Lenape tribe. Despite the presence of these native peoples, William Penn claimed ownership and sold it in 1700 to a Quaker family named Peirce.

The Peirces farmed the land throughout the eighteenth century. As early as 1798, brothers Joshua and Samuel Peirce began planting an arboretum. They traveled far and wide to collect top specimens. The arboretum was well known by the mid-1800s. Joshua's son George Washington Peirce expanded his father's and uncle's vision by developing the land into a public pleasure ground called Peirce's Park, complete with croquet and rowboats.

After George Peirce died in 1880, the trees and land were neglected. In 1906, the trees were about to be logged by a sawmill operator, when Pierre S. du Pont purchased the land and the lumbering contract to save the collection of old trees. Without his intervention, there would be no Longwood Gardens today.

Pierre S. du Pont was a great-grandson of DuPont Company founder Eleuthère Irénée du Pont. Pierre was born in 1870 at the family home in Wilmington, the eldest

Spring comes to Longwood Gardens indoors when there's still snow on the ground outside. LONGWOOD GARDENS/LARRY ALBEE

Visiting Longwood Gardens

U.S. Route 1 at PA Route 52, Kennett Square, PA 19348-0501

Telephone: 610-388-1000; for group visits, use ext. 513 or 512; for Terrace Restaurant information, call 610-388-6771; for recorded information from phones in Connecticut, New York, New Jersey, Pennsylvania, Delaware, Maryland, the District of Columbia, and Virginia, call 800-737-5500.

Website: www.longwoodgardens.org

Hours: Longwood Gardens is open every day of the year, April through October, 9 A.M. to 6 P.M.; November through March, 9 A.M. to 5 P.M. The Conservatory opens at 10 A.M. Longwood remains open several evenings a week during the summer Festival of Fountains and every evening during the Christmas display. The Heritage Exhibit in the Peirce–du Pont House is open daily from 10 A.M. to 5 P.M., until 6 P.M. from April through October, and until 9 P.M. during the Christmas display.

Admission: Fees vary by age and time of year; to verify the fees for the date you plan to visit, call or consult the website.

Audio tours: Visitors may request audio wands, slim, handheld devices that resemble a television remote control, from the desk at the entrance to the Orangery in the Conservatory. After brief instructions on use, visitors are free to explore the Conservatory with the wands as their personal guides. Audio wands are available from mid-January through mid-November beginning at 10 A.M. They are intended for visitors eighteen and older or for closely supervised children. Included in the admission fee.

Special considerations: Longwood is easily accessible to visitors with disabilities. There are forty-five spaces reserved for handicapped parking close to the Visitor Center in the front of the parking lot. Nonmotorized wheelchairs or single-person electric scooters can be borrowed on a first-come basis at no cost from the Information Desk in the Visitor Center. Scooters are not available in rainy or snowy weather, or when the temperature is below 36 degrees Fahrenheit. They must be parked outside the Open Air Theatre, Peirce–du Pont House, or Terrace Restaurant when visiting those facilities.

Food: The Terrace Restaurant has cafeteria and full-service dining, plus special buffets that coincide with holidays, special performances, and fireworks. Special options are available for groups. Gardens admission is required for restaurant access. Picnicking is not permitted on the grounds; it is permitted from spring through fall in Longwood's Picnic Area outside the main Gardens, accessible by car or bus. For hours, information, and reservations where recommended, call or consult the website.

Photography: Visitors are welcome to take still and video pictures for personal use. Tripods may be used any day from 9 to 11 A.M. Stop by the Information Desk in the Visitor Center to fill out a tripod permission form and receive a tripod tag. Monopods may be used at any time, but they cannot be tripods with only one leg extended. The permission form indicates that any photographs or video/film footage taken at Longwood will not be used to advertise commercial products or services. Sessions are limited to garden photography, not wedding photography, individual or family portraits, product photography, or portfolio photography for aspiring models. All photographers must purchase general admission to the Gardens or be valid Frequent Visitor Passholders. Photography sessions must not interfere with the enjoyment of Longwood's other guests.

Shop: The shop, located in the Visitor Center, offers books, horticultural gift items, plants, and gardening tools and supplies. Open the same hours as the Gardens.

Classes: Classes are offered for amateur and professional gardeners, artists, crafters, and cooks. Children's programs are also offered. For a complete list, visit the website or write to Continuing Education, Longwood Gardens, P.O. Box 501, Kennett Square, PA 19348-0501.

son of Lammot and Mary du Pont. Pierre's childhood ended abruptly when his father died in a manufacturing explosion. The fourteen-year-old became head of the family for his mother and ten brothers and sisters.

Despite this responsibility, Pierre was able to graduate from MIT with a degree in chemistry in 1890. He went to work for DuPont, then became president of the Johnson Company in Ohio. Returning to Wilmington in 1902, he joined his cousins Alfred I. duPont and T. Coleman du Pont to purchase a controlling interest in the DuPont Company.

Led largely by Pierre du Pont, the company successfully made the transition from a family firm to a multinational chemical company giant. General Motors also tapped Pierre du Pont's expertise; he guided that company's rapid development as chairman from 1915 to 1929.

In 1915, du Pont married his cousin Alice Belin. The lifelong friends had traveled to many gardens together, including a visit to more than twenty Italian villas and gardens in 1913. Some of these would inspire the development of Longwood Gardens, as would the fifty French châteaux and gardens the couple toured in 1925.

Along with his many business and botanical achievements, Pierre S. du Pont was also a philanthropist. He gave more than $8 million for public schools in Delaware and Pennsylvania, donated $2 million to the University of Delaware, and was generous to local hospitals. He also backed public road improvements and expansions. His wish that Long-

Giant waterplatters unfurl their pads in Longwood's lilypond. LONGWOOD GARDENS/LARRY ALBEE

wood Gardens would be part of the family legacy led to the creation of a foundation to operate the gardens after his death. Pierre du Pont died in 1954, but his personal pride and joy, Longwood Gardens, continues to delight visitors.

Longwood's Water Features

Never underestimate the power of childhood inspiration. When six-year-old Pierre du Pont attended the 1876 Great Centennial Exposition in Philadelphia, he was mesmerized by the waterworks. This sense of wonder never left him. It was reinforced when he attended the 1893 World Columbian Exposition in Chicago and saw the fountain show. Water would play a key part in the development of Longwood Gardens.

The first fountain at Longwood was a modest round one with a single jet, at the intersection of the main paths in the Flower Garden Walk. Subsequent installations became increasingly more elaborate.

Pierre du Pont combined his love of theater with his fondness for fountains and his knack for engineering in the Open Air Theatre starting in 1913. This provided a venue for outdoor performances from such notables as Philadelphia's Savoy Company and John Philip Sousa's band. Simple fountains were in place on the stage from the beginning, but one evening in 1927 a switch was flipped, and the annual "garden party" would never be the same. As the audience gasped, jets of water blasted up fifty feet into the trees, lit from below by more than six hundred colored lights. A newspaper reporter described the new, greatly expanded fountains in Longwood Gardens' Open Air Theatre as "like fireworks, rockets upside down, or weird deep-sea mysteries." Pierre du Pont must have been thrilled. Today performing arts events and fountain shows in the Open Air Theatre still wow visitors.

The Main Fountain Garden in front of the Conservatory has some impressive statistics: Ten thousand gallons of water per minute circulate through 380 fountainheads, scuppers, and spouts; the highest jet soars 130 feet in the air; a 90,000-gallon underground reservoir feeds the fountains and the 50-foot waterfall; the whole system can hold 675,000 gallons. Daily fountain shows are given in the summer, with evening shows three times a week. The after-sunset shows feature musical accompaniment and colored lighting. Fireworks light up the sky on several special nights.

Never one to waste resources, Pierre du Pont had the rocks that were removed during the reservoir's construction built into a tower next to the waterfall. Today the Chimes Tower houses a five-octave carillon on which regular concerts are played.

The Villa Gamberaia near Florence, Italy, inspired du Pont to design the Italian Water Garden. Sometimes called the "frog fountain" by visitors because of the stone amphibians at its far end, the Italian Water Garden has blue-tiled pools surrounded by carved limestone ornaments. Littleleaf linden trees provide shade around the perimeter, while a lush lawn looks just right with the formal pools. Six hundred water jets recirculate 4,500 gallons of water each minute. Pierre du Pont added a unique feature: a staircase down which water cascades. Ever the engineer, du Pont did fifty pages worth of hydraulic calculations before the fountains opened in 1927; when the numbers were checked prior to the Italian Water Garden's 1989 renovation, everything was correct.

The Festival of Fountains takes place daily in summer. LONGWOOD GARDENS/LARRY ALBEE

After Pierre du Pont's death, Longwood Gardens continued to add water features. The courtyard behind the Conservatory is the site of the waterlily ponds. By late summer, waterplatters up to seven feet in diameter spread their pads over the water's surface, while waterlilies, lotus, and other aquatic gems open their blooms. In the Conservatory and around the grounds, the refreshing sound of water against a backdrop of gorgeous plants is a hallmark of Longwood Gardens. One of the loveliest spots in spring is the original, simple fountain along the Flower Garden Walk. Flanked by thousands of tulips and other blooming beauties, the unpretentious fountain is stunning.

The Peirce–du Pont House

The Peirce family of Quaker farmers built the first part of this brick house in 1730. It was enlarged several times over the next century and a half. Pierre du Pont added a wing in 1914 and connected the two parts with a glass-enclosed courtyard.

Visitors may tour the first floor of the house, now the "Longwood Heritage Exhibit." A twelve-minute introductory video gives a good overview of Pierre du Pont's creation of Longwood Gardens. The rest of the exhibits present a fascinating look at his life and legacy.

The Conservatory

Longwood is world famous for its Conservatory, which is divided into twenty distinct "houses" or "gardens." No matter what time of year you visit, spectacular floral displays are always in bloom indoors. Like Pierre du Pont, Longwood's current management focuses on continuous improvement, and nowhere is that more evident than in the Conservatory. Ambitious short- and long-range renovation plans ensure that creative plantings will thrive in the indoor spaces, and that the visitor experience will continue to be enhanced.

The centerpiece of the Conservatory is the Orangery and Exhibition Hall, which opened in 1921 after three years of construction. The original plan was to have orange trees grow and bear fruit here. When they failed to produce as hoped, the trees were replaced by the manicured lawns and flower beds still in place today. Arched windows add to the light that comes through the roof. At the northern end of the Exhibition Hall is the Music Room, always exquisitely decorated during the Christmas display.

The East Conservatory is undergoing a major facelift to create a vibrant interior landscape grounded in Spanish and French classical garden design. Dramatic plantings of subtropical flora and masses of blooming plants are punctuated with water features and restful seating areas. The reopening is scheduled for 2006.

Other highlights of the glass houses include the Mediterranean Garden, redolent of the Côte d'Azur; the Cascade Garden, with bromeliads and a tropical feel; the Silver Garden, where desert plants are at home; and the Palm House, filled with those tropical plants. Orchids, ferns, and roses all have their own distinct spaces.

The bonsai display appeals to many visitors. Through this technique, trees and other plants remain perfect miniatures of their full-size counterparts. Expert horticulturists prune the plants' roots, branches, and leaves to keep them small and to train them to grow in controlled shapes. It's fascinating to look at perfect, tiny trees that are decades old. Autumn is a particularly fine time to see the bonsai, when the leaves on the deciduous specimens turn color and then drop. Several chrysanthemum bonsai are also on display during that time of year.

The Estate Fruit House harks back to the era when Longwood was a country estate, until about 1954. This installation has a sculptural, Zen feel to it with its curved wooden benches and trained trees and vines. Lemons, pomegranates, figs, melons, and other fruits lend structure and texture to the garden. Given Pierre du Pont's penchant for precision, you may not be surprised to learn that when grapes were originally grown indoors, each vine was pruned to produce exactly twelve bunches, with a specific number of grapes in each bunch.

The Conservatory's Ballroom was constructed in 1929 specifically to house the Aeolian organ designed just for Longwood. The world's largest residence organ, it has 10,010 pipes that produce almost every sound you can imagine. Concerts are given frequently; you can also take a behind-the-scenes tour of the instrument. The wood for the original parquet floor came from an unlikely source: surplus World War I walnut gunstock blocks.

Especially for Children

There's plenty for kids to love at Longwood Gardens, and what they enjoy may surprise you. For years, my children didn't even notice the plants; they were fascinated by the drainage system and the work trucks. The topiaries, sundials, and fountains are favorites with the wee ones. There are many places where it's okay for kids to walk on the grass, and lots of good spots where the littlest kids can play peekaboo. They can run back and forth to the fountain in Peirce's Park and examine the insect-eating plants in the Conservatory. Special activities for children are held most weekends.

The newly expanded Children's Garden, scheduled to open by 2007, will be a fanciful, interactive space. All five sections will be wheelchair accessible, and a walkway around the edges will let grown-ups keep watch.

Water features are planned to figure predominantly here: In the Central Cove, flower-shaped water jets squirt while three water pilasters shoot streams of water overhead. Next comes the Secret Room, guarded by a drooling dragon. A bridge over a water curtain leads to a tower; underneath is a "fog-covered" pool, and snakes above drip water. In the Bamboo Maze, visitor-activated water features will surprise maze-goers as they try to find their way through a bamboo jungle. Bring an extra shirt for the kids, and don't sweat it if they get a little wet.

Children have plenty to do at Longwood Gardens. Here, a youngster uses a stamping station in the Idea Garden. LONGWOOD GARDENS

Longwood provides a wonderful stimulus for children's imagination. Ask your youngsters questions like these and see what they come up with: What would it be like to live in the Chimes Tower? If your cactus was up to the ceiling like the one in the Silver Garden, what would you do? What do you think is under the floor in the Conservatory? How did sundial-using people tell time when it was cloudy?

Some Words about Mums

Celebrated in haiku, prized for color and shape, the member of the aster family known as the chrysanthemum has been revered for more than two millennia. Nowhere is a seasonal display of the flowers more spectacular than at Longwood Gardens, where twenty-one thousand plants in the Conservatory provide a dramatic backdrop for performing arts events from late October to just before Thanksgiving.

The Chinese philosopher Confucius wrote favorably about the "yellow glory" as early as the sixth century B.C. Chrysanthemums were objects of meditation and ingredients in wine and medicine. Mums were introduced to Japan in the fourth century A.D., where they were the exclusive purview of nobles for about five hundred years. Considered the imperial flower, the chrysanthemum is part of many Japanese holidays and festivals.

Mums came to Europe in the late seventeenth century. The Swedish taxonomist Carolus Linnaeus named the plant from the Greek *chrysos*, meaning gold, and *anthemom*, meaning flower. About two hundred years later, chrysanthemums crossed the Atlantic. They were exhibited at Longwood in 1921, for the opening of the Conservatory.

Almost all ancient Chinese mums were yellow. Today, thanks to centuries of painstaking breeding, chrysanthemums also come in gold, bronze, pink, lilac, pur-

The annual Chrysanthemum Festival displays mums of every shape and size, including large incurve mums like the yellow ones shown here.
LONGWOOD GARDENS/LARRY ALBEE

ple, white, red, rust, maroon, burgundy, and everything in between. Mums are classified by bloom shape, from the tightly balled pompon to the lanky spider. Longwood presents all varieties of chrysanthemums in ways that are simply breathtaking.

"What we do best is grow the chrysanthemums to a level of perfection not found anywhere else," says floriculturist Sharon Loving. "It's important that we show many different classifications of mums."

The floral fireworks reach their peak in the Orangery and Exhibition Hall. Incurve mums the size and shape of soccer balls are consistent attention-getters. Ditto five-foot-diameter hanging globes, cascades draped over columns, and the mum curtain positioned over the stage in the Exhibition Hall.

Extensive preparation is crucial. "We have to decide a year ahead of time what plants we want and take cuttings from the cultivars we want to use for the baskets and cascades," explains Loving. "They're grown in greenhouses from January to May, then moved outdoors in containers."

In summer, cascade mums undergo training in which they are groomed, pinched, sheared, disbudded, and in some cases, tied to frames. Blooming time is controlled by the plants' light-sensitive internal clock that senses the shortening days. Sometimes growers manipulate the light to make the chrysanthemums flower at a certain time. Cascade mums require particular care, because the plants have to be trained into producing long stems before blooming.

Mums destined for hanging baskets look like giant spiders in the field, since the "legs" are spread out. They're brought inside the first week in October, and the legs are tied together under the baskets to create flawless orbs.

Overall, the effect throughout the Conservatory is one of exotic colors and textures, woven into a beautiful tapestry.

Christmas Magic

For most people who decorate their homes at Christmastime, the installation takes a weekend or two, the planning process not much longer. But for Longwood Gardens, the annual extravaganza involves years of preparation, hundreds of personnel, and thousands of details. Outside, arborists string lights for more than two months. Indoors, crackerjack choreography takes the Gardens from chrysanthemums to Christmas in three days flat. With extensive groundwork, exotic plants, exquisite decorations, and an experienced team to pull it off, it's a production that even Santa and his elves might envy.

The arborist crew begins to install lights in trees the third week of September, with an average of eight people working five days a week. That number increases substantially in November as the Thanksgiving deadline approaches.

When the job is finished, more than 420,000 light bulbs have been installed. Arborists and electricians cover evergreen and deciduous trees up to sixty feet high, as well as wire frames. Shimmering snowflakes and icicles seem to fall from the sky, suspended from the large trees behind the Open Air Theatre's fountains.

Bare lilac bushes are returned to springlike glory with flower clusters of twinkling lights; nearby, tiny light bulbs are massed on the ground to simulate another kind of bulb, spring anemones. Twine frameworks superimpose conifer silhouettes onto trees of any shape. In the informal style that delights Longwood's guests, small colored lights snake along tree branches from trunk to tip.

The result of all this hard work is apparent during the display each evening at 5 P.M. when the switch is flipped, transforming Longwood Gardens into an otherworldly wonderland.

Indoors, work is just as intense. A Herculean effort starts Sunday evening prior to Thanksgiving and ends before the turkey's on the table.

Out go autumn accoutrements by the truckload; in come hundreds of handmade snowflakes and icicles. Good-bye, chrysanthemums; hello, poinsettias. A conga line of Christmas trees snakes its way through the Conservatory, each one labeled so it is dropped off at the appropriate destination. Wiring, plumbing, staging, planting, decorating—all are done according to plan so that nothing is over-

Snowflakes and icicles hang from the trees behind the dancing fountains in the Open Air Theatre at Christmastime. LONGWOOD GARDENS/LARRY ALBEE

Hanging baskets of poinsettias dangle like giant Christmas ornaments in the Conservatory. LONGWOOD GARDENS/LARRY ALBEE

looked. In a synchronized demonstration worthy of Radio City Music Hall's Rockettes, Longwood's cast members work at their tasks in close quarters without ever stepping on each other's toes.

The real showstopper is the "big tree," traditionally a seventeen- to twenty-four-foot-high Douglas fir. This magnificent specimen is installed center stage in the Conservatory, decorated in a unique fashion each year.

Nighttime lights and indoor floral displays are far from the only attractions during Longwood's Christmas celebration. A wildlife tree decorated with edible treats attracts feathered friends; fountains dance to the "Waltz of the Snowflakes" in the Open Air Theatre; hollies flaunt their green leaves and red berries in tribute to the season. Visitors are also treated to a full schedule of concerts and classes. Don't be surprised if you notice a guy in a red suit getting in on the action.

Calendar of Events

Performing Arts and Other Events: Longwood Gardens hosts more than eight hundred such events each year. Most are included in the regular admission fee; some require an additional fee and/or preregistration. For up-to-the-minute information on events and fountain schedules, check the website.

Early January through late March: Welcome Spring. Indoors, profuse bulbs create a kaleidoscope of continuously changing plantings. Outdoors, early bulbs bloom, tinting the landscape.

Late March through early April: Easter Display. Easter lilies and tall-stemmed white calla lilies are complemented by larkspurs, hydrangeas, and fragrant yellow sweet brooms indoors.

Early April through late May: Acres of Spring. Gardens, meadows, and woodlands burst with fragrant flowers, shrubs, and trees. Tulips dominate the Flower Garden Walk in late April and early May; the Wisteria and Peony Gardens bloom in May. The Hillside Garden begins with small bulbs, followed by azaleas, tulips, phlox, and dozens of other rock garden plants.

Late May through late August or early September: Festival of Fountains. Illuminated musical fountain displays follow alfresco entertainment several evenings a week. Fireworks are held on specially ticketed evenings.

September: GardenFest. September's beauty and bounty are highlighted by revisiting the heyday of founder Pierre du Pont's life at Longwood. Vegetables in the Idea Garden are ripe for harvest. A Heritage Trail highlights gardens that bloom just before chilly weather sets in. Waterlilies are at their peak. A garden railway, complete with small structures that resemble Longwood's buildings, chugs near the Idea Garden.

Early October through midmonth: Autumn's Colors. The trees in Longwood's historic arboretum burst into color. Daytime fountain displays provide hourly entertainment.

Late October through Sunday before Thanksgiving: Chrysanthemum Festival. More than twenty thousand mums in all shapes, sizes, colors, and formations are featured.

Thanksgiving Day through early January: A Longwood Gardens Christmas. Indoors, floral displays and concerts celebrate the season. Outdoors, the Gardens are lit by more than 420,000 lights. Weather permitting, fountains "dance" to seasonal music.

ART, ANTIQUES, AND SELECTIVE SHOPPING

Another View
107 W. State St.
Kennett Square, PA 19348
Telephone: 610-444-0146
Hours: Monday through Thursday, 11:30 A.M. to 5:30 P.M.; Friday, 11:30 A.M. to 8:30 P.M.; Saturday, 11:30 A.M. to 8:30 P.M. Open Sundays during Christmas season.
Wheelchair accessible.

Artistic Endeavors of Longwood
808 E. Baltimore Pike (U.S. Route 1)
Kennett Square, PA 19348
Telephone: 610-444-8848
Hours: Monday through Friday, 10 A.M. to 6 P.M. (Thursday until 7 P.M.); Saturday, 10 A.M. to 5 P.M.
Wheelchair accessible.

Artworks Fine Arts & Crafts Gallery
126 S. Union St.
Kennett Square, PA 19348
Telephone: 610-444-6544

Website: www.art2luv.com
Hours: Monday, noon to 9 P.M.; Tuesday through Thursday, 10 A.M. to 9 P.M.; Friday, 10 A.M. to 10 P.M.; Saturday, 10 A.M. to 10 P.M.; Sunday, 10 A.M. to 4 P.M. Monday through Saturday in winter, closing time is one hour earlier.
A full-service arts and crafts gallery offering original works by local artists, signed Wyeth prints, other local prints, and commissions. Dedicated to promoting local artists of superb quality. Not wheelchair accessible.

Brush and Palette
123 E. State St., Kennett Square, PA 19348
Telephone: 610-444-4565
Website: www.brushandpalette.net
Hours: Monday through Thursday, 10 A.M. to 6 P.M.; Friday, 10 A.M. to 7 P.M.; Saturday, 10 A.M. to 5 P.M.
Specializes in custom framing. Eclectic assortment of art from local painters and crafters. Not wheelchair accessible.

Cenzia Arts & Gifts
121 W. State St.
Kennett Square, PA 19348
Telephone: 610-444-9255
Fax: 610-444-9307
E-mail: cenziagifts@aol.com
Hours: Monday through Saturday, 11 A.M. to
7 P.M. Closed Sunday.
An eclectic giftware and contemporary craft
gallery. Over one hundred craft artists who
specialize in art glass, wood, ceramics, and
textiles. Wheelchair accessible.

Equinox
120 W. State St.
Kennett Square, PA 19348
Telephone: 610-444-8275
Hours: Monday through Thursday, 10 A.M. to
7 P.M.; Friday and Saturday, 10 A.M. to 8 P.M.
Closed Sunday. January through March,
closing time is one hour earlier.
Jewelry, gifts, and eclectic garden accents. Not
wheelchair accessible.

Home and Garden Culture of Longwood
908/910 E. Baltimore Pike (U.S. Route 1)
Kennett Square, PA 19348
Telephone: 610-388-6300
Website: www.homeandgardenculture.com
Hours: Monday through Saturday, 10 A.M. to
5 P.M.; Sunday, 11 A.M. to 5 P.M.
A gallery of garden art. Not wheelchair
accessible.

**McLimans Antiques and
Pre-Owned Furniture**
940 W. Cypress St.
Kennett Square, PA 19348
Telephone: 610-444-3876
Website: www.mclimans.com
Hours: July 1 through September 15, Wednes-
day, 10 A.M. to 7 P.M.; Thursday through
Saturday, 10 A.M. to 5 P.M. September 16
through June 30, Wednesday through Satur-
day, 10 A.M. to 5 P.M.; Sunday, noon to 5 P.M.
Fine antique, reproduction, and traditional
furniture in a 13,000-square-foot showroom.
Wheelchair accessible.

Metalworks Fine Arts & Crafts Gallery
124 S. Union St.
Kennett Square, PA 19348
Telephone: 610-444-3648
Website: www.art2luv.com
Hours: Monday, noon to 8 P.M.; Tuesday
through Thursday, 10 A.M. to 9 P.M.; Friday
and Saturday, 10 A.M. to 10 P.M.; Sunday,
10 A.M. to 4 P.M.
Unique gallery specializing in metal arts,
including wall hangings, floor and table pieces,
sculptures, and garden pieces. Not wheelchair
accessible.

Mi Casa Su Casa
106 W. State St.
Kennett Square, PA 19348
Telephone: 610-444-6878
Hours: April through October, Monday
through Thursday, 10 A.M. to 6 P.M.; Friday,
10 A.M. to 9 P.M.; Saturday, 10 A.M. to 5 P.M.
Winter hours: Monday through Thursday,
10 A.M. to 5 P.M.; Friday, 10 A.M. to 7 P.M.;
Saturday, 10 A.M. to 5 P.M. Closed Sunday.
Latin American fine-arts and crafts gallery,
featuring the work of international and local
Latino artists and artisans. Proceeds benefit La
Comunidad Hispaña, an area nonprofit organi-
zation serving low-income families. Not wheelchair accessible.

Nesting Feathers
109 S. Broad St.
Kennett Square, PA 19348
Telephone: 610-444-7181
E-mail: feathers@nestingfeathers.com
Website: www.nestingfeathers.com
Hours: In summer, Monday, 10 A.M. to 3 P.M.;
Tuesday through Friday, 10 A.M. to 4 P.M.;
Saturday, 10 A.M. to 5 P.M. September to May,
Monday, 10 A.M. to 3 P.M.; Tuesday through
Saturday, 10 A.M. to 5 P.M.
Antiques, collectibles, jewelry, furniture, linens,
art, and other rare finds from numerous deal-
ers on several levels. Wheelchairs may be able
to enter via the truck ramp.

Rose's Roses Garden of Art
in Home and Garden Culture of Longwood
Gardens
908 E. Baltimore Pike (U.S. Route 1)
Kennett Square, PA 19348

Telephone: 610-459-5586 for artist, 610-388-6300 for shop.

Hours: Monday through Saturday, 10 A.M. to 5 P.M.; Sunday, 11 A.M. to 5 P.M.

Thomas Macaluso Used & Rare Books
130 S. Union St. (PA Route 82), one block south of State Street
Kennett Square, PA 19348
Telephone: 610-444-1063

E-mail: macaluso@kennett.net

Hours: Monday through Friday, 11 A.M. to 6 P.M.; Saturday, 11 A.M. to 5 P.M. Other times by appointment.

Twenty-five thousand volumes, all subjects and price ranges. Hundreds of old maps and prints in six charming showrooms. Not wheelchair accessible.

RECREATION, LEISURE, AND PERFORMING ARTS

Bicycling

Delaware Valley Bicycle Club
P.O. Box 156
Woodlyn, PA 19094-0156
Website: www.dvbc.org
Check the website for information on road and trail biking.

Mountain Bike Pennsylvania
Website: www.mountainbikepa.com

Disc Golf

Anson B. Nixon Park
North Walnut Street off State Street
Kennett Square, PA 19348
Telephone: 610-444-1416
Website: www.kennett-square.pa.us/KAPA/

Fishing

Anson B. Nixon Park
North Walnut Street off State Street
Kennett Square, PA 19348
Telephone: 610-444-1416
Website: www.kennett-square.pa.us/KAPA/
Two ponds are stocked for fishing. Pennsylvania fishing license required for ages fourteen and over.

Golf

Loch Nairn Golf Club
514 McCue Rd.
Avondale, PA 19311
Telephone: 610-268-2234
www.lngolf.com

Open dawn to dusk. A shotmaker's course. Tree-lined fairways wander over wetlands, lakes, and ponds to undulating bent-grass greens.

Hiking and Walking

Anson B. Nixon Park
North Walnut Street off State Street
Kennett Square, PA 19348
Telephone: 610-444-1416
Website: www.kennett-square.pa.us/KAPA/
Four walking trails.

**Myrick Conservation Center/
Brandywine Valley Association**
1760 Unionville-Wawaset Rd. (PA Route 842)
West Chester, PA 19382
Telephone: 610-793-1090
Fax: 610-793-2813
Website: www.brandywinewatershed.org
Hiking paths meander through 314 acres. Open dawn to dusk. Summer concert series.

Horseback Riding

Gateway Stables Riding Center
949 Merrybell Lane
Kennett Square, PA 19348
Telephone: 610-444-1255
Website: www.gatewaystables.com
Full-service stables. Trail rides and instruction available.

Music

Kennett Symphony of Chester County
105 S. Broad St.
P.O. Box 72
Kennett Square, PA 19348
Telephone: 610-444-6363
Website: www.symphony.kennett.net
Chester County's only professional orchestra.
Concerts held at West Chester University,
Longwood Gardens, Kennett High School,
and other venues. Wheelchair accessible.

TurtleDove Folk Club
P.O. Box 701, Unionville, PA 19375
Telephone: 866-TURTLED
Fax: 610-869-4403
Website: www.turtledove.org
Local concerts, including a series of summer
concerts at Anson B. Nixon Park in Kennett
Square. Promotes traditional, contemporary,
and multicultural folk music and dance.

Park and Playground

Anson B. Nixon Park
North Walnut Street off State Street
Kennett Square, PA 19348
Telephone: 610-444-1416
Website: www.kennett-square.pa.us/KAPA/
Eighty-two-acre park with trails, volleyball,
tennis, bocci, disc golf, children's playground,
and ponds.

Tennis

Anson B. Nixon Park
North Walnut Street off State Street
Kennett Square, PA 19348
Telephone: 610-444-1416
Website: www.kennett-square.pa.us/KAPA/
Two tennis courts.

ACCOMMODATIONS

Kennett House Bed & Breakfast

The Kennett House has a lot going for it: its history and architecture, its location in
the borough of Kennett Square, and most importantly, innkeepers Carol and Jeff
Yetter, who have created a comfortable, informal haven for visitors.

William Scarlett constructed this American four-square home for his son Robert
in 1910. The imposing granite structure stands on part of the property originally
deeded to the Scarlett family by William Penn. After the Battle of Brandywine, the
rise became known as Hessian Hill because it had been occupied by Hessian soldiers aiding the British.

The outside of the three-story Kennett House is a study in solidity. It's constructed of solid granite, unusual for an area in which Pennsylvania fieldstone is
much more typical. Seven stone steps ascend to the spacious wraparound porch.
The overhang is supported by cylindrical stacked stone columns. The thigh-high
wall that encloses the porch is also stone, but in a basket-weave pattern that adds
interest to the exterior. Flowering plants and shrubs placed by the Yetters' son, who
interned at Longwood Gardens, surround the house with color.

Indoors, the woodwork is striking. Floors, doorways, railings, window recesses,
and even some of the fireplace mantels are made of lustrous chestnut that you just
want to reach out and touch. The library is to the right of the foyer, a cozy spot in
which to sit by the fire and appreciate the surroundings.

"When we bought the house, it was decorated in Victorian style," says Carol,
"but the architecture is more Craftsman, and now the furnishings fit that. They're
substantial but not as ornate. We also brought in a lot of oriental rugs to warm
things up without obscuring the floors."

To the left of the foyer is the ladies' parlor, the only room in which the woodwork is rosewood rather than chestnut. There are also two dining rooms on this floor.

Upstairs, the Kennett House has four guest rooms, all with queen-size beds, private bathrooms, ceiling fans, and cable television. There's also a sitting room on the second floor, set off from the hallway with chestnut columns.

The Longwood Suite is visitors' favorite for a romantic getaway. This two-room suite has a four-poster rice bed, walnut armoire, sitting area, and stall shower. The cozy Wyeth Room's art from N. C., Andrew, and Jamie creates a real Brandywine Valley feel. The stenciling in the *en suite* bathroom isn't very Wyeth-esque, but it's charming and looks just right anyway.

The centerpiece of the Brandywine Room, also on the second floor, is a mahogany four-poster canopy bed. In a way, the monumental bed almost echoes the house itself. Rose-colored toile bedding, a mahogany armoire, and an oriental rug complete the room. The private bath is accessed from the hallway.

The Delaware Room has a sitting area and recently added *en suite* bathroom. Floral accents and window treatments make this a very welcoming space.

Maybe it's no coincidence that Carol was a psychology major, because she seems to have anticipated everything her guests could want. "We're kind of casual," she says. "Guests can relax by the fireplace in one of the parlors or sit in a rocking chair on the porch. We stocked the second-floor sitting room with games, a refrigerator, and snacks. People can just help themselves. I think they like not having to come downstairs and ask when they want something. That can be intimidating. We also keep menus up there to help guests select restaurants for lunch and dinner."

The Kennett House Bed & Breakfast is a solid stone structure just a few blocks from the center of town. ALAN B. SILVERMAN

Like the Kennett House Bed & Breakfast itself, this richly appointed library is solid and substantial. ALAN B. SILVERMAN

That's not all. To meet the needs of the Kennett House's corporate guests, the Yetters turned the second dining room, called the Tavern Room, into a business center with high-speed Internet access. Fax and photocopy machines are available.

The innkeepers thoughtfully provide bathrobes to people staying in the Brandywine Room so they can maintain their modesty during the split-second hallway jaunt from the bedroom to their private hall bath. The Yetters are accessible but are also content to leave visitors alone if that's the way they like it.

Carol is a good cook, too, and enjoys making breakfast for her guests. Two of her specialties include baked French toast with Granny Smith apples and cream cheese, and individual egg bakes with mushrooms and tomatoes. "I go with what's in season," Yetter explains. "Fruit and cereal are always available."

The Kennett House is just a few blocks from the center of the very walkable Kennett Square. There are many restaurants, boutiques, and art galleries located here. It's also enjoyable to stroll along the tree-lined side streets, looking at the variety of architectural styles, and then meander back to your anchor, the Kennett House Bed & Breakfast.

Kennett House Bed & Breakfast

503 W. State St., Kennett Square, PA 19348
Telephone: 610-444-9592 or 800-820-9592 • Fax: 610-444-7633
Innkeepers: Carol and Jeff Yetter
E-mail: innkeeper@kennetthouse.com • Website: www.kennetthouse.com
Rooms: 3 with private *en suite* bath, 1 with private hall bath. All have queen beds, ceiling fans, and cable television.
Rates: $119 to $149 per room, with a $25 surcharge for each extra person in room. Includes full breakfast. Reservations must be guaranteed with a credit card. Two-night stay required on weekends from April 1 to December 1.
Credit cards: Visa, MasterCard, American Express, and Discover.
Personal checks: Accepted with proper identification.
Check-in: 4 to 7 P.M.
Check-out: 11 A.M.
Air-conditioned: Yes.
Smoking policy: Nonsmoking.
Wheelchair accessible: No.
Children: Ages ten and up.
Pets: No. A friendly, nonshedding cockapoo is in residence.
Noise: Occasional road noise in front rooms. A white noise machine provided by the B&B mitigates this.
Parking: Ample on-street.

Other Recommended Accommodations

Bancroft Manor Bed & Breakfast
318 Marshall St.
(Mailing address: P.O. Box 654)
Kennett Square, PA 19348
Telephone: 610-444-9101 or 866-447-9101
Fax: 610-444-9101
E-mail: luv2run@ccil.org
Website: www.bancroftmanor.com
Owner: Michael E. Snyder
Rooms: 3 rooms, 1 with private bath and 2 with shared bath. There is a king suite, a queen room, and a full room. Large common rooms are furnished with antiques. Park-like yard.
Rates: $105 to $135, including full breakfast.
Credit cards: Visa, MasterCard, American Express, and Discover.
Check-in: 4:30 P.M.
Check-out: 11:30 A.M.
Air-conditioned: Yes.
Smoking policy: Nonsmoking.
Wheelchair accessible: No.
Children: Inquire.
Pets: No.
Food: Sumptuous breakfast served daily. Many restaurants are nearby in Kennett Square.
Other: A two-time winner in the Victorian category of Kennett Square's Christmas decorating contest, this 1909 house is graced by Tuscan columns, hardwood floors, and two sun porches.

Bed and Breakfast at Walnut Hill
541 Chandler's Mill Rd.
Avondale, PA 19311
(located in Kennett Square)
Telephone: 610-444-3703
Fax: 610-444-6889
E-mail: millsjt@magpage.com
Website: www.bvbb.com/walnuthill
Innkeepers: Tom and Sandy Mills
Rooms: The Laura Ashley Room has a double canopy bed. The second room can be configured with twin beds or as a king. A third room can be combined with one of the others and is appropriate for a single person traveling with a couple.
Rates: $75 to $115, with full breakfast. Two-night minimum most weekends.
Credit cards: Not accepted.
Personal checks: Accepted.

Check-in: Usually late afternoon, but flexible with prior arrangement.
Check-out: 11 A.M.
Air-conditioned: Yes.
Smoking policy: Nonsmoking.
Wheelchair accessible: No.
Children: Welcome. Infants and young children who still awaken in the night may visit as long as the two main rooms are reserved by the family.
Pets: No.
Food: Full breakfast may include French toast with hot peach-orange sauce, cottage cheese pancakes with hot blueberry sauce, a mushroom omelet, or other entree. No breakfast meats are served. Heart-healthy menus. Sandy makes her own bread and jams. Many restaurants nearby in Kennett Square.
Other: The circa 1840 mill house is furnished with antiques. Quiet country road setting. Guests may use the keeping room with fireplace and television, wicker-filled porch, formal rooms, and indoor hot tub. Innkeepers are always available for assistance.

Hilton Garden Inn Kennett Square
815 E. Baltimore Pike (U.S. Route 1)
Kennett Square, PA 19348
Telephone: 610-765-1029 or 800-HILTONS
Fax: 610-444-9186
Website: www.kennettsquare.gardeninn.com
Rooms: 92, including 8 suites. All include refrigerator, microwave, coffeemaker, hair dryer, iron and ironing board, two dual-line speaker phones with voice mail and data ports, cable television with video games and free HBO, clock radio. Rooms have king-size or two double beds. Some have whirlpool tubs.
Rates: $99 to $179. Contact the hotel or consult the website for details on packages.
Credit cards: Visa, MasterCard, American Express, Discover, and Diner's Club.
Personal checks: Accepted.
Check-in: 4 P.M.
Check-out: 12 noon.
Smoking policy: 85 rooms designated nonsmoking.
Wheelchair accessible: Yes, with accessible shower.

Children: Under eighteen stay free with parents or grandparents. Cribs available.

Pets: No.

Food: An on-site café serves breakfast.

Parking: Free on-site.

Other: Fitness center, indoor pool. The Pavilion Pantry convenience mart sells items for cooking, snacking, and personal care. Several shopping centers and restaurants are close by. Longwood Gardens is less than two miles away. Complimentary twenty-four-hour business center. Valet and self-laundry available.

Whitewing Farm Bed & Breakfast

370 Valley Rd.

(Mailing address: P.O. Box 98)

Kennett Square, PA 19348-0098

Telephone: 610-388-2664

Fax: 610-388-3650

E-mail: info@whitewingfarm.com

Website: www.whitewingfarm.com

Innkeepers: Ed and Wanda DeSeta

Rooms: 7 rooms (2 closed December to March) and 3 suites. Rooms have either a queen-size bed or twin beds that can be converted to a king. Suites have king bedrooms, sitting area, and fireplace. A rollaway bed is available in the Hackney Suite. The Gate House Suite also has a den, living room with sofabed, and kitchen.

Rates: $135 to $279, including full breakfast. Two-night minimum on weekends, March 31 to January 10, and on holidays.

Credit cards: Not accepted.

Personal checks: Accepted.

Check-in: 3 to 6 P.M.

Check-out: 11:30 A.M.

Air-conditioned: Yes.

Smoking policy: Nonsmoking.

Wheelchair accessible: No.

Children: Must be at least twelve years old.

Pets: No. There are dogs, cats, rabbits, horses, cows, and birds on the property.

Food: Full breakfast served from 7:30 to 9 A.M. in the Hay Barn. Many restaurants are nearby on U.S. Route 1 and in Kennett Square.

Other: Whitewing Farm is a 1700s Pennsylvania farmhouse with greenhouses, flower gardens, a barn, and stables situated on forty-three rolling acres behind Longwood Gardens. Guests are welcome to enjoy the gathering room and library in the Hay Barn (no spike heels, please). The game room in the main house is open to guests when the owners are in residence, four or five months each year. The lovely grounds feature a swimming pool, Jacuzzi, tennis court, and chip-and-putt golf course.

FOOD

Catherine's Restaurant

1701 Doe Run Rd. (PA Routes 82 and 162)

Kennett Square, PA 19348

Telephone: 610-347-2227

Hours: Dinner served Tuesday through Saturday, seatings begin at 6 P.M.

Prices: $17.29 to $25.95.

Take-out: Yes.

Wheelchair accessible: Yes, including restrooms.

Smoking policy: All nonsmoking.

Dress: Upscale casual.

Credit cards: Visa and MasterCard.

Personal checks: Not accepted.

Other: Reservations recommended. New American menu. Catherine's was previously located in the historic Jamison's Dairy house in West Chester; now in the historic Unionville general store, circa 1851.

Giordano's Restaurant and Sports Bar

633 E. Cypress St.

Kennett Square, PA 19348

Telephone: 610-444-5733

Fax: 610-925-5441

Hours: Sunday through Wednesday, 11 A.M. to 10 P.M.; Thursday through Saturday, 11 A.M. to 11 P.M. Same menu all day.

Prices: $2 to $20.

Take-out: Yes; take-out is handled in a separate area, which opens at 10 A.M.

Wheelchair accessible: Yes, including restrooms.

Smoking policy: Smoking and nonsmoking areas.

Dress: Casual.

Credit cards: Visa, MasterCard, American Express, and Discover.

Personal checks: Accepted with proper identification.

Other: Sports bar open until 1 or 2 A.M. daily. Complete menu available at the bar until 11 P.M. Varied menu, from pizza slices to steak.

Half Moon Restaurant and Saloon

108 W. State St.

Kennett Square, PA 19348

Telephone: 610-444-7232

Website: www.halfmoonrestaurant.com

Hours: Lunch Monday through Friday, 11:30 A.M. to 5:30 P.M.; Saturday, noon to 5:30 P.M. Dinner Monday through Saturday, 5:30 to 10 P.M. Late-night Friday and Saturday until 11 P.M. Closed Sunday.

Prices: Lunch $4 to $12, dinner $7 to $27, with most entrees $16 to $17.

Take-out: Yes.

Wheelchair accessible: Yes, including restrooms.

Smoking policy: Smoking and nonsmoking sections; some secondhand smoke.

Dress: Casual.

Credit cards: Visa, MasterCard, and American Express.

Personal checks: Accepted with proper identification.

Other: Twenty-one draft beers on tap. Rooftop deck open in spring and summer. Live music Thursday and Saturday evenings. Late-night light menu.

Harrington's Coffee Company, Ltd., and Collectibles

127 E. State St.

Kennett Square, PA 19348

Telephone: 610-444-9992

Fax: 610-444-8388

Hours: Monday through Friday, 6:30 A.M. to 5 P.M.; Saturday, 7:30 A.M. to 3 P.M.; Sunday, 8 A.M. to 1 P.M.

Take-out: Yes.

Wheelchair accessible: Yes, including restroom.

Smoking policy: All nonsmoking.

Dress: Casual.

Credit cards: Visa, MasterCard, and American Express.

Personal checks: Yes, with proper identification.

Other: Gourmet coffees and teas, espresso drinks, pastries, and soups. Friendly, neighborhood atmosphere. Located in the heart of Kennett Square. Bulk coffees and teas available. Country antiques, collectibles, and gifts for sale.

Peacock Gourmet Cafe at Nesting Feathers

109 S. Broad St.

Kennett Square, PA 19348

Telephone: 610-925-4686

Website: www.nestingfeathers.com

Hours: Monday through Friday, 11 A.M. to 3 P.M.; Saturday, noon to 3 P.M.

Prices: Sandwiches and wraps average $6.95 to $7.95.

Take-out: Yes.

Wheelchair accessible: No.

Smoking policy: All nonsmoking.

Dress: Casual.

Credit cards: Visa, MasterCard, and Discover.

Personal checks: Accepted with proper identification.

Other: Homemade soups, salads, and gourmet sandwiches. Fresh-baked goods. Gift baskets available. Cozy atmosphere with peacock theme. Located in Nesting Feathers, an antique and decorative arts shop with booths from more than twenty dealers.

State Street outside Harrington's Coffee Company has a welcoming feel. BOROUGH OF KENNETT SQUARE/SAM MELDRUM

Kennett Square Inn

The borough of Kennett Square has a solid, comfortable feel. So does the Kennett Square Inn, located in the center of town. The three-story structure was built between 1820 and 1839 and has served as an inn since 1835.

Outside, the building's facade has a bit of a split personality. The left side is typical of a two-bay Penn plan, while the right side is a four-bay Federal style. A modern addition is the cheerfully striped awning that shades the patio.

Inside, the inn has two distinct demeanors as well. There's the formal dining room, appointed with wooden chairs and white tablecloths. Fresh flowers, a fireplace with wooden mantel, and thick carpeting give the room a refined atmosphere.

In contrast to this elegant space is the wood-paneled tavern room with its warm, clubby style. Locals and visitors gather here to eat, drink, and be merry.

No matter which room you choose, you'll find food that emphasizes fresh, local ingredients. As is fitting in this "Mushroom Capital of the United States," the fungi figure prominently on the menu. Lunch appetizers include stuffed mushrooms with a vegetable puree, grilled marinated portabella, and sautéed exotic mushrooms. Mushroom soup is a menu staple. There are many salads and sandwiches, as well as a large selection of entrees.

Main dishes at dinner come with salad, fresh-baked bread, vegetables, and a starch side dish. The impressive menu includes crab imperial, steak Diane, bouillabaisse, and a sauté of exotic mushrooms and garden vegetables in an oriental sauce, served over pasta.

The bar menu offers hot and cold sandwiches plus light bites. Again, there are lots of creative mushroom dishes to try out, including shiitake mushrooms and tortellini in a garlic cream sauce.

Libations did not always flow freely here. During Prohibition, the inn was remade into the Green Gate Tea Room. A major renovation in 1976 brought the Kennett Square Inn full circle, restoring the building to the formal dining and tavern arrangement that exists today.

The restaurant and tavern at the Kennett Square Inn serve lunch, dinner, and a bar menu.
KENNETT SQUARE INN

VISITING THE KENNETT SQUARE INN

201 E. State St., Kennett Square, PA 19348
Telephone: 610-444-5687 • Fax: 610-444-4904 • Website: www.kennettinn.com

Hours: Lunch Monday through Saturday, 11:30 A.M. to 5 P.M. Dinner Monday through Saturday, 5:30 to 9:30 P.M. Sunday a la carte brunch, 11 A.M. to 3 P.M. Bar menu available all day.
Prices: Lunch $6 to $15, dinner $15 to $25.
Take-out: Yes.
Wheelchair accessible: Yes, but not restrooms.
Smoking policy: Dining room all nonsmoking. Smoking permitted in tavern.
Dress: Upscale casual.
Credit cards: Visa, MasterCard, American Express, and Diner's Club.
Personal checks: Not accepted.

Sovana Bistro
696 Unionville Rd., at the intersection of
PA Routes 82 and 926 in the Willowdale
Town Center
Kennett Square, PA 19348
Telephone: 610-444-5600
Website: www.sovanabistro.com
Hours: Monday through Saturday, 11 A.M.
to 10 P.M.; dining room closed 3 to 5 P.M.,
but take-out desk is open.
Prices: Lunch averages $8, with gourmet and
traditional pizzas from $6.75 to $14 depend-
ing on size and ingredients; dinner entrees
range from $12 to $26.
Take-out: Yes.
Wheelchair accessible: Yes, including restrooms.
Smoking policy: Nonsmoking.
Dress: Casual.
Credit cards: Visa and MasterCard.
Personal checks: Accepted with proper identifi-
cation.
Other: BYOB. Relaxed atmosphere with excel-
lent food. Patio in season.

State Street Grille
115 W. State St.
Kennett Square, PA 19348
Telephone: 610-925-4986
Fax: 610-925-4984
E-mail: cheftotman@zoominternet.net
Website: www.streetgrille.com
Hours: Lunch Tuesday through Friday, 11:30
A.M. to 2:30 P.M. Dinner Tuesday through

Thursday, 5 to 9 P.M.; Friday and Saturday, 5
to 10 P.M.; Sunday, 5 to 9 P.M. Closed Monday.
Prices: Lunch entrees average $6.50, dinner is
$28 for a three-course meal that includes an
appetizer, entree, and dessert.
Take-out: Yes.
Wheelchair accessible: No.
Smoking policy: All nonsmoking.
Dress: Casual.
Credit cards: Visa and MasterCard.
Personal checks: Accepted with proper identifi-
cation.
Other: Fun and lively American upscale bistro.
Creative cuisine on extensive menu.
ZAGAT Survey–rated. BYOB.

The Stone Barn
Route 842, 3 miles north of U.S. Route 1
Unionville, PA 19348
Telephone: 610-347-2414
Fax: 610-347-0332
Website: www.thestonebarn.com
Hours: Sunday brunch only, 10 A.M. to 3 P.M.
Price: Fixed price $14.95 for brunch buffet.
Take-out: No.
Wheelchair accessible: Yes, including restrooms.
Smoking policy: Separate smoking and non-
smoking areas.
Dress: Casual.
Credit cards: Not accepted.
Personal checks: Accepted with proper identifi-
cation.
Other: 1700s stone barn on sixty-two acres in
horse country.

Wilmington and Environs

A visit to Wilmington will turn your "Dela-where?" into "Dela-WOW!" The First State's largest city (though not its capital—that's Dover), this "Gateway to the Brandywine Valley" is a convenient destination, with history, culture, shopping, fabulous hotels and restaurants, and activities for every interest. In the nearby "château country," picturesque estates and villages dot the rolling hills. Delaware has no tax on shopping or dining, and the lodging tax is just 8 percent (10 percent within Wilmington city limits), making a visit to the state a good value as well.

With the 1638 arrival of the Swedish warship *Kalmar Nyckel,* the Delaware Valley's earliest permanent European settlement was accomplished. The colonists of New Sweden built Fort Christina, which included the first two log cabins in the New World. Agriculture and fur trading were predominant, soon supplemented by the milling of corn and wheat. Water power from the Brandywine was the essential element for the success of the mills.

Control of New Sweden passed to the Dutch and then the English. In 1731, on the Christina River about a mile upstream from the original settlement, Thomas

Move over, Washington. The cherry trees in Josephine Gardens along the Brandywine River in downtown Wilmington show off their springtime glory. GREATER WILMINGTON CONVENTION & VISITORS BUREAU/J. HARRY FELDMAN

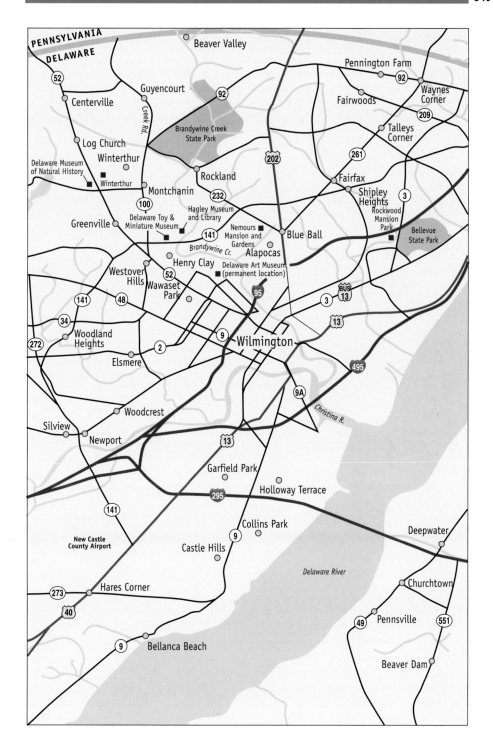

PENNSYLVANIA
DELAWARE

Beaver Valley

Pennington Farm

52

92

Guyencourt

92

Fairwoods

Waynes
Corner

Centerville

209

Talleys
Corner

Creek Rd.

Brandywine Creek
State Park

202

261

3

Log Church

Delaware Museum
of Natural History

Winterthur

Rockland

Fairfax

Shipley
Heights

Winterthur

Montchanin

232

Rockwood
Mansion
Park

Bellevue
State Park

100

Delaware Toy &
Miniature Museum

Hagley Museum
and Library

141

Nemours
Mansion and
Gardens

Blue Ball

Greenville

Brandywine Cr.

Alapocas

Henry Clay

Delaware Art Museum
(permanent location)

3

BUS
13

Westover
Hills

52

Wawaset
Park

141

48

13

34

272

Woodland
Heights

2

9

Wilmington

Elsmere

495

Woodcrest

9A

Christina R.

Silview

Newport

13

Garfield Park

Holloway Terrace

295

141

Collins Park

New Castle
County Airport

9

Deepwater

Castle Hills

Delaware River

Churchtown

273

Hares Corner

40

49

Pennsville

551

9

Bellanca Beach

Beaver Dam

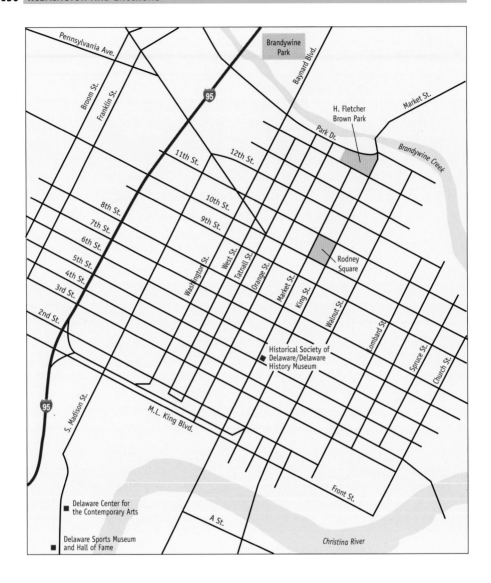

Willing laid out Willingtown. In 1739, the area was chartered by the Crown and renamed Wilmington. Delaware earned its nickname of the "First State" when it ratified the newly drafted U.S. Constitution on December 7, 1787.

Paper and cotton mills joined the flour mills along the Brandywine. Then Wilmington was changed forever with the arrival of Eleuthère Irénée du Pont de Nemours in 1802. The DuPont black powder mills supplied American hunters, soldiers, and construction projects for more than a century. The company evolved into the modern chemical industry giant still headquartered here. DuPont's presence helped make Wilmington an industrial, financial, and shipping hub. Today, more than 60 percent of Fortune 500 companies are incorporated in Delaware. Wilmington is a major electronic banking center.

Over 100 performances a year are held in the 1,200-seat Grand Opera House, famous for its excellent acoustics, stunning interior, and cast-iron facade. GREATER WILMINGTON CONVENTION AND VISITORS BUREAU

You can board a replica of the *Kalmar Nyckel,* explore the original DuPont powder works and mansion at Hagley Museum, and tour the du Pont estates Winterthur and Nemours. Rockwood Mansion Park, once owned by Joseph Shipley, is also open to visitors. Using interactive exhibits, the Delaware History Museum in the center of town traces life in Delaware from Native American times through today.

Wilmington's newly revitalized Christina Riverfront offers museums, outlet shops, a farmers' market, and a mile-long walking trail. The *Kalmar Nyckel* is berthed here, and water taxi service is available. Tubman-Garrett Riverfront Park is named for Harriet Tubman, the escaped slave who helped many others achieve freedom, and Thomas Garrett, a local "station master" on the Underground Railroad.

Art lovers will appreciate the Delaware Art Museum on Kentmere Parkway and the Delaware Center for the Contemporary Arts along the river. For sports fans, the Delaware Sports Museum and Hall of Fame is located at Frawley Stadium, where the minor league Wilmington Blue Rocks play.

There are numerous public gardens, parks, playgrounds, even a small zoo. Newcomers to the city often comment on how much green space the area has. Brandywine Creek State Park has the most trail space; other parks have their own character and appeal.

No matter what kind of performing arts you prefer, you'll find it in Wilmington. Ballet, theater, classical music, opera, jazz, gospel, blues—your only problem will be deciding among the many choices.

The Greater Wilmington Convention and Visitors Bureau at 100 W. Tenth St. has a guide to notable sites of African-American culture and heritage, *Wilmington: Last Stop to Freedom.* Another guide is

Active rowing clubs use one-, two-, four-, and eight-person shells on the Christina River in Wilmington. GREATER WILMINGTON CONVENTION AND VISITORS BUREAU/J. HARRY FELDMAN

a walking tour of the city's outdoor sculpture. Don't miss the water-borne spinning granite spheres outside the Hercules Building.

Quiet Montchanin Village north of Wilmington was once a millworkers' community. It's been restored as an inn and restaurant that retains its historical charm while offering every modern amenity.

Nearby Greenville is known for its shops and boutiques. Farther north on DE Route 52 (Kennett Pike), you'll come to the Delaware Museum of Natural History and Winterthur, An American Country Estate.

Also on Route 52 is Centreville, a scenic, rural area on the ridge between the Brandywine and Red Clay Creeks. Many vintage estates are located among the woods and hills. You may see some attractive Belted Galloway cattle, nicknamed "Oreo cows" for their black-white-black coloring. The village hub of Centreville has many historic structures and is home to antique shops, art galleries, boutiques, and restaurants. It's a lovely place to walk around before resuming your tour of northern Delaware's lovely enclave of open space.

Getting Around

Wilmington is easy to reach from Interstates 95, 495, and 295, as well as the New Jersey Turnpike. All Northeast Corridor Amtrak trains stop at the Wilmington station, as do SEPTA commuter trains from Philadelphia. Philadelphia International Airport is thirty minutes north of Wilmington along Interstate 95. The New Castle County Airport, which serves private aircraft and charters, is fifteen minutes away.

You can cover much of Wilmington's downtown area on foot. City hotels are convenient to most performing arts venues, as well as shops, galleries, and restaurants. Neighborhoods like Little Italy (www.discoverlittleitaly.com) and the Village of Trolley Square (www.visittrolleysquare.com) are lively and fun.

A downtown rubber-tire trolley, Wilmington Trolley Route 32, stops at popular tourist spots; each ride costs only a quarter. It makes a loop from Rodney Square Transit Center to Downtown Wilmington (several stops) to the Riverfront (also several stops). Pick up a route map at any stop or at the Greater Wilmington Convention and Visitors Bureau. It's a great way to reach Wilmington Riverfront shops and museums. For more information, call 800-652-DART or visit www.DartFirstState.com.

A car is essential for exploring the countryside. It's a short drive to reach Hagley Museum, the Delaware Toy & Miniature Museum, Montchanin Village, the Delaware Museum of Natural History, Winterthur, Centreville, and the Brandywine Valley attractions in Pennsylvania.

Calendar of Events

Many of Wilmington's events are sponsored by organizations listed under "Featured Attractions," "Performing Arts," and "Spectator Sports." Check those for details.

Monthly except January, July, and August, first Friday, 5:30 to 8 P.M.: Art on the Town. Museums and galleries in and around Wilmington are open late for visitors. Sponsored by the Mayor's Office of Cultural Affairs/Wilmington Arts Commission. Call 302-576-2137, or visit www.ci.wilmington.de.us.

March, Saturday before St. Patrick's Day: St. Patrick's Day parade in downtown Wilmington. Call 302-656-0317

May, first Saturday, 10 A.M. to 5 P.M.: Wilmington Garden Day. A tour of distinctive gardens and homes in the greater Wilmington area. Tickets $15. Order form and information on website, www.gardenday.org, or call 302-428-6172.

May, one weekend early in month: Wilmington Flower Market. Rockford Park, 1021 W. 18th St. near DE Route 52. Call 302-995-5699.

May, early in month: Polish Festival. St. Hedwig's Church, 408 S. Harrison St. Call 302-594-1400.

June: Delaware Chamber Music Festival. Performances held at a variety of venues, including Winterthur and the Wilmington Music School. Admission fee. Call 302-239-8440, or visit www.dcmf.org.

June, one weekend early in month, 11 A.M. to 11 P.M.: Greek Festival. Holy Trinity Greek Orthodox Church, 808 N. Broom St. Call 302-654-4447. Free lunch shuttle service 11 A.M. to 2 P.M. daily from Ninth and Market Streets.

June, one Sunday early in month: Taste of Wilmington Festival. Frawley Stadium, 801 S. Madison St. A family, food, and fun festival with cooking demonstrations, food from over forty local restaurants, and games. Admission fee. Call 302-765-1160, or visit www.wjbr.com.

June, Friday and Saturday the week before Father's Day: Greenville Summer Art Show. DE Route 52 in Greenville Crossing One shopping center. Original art by Brandywine Valley artists. Call 302-475-8796.

June, one week midmonth: St. Anthony's Italian Festival sponsored by St. Anthony of Padua Church. Festival held at 901 N. Du Pont St.; parking is available at Delaware Avenue and Van Buren Street, and at 8th and Orange Streets. Shuttle buses run continuously. Call 302-421-3790, or visit www.stanthonynet.org/festival/index.html.

June, one week midmonth: Clifford Brown Jazz Festival. Locations vary. Admission charged. Call 302-576-2137, or visit www.cliffordbrownjazzfest.com.

July 4, 3 to 11 P.M.: Independence Day Celebration along the Christina Riverfront. Call 302-576-2137, or visit www.riverfrontwilmington.com.

Late July through early September: Summer Concert Series. Dravo Plaza along the Christina Riverfront. Call 302-425-5000, or visit www.riverfrontwilmington.com.

August, one weekend midmonth: Cool Blues, Brews, and BBQs. Downtown Wilmington. Call 302-576-2137, or visit www.ci.wilmington.de.us.

August or September: Caribbean Festival. Frawley Stadium, 801 S. Madison St. Call 302-658-4095, or visit www.cariculture-de.org.

September, one Saturday late in month, 10 A.M. to 5 P.M.: DuPont RiverFest & Delaware Transportation Festival. Tubman-Garrett Riverfront Park and along the Christina Riverfront. Children's entertainment, water taxi rides, love music, and refreshments. Admission fee. Call 302-658-1870, or visit www.dupontriverfest.com

October, first week: Wilmington Independent Film Festival. Call 302-576-2135, or visit www.wilmingtonfilmfest.com.

FEATURED ATTRACTIONS

Delaware Art Museum

Driving through a quiet neighborhood of stately houses, one hardly expects to come upon a cultural treasure around the next tree-lined bend. But that's exactly what happens along Kentmere Parkway, where the Delaware Art Museum makes its home. Three major permanent collections—"American Illustration," "English Pre-Raphaelite Art," and "American Art from 1840 to the Present"—are joined by temporary exhibits in a newly expanded and renovated building that is fully integrated into its scenic setting. A cafe, shop, and sculpture garden are added attractions.

Temporarily located at the Bank One Center on the Riverfront at 800 S. Madison St. in Wilmington, the greatly expanded Delaware Art Museum will reopen on Kentmere Parkway in October 2004.

Origins and Evolution

The Delaware Art Museum owes its genesis to fans of native son Howard Pyle. In 1912, the year after the artist died, a grassroots group of art lovers formed the Wilmington Society of the Fine Arts. Their goal: to keep the works of lifelong Wilmington resident Pyle together and in the area. The Society purchased four dozen original paintings and drawings, housing them first at downtown Wilmington's Hotel du Pont, then in a more permanent setting at the Wilmington Institute Free Library starting in 1923.

As word spread, the Society received donations of Pyle's work. Many of his

most famous pictures, familiar from magazine and book illustrations, were put on display for the public to enjoy. The next logical step was for the Society to acquire works from Pyle's students, famous in their own right as artists of the Brandywine School. Works by key people in the "Golden Age of American Illustration," such as Maxfield Parrish, Frank Schoonover, and N. C. Wyeth, joined those of their teacher.

Starting in the mid-1920s, the Society expanded its vision to include other genres of nineteenth- and twentieth-century American art, not just illustration. Masterpieces by Winslow Homer,

The desire to keep native son Howard Pyle's work in Wilmington was the impetus for the founding of the Delaware Art Museum. This is Pyle's *The Flying Dutchman,* 1900, watercolor on paper, seven-and-one-quarter inches by four-and-three-eighths inches. DELAWARE ART MUSEUM

Visiting the Delaware Art Museum

Until October 2004: 800 S. Madison St.
along the Christina Riverfront, Wilmington, DE 19801
After October 2004: 2301 Kentmere Parkway, Wilmington, DE 19806
Telephone: 302-571-9590 • Website: www.delart.org

Hours: For museum hours and the hours of the Art Sales & Rental Gallery, call the museum or visit www.delart.org.

Admission: Adults $7, seniors $5, students with valid identification $2.50, six and under free. The Museum Sales Gallery and the Art Sales & Rental Gallery are open to all visitors at no charge. Contact the museum regarding free admission periods.

Credit cards: Visa, MasterCard, American Express, and Discover.

Group tours: Guided tours are offered to schools, organizations, and private groups of ten or more by appointment. Make reservations at least four weeks in advance. Contact the Museum's Tour Services Office for information.

Special considerations: All public areas of the museum are accessible to wheelchairs. Wheelchairs are available upon request at the Information Desk. Strollers are permitted in the museum and on paved paths in the sculpture park. The Children's Participatory Gallery is a special attraction for youngsters.

Food: An on-site café serves light fare and gourmet coffees during regular museum hours. Patio seating available (Kentmere Parkway location only).

Art Sales and Rental Gallery: Original art by regional artists.

Library: The Helen Farr Sloan Library contains more than forty thousand volumes of art reference and study materials. Contact the museum for hours and information.

Store: The museum store sells art-related gifts, including crafts, jewelry, books, posters, prints, and postcards, plus toys, books, and other items for children. Open during regular museum hours.

Gallery: The museum also runs a satellite gallery, the Downtown Gallery, located at 919 Market St. in the lobby of an eighteen-story office building in the heart of the revitalized downtown. The gallery exhibits regional art and works from the museum's permanent collection. Open Monday through Friday, 9 A.M. to 6 P.M. Free admission. Wheelchair accessible. Telephone: 302-571-9590.

Thomas Eakins, George Luks, Edward Hopper, and Andrew Wyeth eventually became part of the collection. The Delaware Art Museum now houses American art from the nineteenth century through today. Major aesthetic movements including historical portraiture, landscapes, Impressionism, figuration, and abstraction are represented in art, photography, mixed media, and sculpture.

The Society received a life-altering donation in the mid-1930s, when the family of Samuel Bancroft Jr. (1840–1915) gave his collection of Pre-Raphaelite works, along with eleven acres of land for a museum. When the Wilmington industrialist saw his first Pre-Raphaelite painting, Rossetti's *Fiamma,* in London in 1880, Bancroft immediately pronounced himself a Pre-Raphaelite "fiend" and became an avid collector of art and objects from this Victorian movement.

The Delaware Art Museum's Samuel and Mary R. Bancroft Collection has an outstanding Pre-Raphaelite collection, including Dante Gabriel Rossetti's *Veronica Veronese,* 1872, oil on canvas, forty-one-and-a-half inches by thirty-four inches. DELAWARE ART MUSEUM

A Georgian building designed by architects Victorine and Samuel Homsey of Wilmington was erected on the Bancroft land and opened in 1938 as the Delaware Art Center. It faces a beautiful parkway designed by landscape architect Frederick Law Olmstead. Immediately the Pre-Raphaelite collection vaulted to international renown. The Samuel and Mary R. Bancroft Memorial Collection, along with the accompanying Janson Collection of decorative arts, remains the top collection of Pre-Raphaelite art outside of England. With the artwork displayed in a manner appropriate to the period, everything from the picture frames to the wallpaper transports viewers to the heyday of the Pre-Raphaelites.

One visitor who was mightily impressed with the Delaware Art Center and its staff was Helen Farr Sloan, widow of John Sloan. She first visited in 1961 to help organize an exhibition of her late husband's work and decided to make the arrangement permanent. Since then, Helen Farr Sloan deserves most of the credit for increasing the museum's holdings of Sloan's works to more than three thousand paintings, prints, and drawings. These are joined by works from Sloan's contemporaries, collectively nicknamed the "Ashcan School" for their honest portrayals of real-life urban scenes.

The Delaware Art Center received accreditation from the American Association of Museums in 1972 and was renamed the Delaware Art Museum. Expansions were made in 1957 and again in 1987, but the museum's twelve thousand or so works of art were straining its capacity. The need for new classrooms, flexible space in which to mount traveling exhibitions, updated technology, and rejuvenated landscaping called for a major renovation.

Enter Ann Beha Architects of Boston. Beha's dramatic $25 million expansion uses the 1938 building as its core, while adding wings on either side that embrace the sculpture park and terrace. Traditional local materials like stone and brick, complemented by large expanses of glass, take advantage of the views and closely integrate the interior and exterior. The old stone reservoir, once used to provide water power for the Bancroft textile mills on the Brandywine River, is a central feature and a fitting nod to the past.

Howard Pyle: Illustrious Illustrator

Howard Pyle's sense of drama translated itself onto his canvases and into the hearts of millions. The "Father of American Illustration" was a powerful presence, an influential teacher, and above all, a master storyteller.

Born in 1853 to a Wilmington, Delaware, family, Pyle attended the Friends' School in Wilmington. Drawing interested him more than traditional studies, so from age sixteen to nineteen, he commuted to Philadelphia to study with Antwerp-trained artist F. A. Van der Weilen.

Back in Wilmington in 1872, Pyle helped in the family leather business but also chose to dedicate himself to a career in art. After his first illustration appeared in *Scribner's Monthly* in 1876, Pyle moved to New York City to be near the top publishers. During his three years in New York, he took classes at the Art Students League and continued to publish illustrations, short stories, and poems in major periodicals like *Harper's Weekly*.

Pyle revolutionized the interaction between picture and viewer. The stagnant, uninvolving illustration styles of his predecessors gave way to intense drawings in which every line, every shadow, every nuance of color heightened emotion and created action in which the viewer was immersed. The combination of imagination and attention to detail paid off in spades: Pyle's illustrations told a story, but he made it seem as real as the words they accompanied.

When Pyle returned to Wilmington, he continued to write, paint, and raise a family. Throughout his career, he taught extensively: at the Drexel Institute of Arts and Sciences in Philadelphia, his own school in Wilmington, and summer classes in Chadds Ford. The list of those who studied with Pyle reads like a *Who's Who in American Illustration*: Maxfield Parrish, Jessie Willcox Smith, Stanley Arthurs, Frank Schoonover, and N. C. Wyeth, to name a few. Teacher and students came to be known collectively as the "Brandywine School."

Pyle inspired his students with his high standards and work ethic, as well as his technical expertise and imaginative approach to illustration. He was a generous mentor who put his students—when he felt they were ready—in contact with editors at *Harper's, St. Nicholas, Collier's Weekly, Scribner's*, and other leading magazines. Many of Pyle's students owe their long and productive careers in large part to their teacher. Still, some students eventually resented Pyle, feeling that his emphasis on commercial success thwarted their chances to be serious painters.

"Prolific" does not begin to describe Pyle's output. During his thirty-five-year career, he published more than three thousand illustrations. About half of them accompanied his own writings, an astonishing two hundred magazine stories and nineteen books. Some of his beloved titles are *The Merry Adventures of Robin Hood, The Wonder Clock, The Garden behind the Moon*, and the four-volume Arthurian legends, starting with *The Story of King Arthur and His Knights*.

In 1910, Howard Pyle and his family moved to Florence, Italy, where the artist planned to study and paint murals in the Old World tradition. Pyle died there of a kidney inflammation on November 9, 1911, at age fifty-eight. Almost a century later, his illustrations, and those of his students and their students, still pack a powerful emotional punch.

John Sloan: American Realist

When John Sloan and seven of his artist colleagues opened a collective exhibit at New York City's Macbeth Gallery in 1908, the gasp from the American art establishment was almost audible. "The Eight" rejected idealized subject matter, prefer-

The Delaware Art Museum's Helen Farr Sloan Collection has more than 3,000 of John Sloan's paintings, prints, and drawings, including *Spring Rain*, 1912, oil on canvas, twenty-and-one-quarter inches by twenty-six-and-one-quarter inches. DELAWARE ART MUSEUM

ring an authentic portrayal of urban life. Just like jazz revolutionized American music, the new realism of Sloan, Arthur Bowen Davies, William Glackens, Robert Henri, Ernest Lawson, George Luks, Maurice Prendergast, and Everett Shinn altered the content of American art.

Sloan was born in 1871 in Lock Haven, Pennsylvania, and moved to Philadelphia with his family at age five. Largely self-taught, Sloan became skilled at etching, drawing, and lettering. He became a newspaper illustrator, first with the *Philadelphia Inquirer* from 1892 to 1895, then the *Philadelphia Press*. By November 1903, with the advent of photomechanical reproduction, hand-rendered illustrations were no longer cost-effective. Sloan lost his newspaper job.

In Philadelphia, Sloan had attended night classes at the Pennsylvania Academy of the Fine Arts. There he met Robert Henri, who favored real-world subjects. With his Philadelphia employment severely diminished, Sloan and his first wife, Dolly, followed Henri and other artists to New York City. Sloan was commercially successful doing illustrations for magazines including *Collier's* and *The Century*. He was commissioned to do more than fifty etchings to illustrate French novelist Charles Paul de Koch's books.

Sloan continued to develop as a fine artist and a personal force. His paintings were exhibited at the Pennsylvania Academy of the Fine Arts and the Chicago Art Institute. Sloan joined the Socialist Party in the 1910s and was art director of the

Who Were the Pre-Raphaelites?

Despite the name, the "Pre-Raphaelite Brotherhood" of English artists and poets postdated the Italian Renaissance painter Raphael by several hundred years. The members coined the title in 1848 when the group formed in mutual disdain for what they saw as declining standards in British art. They eschewed the painterly style that had become representative of the artists of the Royal Academy, presided over by Sir Joshua Reynolds, whom they nicknamed "Sir Sloshua." Their goal was to return to the honesty found in the work of painters prior to Raphael.

The seven young people who formed the group were visual artists Dante Gabriel Rossetti, William Holman Hunt, John Everett Millais, and James Collins; sculptor Thomas Woolner; and writers William Michael Rossetti (Dante's brother) and Frederick George Stephens. The painters were supported by noted art critic and social theorist John Ruskin, who defended their endeavors in two benchmark letters published in the *London Times*.

The group chose nostalgic, often mythological or medieval subjects, laden with emotion. Sometimes the references were literary, evoking Chaucer or Tennyson. At other times, the artists depicted social problems brought about by rapid industrialization and urbanization. Therefore, the art worked on several levels: Viewers could appreciate the paintings simply for their beauty or—with some knowledge of literature or a sensitivity to societal conditions—could understand more deeply the meaning with which the paintings were imbued. The Brotherhood did face suspicion, though, from viewers who found their work too "popish," or Catholic.

The artists favored a bright color palette painted on a light background, as opposed to the dark tones on a brown background that were representative of the time. This vivid infusion of color brought a breath of fresh air to the dullness of Victorian England. The techniques they used were a return to practices that had been used in the early Renaissance.

Another hallmark of Pre-Raphaelite work is the meshing of paintings with other design elements. For example, intricate picture frames were designed to complement the paintings, not just added as an afterthought. One man who was influenced by the Pre-Raphaelites was William Morris. Known as a poet, artist, craftsman, social reformer, and printer, as well as a designer, Morris studied the Middle Ages and was instrumental in reviving handmade decorative arts. An avowed anti-industrialist, Morris founded his own decorating firm in 1861. The intricate designs that artists created for Morris's firm, especially for furniture, wall coverings, and textiles, are still popular today.

Seeing the paintings in person, it's impossible not to be drawn into the minutely rendered scenes of beautiful women, rich patterns, and symbolic objects. One can't help but feel that there are many messages in the artwork, which probably would have pleased their creators greatly.

The Pre-Raphaelite Brotherhood officially disbanded in 1853, but the philosophy of its proponents exerted its influence through the end of the nineteenth century.

magazine *The Masses* for a time. He was also a teacher, notably at the Art Students League beginning in 1916; in 1918, he became president of the Society of Independent Artists. Critical acclaim continued, and his paintings were displayed at the Phillips Memorial Gallery in Washington, D.C., and New York's Metropolitan Museum of Art.

This blown glass on wooden lattice is called *Persian Window*. It is fifteen feet by thirty feet and was exclusively designed for the Delaware Art Museum by Dale Chihuly in 1999. DELAWARE ART MUSEUM

Always ready to try something new, Sloan embraced the color system of Hardesty Maratta, which Henri had introduced him to in 1909. This technique is based on tonal relationships and uses paints mixed to specific color intervals. Sloan quickly mastered the system, eventually altering some of the pigments to make his own palette. Later, Sloan added underpainting, glazing, and cross-hatching to give his paintings dimensionality.

Summers were spent at the artists' colony in Gloucester, Massachusetts, and then in Santa Fe, New Mexico. Sloan found the Southwest so enchanting that he vacationed there annually for almost thirty years. The nudes and *plein air* landscapes Sloan painted in Santa Fe provide a counterpoint to the often gritty New York street scenes for which he is best remembered.

A year after Dolly Sloan died in 1943, John Sloan married Helen Farr, a former student. She helped him edit his lecture notes and philosophy into *The Gist of Art*, useful to art students to this day.

John Sloan received a Gold Medal from the American Academy of Arts and Letters in 1950. He died in 1951, but his artistic legacy endures. For more than four decades, Helen Farr Sloan has been a supporter and advocate of the Delaware Art Museum. Her donation of over three thousand Sloan works of art, as well as archival and library materials, has made the museum a national center for the study of John Sloan and his art.

Calendar of Events

Wednesdays: Art After Hours, 4 to 9 P.M. Free admission to museum's permanent collections, special exhibitions, and a variety of concerts, tours, entertainment, and educational programs (Kentmere Parkway location only).

Bi-monthly: Featured Artist of the Month. Regional artists are featured in the Art Sales & Rental Gallery, with a "meet the artist" reception.

Every other year: Regional "Biennial," a juried exhibit of works by artists from Philadelphia to Baltimore who are breaking ground in a variety of media.

February, resuming in 2005: Howard Pyle's Pirate Party. Inspired by the museum's collection of Howard Pyle pirate illustrations, this children's event features art activities, storytelling, and more. Contact the museum for exact date, time, and fee.

June, resuming in 2005: Craft Fair. Juried show featuring original works by craft artists of the mid-Atlantic region. Contact the museum for information.

December, second Saturday: Holiday House Tour. Decorated private homes, artists' studios, and the museum are open to guests. Admission fee includes a discount for lunch at some local restaurants. Reservations are required. Call or visit the website for information.

The Delaware Center for the Contemporary Arts

A rebuilt railroad-car factory along the revitalized Wilmington waterfront is home to the Delaware Center for the Contemporary Arts (DCCA), where art and community intersect with passion and energy.

"We believe art can affect how the community responds to current issues," says Jessi LaCosta, director of marketing and public relations. "Art can spark a dialogue, and the DCCA provides a forum for this kind of discussion. In some ways, this differentiates us from other museums."

You don't have to worry about being "shooshed" here. Open dialogue isn't just tolerated, it's encouraged. At the DCCA, people often express their reactions to the

This rebuilt railroad-car factory houses the Delaware Center for the Contemporary Arts. DELAWARE CENTER FOR THE CONTEMPORARY ARTS

Visiting the Delaware Center for the Contemporary Arts

200 S. Madison St. at the Wilmington Waterfront, Wilmington, DE 19801
Telephone: 302-656-6466 (for tours, ext. 7103 or 7101)
Fax: 302-656-6944 • E-mail: info@thedcca.org • Website: www.thedcca.org

Hours: Tuesday, and Thursday through Saturday, 10 A.M. to 5 P.M.; Wednesday and Sunday, noon to 5 P.M.

Admission: Adults $5, students and seniors $3, children twelve and under and DCCA members free. Free admission for everyone Saturday, 10 A.M. to noon. For a guided tour, add $1 to admission price. Call for information about times and availability. For a guided tour with hands-on workshop, for school groups only, call for price structure.

Special considerations: Wheelchair accessible.

Food: None on-site. Numerous restaurants nearby along waterfront.

Cyber café: Free to anyone visiting the DCCA. Internet access only, no printers or other applications.

Gift shop: Same hours as museum.

installations and exhibits. Insights and comments are shared. The museum has created a healthy environment in which mutual exchanges like this take place.

Other features of the DCCA are also unique among institutions in this area. It's a "noncollecting" museum, which means that all exhibits are temporary. Installations are generally on display from six to nine weeks, so repeat guests can look forward to seeing something new with each visit.

More unusual aspects are the DCCA's deep commitment to active local artists and the interaction the museum fosters between artists and visitors. The site leases twenty-six artists' studios right in the building. This support enables artists to explore their talents in a synergistic, accepting environment. About half the artists open their studios during the monthly Art on the Town evenings sponsored by the Mayor's Office of Cultural Affairs, giving the public direct access to artists and their creative processes. Studio artists have the opportunity to display their work in the DCCA's Elizabeth Denison Hatch Gallery. Professional development takes the form of workshops and visits from guest critics, plus the invaluable benefits the artists gain from interacting with each other.

The artwork at the DCCA is always fresh, thought-provoking, sometimes experimental. In the past, the site has exhibited Ava Blitz's cast cement waveforms; Kiwon Wang's jewelry of paper, silver, and pearls; and trees sculpted by Emilie Benes Brzezinski, wife of Zbigniew Brzezinski, Jimmy Carter's national security advisor. Abstract photographs, computer and video art, and walk-in installations reveal the endless possibilities of the visual arts. The industrial origin of the building enables the concrete-floored galleries to accommodate large, heavy works, moved on rollers from the loading dock. Emerging and established artists from around the corner and around the world are represented.

Contemporary art is known for its willingness to confront global and personal issues—from pollution to domestic abuse—head-on. Some of the art can be unsettling, not because of its inherent qualities, but because it challenges us to think about things in a different way. The warm and welcoming atmosphere at the DCCA provides a safe, friendly atmosphere in which to approach socially relevant topics as explored through art. The large lobby has the feel of a town square, and the galleries flow one into the next, kind of like a system of streets. As "neighbors" explore, they can share their reactions and observations with other passersby. At their most powerful, the installations encourage discussions that can then serve as a catalyst for change.

The center's history dates back to 1979, when a small group of artists and patrons banded together with the goal of promoting contemporary arts in Delaware. They opened a gallery in downtown Wilmington in 1980, then relocated to the Waterworks complex on the banks of the Brandywine in 1984. Renovations in 1987 increased gallery space from five hundred to twenty-two hundred square feet.

The 1990s brought increasing interest and steady growth. First an executive director was hired, then educational staff and a professional curator/program director. Various grants enabled the museum to expand its artists' residency program, increase awareness about contemporary arts and museum programs, and expand educational programs, public symposia, and publications.

Thanks to a successful capital campaign, in September 2000 the DCCA was able to open its current facility. Along with the artists' studios, the thirty-three-thousand-square-foot building contains seven galleries, an auditorium, a classroom, a cyber café, and a gift shop. The large, well-equipped facility gives the DCCA a strong presence in the community and helps it better serve artists and the public.

The Carole Bieber & Marc Ham Gallery, DuPont Gallery I, and DuPont Gallery II house changing curated thematic and one-person exhibitions (national and regional); the Constance S. & Robert J. Hennessy Project Space highlights experimental projects and community collaborations; the E. Avery Draper Showcase is for curated one-person exhibitions by national contemporary craft artists; the Beckler Family Members' Gallery displays one-person exhibitions of DCCA members' work; and the Hatch Gallery is reserved for artists who use studio space here.

The DCCA's commitment to community outreach includes Contemporary Connections, a program in which artists work on two-month projects with schools to integrate contemporary art with subjects like math, science, and social studies. The Artist in Residence program pairs artists with community groups such as homeless shelters, inner-city community centers, and Boys and

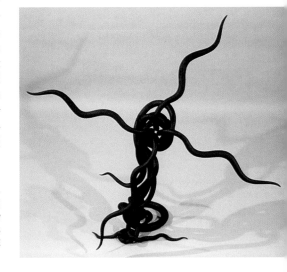

Art at the Delaware Center for the Contemporary Arts, like this George Lorio painted wood piece called *Medusa's Fan* (thirty-four inches by thirty-seven inches by fifteen inches), invites discussion among visitors. DELAWARE CENTER FOR THE CONTEMPORARY ARTS

Girls Clubs for collaboration. Public symposia and panel discussions are regular events. The facility also hosts concerts.

This dedication to art, artists, and community makes the DCCA a vital participant in the Brandywine Valley arts scene.

Calendar of Events

First Friday of every month except January, July, and August: Art on the Town. Sponsored by the Mayor's Office of Cultural Affairs, this is Wilmington's open house for the arts. The DCCA participates, as do some of the artists who have studio space here. For information, call 302-576-2137 or visit www.ci.wilmington.de.us.

Occasional Saturdays: Workshops for ages six through twelve. Contact the DCCA for details. Reservations required.

April and May (some years): Community Open. Nonjuried, fund-raising exhibition of artwork by individuals, community groups, and businesses who rent space on the gallery walls. Many of the center's more than fifty past and present community collaboration partners participate by decorating an object chosen by the DCCA. Funds raised benefit education and outreach programs.

Delaware Museum of Natural History

A visit to the Delaware Museum of Natural History (DMNH) is a family-friendly voyage of discovery. You'll sense the heat of the African plains, the humidity of the Philippine forests, and the refreshing waters of the Great Barrier Reef. Faster than you can say, *"Tuojiangosaurus multispinus,"* you'll be transported back 150 million years among the dinosaurs in prehistoric China. Before your journey ends, you'll return safely to the familiar flora and fauna of Delaware.

Built in 1972 by John E. du Pont, the Delaware Museum of Natural History houses both a laboratory for professional scientists and a treasure chest of wonders for the public. With the second-largest collection of birds' eggs in North America, and among the top ten in the United States in mollusk and bird collections, DMNH is a valuable resource to professional and private collectors, as well as any-

one eager to learn more about the natural world. The Curatorial & Research Division publishes *Nemouria,* a scientific journal. Regional artists also use the museum as a resource.

Scientific collections teach valuable lessons about the world around us. The Delaware Museum of Natural History's strong research and educational focus comes through in the exhibits. Specimens are explained in terms of their

Meat-eater meets plant-eater as this allosaur and stegosaur share center stage at the Delaware Museum of Natural History. DELAWARE MUSEUM OF NATURAL HISTORY

Visiting the Delaware Museum of Natural History

4840 Kennett Pike (DE Route 52), between Greenville and Centreville (Mailing address: P.O. Box 3937), Wilmington, DE 19807 Telephone: 302-652-7600 for recorded message; 302-658-9111 for more information • Website: www.delmnh.org

Hours: Monday through Saturday, 9:30 A.M. to 4:30 P.M.; Sunday, noon to 4:30 P.M. Closed New Year's Day, Easter Sunday, July Fourth, Thanksgiving Day, and Christmas.

Admission: Adults $6, sixty and over $4, ages three to seventeen $4, ages two and under free.

Special considerations: Fully wheelchair accessible. Level or ramped access throughout the public galleries and into the theater. Two wheelchairs are available in the coatroom.

Group tours and workshops: Available with reservations.

Museum store: Open during museum hours. The shop offers items related to natural history, including toys, games, stuffed animals, kits, jewelry, and decorative objects.

Food: Snacks and drinks are available from vending machines. Visitors may eat in the vending area or at picnic tables outside.

ecology, physiology, and evolution; conservation, endangerment, and extinction are also addressed in the accompanying text.

It's a pleasure to visit a natural history museum that's in as good shape as this one. Since its opening in 1972, the displays have been maintained and updated. Explanatory information is easy to use and is altered whenever new facts come to light. Interactive exhibits help make a visit more memorable, while daily films and frequent special events keep things lively. A butterfly garden and one-mile hiking trail with markers distinguishing two different trail options on the museum's grounds are added attractions in good weather. Outdoor scavenger hunt activity sheets are available at the front desk.

The public galleries of the Delaware Museum of Natural History are seventeen thousand square feet all on one floor, arranged mostly in a rectangle. Keep going in the same direction, and you won't miss anything.

The front gallery packs a punch, with a *Yangchuanosaurus magnus* (an allosaur) and a *Tuojiangosaurus multispinus* (a stegosaur) looming large. The temporary exhibition gallery also features exciting exhibits that change about four times a year, on subjects as diverse as ancient marine reptiles, live insects, or biodiversity conservation. Call the museum or visit the website for exhibit schedules and information.

A popular area with kids is the Discovery Room, where "hands-on" is the rule. This well-stocked space includes puzzles and books; working microscopes and a selection of slides; bones, horns, and teeth to examine; a habitat activity wall; a live saltwater fish tank; and a comfortable area in which to explore and learn. Lockers are stocked with the garb scientists might wear, including a marine biologist's wet-

Life can be a struggle at the African watering hole. DELAWARE MUSEUM OF NATURAL HISTORY

suit and an entomologist's field jacket. Kids have a blast trying the stuff on, though they may have to wait a while for a turn when it's crowded.

Continue on to the Egg Gallery, an amazing display of ova, from the tiny hummingbird egg to the world's largest, the elephant bird egg (maybe Dr. Seuss was right in *Horton Hatches the Egg*). What's displayed is but a small subset of the complete collection, which includes thirty-six thousand clutches of eggs.

To continue your tour, you have to cross the Great Barrier Reef. This unique display is actually installed under the floor, covered with clear Plexiglas that visitors walk across. It's only a step or two wide, but there are many interesting specimens underfoot.

Next stop is the Shell Gallery. The museum owns two million specimens representing more than seventeen thousand species in all seven living classes of mollusks. Many of these shells are on display here, including a five-hundred-pound clamshell. One beautiful arrangement has shells positioned in a circular fashion on the ends of sticks, creating an orb of mollusks reminiscent of a sea urchin's spines. The gallery also showcases the ways people have used shells for function and as decoration. Utensils, containers, and beautiful shell jewelry are on view in well-lit cases. Before you leave the gallery, make sure you find out what makes those little round holes in the clamshells you find on the beach. You may be surprised.

Research is done on-site, and the museum shares that with visitors through its Science in Action Lab. You'll get to interact with a professional who may be identifying carnivorous plants, numbering bones, pressing leaves, or preparing fossils. It's a nice inspiration for future scientists. The lab is a permanent feature of the museum; open lab times vary.

A roar coming from around the corner might be one of the big cats at the African Watering Hole in the Hall of Mammals. This display of taxidermy specimens features a variety of animals that all visit watering holes during the dry season, giving visitors an up-close look at these individual animals. Interactive touch-screen computers offer more information on the animals, the characteristics of watering holes in general, and the geography of Africa. North American mammals are also exhibited in this area.

Around the corner are exhibits on Delaware woodland and stream wildlife, showcasing the flora and fauna found in many local backyards. These include familiar birds and mammals such as cardinals, blue jays, woodpeckers, mink, otter, white-tailed deer, and cottontail rabbit.

Calendar of Events

Sundays and Mondays, 1 to 4:30 P.M.: Make-It-Take-It. Children with a parent make a craft.

Monday, last one of every month, 2 to 3 P.M.: Meet an Animal. A live animal is introduced to visitors.

Thursdays, 2 to 2:30 P.M.: Read and Explore. Nature-related story program.

Annually: Special events and programs include Family Music Festival, Summer Camps, and Dino Days (every December 27 and 28). For more information, call the museum or check the website.

Delaware Sports Museum and Hall of Fame

For anyone who likes sports or history, or who wants an interesting diversion before a Blue Rocks game or after shopping along the Wilmington Riverfront, a visit to the Delaware Sports Museum and Hall of Fame is a pleasant way to spend an hour or so. The five-thousand-square-foot space covers the sports history of the First State from the Civil War to the present. Photographs, artifacts, and displays of memorabilia are complemented by high-tech computer access to inductee biographies and on-line links to national and local sports halls of fame. Athletes, coaches, administrators, officials, and media luminaries in more than thirty sports ranging from javelin throwing to major-league baseball are honored, with emphasis on inductees in the Delaware Sports Hall of Fame. The Special Olympics gets well-deserved attention, with a section devoted to its athletes and volunteers.

The Delaware Sports Hall of Fame was created in 1976 in conjunction with the nation's bicentennial. Eight sports figures were inducted that first year. Since then, six to ten new inductees have been added annually; the current total is over two hundred.

Items associated with Hall of Fame members were not assembled in one place until Frawley Stadium added right-field seating in 2001. Space on the ground level was designed specifically for the museum, which opened in 2002.

This bicycle is one of the many fascinating items that trace this history of sports in Delaware.
DELAWARE SPORTS MUSEUM AND HALL OF FAME

Visiting the Delaware Sports Museum and Hall of Fame

Frawley Stadium, 801 S. Madison St.
Wilmington, DE 19801 • Telephone: 302-425-FAME
E-mail: dsmhof1@aol.com • Website: www.desports.org

Hours: April 1 to October 31, Tuesday through Saturday, noon to 5 P.M. November 1 through March 31, open for school tours and other groups by appointment weekdays, 10 A.M. to 5 P.M.

Admission: Adults $4, seniors $3, students over twelve $2, ages twelve and under free.

Group tours: Groups welcome; advance reservations suggested. Entertaining and informative two-hour school field trip programs for grades four through seven. A history of sports scavenger hunt is one of the activities offered. Contact the museum for details and reservations.

Special considerations: Wheelchair accessible.

Shop: A modest gift shop offers sports- and museum-related items.

Special events: Call the museum or check the website to find out about special events and promotions.

The museum lobby has displays about the newest Hall of Fame inductees and a variety of sports photographs. A ten-minute film sets the stage for what's to come: Delawareans talk about their sports experiences, such as ice skating on the Brandywine or going to the old Blue Rocks stadium at Thirtieth and Northeast Boulevard. The film reinforces the museum's dedication to all the state's sports, not just baseball, football, and basketball.

The rest of the exhibits are organized chronologically, starting with the Lenni-Lenape Indians playing lacrosse. Decade by decade, the museum traces the state's sports history. Photographs and artifacts give way to old radio broadcasts and black-and-white newsreels, bringing back fond memories for older persons, while youngsters are fascinated with sights and sounds that are so different from what they're used to.

Delaware certainly can be proud of its sports figures. Among the athletes represented is Elsmere's Bill Hawke, who is credited with pitching the first no-hitter on August 16, 1893, at the current mound-to-home plate distance of sixty feet, six inches.

Delaware has sent athletes to the Olympics since 1908. Participants from the First State have brought home four gold medals and a silver, so far. Dionna Harris played on the gold medal softball team in 1996; four years later, Mike Neill stood on the top podium with his Olympic championship baseball teammates.

The museum also pays homage to athletes who have been inducted into other sports halls of fame. Delawareans are represented in the National Baseball Hall of Fame in Cooperstown, New York, the Pro Football Hall of Fame in Canton, Ohio, and other college and professional associations. Defensive tackle Randy White, a nine-time Pro Bowl selection who was a leader of the Dallas Cowboys' "Doomsday Defense," is from Delaware.

The equipment is as interesting as the players. An old tool much like a bicycle wheel was used to mark foul lines on the baseball field. A collection of football helmets shows the evolution from a leather model to the current high-tech composite materials. Also on display are the twelve-foot-long oar used in the 1952 Helsinki Olympics eight-oared shell competition, the luge used at the 1980 Lake Placid Olympics, and a collection of field hockey and lacrosse sticks.

Audiotapes such as a recitation of "Casey at the Bat" make a nice break from reading interpretive displays.

William Julius "Judy" Johnson

A favorite exhibit is a lifesize figure of "Judy" Johnson sharing some memories with a young boy. An audiotape takes visitors back to Johnson's career as a standout third baseman in the Negro Leagues of the 1920s and 1930s, which led to his 1975 induction into the National Baseball Hall of Fame in Cooperstown, New York.

Born on October 26, 1899, in Maryland, Johnson grew up and spent much of his life in Wilmington. His father was an athletic director of the Negro Settlement House and a licensed boxing coach. Believing fitness was important, the elder Johnson set up athletic equipment for an outdoor gym for neighborhood children to use. Young Johnson got to watch plenty of baseball during his stint as batboy on his dad's local team.

Johnson left school after tenth grade and was a dockworker in New Jersey during World War I. In 1918, he got his first professional baseball contract with the Atlantic City team, the Bacharach Giants. Their pay: $5 per game. The following year, Johnson tried out for the elite Hilldale club in Darby, Pennsylvania, but he didn't make the cut. He dropped down to a semipro club to hone his skills and finally became a Hilldale player in 1921. In the inaugural Negro League World Series in 1924, John-

Hall-of-famer William Julius "Judy" Johnson, for whom the field at Frawley Stadium is named, "chats" with a young fan. Visitors get to hear the story of his life and baseball career. DELAWARE SPORTS MUSEUM AND HALL OF FAME

son led both clubs with a .341 average, contributing five doubles, a triple, and a homer in his team's losing effort.

At five feet, eleven inches and about 145 pounds, the right-handed third baseman was not known for his power. However, Johnson was recognized as a consistent hitter, an outstanding fielder, and a smart base-runner. He studied opposing pitchers carefully, and he frequently seized the opportunity to steal a base. In 1929, he hit .390 and was named the league's most valuable player.

Johnson became player-manager for the Homestead (Pennsylvania) Grays in 1930. He then returned to the Darby Daisies, a spin-off of the Hilldales, in 1931. Midway through the 1932 season, he switched to the Pittsburgh Crawfords, a dynasty in the Negro Leagues, where Johnson continued his reliable hitting with averages of .332, .333, and .367. He was named captain of the Crawfords in 1935.

Johnson played in his last Negro League World Series in 1935, the Crawfords versus the New York Cubans. Fittingly, Johnson got a clutch hit in the ninth inning of the sixth game, with the bases loaded, the score tied, and the Crawfords trailing three games to two. His RBI single won the game for the Crawfords; they took the series the next day. Johnson ended his playing career with the Crawfords in 1936.

After retiring, Johnson coached the Alco Flashes, a semipro basketball team that was Delaware State Champion in 1937. He also drove a cab in Wilmington before becoming a major-league scout for the Milwaukee Braves and the Philadelphia Phillies.

The superb fielder's .349 lifetime batting average over a nineteen-year career in the Negro Leagues qualified Johnson for induction into the National Baseball Hall of Fame in 1975. The city of Wilmington, in recognition of his contribution to baseball and to improving the quality of life for young adults, named the park at Second and du Pont Streets "Judy Johnson Park."

Johnson died in Wilmington on June 15, 1989. His statue stands outside Frawley Stadium, where the field is named in his honor. Former Negro League players are invited to a Wilmington Blue Rocks game every year, where they are honored in a ceremony on the field.

Delaware Toy and Miniature Museum

Some of the Brandywine Valley's most opulent mansions are barely three feet high. You'll find them at the Delaware Toy and Miniature Museum, where more than a hundred dollhouses and rooms showcase small wonders that duplicate, even surpass, the real thing. Furniture, dolls, toys, and trains provide a historical reference that spans three centuries, interpreted with signage and by docents. The museum also houses a wardrobe of tiny haute couture fashions, a variety of Noah's arks, and an unparalleled collection of miniature vases.

Located near the Brandywine River in a historic building on the grounds next to the Hagley Museum entrance, the Delaware Toy and Miniature Museum is fun for families and a must for collectors. Most of the items on display are for looking at, not for touching, but little ones seem to enjoy the format anyway. The glass cases extend low, making it easy for children to get a good view. The working train layout is also a kid pleaser.

When Beverly Thomes and her mother, Gloria R. Hinkel, founded the not-for-profit museum in 1994, their mission was both to entertain and to educate. Tracing

Visiting the Delaware Toy and Miniature Museum

6 Old Barley Mill Rd., adjacent to Hagley Museum entrance off DE Route 141
(Mailing address: P.O. Box 4053), Wilmington, DE 19807
Telephone: 302-427-TOYS • Fax: 302-427-8654
Website: www.thomes.net/toys

Hours: Tuesday through Saturday, 10 A.M. to 4 P.M.; Sunday, noon to 4 P.M. Closed
Monday.

Admission: Adults $6, seniors $5, children $3, ages two and under free. Group
rates available.

Groups: Welcome. Call to make arrangements and reservations.

Special considerations: The first floor and bathroom are wheelchair accessible.
The second floor is wheelchair accessible on weekdays only.

Shop: A small shop carries antiques and collectibles, educational items, and
doll- and toy-related items and books.

Reference library: The museum maintains an extensive library of books and
magazines related to toys and miniatures. Interested people are welcome
to use this for research.

the evolution of dollhouses from the eighteenth through twentieth centuries provides visual documentation of history and customs. Furniture and accessories are a window to the tastes of past generations. The museum does a good job of explaining the origins of the items, how they were used, and what that tells us about the people and lifestyles of the time.

The houses and their contents are magnificently detailed. The Lines House from 1895 London has working plumbing, even though indoor plumbing was not universal in the full-size homes of the time. Water from a pan on the dollhouse's top floor drains through pipes to the kitchen sink. The house is also interesting because of its removable exterior. When playtime was over, the facade could be put back in place. The same manufacturer created Queen Mary's famous dollhouse, on display at Windsor Castle in England.

Another striking item is a miniature American dining room originally from the collection of Jean Austin du Pont. It takes hours just to set the table for eight with English sterling silver. The room is embellished with molding, carpeting, window treatments, a chandelier with tiny candles, even a little birdcage.

Along with items from Jean du Pont, the museum acquired collections from other European and American estates, including those of Helena Rubenstein and the Strassburger family, of Singer sewing machine fame.

To say that the artisans who created these miniatures were obsessed with detail is an understatement. They fashioned everything from hemmed cloth napkins to paintings whose detail is done with brushes made from one hair.

The museum has an 1860 replica of Maryland's Readbourne House, an 1875 French opera house where *Little Red Riding Hood* is playing, and lithographed German houses dating from 1880. Also from that year, a Victorian parlor depicts a traditional Christmas scene with a "goose feather" tree. Noah's arks—the only toys

Originally in the collection of Jean Austin du Pont, this American dining room with English sterling silver service for eight is displayed at the Delaware Toy and Miniature Museum. DELAWARE TOY AND MINIATURE MUSEUM

strict Sabbath observers in early America let the children play with on Sundays—have animals as small as a fingernail clipping.

The museum's doll and toy collection presents Asian, Native American, and fragile Bisque dolls, including Madame Alexander specimens; trains, trucks, and Erector sets; French parlor games; a Schoenhut circus made in Philadelphia; lots of tea sets; and "Armies of the World," a display of miniature soldiers and figurines.

Not everything in the museum is old; contemporary items of museum quality are also on display. In fact, some of the twentieth-century settings are a real hoot. Get a load of the purple pit room with its mirrored wall. It was made in the Art Deco era but would have been right at home in the days of disco.

Another interesting collection is a hundred enameled brass figures crafted and dressed in haute couture by the late New York fashion designer Lee Menichetti. Known for his brass relief sculptures and his opera costumes, he worked for Swarovski Crystal and Cartier Jewelers. The eight-inch-tall statues trace the history of costume in a big way. These are the kind of designer duds your average Barbie could only dream of.

The museum also features a permanent collection of more than seven hundred miniature vases dating back to 600 B.C. These tiny jewels, ranging in height from a half inch to five inches, were amassed by a gentleman in the Midwest and were displayed in prominent venues, including the Art Institute of Chicago. The collector's family searched carefully for a good home for the grouping, narrowing the choices to five museums. In 1996, Beverly Thomes made a personal visit to Chicago, after which the collector's widow decided to donate the collection to the Delaware Toy and Miniature Museum. It was important that the vases were going to someone who appreciated miniatures as much as the collector and his family had.

It's amazing to see something sixteen centuries old, like the Roman and Corinthian bottles and vases. No one knows why these ancient vessels were made, whether for decoration, funerary purposes, play, or another reason. Modern pieces are also on display, from such famous names as Tiffany, Staffordshire, Lalique, and Royal Crown Derby. The materials are as rich as the craftsmanship, with vases made of crystal, jade, and amethyst. Faberge flowers have gold stems, jade leaves, and carnelian and diamond petals and centers.

Miniature Satsuma vases are examples of the intricate hand-painted ceramics crafted in eighteenth- and nineteenth-century Japan. Unusual shapes characterize these pieces. For Satsuma artists, making the minuscule vases was hardly child's play. The eyestrain caused many artisans to go blind, resulting in an edict forbidding the making of miniature vases.

Calendar of Events

Every six to eight weeks: Doll appraisals, at $5 per doll. Contact the museum for dates and details.

For information about upcoming events and shows, contact the museum.

Hagley Museum and Library

It's almost a shame to call Hagley a "museum," since it's so much more than the term implies. Located on 235 scenic acres along the Brandywine River, on the site of the first du Pont black powder works, Hagley tells the story of life and industry in the nineteenth century through exhibits, tours, restorations, and demonstrations.

The grounds at Hagley Museum and Library are a beautiful place to walk, especially in spring when the dogwood trees are in bloom. HAGLEY MUSEUM AND LIBRARY

Visiting Hagley Museum and Library

DE Route 141 just north of DE Route 100. Museum entrance is at the western end of the Tyler-McConnell Bridge. (Mailing address: P.O. Box 3630), Wilmington, DE 19807-0630 Telephone: 302-658-2400 • Website: www.hagley.org

Hours: March 15 through December 31, daily, 9:30 A.M. to 4:30 P.M. On weekdays during January, February, and March 1 through 14, only one guided tour of the property by bus is held, at 1:30 P.M.; the Henry Clay Mill opens at 1 P.M. for ticket sales. The museum is open weekends year-round, 9:30 A.M. to 4:30 P.M. Closed Thanksgiving Day and Christmas.

Admission: Adults $11, students and seniors $9, ages six through fourteen $4, ages five and under free. Family admission rate: $30. Admission to Henry Clay Mill exhibits only: adults $5, ages six to fourteen $2, ages five and under free.

Group tours: Groups of fifteen or more should call to schedule their visits in advance. Group rates are available. If ordered ahead of time, a group lunch in a historic building can be served for an additional fee. Several focus tours are available, including a Brandywine Tour centered on Eleutherian Mills, Workers' World Tour, Great Trees and Gardens, and the Extended Brandywine Tour. Call for details.

Special considerations: Many, but not all, facilities are wheelchair accessible. Twenty-four hours' notice is required to ensure the availability of the wheelchair-accessible bus. Call for more detailed information.

Food: Hagley's Belin House Restaurant, serving coffee and light lunch, is located on Blacksmith Hill. Open daily March 15 through November, and on weekends in December, from 11:30 A.M. to 4 P.M. Picnicking is also permitted.

Store: The Hagley Store carries decorative items, reading materials, and gifts. Located in a historic building once used for cotton and wool picking.

There really is something for everyone at this National Historic Landmark and National Recreation Trail. Fans of architecture and decorative arts will enjoy touring Eleutherian Mills, the du Pont family home. Car enthusiasts should check out the nineteenth-century vehicles in the barn. People who like horticulture will appreciate the French-style garden.

Interactive exhibits in the Henry Clay Mill building make science fun for all ages. The restored workers' community on Blacksmith Hill immerses visitors in a lifestyle now gone and shows how technology altered the lives of the families who lived here. Everyone is fascinated by the machinery demonstrations and rocky ruins in the powder yard. Light lunch is available at the Belin House on Blacksmith Hill. To top it all off, Hagley is a beautiful spot just to walk along the water near the sluice gates and millraces.

Plan to spend at least three hours here. Check in at Reception in Henry Clay Mill, where you can visit the exhibits now or later. Then take the shuttle to Eleutherian Mills for the half-hour house tour. Visitors with small children may want to skip the house but ride to Eleutherian Mills anyway to explore the garden and barn. The bus also stops at Blacksmith Hill and in the powder yard before returning to Henry

Clay Mill. If it's nice out, you may prefer to walk the mile and a half along the river back from Eleutherian Mills.

Hagley holds special events throughout the year, but a visit here is special even when there's nothing extra going on.

History of the Site

In 1802, the French immigrant Eleuthère Irénée du Pont started a black powder factory on this site. The location had all the ingredients necessary for success: the Brandywine's water power; a ready supply of timber to make the charcoal required for superior black powder; proximity to the Delaware River for shipping raw materials in and finished products out; and granite that could be quarried for building materials.

The name Hagley predates the du Ponts. As early as 1797, the previous owner, Philadelphia Quaker merchant Rumford Dawes, applied for insurance on buildings at "Hagley on the Brandywine." Dawes may have taken the name from the poem "The Seasons," by James Thomson, in which the "Spring" section refers to Hagley Park, the West Midlands estate of Lord Lyttleton.

E. I. du Pont de Nemours & Company's black powder manufactory went on to become the largest in the world, spawning a business dynasty that continues to this day. DuPont expanded and diversified, building many factories, laboratories, and offices nearby.

The mills closed in 1921, but Hagley was not forgotten. When the DuPont company celebrated its 150th anniversary in 1952, plans for the site were made. Hagley Museum was dedicated in May 1957 with the opening of the Henry Clay Mill building. The Millwright Shop followed in 1962, then Eleutherian Mills in 1964. In 1966, Hagley was designated a National Historic Landmark.

Hagley Museum continued to grow. Blacksmith Hill was ready for visitors in 1982. In 2002, two new exhibits, "DuPont Science and Discovery" and "DuPont: The Explosives Era," opened to commemorate the company's two hundredth anniversary. Altogether, more than sixty original structures have been restored.

Hagley also has an extensive research library and a scholarship center. The library is internationally known for its focus on business, technology, economics, and history.

Once you enter through the iron gates installed for DuPont's 1902 centennial, you'll begin your adventure back to where the du Pont story begins. All of the other fabulous places that family created in this area—including Winterthur, Nemours, and Longwood Gardens—owe their origins to the fortune the du Ponts made with their black powder enterprise right here.

Henry Clay Mill

The three-story Henry Clay Mill, constructed in 1814 for a cotton-spinning venture, is Hagley Museum's reception center and ticket office. An orientation film covers two centuries of DuPont Company history.

Two permanent exhibits trace the way the gunpowder manufacturer transformed itself into a chemical company giant. On the first floor, "DuPont: The Explosives Era" looks at the company's first hundred years; "DuPont Science and Discovery" on the third floor examines the company's second hundred years. Both include lots of hands-on activities.

The exhibits begin by explaining the du Pont family's decision to leave France for the United States and the factors that influenced their choice of where to settle. They also delve into the role of explosives in the nineteenth and early twentieth centuries.

By the time World War I broke out in Europe in 1914, DuPont had mastered the art and science of making smokeless powder. The factory's maximum output was about seven hundred thousand pounds per month, although this amount wasn't produced on a regular basis. Over the next four years, the Allies placed such extensive orders that the company had to—and could afford to—add more capacity. By 1918, DuPont was making thirty-eight million pounds of powder a month.

The company's success had a downside. During the last third of the nineteenth century, DuPont purchased competitors' operations, completely dominating the explosives industry. This didn't sit well with the U.S. Justice Department, which filed an antitrust suit in 1907. DuPont lost, and the company was forced to divest Hercules and Atlas.

DuPont overcame this temporary setback. As it had since the days of its founder, the company continued to strive for technological discoveries and improvements. Now management began to apply the same approach to diversification. One of the ingredients in their smokeless powder, nitrocellulose, is also the basis of celluloid, an early plastic.

Scientists searched for peacetime uses for nitrocellulose. They developed plenty, many of which were used by the burgeoning automobile industry. An artificial leather, Fabrikoid, was used for upholstery. Pyralin, when sandwiched between two sheets of glass, kept car windshields from shattering. Duco auto lacquer improved the painting process. A 1931 Chevrolet on display showcases these innovations and plays a "radio broadcast" explaining their use. Today's cars, like Jeff Gordon's #24 DuPont NASCAR, greatly benefit from more recent DuPont inventions like the fire-resistant material Nomex®.*

From household items to satellite materials, DuPont products have changed the way people live and work. The bases for many of these items are long chains of molecules called polymers. A giant blow-up model of a nylon molecule shows just how complex the molecular structure is. Computer stations surrounding the floor-to-ceiling installation provide interactive fun. Visitors also have a chance to see a space suit and look through an astronaut's helmet. Microscopes give a close-up view of some polymer chains. Videos about nylon and Teflon®,† and a film in which present-day DuPont scientists discuss their work, round out the exhibits.

The second floor in the Henry Clay Mill provides space for changing displays.

Eleutherian Mills

Eleutherian Mills, built by E. I. du Pont in 1803, was the family's first home they built in America. The Georgian-style mansion sits on a hill with a view of the Brandywine. It's furnished with antiques that recall the five generations of du Ponts that lived here.

The family vacated the house after it was damaged in an 1890 powder blast. Three years later, Eleutherian Mills was converted to a clubhouse for company work-

---

*Nomex® is a registered trademark of the DuPont Company.
†Teflon® is a registered trademark of the DuPont Company.

Georgian-style Eleutherian Mills, the du Ponts' family home built in 1803, is open for tours. HAGLEY MUSEUM AND LIBRARY

ers. In 1921, the mills closed and parcels of the land were sold off; in 1923, Henry Algernon du Pont, one of Irénée's grandsons, bought and renovated the house for his daughter, Louise Evelina du Pont Crowninshield. She spent one month in spring and another in fall here at her country home each year until she died in 1958.

On the first floor, the morning room features Queen Anne and Chippendale furniture. Don't miss the French block-printed wallpaper in the dining room. On the second floor, period rooms are decorated in the Federal, Empire, and Victorian styles. The Blue Room contains some of E. I. du Pont's furniture from the period of 1800 to 1830. A nursery is connected to Sophie and E. I. du Pont's bedroom.

Eleutherian Mills is especially beautiful at Christmas. The dining room table is set with an exquisite dessert service for a Twelfth Night Celebration.

Also at this part of the property is the First Office of the DuPont Company. It has been restored the way it would have looked in about 1850, complete with Henry du Pont's desk.

The barn is filled with antique vehicles that were used for transportation, to do farm chores, and in the powder yard. A real Conestoga wagon is a favorite of visitors. There's a small workshop and laboratory in the barn as well.

Like many members of his extended family, E. I. du Pont loved horticulture and gardening. Eleutherian Mills boasts an authentically restored nineteenth-century French garden, with vegetables, perennials, bulbs, and flowering shrubs. It's laid out in the parterre, or sectioned, style, with espaliered fruit trees and a charming gazebo.

Powder Yard

For Eleuthère Irénée du Pont, the Brandywine River meant power: the waterpower to generate energy that ran gunpowder-producing machinery. Today visitors to the Hagley Powder Yard can see the operation in action. Working models, restored equipment, and exhibits bring the past to life.

Equipment in the machine shop at the old Du Pont Powder Mills still works; demonstrations are scheduled regularly. HAGLEY MUSEUM AND LIBRARY

Join a powderman at Eagle Roll Mill, where gunpowder ingredients were mixed under the weight of two eight-ton waterwheels. Watching the rushing water spin the wheels is living history at its best. You'll also see—and hear—how the powder was tested and learn about the extensive safety precautions that were taken to minimize the ever-present danger of explosion.

A restored machine shop of around 1880 hums with activity. Leather belts and pulleys power metal-working machinery that is demonstrated to visitors and is still used to repair the site's machinery.

Just opposite the Millwright Building housing the Machine Shop, a stone quarry with tools is a reminder of the granite that was used to build many of the structures at Hagley. A few steps away in the engine house, an 1870 engine operates under live steam. Step inside to get a feel for the heft of the metal wheel and the speeds it achieves. A whistle blows when the boiler is ready.

Blacksmith Hill

The restored buildings on Blacksmith Hill focus on the social and family lives of powder mill workers. Interpreters in period dress introduce visitors to the late nineteenth century in the Gibbons House, which was home to foreman John Gibbons from the late 1850s to the 1880s.

A variety of ethnic groups lived and worked at Hagley, including many Irish. Learning about their traditions, foods, and conveniences helps visitors understand the rhythms that structured people's lives.

The Brandywine Manufacturers' Sunday School, constructed in 1817, is where mill workers' children learned to read, write, and do arithmetic before Delaware provided public education. Lessons are given just as they would have been back then. Try your hand with a quill pen; it's not as easy as it looks.

The Belin House was home to several generations of company bookkeepers. Currently it's a coffee shop where visitors can get a light bite. As you sit and enjoy a sandwich, take time to reflect on the contrast between then and now at Hagley.

Calendar of Events

Unless noted otherwise, events are included with general admission, not discounted or surcharged. Special parking instructions are listed when appropriate; otherwise, use the main entrance and parking area.

January, the Saturday, Sunday, and Monday including Martin Luther King Jr. Day, 10 A.M. to 4 P.M.: Invention Convention. Hands-on science activities in the Soda House. Adults $4, ages six through fourteen $2.50, ages five and under free. Creative hands-on activities challenge youngsters to develop their own products and get a "Hagley Patent." Use Hagley's Buck Road East entrance via Route 100.

February, the Sunday before Valentine's Day, 12:30 to 4 P.M.: Victorine's Valentine Day. Victorine du Pont, the daughter of E. I. du Pont, spent time as superintendent of the Brandywine Manufacturers' Sunday School during the nineteenth century. Today's "Victorine" tells love stories from the nineteenth century. Visitors can make Victorian Valentines and bake gingerbread hearts on a wood stove.

March, one Sunday midmonth, 12:30 to 4 P.M.: St. Patrick's Day celebration. Blacksmith Hill features tea and Irish soda bread served in the Gibbons House, along with Irish storytelling and music.

March, one weekend, Saturday 10 A.M. to 4:30 P.M., Sunday 11 A.M. to 4 P.M.: Art and Antiques Show at Hagley Soda House. Art from more than fifty artists and antiques for sale. Admission $5, under eighteen free. Use Hagley's Buck Road East entrance via Route 100.

July, Tuesdays, 12:30 to 4 P.M.: The Creek Kids. Young volunteer interpreters add games, music, snacks, and hands-on activities to the museum visit.

July and August, Saturdays: Summer Dollar Days. Visitors admitted for $1.

August, some Sundays, 12:30 to 4 P.M.: Summer Science Sundays. Explore different science themes each Sunday with workshops and hands-on activities for the whole family. A nominal materials fee may apply on some Sundays.

August, Wednesdays, 5 to 8 P.M.: Bike and Hike. Visitors are welcome to hike, bike, or just enjoy a summer evening outdoors at Hagley. Dinner available at the Belin House Restaurant. Picnicking permitted. Admission $1.

September, one Sunday midmonth, 10 A.M. to 4 P.M.: Hagley Car Show. More than five hundred antique cars and trucks present a display of automotive history. Admission: adults $5, ages six to fourteen $3, free for ages five and under. Family rate: $12. Park at the DuPont Company's Barley Mill Plaza, at the intersection of DE Routes 141 and 48; shuttle buses take visitors to Hagley.

Fall, three Sundays: Concert Series at the Soda House. Tickets $7. Use Hagley's Buck Road East entrance via Route 100. Various music and starting times. Call for information.

October, one weekend midmonth, 10 A.M. to 5 P.M.: Craft Fair. Artisans demonstrate, display, and sell their crafts. Daily admission $4, ages five and under free. Use Hagley's Buck Road East entrance via Route 100.

November, a Friday, Saturday, and Sunday early in month, 10 A.M. to 5 P.M. (9 P.M. on Friday): Festival of Museum Shopping. Gift shops from more than twenty regional museums assemble to present a unique holiday shopping opportunity. Daily admission $4, ages five and under free. Use Hagley's Buck Road East entrance via Route 100.

November, day after Thanksgiving through early January (closed December 25), 9:30 A.M. to 4:30 P.M.: Christmas at Hagley. Eleutherian Mills, the 1803 Georgian-style estate E. I. du Pont built for his family, is trimmed for the holidays.

Historical Society of Delaware/Delaware History Center

The Historical Society of Delaware is dedicated to making sure the rich history of the First State is understood and appreciated. Founded in 1864, the nonprofit educational organization collects and preserves relevant materials and makes them available to the public through exhibitions, programs, and publications.

Four sites in downtown Wilmington, all located on the same city block, are collectively known as the Delaware History Center: the Historical Society of Delaware's headquarters and research library, Willingtown Square Historic Park, Old Town Hall, and the Delaware History Museum. A red arch spanning the 500 block of Market Street points visitors to the right place.

The headquarters and library are housed in an Art Deco building that used to be a bank. Visitors are welcome to see the small displays that highlight a portion of the Society's collections, perhaps postcards, dolls, or old letters. These exhibits change every four to six months. The library is a repository of genealogical and historical information, including maps, manuscripts, and photographs.

Next to this building is Willingtown Square, a park bordered by six eighteenth- and nineteenth-century homes. The buildings were moved here to save them from demolition, and the resulting urban green space is a lovely area with a historic feel that's great for a picnic lunch.

Across Market Street is the Old Town Hall, a fine example of Federal architecture and craftsmanship. The building once hosted abolitionist meetings and was also the city jail where fugitive slaves were imprisoned. Old Town Hall is currently used for occasional special events.

The big red arch across Market Street welcomes visitors to the Historical Society of Delaware's complex, which includes the Delaware History Museum in a restored Woolworth's store. HISTORICAL SOCIETY OF DELAWARE

Visiting the Historical Society of Delaware/ Delaware History Center

504 Market St., "Under the Red Arch," Wilmington, DE 19801
Telephone: 302-655-7161 • Fax: 302-655-7844
E-mail: hsd@hsd.org • Website: www.hsd.org

Hours: Monday through Friday, noon to 4 P.M.; Saturday, 10 A.M. to 4 P.M.

Admission: Adults $4, seniors and students $3, ages three to eighteen $2, ages two and under free.

Research library and Willingtown Square Gallery free to the public, Monday, 1 to 9 P.M.; Tuesday through Friday, 9 A.M. to 5 P.M.

Special considerations: Buildings are wheelchair accessible.

Shop: The Delaware History Museum has a gift shop that sells books and other items relating to Delaware.

Food: No food available on-site; there are dozens of restaurants within walking distance of the Historical Society's buildings.

Parking: Parking lots are at Fourth and King Streets, Seventh and King Streets, Sixth and Shipley Streets. Parking is also available at street meters.

The Delaware History Museum, just steps from Old Town Hall, is the anchor of the Delaware History Center. Here the state's history is brought to life in an entertaining, interactive environment.

Delaware History Museum

The Historical Society of Delaware's museum division collects, preserves, and interprets every kind of object imaginable, as long as they were made by, used by, owned by, collected by, or otherwise have relevance to Delawareans. These artifacts include items from a Revolutionary War flag to the world's largest frying pan.

Some of these treasures are exhibited in the Delaware History Museum, a worthwhile destination for an hour or two. Even before you go inside, you'll be able to tell that this museum is fun—it's in a refurbished 1940s Woolworth's that still has its appealing red and gold facade. The Society acquired the building in the 1990s.

Indoors, the main installation is a permanent exhibit, Distinctively Delaware™. It's an innovative display that combines high technology with traditional museum techniques to examine the people, places, events, and industries that make Delaware unique. Arranged in chronological order, approximately two dozen scenes and set pieces cover four centuries of the First State's history, beginning with Native American life and culture. Some areas are grouped thematically, including "Delaware as a Crossroads," "The Many Faces of Delaware," and "Made in Delaware."

The multimedia approach is very appealing, and there are plenty of things to touch. In the Native American section, you may handle furs, turtle shells, baskets, and drums; in Transportation, you are welcome to climb inside an old railroad car. In the Early Explorers area, mannequins speak on tape; throughout the museum, actors' taped voices bring more than two dozen significant Delawareans to life.

Displays at the Delaware History Museum, like this one in the Transportation section, include audio-visual components, computer stations, and hands-on activities that trace the First State's history from Native American times to the present. HISTORICAL SOCIETY OF DELAWARE

There are eighteen short videos, six computerized learning stations, and four computer games where you can test your "DelAwareness."

Delaware's singular features such as its coastline, Dover Air Force Base, and Fort Delaware are explored. Historic times including the Civil War and the Underground Railroad in the state are examined, as are modern-day industries.

The important role of chicken farming is brought home with a giant frying pan ten feet in diameter. Used at the Delmarva Chicken Festival, it can hold 180 gallons of oil and 800 chicken quarters.

On the museum's second floor, the well-stocked "Grandma's Attic" provides a hands-on experience for ages two to ten. An old-fashioned corner store, puppet theater, and historic games and toys join vintage dress-up clothes and an old-fashioned marketplace in this discovery room. Special programs are held some Saturdays; contact the museum for details.

The museum also mounts changing exhibitions. Past shows have included Caesar Rodney's Journey to Independence; Delaware in the Civil War; and Inside and Out: Two Centuries of DuPont Products in the Home.

The museum's interactive nature, combined with the memorabilia, artifacts, and art on display, make a visit fulfilling and educational.

Calendar of Events

Regular lectures, programs, and events: For details, call the Society or consult the website.
Saturdays, usually one per month: Family Saturday at the Delaware History Museum.
Programs are presented that tie in with whatever is on exhibit at the time.

January, Martin Luther King Jr. Day, noon to 4 P.M.: Relevant program.

April, late month, 10 A.M. to 4 P.M.: Dr. Carothers' Day Program. Hands-on touch-it lab for kids at the Delaware History Museum.

Nemours Mansion and Gardens

It may seem strange to call a forty-seven-thousand-square-foot Louis XVI château set on a three-hundred-acre estate "homey," but that's the feeling one gets at the Nemours Mansion and Gardens. The former residence of Mr. and Mrs. Alfred I. duPont, Nemours is like Winterthur's low-key cousin. There are no period rooms here; these duPonts collected things they liked, regardless of the objects' style or year of origin. The furnishings, though unabashedly elegant, are also appealingly eclectic.

To visit, you'll have to plan ahead: Tours are offered only in May through October and on a limited schedule in November and December. A guided tour covers about thirty-six rooms in the mansion, then takes visitors on a bus ride through the gardens, concluding with a stop to see the antique automobiles in the chauffeur's garage. Be prepared to climb up and down several flights of steps at a brisk pace. There is no operational elevator.

Visiting Nemours

1600 Rockland Rd., between U.S. Route 202 and DE Route 141
Wilmington, DE 19803
Telephone: 302-651-6912 or 800-651-6912;
Reservation Office open Monday through Friday, 8 A.M. to 4 P.M.
E-mail: tours@nemours.org • Website: www.nemoursmansion.org

Hours: May through October, tours are given Tuesday through Saturday, 9 A.M., 11 A.M., 1 P.M., and 3 P.M.; Sunday, 11 A.M., 1 P.M., and 3 P.M. Closed Mondays, Thanksgiving, and Christmas Day. Open for holiday tours on a limited basis in November and December. Visitors must arrive at the Reception Center on Rockland Road at least fifteen minutes before tour time. Tours last two to two and a half hours and include a guided tour through the mansion followed by a bus tour through the gardens and a visit to the chauffeur's garage.

Admission: $12

Credit cards: Not accepted.

Personal checks: Accepted.

Reservations: Highly recommended for individuals, required for groups. When you write, call, or e-mail for reservations, include two alternative dates, a daytime telephone number, and your zip code. The office is closed on weekends. The Reservation Office must confirm all reservations and changes.

Group tours: Can accommodate groups of up to sixty.

Special considerations: Not accessible to wheelchairs. Visitors must be capable of walking up and down several flights of steps at a brisk pace and remaining on their feet for more than an hour. No visitors under age twelve. No indoor photography. Cell phones and audible pagers must be turned off.

Food service: None. Picnicking not permitted. Restaurants are located nearby on Concord Pike (U.S. Route 202).

In the Main Staircase, the stained glass window designed by Alfred I. duPont's son, Alfred Victor, and Alfred Victor's partner, Gabriel Massena, depicts the family coat of arms. NEMOURS MANSION AND GARDENS

Along the way, your professional guide will share information about the home, its contents, and the duPont dynasty. It's hard to decide which topic is the most fascinating.

The Man and His Mansion

Nemours is named for the town in France that Alfred I. duPont's great-great-grandfather, Pierre Samuel duPont de Nemours, represented in the Estates General in 1789. After the French Revolution, Pierre Samuel and his family emigrated to the Brandywine Valley, where they purchased land for their homes and businesses.

Alfred I. duPont's mansion was designed by the New York firm of Carrère and Hastings. It was constructed in 1909–10 by Smyth and Son from Wilmington. Based somewhat on Le Petit Trianon, the Neoclassical house at Versailles built for Madame de Pompadour, Nemours contains some of duPont's own modifications, including a recessed portico and a front veranda. The house is made of granite quarried on the estate, trimmed with Indiana limestone. DuPont must have had a good relationship with the builder, because the two parties never signed a formal contract; a handshake sealed the deal.

Alfred I.'s marriage to his cousin Bessie Gardner duPont, the mother of his four older children, ended in divorce. Wife number two was another cousin, Alicia Bradford, for whom duPont built Nemours. Alfred I. became the legal guardian of Alicia Maddox, Alicia's daughter, and in 1915 the couple adopted a French orphan, Denise.

When Alicia died, Alfred married Jessie Dew Ball, a collateral descendant of George Washington's mother. The couple's union lasted until Alfred I.'s death in 1935.

Even though duPont and two male cousins had transformed the DuPont Company from the brink of sale into a chemical company giant, his extended family was unable to overlook what they considered his scandalous personal life. A feud that started with his marriage to Alicia resulted in his ouster from the company in 1916. DuPont hardly missed a beat, entrepreneur-wise: he made a second fortune in Florida, where he was instrumental in the development of the banking, transportation, and paper industries.

DuPont had built Nemours during his marriage to Alicia, but it was he and Jessie who really enjoyed the estate and put their own signature on it. They traveled abroad extensively, collecting furniture, rugs, tapestries, paintings, and other items. When stateside, the duPonts were regular customers of antique dealers in New York and Philadelphia.

After her husband's death, Jessie Ball duPont remained at Nemours until she died in 1970. As per the couple's wishes, the mansion and gardens were to be opened for public enjoyment. Nemours, in all its historic splendor, opened for tours in April 1977.

Alfred I. duPont's legacy extends far beyond his home. He provided for the founding of what is now the Alfred I. duPont Hospital for Children, located on the Nemours estate. His philanthropy also created the Nemours Children's Clinics in Wilmington and in Jacksonville, Orlando, and Pensacola, Florida, as well as the Nemours Health Clinic for the elderly in Wilmington.

Jessie Ball duPont surveys Alfred I.'s Steinway piano and his violin in the music room. NEMOURS MANSION AND GARDENS

The House Tour

Your visit to the mansion begins in the reception hall, where Mr. and Mrs. duPont would have greeted their guests. The black and white marble floor and elaborately painted, coffered ceiling give the hall an aura of elegant sophistication. A large portrait of Alfred I. duPont occupies the position of prominence above the gilded stone mantel, while two portraits of George Washington are relegated to less important wall space. The family motto, "Aimer et Connâitre," "To Love and To Know," is carved on the fireplace.

In contrast to the reception hall's powerful space, the drawing room is a study in gorgeous, creamy femininity. Here a portrait of Jessie Ball duPont watches over a symmetrical arrangement of delicate gilded wood French furniture atop an Aubusson carpet. The decorative arts in the room are a name-dropper's dream: a Tiffany vase here, a Rosenthal puppy there, a Sèvres vase nearby. The sun shining in makes the inviting room even more delightful.

In the music room, decorative elements are unabashedly thematic. Harps are formed in the gold leaf trim, sconces are shaped like lyres, and there are musical scenes in the lace curtains. Alfred I. duPont was a musician and composer; the orchestra he started with friends and coworkers eventually became the Delaware Symphony. This room houses his Steinway grand, his violin, and a rare lyre guitar.

The kitchen was clearly designed for a home where people did a lot of entertaining. For one thing, it's huge. Zinc-topped worktables provided ample preparation surfaces. Gleaming copper pots hang above and alongside the tables for easy access. The cork floor would have eased the strain of standing for long periods. Banks of refrigerators in the adjoining butler's pantry were originally cooled with large blocks of ice made in the basement.

Guests would have eaten this fine food in the dining room. The table here could be expanded with sixteen leaves for large dinner parties. The room's most dramatic feature is the massive crystal chandelier that is believed to have originally hung in the Schönbrunn Palace just outside Vienna. The Nemours staff keeps the table set with china and crystal; place settings are changed every six weeks or so to showcase other items from the collection.

The conservatory may be the mansion's most charming room. With its black-and-white-tiled floor, pale green treillage covering the walls, and parakeets and canaries twittering away in Victorian cages, it's delightful no matter where you look. A bamboo motif and an aquarium with a pagodalike cover give the room a Chinese feel.

Downstairs, the duPonts had a billiard room and pool room. There is also a two-lane bowling alley, which did double duty as a movie theater. A screen came down from the ceiling, and a room behind the bowling alley housed a carbon arc projector.

Alfred I. duPont was a talented inventor, with more than two hundred patents. He liked machinery and technical innovations, and his home contained a dark-room and photo laboratory, a water-bottling plant (fresh and carbonated), a central vacuuming system, and ammonia compressors and a condenser for ice making.

Before leaving the house, you'll see one of the most beautiful objects the duPonts owned: a Louis XVI compound musical clock, made about 1785 for Marie Antoinette. The clock plays four tunes on dulcimer and pipe organ. Like the mansion that houses it, it has been restored to perfection.

The Gardens and Garage

The gardens at Nemours are a slice of France in the Brandywine Valley. Statuary and other architectural pleasures grace the greenery. The pools, steps, and flower-filled urns are typical of the French Renaissance tradition.

Your tour includes a bus ride through the gardens. In addition, you may choose to stroll through them at your leisure. There are shady places and strategically placed benches for cooling off on a hot day. A reflecting pool and several smaller ponds and fountains provide invigorating splashing sounds.

Extending from the mansion to the reflecting pool is a one-third-mile-long tree-lined vista. When the water jets are turned off, the one-acre pool clearly reflects its environs. The pool is surrounded by white marble statues representing the seasons. Past the reflecting pool is a maze garden, dominated by a bronze statue titled *Achievement*.

The 157 jets of the Reflecting Pool provide a stunning foreground to the Nemours Mansion.
NEMOURS MANSION AND GARDENS

A colonnade is next, dedicated to the memory of Pierre Samuel duPont de Nemours and his son, Eleuthère Irénée duPont. The grounds continue with the sunken gardens, designed by Alfred I. duPont's son Alfred Victor duPont and his architectural partner, Gabriel Massena. At the farthest point from the mansion is the classical Temple of Love, a fitting setting for a lifesize statue of Diana the Huntress.

The scene is just as lovely in the opposite direction, with three gardens to the mansion's south. First is a French parterre garden, meaning that the pattern is low to the ground. This parterre is done in boxwood, with a fetching faun fountain in the middle. Steps descend into a four borders garden. At the far end is *Tendresse,* a bronze statue by G. Loiseau-Bailly. The third section is known as the frog pond and contains a whimsical statue of a child.

After the gardens, the tour wraps up at the chauffeur's garage. Alfred I. duPont was the first Delawarean to own a car, an 1897 one-cylinder Benz. Some of his other automobiles are on display here, including a 1924 Cadillac limousine and a 1921 Renault with cane bodywork. There are two Rolls Royces: a 1951 Silver Wraith and a rare 1960 Phantom V, one of only ten made.

Rockwood Mansion Park

Rockwood proves that historic sites don't have to be stodgy. Along with tours of the Gothic Revival mansion, Rockwood offers six acres of formal landscape; seventy-two acres of woods and meadows; two and a half miles of paved, lighted trails; and a café where visitors can enjoy a light bite in a Victorian parlor or on one of the mansion's porches. It's wonderful to see how well a treasure listed on the National Register of Historic Places can be integrated into the community. Rockwood Mansion Park is owned and operated by New Castle County.

History

The force behind Rockwood was Joseph Shipley, born in Wilmington on December 4, 1795, into a Quaker family. Shipley attended Westtown School, then moved to Philadelphia. In 1819, he was hired by James Welsh to concentrate on the Anglo-American trade for that Philadelphia merchant's firm. The twenty-three-year-old Shipley sailed for Liverpool in October of that year, planning to stay a short time. More than thirty years would pass before he made his permanent return stateside.

While in England, Shipley rose through the ranks of merchant banking.

Joseph Shipley returned to Wilmington after years in England and had Rockwood Mansion built to his specifications. ROCKWOOD MANSION PARK

Visiting Rockwood Mansion Park

**Just south of Shipley Road on the Washington Street Extension
Wilmington, DE 19809, (Mailing address: Rockwood Mansion Park,
NCC Government Center, 87 Reads Way, New Castle, DE 19720)
Telephone: 302-761-4340 • Fax: 302-761-4345
Website: www.rockwood.org
(New Castle County website; click on the Rockwood Mansion Park link)**

Hours: Grounds open daily, 6 A.M. to 10 P.M.

Food: The Butler's Pantry Cafe, a self-service café in the mansion offering coffee, tea, pastries, and light lunch fare, is open daily from 7 A.M. to 7 P.M. except major holidays. Cash or checks only, no credit cards.

Admission: Free to mansion and grounds.

Tours: Guided tours of the mansion are available daily on the hour from 10 A.M. to 3 P.M., except major holidays. Groups of six or more should call for reservations.

Special considerations: Mansion tour not wheelchair accessible; café and restrooms are accessible.

He led Shipley, Welsh and Co. and also became a limited partner with William and James Brown & Co.

Then came the Panic of 1837, difficult financial times in England and the United States. Shipley pulled off an especially difficult feat, securing a loan from the Bank of England for the firm of William and James Brown & Co., even though the bank had previously refused to lend money to Anglo-American firms. Thanks to Shipley's meticulous documentation and powers of persuasion, Brown & Co. borrowed the largest sum ever loaned to a private firm, and the company was saved from ruin. The money was repaid in full. Shipley went from limited partner to participating partner at Brown, and the firm changed its name to Brown, Shipley Co. It is still in business today, providing banking, investment management, and other services to private, institutional, and corporate clients.

Shipley amassed a fortune. He wanted, and could afford, a quiet country house. In 1846, he moved to Wyncote, an estate near Liverpool that had been designed by Arthur and George Williams. Shipley knew that he would return to Delaware eventually, so he hired architect George Williams to draw up a design for his future home.

Debilitating attacks of gout accelerated the timetable for Shipley's retirement. He arrived back in Wilmington sometime in the summer of 1851. But the city was too hectic for him, and he longed for a more peaceful atmosphere like that of Wyncote. He had started purchasing farmland, woods, and rocky meadows, eventually amounting to three hundred acres, in 1850. Armed with this parcel, and with the design from George Williams, Shipley began Rockwood.

The House

The style of the mansion's exterior is known as Gothic Revival. Americans largely rejected this style, associating it with churches and ascribing an almost undemocratic aspect to it. It's even more unusual to find a house of this type in northern

Wood embellishments, like the molding, finials, and pendants around the doorway, are characteristic of Rockwood Mansion. You may dress more casually than these greeters when you visit. ROCKWOOD MANSION PARK

Delaware, nicknamed "château country" because of the many French-style mansions built here by members of the Du Pont family.

But Joseph Shipley had no anti-Gothic bias and was obviously not motivated by a desire to "keep up with the du Ponts," so he forged ahead. Rockwood was constructed between 1851 and 1854. The home's exterior expresses the Rural Gothic idiom in several ways. The stone is primarily dark Brandywine granite, with lighter stone quoining and window surrounds for contrast. There is a lot of wood embellishment: pendants hanging from roof angles, bargeboards, gables, finials above doors, and even the doors themselves. The huge veranda off the structure's south side, however, is a departure from Rural Gothic, a distinctly American feature.

Inside, the design is eclectic, mixing architectural features from different periods. The staircase in the two-story entry hall is part Jacobean, part Greek Revival, and part William and Mary, with a little Roman Revival thrown in. This part of the house, the first space that guests would see, showcases the owner's wealth. There are more than a dozen types of plaster moldings, including ogee, scroll, and egg-and-dart. Twelve-inch-high baseboards have inset panels.

The drawing room is also an elegant space, with its plaster ceiling rosette and large windows. It is decorated with two big mirrors, carpet, elaborately folded curtains, and Baroque furniture. The most important room in the house, it was situated with views of, and direct access to, the conservatory, veranda, and gardens. The dining room, symmetrical with the drawing room, is Gothic, with gilded woodwork and mahogany furniture.

Rooms at the time were often characterized as masculine or feminine. The drawing room, as a feminine space, had dainty furniture with lots of curves, while the dining room was considered masculine and had heavy, angular furniture to fit in with this idea.

A conservatory was *de rigueur* for any mansion built in the mid-nineteenth century. Shipley used innovative construction for this outstanding functional and decorative element. The choice of cast-iron columns to support the glass explains why this is the only conservatory of its type and era still standing today. Shipley had originally planned to use wood, but architect George Monier Williams insisted on importing iron and glass from England.

Upstairs, the bedroom spaces are a little plainer. The white marble fireplaces are less ornate, as was the furniture here during Shipley's time.

Shipley was on the cutting edge of technology for his home. He installed central heating from a coal furnace in the cellar. A separate furnace piped hot water under the sandstone floor to heat the conservatory. There was an acetylene gas plant on the property so the house could be lit this way. Rockwood had indoor plumbing with flush toilets.

Joseph Shipley moved into his new home in 1855. An 1857 addition tacked on a summer kitchen and three upstairs rooms that could be used for servants. Two sisters, Sarah and Hannah, who survived after Joseph Shipley's death in 1867, inherited the property. Sarah died in 1872. Hannah lived there until her death in 1891, when her niece Sarah Shipley Bringhurst purchased the mansion and grounds.

In 1892, a third-floor section with another servant's bedroom was added. Sarah turned over the house and 160 acres to her son Edward Bringhurst and his wife, Anna. The family lived there with their three youngest children. Their eldest daughter, Elizabeth "Bessie" Shipley Bringhurst Galt-Smith, was married and living in Ireland.

During the Bringhursts' tenure at Rockwood, they raised the west tower circa 1900 and added a west wing in 1912–13. That construction gave the mansion five more rooms on the first floor, plus three rooms, a sleeping porch, and a winter garden on the second floor.

Although Bessie was overseas, she had strong opinions about how Rockwood should be decorated, and she expressed those preferences in hundreds of letters. Status was very important to her, so she sent suggestions on how to make things look even grander than they really were. Bessie was widowed in 1899, but she remained in Ireland until after World War I ended, when she returned to Rockwood and joined her mother and unmarried siblings, Edward Bringhurst III and Mary Bringhurst, in the mansion.

The interior rooms interpreted to the Bringhurst period show the family's fondness for decorating and concern with image. Edward III liked to collect antiques. The Bringhursts followed the latest decorating trends in paint colors, wallpaper, and accessories.

Bessie died in 1932, followed by Edward III in 1939. Mary was forced to sell a number of parcels between 1940 and 1951, and the estate began to decline. She lived at Rockwood until her death in 1965 at age one hundred. Mary left Rockwood to two nieces. One, Nancy Sellers Hargraves, lived at Rockwood with her husband, Gordon, until her death in 1972. She left it to be maintained and preserved for the "enjoyment and enlightenment of the present and future generations." Rockwood was conveyed to New Castle County in 1973. It was added to the National Register of Historic Places in 1976 and opened as a public museum on September 23 of that year.

By the mid-1990s, it was agreed that the mansion needed restoration, but there were a lot of details to work out. A task force in 1999 concluded that the most important period to interpret was the Joseph Shipley era. However, not much information was available about the interior and furnishings of Rockwood during that time. Therefore, the decision was made to focus on Shipley's period for the exterior and the early period of the Bringhursts' residency, during the Gilded Age around 1895, for the interior.

Paint chips were studied. Wallpaper and floor coverings were researched, with replacements matched as closely as possible to the originals, no longer manufac-

The Bringhurst Bedroom has been restored with solid furniture and an emphasis on floral patterns.
ROCKWOOD MANSION PARK

tured today. Out went lead paint. In came central air-conditioning. Water damage, chipped marble, and crumbling plaster were repaired.

Sometimes different is better, and that's the case with the first floor of the West Wing. Rather than make that section part of the museum, the task force wanted the space to be inviting and accessible to visitors every day, so they installed a self-serve café. The stone vestibule welcomes guests with stenciled climbing vines on the walls. There are four beautiful parlors where visitors can sit, eat, chat, and feel right at home. The rooms are decorated and furnished in Victorian style. The ladies room is decorated with beautifully hand-painted walls, and the men's room has interesting wallpaper. Those who wish to take the mansion tour see a short video, then are guided by docents in period dress on the forty-five-minute tour.

The short-term improvement plan centers on renovating the carriage house into a wheelchair-accessible Visitor Center and Conference Center. Long-term, the site hopes to add a Victorian playhouse, croquet court, and garden maze.

The Gardens

The grounds of Rockwood are described as "Gardenesque." This doesn't mean "like a garden," but refers to a particular landscaping philosophy. Gardenesque style was popularized in England by John Claudius Loudon and brought to the United States largely by Andrew Jackson Downing's book, *A Treatise on the Theory and Practice of Landscape Gardening Adapted to North America.*

Gardenesque landscaping, popular in the 1840s and 1850s, evolved from other theories, including the Sublime, Beautiful, and Picturesque. It took some elements of each—the surprises of the Sublime, the curves of the Beautiful, and the jagged irregularity of the Picturesque—and added ornamentation and flowerbeds. A key component of the Gardenesque style was to focus attention on individual plants, especially exotic ones. They were to be placed far enough apart, and with enough seeming randomness, so each one could be appreciated but the whole didn't look boring.

Joseph Shipley embraced the Gardenesque style and integrated house and garden according to that philosophy. The layout of the garden influenced the way the mansion was arranged; the garden was arranged based on how it would look from the house.

There also were practical considerations. A kitchen garden provided fruits, vegetables, and herbs. It was surrounded by a stone wall that kept animals out and transferred solar heat. The stables were placed near the kitchen garden but downwind from the house, so fertilizer could be moved easily but the residents wouldn't be assailed by unpleasant odors.

The Gardenesque plan starts with the curving drive that leads up to the house from the entrance gates. Natural rock formations, or groupings made to look natural, emphasize the native setting. Closer to the mansion, the plantings become more exotic and the space opens onto a lawn.

Rockwood's grounds also boast a "ha-ha," a sunken stone wall to keep livestock out, but invisible from the house. It gets its name because it would surprise unsuspecting walkers who came upon it. From the south veranda, the view was uninterrupted to the Delaware River and across to New Jersey.

Rockwood Mansion in winter is the perfect spot for a hot cup of tea. The Butler's Pantry serves snacks and drinks, which visitors are welcome to enjoy in one of the parlors. ROCKWOOD MANSION PARK

A pleasure garden with walkways was a highlight of Shipley's plan. The gently curved paths were designed to be wide enough to accommodate the wheelchair he used because of his gout. Farther from the house, Shipley planted trees with varying shapes, textures, and colors. A pinetum boasts specimens of larch, cedar, spruce, elm, hemlock, fir, and other evergreens. These are just some of the twelve hundred trees, shrubs, flowers, and tropical plants Shipley purchased for Rockwood.

Visitors are welcome to stroll the gardens and hike the trails in the park. Rockwood is part of Delaware's Greenways and Trail Program, and as such, recreation and conservation are primary values.

Calendar of Events

Spring and fall: Sleep under the Stars Campout. Bring a tent and enjoy planned activities, then camp overnight on Rockwood's grounds. Call or check the website for more information.

June: Concert series on the South Lawn. Bring a picnic supper and enjoy a variety of music styles. Call or check the website for more information.

July, second weekend, Saturday 11 A.M. to 9 P.M., Sunday 11 A.M. to 10 P.M.: Ice Cream Festival. From blacksmithing to quilting, interpretive historical demonstrations offer a look at Victorian life. A variety of entertainment and music, featuring the Delaware Symphony Orchestra Saturday evening and fireworks Sunday evening, as well as Victorian-era games, strolling performers, antique bicycles, food, and ice cream. Admission is free. For a fee, visitors may enjoy a catered meal in an air-conditioned tent during the Saturday evening concert, or a catered Sunday brunch. Free shuttle parking is available at the Merchant's Square Shopping Center on Governor Printz Boulevard. Handicapped parking is available at the Rockwood Office Park, 505 Carr Rd.

Early October through late November: Hayrides for groups. Rent a hay wagon for a tractor-pulled ride through the woods. Each thirty-minute ride is accompanied by a one-hour bonfire. Wagon rentals $75 for up to twenty-five people. Reservations required. Hayrides can be booked on the hour from 5 to 8 P.M. Call for information or a reservation.

Early December through mid-January, dusk to 10 P.M.: Winter Wonderland Festival of Lights. Drive or walk through this spectacular display featuring a million lights.

December, weekends until Christmas, Friday 6 to 9 P.M., Saturday and Sunday, 5 to 8 P.M.: Holiday Open House Weekends with Santa. See the mansion decorated for the season, and enjoy carolers and other performers. Kids can have a free photo taken with Santa and receive a special treat.

Winterthur, An American Country Estate

When the late Henry Francis du Pont organized every square inch of Winterthur, he had strict rules for everything from flower arranging to furniture placement. This obsessive attention to detail paid off. Du Pont made his 175-room mansion a world-renowned center for American decorative arts set amidst a spectacular garden.

The same meticulousness is very much in evidence at Winterthur (pronounced "winter tour") today. From the impeccably trained guides to the copious literature available at the information desks to the clean restrooms, nothing in the mansion, gardens, and galleries has been overlooked.

But that doesn't mean Winterthur is inflexible. The institution is remarkable for its willingness to adapt its programs to meet visitors' wants and needs, while staying true to H. F. du Pont's ideals. Winterthur now offers a variety of tours so that visitors can see a different part of the mansion on each visit. The twenty-two-thousand-square-foot Winterthur Galleries hosts permanent and changing exhibitions in a museum setting and shares a spacious entry area with the mansion. A full calendar of special events brings music, crafts, and even horse racing to the estate.

Children are welcome at Winterthur, something one might not expect at a chateau full of priceless antiques. The Touch-It Room to the left of the Galleries Reception Area encourages little ones to have fun with early American objects. The Enchanted Woods in the gardens is a paradise for kids; paved paths make it easy to get a stroller there. The cafeteria has high chairs. Some tours permit children, others don't; stick with the kids-okay tours for an experience the whole family will enjoy.

Winterthur deserves special kudos for its commitment to accessible programming. Most tours are wheelchair accessible. So are paths throughout the garden, though the terrain is steep in spots. Vans and trams have ramps or lifts and wheelchair-securing devices. Visually impaired visitors may take guided tours with detailed verbal descriptions; audiotapes and players, high-contrast photographs, and large-print scripts are available for some exhibitions. For hearing-impaired visitors, assistive listening systems are available for guided tours and special presentations, as are printed scripts. Winterthur will even hire a sign language interpreter, given at least a week's notice.

Along with the incredible collections and grounds, it's this detail-oriented, caring attitude that makes a visit to Winterthur so memorable.

The Chinese Parlor was created from two rooms in the original Winterthur house; its size was defined by the wallpaper. WINTERTHUR/GAVIN ASHWORTH

Visiting Winterthur,
An American Country Estate

Route 52, 6 miles north of Wilmington and Interstate 95,
and 5 miles south of U.S. Route 1, Winterthur, DE 19735
Telephone: 800-448-3883 or 302-888-4600; TDD 302-888-4907.
Information and tours office open Monday through Friday,
8:30 A.M. to 4:30 P.M.
Website: www.winterthur.org

Hours: Tuesday through Sunday, 10 A.M. to 5 P.M. Touch-It Room open Monday through Friday, 2 to 4:30 P.M.; Saturday and Sunday, noon to 5 P.M. Last admission tickets sold 3:30 P.M.; last period room tour departs 3:45 P.M. Closed Mondays (except for holidays), New Year's Day, Thanksgiving Day, and Christmas.

Admission: The Galleries & Garden Pass offers admission to the Galleries, Touch-It Room, gardens, and garden tram weather permitting. Adults $15; discounts for seniors, students, children, and groups. The Winterthur Experience package includes a one-hour Discovery Tour—Elegant Entertaining, Private Spaces and Gaming Places, Stylish Suites, Gracious Living, Distinctive Collections, or Yuletide at Winterthur. Tickets $20; for $5 extra, you may add another Discovery Tour. For $10, you may add a two-hour Focus Tour or Conservation Tour.

Tours: Tours run continuously every day; to ensure a specific time or tour, call in advance. Discovery Tours run more frequently than Focus Tours and the Conservation Tour. From early November through early January, Yuletide Tours are the primary offering. These tours fill quickly; reservations strongly suggested. Arrive at least fifteen minutes before your scheduled tour to allow time for the tram ride from the Visitor Center to the Galleries. Wear comfortable walking shoes.

Special considerations: Wheelchair accessible. Vehicles with official permits may use designated parking spaces next to the Visitor Pavilion and near the museum entrance. During regular public hours, a wheelchair accessible shuttle stops at the Visitor Pavilion, the Museum Store on Clenny Run, and the museum entrance, where wheelchairs are available. All garden trams also are wheelchair accessible. For accommodations or details on physical access, call for information or to make arrangements. Assistive listening systems are available for guided tours and special presentations. Printed scripts of audio portions of exhibitions are available at the museum reception desk. With at least one week's notice, a sign language interpreter can be hired. Visually impaired guests may make advance reservations for guided tours that include detailed verbal descriptions. Audiotapes and players, high-contrast photographs, and large-print scripts are available for selected exhibitions; ask at the museum reception desk. Demonstration objects and items in the Touch-It Room are available for touching.

Children: Strollers are available in the Visitor Center and the Galleries Reception Area.

Food: The Garden Cafeteria (302-888-4910) in the Visitor Center offers lunch, snacks, and Sunday brunch. Open 10 A.M. to 4 P.M. (hot food available from 11 A.M. to 3 P.M.); Sunday brunch, 10 A.M. to 2 P.M. The Cappuccino Cafe near the Galleries features soup, sandwiches, snacks, and specialty drinks. Open Tuesday through Friday, 8 A.M. to 4 P.M.; Saturday and Sunday, 10 A.M. to 5 P.M. Ticketed guests may use picnic tables near visitor parking area and on either side of the Galleries.

Photography: Still and video photography for personal use only is permitted in the Galleries and on the Elegant Entertaining tour, as well as in the garden and around the estate.

Shops: Museum Store at Clenny Run and Bookstore in the Visitor Center. Open Tuesday through Sunday, 10 A.M. to 5 P.M. The bookstore includes resources on antiques and decorative arts, Winterthur, gardening, and architecture, home accents, and children's books and toys.

Research library: Open weekdays for ages twelve and up. Rare manuscripts and other items are displayed in the entry hall and elsewhere in the library.

Henry Francis du Pont and the Winterthur Estate

Winterthur was named for the ancestral Swiss home of Jacques Antoine Bidermann, who in 1837 purchased 450 acres of Delaware land with his wife, Evelina Gabrielle du Pont. They bought it from her father, the founder of the E. I. du Pont de Nemours and Co. black powder manufacturing firm. The Bidermanns built a three-story, twelve-room Greek Revival home above Clenny Run.

The property passed to their son, who then sold it to his uncle Henry du Pont in 1867. Henry invited his son and daughter-in-law, Henry Algernon and Pauline du Pont, to live in the house. They inherited Winterthur in 1889.

Henry Algernon made substantial improvements to the estate and enlarged the house twice. By the early twentieth century, Winterthur was a self-sustaining agricultural community. Up to two hundred tenant farmers and their families living on the property raised turkeys, chickens, sheep, pigs, and cattle and grew vegetables and grains in the fields. Gardens and greenhouses provided flowers year-round. Winterthur also had a sawmill, machine shops, milk-bottling plant, post office, and its own train station.

Henry Francis du Pont was born at Winterthur in 1880. He studied horticulture at Harvard's Bussey Institution, then returned to Winterthur to manage the farm. He was especially interested in dairy operations and began a long-term Holstein-Friesian breeding program to increase the butterfat content of the milk. Du Pont's herd broke records; he had permanently altered the breed, and his cows were in great demand by other dairy farmers.

Du Pont married Ruth Wales in 1916. Along with their home at Winterthur, by 1923 they had houses on Long Island and in Boca Grande, Florida, plus a New York City apartment. As was fashionable at the time, the couple favored European furniture.

That changed dramatically in 1923, when du Pont traveled to Vermont to see a friend's dairy operation. While visiting Watson and Electra Havermeyer Webb, he saw an American pine dresser filled with pink china. Apparently, du Pont was smitten with the sight and resolved then and there to turn his attention to early American objects.

Du Pont collected with a vengeance. Over the years, he purchased more than sixty thousand objects—supplemented since his death to total eighty-five thousand—made or used in America between 1640 and 1860. He acquired furniture, textiles, silver, clocks, needlework, porcelain, oriental rugs, and paintings, as well as architectural features, sometimes entire buildings, to serve as backdrops.

Originally, du Pont intended to outfit his Long Island home with the items, but that quickly became impossible. The solution: use some of the existing spaces at Winterthur, such as the Visiting Children's Maids' Pressing Room, as display areas, put a nine-story addition on the mansion, and furnish the whole thing with the world's premier collection of early American decorative arts.

Du Pont's discerning eye, artist's sensibilities, and penchant for massing like objects together has created maximum visual impact in the period rooms. He took entire rooms, initially from the first thirteen colonies, interpreted them according to his own sensibilities, and lived in them. Appropriate woodwork and other architectural details provide context that would be absent in a typical museum setting. Taken as a whole, Winterthur is a tribute to early American artisans and their useful, beautiful products. Du Pont used his settings, vignettes, and architecture to create a home and museum that continues to inspire, especially when it comes to his ideas of balance, color, and decorating with textiles.

George Washington didn't stay here, but some of his dishes from Mount Vernon do. They're decorated with the emblem of the officers' club from the Revolution, the Society of the Order of the Cincinnati. The plates were hand-painted in Canton—that's China, not Ohio.

Du Pont received well-deserved recognition for his accomplishments. In 1961, Jacqueline Kennedy invited him to become chairman of the new Fine Arts Committee and oversee the renovations for the White House. He, in turn, hosted her at Winterthur.

The Henry Francis du Pont Winterthur Museum opened to the public in 1951. Ruth and H. F. du Pont moved to a Regency-style "cottage" on-site, now

Winterthur's Federal-style dining room includes icons of American history like Benjamin West's unfinished painting, *Peace Commissioners*. WINTERTHUR/GAVIN ASHWORTH

the Museum Store on Clenny Run. Ruth died in 1967, H. F. du Pont two years later. Winterthur, An American Country Estate continues to awe and delight visitors from around the world.

Tours

General admission, known as the Galleries & Garden pass, gives access to the gardens, including the narrated tram tour, and the Galleries, Winterthur's museum-type space. Passports are valid for two days. The narrated tram tour provides panoramic views of the estate as it drives through many sections of the garden.

To tour the house, Winterthur offers five Discovery Tours that cover the mansion and grounds. The Winterthur Experience ticket includes one of these tours along with everything covered by the Galleries & Garden pass; additional tours can be added for a $5 upgrade. All tours begin with a brief shuttle ride from the Visitor Center to the Galleries, or guests may choose to walk. Discovery Tours last between forty-five minutes and an hour.

Two-hour tours that focus on special interests are available. The Focus Tours' theme changes seasonally. Past tours have highlighted ceramics, furniture, and decorating with textiles. The Conservation Tour gives a behind-the-scenes look at Winterthur's laboratories. It's a rare chance to see the intriguing way art and science—and a lot of detective work—combine to help Winterthur's professional staff assess and conserve items.

Special-Subject Tours can be arranged to study a specific type of item in the collection. Call at least one week in advance for details, reservations, and costs.

If you plan to visit Winterthur with children, mention this when you call to make reservations. Some tours accommodate children; others are limited to ages twelve and over. Winterthur's website lists this information too.

All of the tours give an education about life in early America and showcase one-of-a-kind antiques. For first-time visitors, Elegant Entertaining is a good tour to start with. This tour visits the mansion's most elegant rooms, where the du Ponts hosted guests and celebrated special occasions. Private Spaces and Gaming Places focuses on the rooms in which the du Ponts relaxed during their leisure time and offers an overview of how styles changed from the 1600s, through pre-Revolutionary times, to the period of early nationhood. Stylish Suites offers a peek into the spaces where guests received du Pont hospitality. The Gracious Living tour has a spectacular array of American high-style urban and country furnishings shown off to their best advantage in rooms designed by H. F. du Pont.

Winterthur has many exceptionally strong collections among its fine antiques: Shaker furniture, Pennsylvania German items, glass, ceramics, and metals. To see these items and learn more about du Pont's collecting philosophy, take the Distinctive Collections tour.

The Galleries

Twenty-two thousand square feet of display space in the Galleries gives Winterthur the opportunity to mount permanent and temporary exhibitions related to its collections; some of these are created by Winterthur, others come from across the country. A short film gives a good overview of Winterthur and the objects.

The Yuletide Tour

Seasonal tours at Winterthur re-create holiday celebrations of days gone by. The specially decorated period rooms are breathtaking to look at, and the displays, interpreted by tour guides, are informative about early American traditions.

In America's earliest days, New Year's Day, not Christmas Day, was considered the highlight of the winter season. Puritans in the North rejected any frivolity surrounding Christmas, but people in the South were more flexible. In the mid-Atlantic, customs varied from one religious group to the next: The Anglicans celebrated the holiday with gusto, while their quiet Quaker neighbors didn't observe it at all.

The kinds of decorations used in early America were very different from what we're used to today. The earliest reference to a Christmas tree appears in a 1747 Moravian Church diary and refers to a wooden pyramid decorated with evergreens. The Yuletide Tour features nineteenth-century displays, including small tabletop trees with ornaments appropriate to different eras, such as dolls, paper cornucopias, or paper or felt flowers.

Yuletide Tours begin in the Reception Area, then move down a long hallway to emerge, surprisingly, in a cobblestoned courtyard. Surrounded by the facades of three historic buildings du Pont purchased, you'll feel like you're outdoors. Streetlamps and candlelight shining from windows illuminate the faux snow and trees to complete the illusion. This enclosed area used to be the du Pont family's indoor badminton court.

The rooms seen on Winterthur's Yuletide Tour and the holiday celebrations depicted in them vary from year to year, but some special areas are often repeated. At the top of the list is the Montmorenci Stair Hall, swagged in greens and adorned with poinsettias. Du Pont had purchased architectural elements, including a spiral stairway and woodwork, from the 1822 Montmorenci plantation in North Carolina. His plan was to use the staircase to replace the existing Beaux-Arts style marble one. Unfortunately, the new stairway didn't fit, and it wasn't structurally sound, either. Du Pont, in consultation with architect Thomas Waterman, came up with a design for new steps consistent with the Neo-classical design of the Montmorenci Stair. They elongated the circular shape into an ellipse and sent the stairs soaring two stories instead of one. The result is the successful completion of a 360-degree turn from bottom to top. The floating staircase, not anchored to any walls, looks particularly stunning decorated for Christmas.

You'll also visit the Conservatory, where a fifteen-foot Christmas tree is covered in hundreds of dried flowers. The du Ponts' tree would have been in the same spot, atop the green marble floor, surrounded by a spectacular show of blooming trees and plants.

The elegant Montmorenci Stair Hall is swagged in greens for Yuletide. WINTERTHUR

Some of the twenty rooms on the tour present vignettes of the winter experiences of diverse groups. You may see a holiday celebration from such varying viewpoints as an early-1800s Pennsylvania German farm household or a prosperous New England household in the 1870s. An eighteenth-century menorah, the centerpiece of a Hanukkah vignette, reminds us of the diversity of the early European settlers of North America.

Other rooms evoke the festivities—and craziness—of New Year's Day. Trumpet fanfares, raucous behavior, and gunfire were typical ways to greet the new year. Men tore from house to house trying to visit as many friends and relatives as possible, while the women played hostess to these impatient guests. Ruth Wales du Pont invited her callers to the Port Royal Parlor and offered them a selection of cakes and cookies, with coffee or hot mulled wine to wash them down. You'll see some of these incredible delicacies on display, but don't try to sneak a snack. It's hard to believe, but all the luscious-looking foods on display are clever fakes concocted by Winterthur's staff.

Yuletide at Winterthur is beautiful outdoors as well. As dusk falls, the property glows with more than one hundred thousand lights. On select evenings, children are invited for festivities in the Enchanted Woods, followed by storytelling in the Museum Store while Mom and Dad do their shopping. On December Saturdays, Santa comes for breakfast and welcomes company.

The tours and events are popular and sell out quickly. Make reservations as soon as you have a date in mind.

The gallery known as In Style compares and contrasts eight design styles popular in America during the period covered by H. F. du Pont's collections, including Chippendale, Federal, Queen Anne, and William and Mary. Each has distinguishing characteristics. Learning how to recognize each style helps deepen one's appreciation for the objects in Winterthur's period rooms.

In Wood focuses on furniture and cabinetmaking. Like the wallpaper books we can look through today, pattern books for furniture were available in early America. The "Chairs Chairs Chairs" section of this gallery shows the regional and chronological evolution of seating from the 1750s through 1850s.

Fine gowns, wall hangings, and quilts are some of the items featured in the Textiles and Needlework gallery. Paintings and Prints showcases the fine art that complements Winterthur's decorative crafts. The Metalworks gallery has useful and beautiful metal objects and explains the smiths' choice of materials and design.

Changing displays of earthenware, stoneware, porcelain, and glass are featured in the Ceramics and Glass gallery.

The Dominy Shops re-create an actual woodworker's enterprise and a clock shop used by the Dominy family from Long Island and transported here to Winterthur. Finished objects are displayed near the equipment that was used to make them. It's a nice nod to the artisans, without whom collectors would have nothing to collect.

The Touch-It Room is a space that encourages children to learn more about early American objects by using them. Colonial toys and games, costumes, a shop, and other items make this a fun place to play and explore.

This rabbit tureen, made of soft-paste porcelain with hand-painted decoration in enamel colors, was manufactured at the Chelsea Porcelain Factory in London. Catalogues list the piece as "Fine tureen in the form of a rabbit as big as life." WINTERTHUR

Winterthur mounts at least one major and several smaller changing exhibitions every year. The exhibition schedule is on the website, or you may call for this information.

More than 125 soup tureens and other soup-related items are displayed in the Campbell Collection of Soup Tureens. The items are housed in the Dorrance Gallery, named for the family whose members have been involved with the Campbell Soup Company since 1876. Bright light and airy shelves make this gallery just the right setting for this unique assemblage of serving pieces.

Soup, porridge, and stew were inexpensive meals common on sixteenth-century menus and were often eaten right out of the pot. By the eighteenth century, however, soup was the first course on upscale menus, and the containers had to be just as sophisticated as their wealthy owners. Artisans responded by making fashionable vessels from bronze, silver, and ceramics, in an incredible array of forms. Metal tureens on display have minute details, such as anchors hanging from ships, woodland scenes, or royal insignia. Many of the items collected by the late John T. Dorrance Jr., former Campbell's board chairman, were actually made for European royalty. The two lifesize rabbit tureens were made in England's Chelsea Porcelain Factory. If you care to add some whimsy to your own table, reproductions are for sale in the Museum Shop.

The Gardens

The sixty-acre Winterthur gardens, nestled in the almost one-thousand-acre estate, are blessed with many natural advantages. Rolling hills, flowing streams, and lush native greenery present a visually appealing, parklike landscape. In this once-private setting, Henry Francis du Pont created unity between the collection of American arts inside and a floral kaleidoscope outside. Estate Passport admission includes a narrated tram ride through the gardens.

As children, du Pont and his sister, Louise, were immersed in gardening. Their mother, Pauline, taught them the practical aspects, while their father, Henry Algernon, made sure they knew the Latin names of plants and trees. H. F. du Pont went on to study horticulture and practical agriculture at Harvard's Bussey Institution. At the same time, family friend Marian Cruger Coffin was in training in landscape architecture at MIT. Coffin and du Pont later collaborated on many of Winterthur's outdoor spaces.

Du Pont applied a naturalistic philosophy to the garden, an approach that might be described as going nature one better. Every plant looks as if it belongs, but it's

A spectacular assemblage of azaleas provides masses of color in spring. Henry Francis du Pont used this technique in his home as well as in the garden. WINTERTHUR

Kids can "hatch" in the huge bird's nest that's part of the Enchanted Woods™. WINTERTHUR/RICH DUNOFF

obvious—and acceptable—that human planning was involved. Plantings were arranged in layers like a natural understory and canopy. Curved paths snaked through the gardens, offering fresh viewpoints with every turn. Exotic plants joined familiar native ones, but all were carefully selected to be well suited to their location.

Winterthur's founder was keenly interested in color. He kept copious notes about tints and shades, as well as blooming times and care requirements. Yellow and lavender was a favorite combination. Just as he massed similar objects in the mansion, he assembled huge amounts of color in the garden. He often chose plants with highly contrasting colors to be massed near each other, a counterpoint that made each color seem more intense.

One of du Pont's goals was to have a succession of blooming plants for as long as possible. To that end, he planted the March Bank with thousands of bulbs, which over time have propagated into millions, and perennials that start flowering in late January and don't quit until early May, followed by other areas of the gardens. A few hundred bulbs in an area the size of du Pont's bulb garden would have been ludicrous; in two of his more expansive purchases, he reportedly ordered twenty-five thousand bulbs in 1909, and another thirty-nine thousand in 1913. Snowdrops, crocus, squill, and glory-of-the-snow by the thousands remind visitors that spring is on the way.

The Sundial Garden, developed in conjunction with Marian Cruger Coffin, is a highlight in April. A pastel rainbow starts with pink magnolias and blooms through the month until the lilacs blossom.

For show-stopping color, the eight-acre Azalea Woods in May is without equal. Oaks, tulip poplars, and beech trees give structure to the hundreds of azaleas and rhododendrons below.

Other garden highlights include the views from Sycamore Hill; a boggy, rocky area called the Quarry Garden; and the Pinetum, which contains an extensive array of rare conifers. Everyone enjoys the Reflecting Pool area, even frogs and the occasional snake in the summertime; the du Pont family used this attractive water feature as a swimming pool.

A wonderful recent addition to the gardens is the Enchanted Woods, a three-acre themed area named "Best Children's Garden" by *Philadelphia* magazine. Winterthur has concocted a story about the fairies who created the garden; some kids get into it and show up wearing fairy wings, but even kids who are indifferent to the story enjoy visiting. And why not? It's magical and fun. Kids and adults can step over the Story Stones, wind along the S-S-Serpentine Path, then rumble across the Troll Bridge. A huge bird's nest makes for great photographs. A working pump provides a cooling splash, and there are spaces to climb into, hide behind, and explore.

For anyone interested in horticulture, Winterthur offers brochures on the gardens' plants and on what's in bloom at certain times.

Calendar of Events

Programs, exhibitions, classes, and events: Call 800-448-3883 or visit www.winterthur.org for the latest updates on Winterthur's active schedule. Unless otherwise specified, events are included in the price of admission.

January, third Monday: Martin Luther King Jr. Day Celebration.

March through June: Spring garden walks. One-hour guided tours. $5 admission in addition to Estate Passport fee. Reservations recommended.

Easter Sunday, 10 A.M. to 3 P.M.: Easter in the Garden. Music, face painting, other entertainment, and a visit from the Easter Bunny in the Enchanted Woods.

May, first Sunday: Point-to-Point races. Enjoy the excitement of horse racing, an antique carriage parade, bagpipers, and family fun. Tickets go on sale March 1: adults $25, ages twelve to twenty $10, ages two to eleven $5, ages two and under free. General admission includes remote parking. Preferred parking available for additional fee, which varies depending on the desirability of the parking area. Contact Winterthur for information about parking and the tailgate party competition. Races run rain or shine; no refunds.

July and August, Tuesdays: Terrific Tuesdays for children four to eight. Admission $5 per child; one adult admitted free with each child. Children's activities and craftmaking related to a current exhibit.

A Windsor chair takes shape at Winterthur's Crafts Festival. WINTERTHUR/STUDIO A

November, one weekend early in month: Delaware Antiques Show, held at the Bank One Center on the Riverfront in Wilmington. Features more than fifty of the country's top dealers of American antiques. Admission $12.

Early November through early January: Yuletide. Discover the winter holidays as experienced by early Americans. The mansion and estate are spectacularly decorated. Adults $15, seniors and students $13, ages five to eleven $9, ages four and under free. Reservations required.

November and December, selected evenings, 4:30 to 6:30 P.M.: Nights of Enchanted Lights for families. Admission $6 per person; advance tickets required. Families can tour the lighted Enchanted Woods. Music or other entertainment. Shoppers receive a 10 percent discount in the Museum Shop on Clenny Run.

December, selected Saturdays before Christmas: Breakfast with Santa. Buffet breakfast, scavenger hunt, make a Victorian tree ornament. Reservations required. Members $14, nonmembers $16, children two to twelve $11, under two free.

OTHER ATTRACTIONS

Afro-American Historical Society of Delaware
512 E. Fourth St.
Wilmington, DE 19801
Telephone: 302-571-1699
African-American heritage with emphasis on Delaware. Conducts tours and lectures. Gallery open by appointment. Wheelchair accessible.

Bank One Center on the Riverfront (Riverfront Arts Center)
800 S. Madison St.
Wilmington, DE 19801
Telephone: 888-862-ARTS
Fax: 302-425-4897
Website: www.riverfrontwilmington.com
Grand and spacious facility houses traveling art and historical exhibitions. Wheelchair accessible.

Brandywine Zoo
1001 N. Park Dr.
Brandywine Park
Wilmington, DE 19802
Telephone: 302-571-7747
Fax: 302-571-7787
Website: www.brandywinezoo.org
Located along the Brandywine River. Open year-round, 10 A.M. to 4 P.M. Admission charged

March 15 through November 15. Wheelchair accessible. Special events. Siberian tigers, llamas, river otters, monkeys, and birds are some of the animals in residence.

Fort Christina
7th St. East at river
Wilmington, DE 19801
Telephone: 302-652-5629
Site of first settlement in Delaware.

Gibraltar Gardens
1405 Greenhill Ave.
Wilmington, DE 19806
Telephone: 302-651-9617
Fax: 302-651-9603
Website: www.preservationde.org
Hours: Self-guided tours Monday through Friday, 9 A.M. to 5 P.M. Groups by appointment. Admission: Free.
Italianate-style historic gardens designed by Marian Coffin feature terraces, marble staircase, ironwork, fountains, garden ornaments, reflecting pool, shrubs, perennials, and annuals. Formal gardens are wheelchair accessible, the rest of the property is not.

Goodstay Gardens
Goodstay Center, University of Delaware
   Wilmington Campus
2600 Pennsylvania Ave. (DE Route 52)
   at Greenhill Ave.
Wilmington, DE 19806
Telephone: 302-573-4450
Hours: Daylight hours.
Admission: Free.
Gravel paths, perennial borders, boxwood-lined
"rooms" (iris, rose, peony), woodland area,
stream, magnificent magnolia alley. Partially
wheelchair accessible. Visitors Center open
weekdays from 8 A.M. to 3 P.M. in good weather.

Greenbank Mill
500 Greenbank Rd.
Wilmington, DE 19808
Telephone: 302-999-9001
Website: www.greenbankmill.org
Living-history museum with farmhouse, water
wheel, and barn. Open April through November, Friday and Saturday, 10 A.M. to 4 P.M. Regularly scheduled events include sheep-shearing
and archaeological excavations. Admission fee.
Programs available for groups. Call for rates
and reservations. Partially wheelchair accessible; call for details.

Holy Trinity (Old Swedes) Church and Hendrickson House Museum
606 Church St.
Wilmington, DE 19801
Telephone: 302-652-5629
Fax: 302-652-8615
E-mail: oldswedes@aol.com
Website: www.oldswedes.org.
Experience the timeless beauty of Old Swedes
Church, built in 1698. Hendrickson House
Museum holds artifacts from colonial days.
Open Wednesday through Saturday, 10 A.M.
to 4 P.M. Group reservations required. Partially
wheelchair accessible; wheelchairs available.

Kalmar Nyckel–Delaware's Tall Ship
1124 E. Seventh St.
Wilmington, DE 19801
Telephone: 302-429-SHIP
Fax: 302-429-0350

Old Swedes Church was built in 1698 by descendants of the original Swedish settlers. It is the
oldest house of worship in American in continuous use for that purpose. GREATER WILMINGTON CON-
VENTION AND VISITORS BUREAU

Website: www.kalnyc.org
This tall ship, ten stories high and 139 feet
long, is a magnificently detailed re-creation
of her ancestor that landed on the Christina
River in 1638. Open for dockside tours, public
day sails, and private charters. Not wheelchair
accessible.

Ahoy, there! The tall ship *Kalmar Nyckel,* a reproduction of the Swedish warship that brought the
first settlers to the area, is often moored along
the Christina Riverwalk. Tours are available.
GREATER WILMINGTON CONVENTION AND VISITORS BUREAU

Patrons enjoy the outdoor ambiance at restaurants along the Christina Riverwalk. GREATER WILMINGTON CONVENTION AND VISITORS BUREAU

Mt. Cuba Center, Inc.
Box 3570
Barley Mill Rd.
Greenville, DE 19807-0570
Telephone: 302-239-4244
E-mail: jfrett@mtcubacenter.org
Hours: Prescheduled tours in spring and fall.
Admission: $5.
Dedicated to the study of Piedmont flora. Rural pastures, native forest, woodland wildflower gardens, and formal landscapes. Not wheelchair accessible.

Peter Spencer Heritage Hallway Museum
Mother African Union FCMP Church
812 N. Franklin St.
Wilmington, DE 19806
Telephone: 302-658-3838

Interactive living-history museum of African-Americans in Delaware and the United States. Emphasizes the Underground Railroad and the journey toward freedom. Call for reservations.

Wilmington Library
Tenth and Market Streets
Wilmington, DE 19801
Telephone: 302-571-7408
Wheelchair accessible. Eighteen original N. C. Wyeth paintings done for *Robinson Crusoe*.

Wilmington Riverfront/Christina Riverfront
800 S. Madison St.
Wilmington, DE 19801
Telephone: 302-425-4890
Ample parking available in lots near Tubman-Garrett Riverfront Park, the Riverfront Market, and Shipyard Shops. A series of twenty-one colorful panels traces the history of Wilmington along the banks of the Christina River. Start at Tubman-Garrett Riverfront Park. The Riverfront Market (302-425-4454) is open Tuesday through Friday, 9 A.M. to 6 P.M.; Saturday, 9 A.M. to 6 P.M. Market not wheelchair accessible.

Wilmington Savings Fund Society
838 Market St.
Wilmington, DE 19801
Telephone: 302-792-6000 or 888-WSFSBANK
Website: www.wsfsbank.com
An example of Greek Revival architecture, this 1920 building is on the National Register of Historic Places. Houses N. C. Wyeth's monumental mural *The Apotheosis of the Family*. Wheelchair accessible.

ART, ANTIQUES, AND SELECTIVE SHOPPING

Good shopping opportunities abound in Wilmington and Northern Delaware. Centreville and Greenville boast a wide selection of galleries, antique stores, specialty shops, and restaurants, as does the Trolley Square area. Outlet stores are located at the Wilmington Riverfront. You'll find shopping centers up and down U.S. Route 202, including Concord Mall at the intersection with DE Route 92. A fringe benefit to shopping in Delaware: no sales tax!

Art on the Town is held every first Friday of the month except January, July, and August. To find out which galleries are on the loop, consult the website www.ci.wilmington.de.us.

Somerville Manning Gallery

An art gallery's success is based on relationships—between owners and artists, owners and clients, and gallery staff. The Somerville Manning Gallery is a stellar example of what can be achieved when good relationships are created and developed. Since 1981, Sadie Somerville and Victoria Manning have used their knowledge and integrity to cultivate long-term associations with artists and collectors, and to create a harmonious, welcoming environment. As a result, their gallery is *the* place for high-end art of the Brandywine tradition and twentieth-century American realism.

Breck's Mill along the Brandywine, where the Somerville Manning Gallery is located, has plenty of charm with its wooden floors and crisp white interior walls. The stone building, listed on the National Register of Historic Places, was built in 1814 as a textile mill. It was purchased in 1852 by the Du Pont Company, whose black powder manufactory was next door at Hagley. Cotton and wool fabric were made here until 1880. After that, the building became a community center for arts, recreation, education, and entertainment. This continued after Mary A. B. du Pont Laird acquired the building in 1922. During her ownership, musical and theater groups used the mill. In 1970, Mary's son W. W. "Chick" Laird donated the building to Hagley Museum, which used the facility primarily for office space.

"Finding this place was like a blessing from heaven," says Manning. "Hagley Museum heard we were planning to move from the shopping center in Greenville, where we had been for eleven years. They didn't want to use this building for offices anymore, so the timing was right.

"Hagley gave us carte blanche in designing the inside. After being in our previous space for so long, we knew what we didn't want. Our goal was to make things more accessible and efficient." Manning and Somerville hired a space planner to arrange the 1,850 square feet before relocating here in 1993.

The resulting floor plan is clean and free-flowing. There's a good balance between windows, which permit views of the Brandywine, and solid wall space for artwork, plus ample floor space for sculpture. Twelve rolling storage racks allow a large inventory to be kept on hand.

Somerville and Manning both have art education backgrounds. The business partners met in a fiber-arts class. When they were planning their venture, they set their sights high. "We were determined to open an art gallery, not a frame shop," Manning recalls. "What developed was an

(continued on page 210)

"The savage gave a yell and came bounding across the open ground flourishing a tomahawk." N. C. Wyeth illustrated these words from James Fennimore Cooper's *The Deerslayer*. Some of Wyeth's works are represented by the Somerville Manning Gallery. *The Deerslayer,* 1927, oil on canvas, forty inches by thirty-two inches. SOMERVILLE MANNING GALLERY

(continued from page 209)

adaption of our own visions and a recognition of where we are. For us, this meant that we needed to stay primarily in a realism tradition. Along with historically significant art, we present the best of regional artists. We also bring works from artists of national and international stature here to Wilmington."

In appreciation of the Brandywine Valley's rich heritage in illustration, the gallery has mounted exhibits in that genre and has handled pieces by Howard Pyle and other artists from his Brandywine School. One show was "Howard Pyle and His Students," then the lineage continued to Frank Schoonover and Gayle Hoskins, and to Pyle's most famous student, the late N. C. Wyeth.

Interestingly, the exhibit of Wyeth's art was motivated by one of Somerville Manning's collectors who was interested in purchasing one of his works. The Wyeth extended-family connection has grown to include art by Andrew Wyeth, Carolyn Wyeth, Jamie Wyeth, John McCoy, Anne Wyeth McCoy, and Anna B. McCoy.

The trust that Somerville and Manning have gained from their artists and collectors, combined with their interest in learning and in educating people, has enabled them to introduce new artists and styles to the Brandywine Valley. They present contemporary art—as long as it meets their standards for high quality—including sculpture and jewelry, as well as paintings and other works on paper. Artists like Peter Sculthorpe, J. Clayton Bright, Greg Mort, Donald Pywell, and others regularly exhibit at Somerville Manning.

"Art has unlimited potential for growth and change," says Manning. "The last few years we've gotten into nineteenth-century marine painting. That's the exciting part: Sometimes it's us finding something, discovering something. We also enjoy promoting living artists. A lot of people we represent have been trained at the Pennsylvania Academy of the Fine Arts. It's gratifying to mount a show you believe in and have people respond to that."

Adds Sadie Somerville, "It's so fulfilling to build a collection for someone; to find someone who's excited about what you're excited about. The part of this job I like best is having the relationships with artists and customers, and making the connection between them."

VISITING SOMERVILLE MANNING GALLERY

Breck's Mill, Second Floor, 101 Stone Block Row
Greenville, DE 19807 • Telephone: 302-652-0271
Fax: 302-652-1946 • Website: www.somervillemanning.com

Hours: Monday through Saturday, 10 A.M. to 5 P.M.

Sculptor André Harvey has a studio on the floor above the Somerville Manning Gallery. Harvey's bronze sculptures, including many animals, and gold sculptural jewelry are displayed. If possible, set aside time to visit both galleries in Breck's Mill. Somerville Manning has a wheelchair lift. Contact the gallery for details.

CALENDAR OF EVENTS

Somerville Manning Gallery hosts regular openings and exhibitions. Contact the gallery for details.

Spring and Fall: Somerville Manning Gallery participates in Art on the Town, Wilmington's open house for the arts on the first Friday of certain months.

André Harvey Studio
Breck's Mill
101 Stone Block Row, top floor
Greenville, DE 19807-3038
Telephone: 302-656-7955
Fax: 302-656-7974
E-mail: info@andreharvey.com
Website: www.andreharvey.com
Hours: Monday through Saturday, 10 A.M.
  to 4:30 P.M. or by appointment.
More than forty bronze sculptures of animals
and people, and 18K gold sculptural jewelry.
Not wheelchair accessible.

Barbara's Antiques & Books
5900 Kennett Pike
Centreville, DE 19807
Telephone: 302-655-3055
Hours: Monday through Saturday, 10 A.M. to
  5 P.M., but call first.
Collectible out-of-print books, regional items,
children's art, antiques, postcards, ephemera,
photographica, small antiques. Wheelchair
accessible inside, but there are two steps at
the entrance.

Blue Streak Gallery
1721 N. Delaware Ave.
Wilmington, DE 19806
Telephone: 302-429-0506
Website: www.bluestreakgallery.com
Hours: Monday through Friday, 10 A.M. to
  5 P.M.; Saturday, 10 A.M. to 4 P.M.
Contemporary crafts with a twist. Trolley
Square area. Not wheelchair accessible.

Carspecken-Scott
1707 N. Lincoln St.
Wilmington, DE 19806
Telephone: 302-655-7173
Fax: 302-655-8971
E-mail: carspeckenscott@aol.com
Hours: Monday through Friday, 9 A.M. to
  5:30 P.M.; Saturday, 10 A.M. to 3 P.M. Trolley
  Square area. Wheelchair accessible.

Delaware College of Art & Design (DCAD)
600 N. Market St.
Wilmington, DE 19801
Telephone: 302-622-8000
Fax: 302-622-8870

E-mail: ahill@dcad.edu
Website: www.dcad.edu
Hours: Variable, depending on whether school
  is in session. Wheelchair accessible.

Hardcastle Gallery
Frederick's Country Center
5714 Kennett Pike
Centreville, DE 19807
Telephone: 302-655-5230
Website: www.hardcastlegallery.com
Hours: Monday through Friday, 10 A.M. to
  6 P.M.; Saturday, 10 A.M. to 4 P.M.
Original artwork from scores of local and
regional artists. Wheelchair accessible.

Mezzanine Gallery
Delaware Division of the Arts
820 N. French St., Carvel State Office Bldg.
Wilmington, DE 19801
Telephone: 302-577-8278
Fax: 302-577-6561
Website: www.artsdel.org
Hours: Monday through Friday, 8 A.M. to
  4:30 P.M. Wheelchair accessible.

My Thai: Made in Thailand
21A Trolley Square
Wilmington, DE 19806
Telephone: 302-428-1040
Website: www.picturetrail.com/mythai
Hours: Monday through Friday, 10 A.M. to
  7 P.M.; Saturday, 10 A.M. to 6 P.M.
Hand-woven silks, accessories, jewelry, crafts,
and gifts from Thailand. Trolley Square area.
Wheelchair accessible.

Ronald C. Bauman, Inc.
5722 Kennett Pike
Centreville, DE 19807
Telephone: 302-655-4466
Hours: Tuesday through Saturday, 10 A.M. to
  5 P.M., but call first. Closed Saturdays in July
  and August.
High-end items of the Queen Anne, Chip-
pendale, Federal, and Empire periods (circa
1740–1860). Also offers Chinese export, Eng-
lish and Dutch Delft accessories, and clocks.
Located in the circa 1817–20 Historic
Delaplaine House. Not wheelchair accessible.
Strollers not permitted.

Peter Sculthorpe: Capturing a Mood

Peter Sculthorpe's watercolors are perfect examples of art imitating life. A Peter Sculthorpe watercolor of a winter sunset in the Brandywine Valley, with the saturated pinks and purples of the sky, the exquisitely sharp silhouettes of bare trees, and the welcoming warmth of a not-too-distant fieldstone farmhouse, has as much impact as the real thing. Such is the beauty of the place, and such is the skill of the artist.

Born in Canada in 1948, Sculthorpe received early training from an artist uncle before the family relocated to Pennsylvania in 1962. He showed so much artistic promise during high school that local watercolorist Philip Jamison gave him a college scholarship.

After attending Hussian School of Art in Philadelphia, Sculthorpe took classes at the city's Pennsylvania Academy of Fine Arts but dropped out after a favorite professor retired. "I started out on my own, from my bedroom," he says. Sculthorpe opened a West Chester studio in 1969 and held his first show the following year. Now he has a dedicated following of collectors and has exhibited at galleries and museums countrywide.

Sculthorpe's work celebrates the Brandywine Valley's connection to the past. "There's a huge history here," he says. "That's a validating feature, when it comes to what the landscape has given to artists. Early American domestic architecture has been important in my work. More than any other area in the country, this has it."

The artist chooses his subjects more by osmosis than by picking a specific theme. "There's a subconscious gestation period of seeing subject matter and having the brain digest it," he explains. "A lot of times I build an image of a mood or a source of light."

The watercolor work is a slow process. "I'm not a very spontaneous watercolorist," the artist says. "I use an old English method of cross-hatching the color as

Peter Sculthorpe's *East Coventry Farm* captures the essence of the Brandywine Valley; the winter sky is particularly evocative. Belted Galloway cattle are nicknamed "Oreo cows" for their black-white-black coloring. Watercolor on rag panel, fifteen inches by thirty inches.
PETER SCULTHORPE

an overlay." This meticulous technique gives Sculthorpe's watercolors the complex textures and colors for which they are known.

Size is another hallmark of Sculthorpe's paintings. He started out at forty by sixty inches but "just had the need to go bigger," he says. "I probably did several dozen paintings in monumental image, four feet high by eight feet long. The textures I was working with needed some room to really happen."

Sculthorpe is also adept in oils and has painted powerful scenes of Maine and Newfoundland. But it's the poignancy of the Brandywine Valley watercolors that have captured the hearts of Sculthorpe fans far and wide. It's obvious that the artist loves the area, and people respond to that passion.

"I haven't regretted a minute of it," says Sculthorpe, who still seems slightly astonished at his own success. "I feel very honored that I can leave something behind me. All I want to be remembered as is an American landscape painter of note."

He needn't worry. With every sunset, the name Peter Sculthorpe will spring to mind.

Contact Peter Sculthorpe through the Somerville Manning Gallery, 302-652-0271, or visit www.somervillemanning.com.

Shipyard Shops
(factory outlets along Christina Riverfront)
900 S. Madison St.
Wilmington, DE 19801
Telephone: 302-425-5000
Website: www.shipyardshopsoutlets.com
Hours: January through April, Monday through Thursday, 10 A.M. to 6 P.M.; Friday and Saturday, 10 A.M. to 9 P.M.; Sunday, 11 A.M. to 5 P.M. May through December, Monday through Saturday, 10 A.M. to 9 P.M.; Sunday, 11 A.M. to 5 P.M. Holiday hours Christmas Eve, New Year's Eve, Memorial Day, July Fourth, and Labor Day, 11 A.M. to 5 P.M. Closed New Year's Day, Easter, Thanksgiving, and Christmas.
Shops: Big Dogs, Blair Catalog Outlet, Bon Worth, Claire's, Coldwater Creek, Dress Barn/Dress Barn Woman, Factory Brand Shoes, L. L. Bean Factory Store, L'eggs/Hanes/Bali/Playtex, Lillian Vernon, Nautica, Totes/Isotoner/Sunglass World, Twenty/20, VF Factory Outlet, Westpoint Stevens.
Food: Molly's Old Fashioned Ice Cream and Deli (302-984-2773) and Timothy's Riverfront Restaurant (302-429-7427).

The Station Gallery
3922 Kennett Pike
Greenville, DE 19807

Telephone: 302-654-8638
Fax: 302-654-8973
Hours: Monday through Friday, 9 A.M. to 5 P.M.; Saturday, 10 A.M. to 3 P.M. Wheelchair accessible; threshold is about 1.5 inches high.

Twice Nice Antiques & Collectibles
5714 Kennett Pike (Delaware Route 52)
Frederick's Country Center
Centreville, DE 19807
Telephone: 302-656-8881
Hours: Monday through Friday, 10 A.M. to 4:30 P.M.; Saturday, 10 A.M. to 5 P.M.
Hand-refinished preowned furniture, antiques, and accessories. Entrance is wheelchair accessible, but negotiating the aisles might be difficult.

Windle's Fine Antiques
5714 Kennett Pike (second floor)
Frederick's Country Center
Centreville, DE 19807
Telephone: 302-651-9222
Hours: Monday through Saturday, noon to 4:30 P.M.; Sunday, 1 to 3:30 or 4 P.M.
Pre-1830s country painted and formal period furniture and accessories. Largest area selection of antique quilts and Shaker items, fine jewelry, and documented antique northern decoys. Wheelchair accessible.

PERFORMING ARTS

Academy of the Dance
209 W. Fourteenth St.
Wilmington, DE 19801
Telephone: 302-656-8969
Website: www.academyofthedance.net
Professional training school of classical ballet presents performances at the DuPont Theatre in the historic Hotel du Pont. Performances feature international professional dancers and a live orchestra. Wheelchair accessible.

Baby Grand
818 N. Market St.
Wilmington, DE 19801
Telephone: 800-374-7263
Website: www.grandopera.org
Intimate 300-seat venue for chamber music and other entertainment. Affiliated with the Grand Opera House.

Best of Broadway Dinner Theater at the Bank One Center on the Riverfront
800 S. Madison St.
Wilmington, DE 19801
Telephone: 302-478-6178 or 877-313-4411
Website: www.de-bestofbroadway.com
Intimate 280-seat musical dinner theater. Tables of ten. Live music and dance before and during the show. Friday and Saturday, curtain at 8 P.M.; Thursday and Sunday matinees, curtain at 2 P.M. Doors open two hours before curtain. Wheelchair accessible.

Brandywine Baroque
P.O. Box 730
Wilmington, DE 19801
Telephone: 302-594-4544
Fax: 302-594-4938
Website: www.brandywinebaroque.org
Delaware's award-winning early music ensemble and orchestra is known for its energetic performances using period instruments. Performances at Christ Church in Greenville and other venues. Wheelchair accessible.

The Brandywiners Ltd.
P.O. Box 248
Montchanin, DE 19710
Telephone: 302-478-3355 or 800-338-6965
Website: www.brandywiners.org
Presents high-quality musical productions at various venues throughout the Delaware Valley, including Longwood Gardens. Check with specific venue for wheelchair access. Longwood is wheelchair accessible.

Candlelight Music Dinner Theatre
2208 Millers Rd.
Ardentown, DE 19810
Telephone: 302-475-2313
Fax: 302-475-2320
Website: www.candlelightdinnertheatre.com
Fine dining and superb musical theater entertainment at Delaware's first dinner theater. Reservations at $32 include buffet and performance. Thursday through Sunday. Wheelchair accessible.

Delaware Symphony Orchestra
818 N. Market St.
Wilmington, DE 19801
Telephone: 302-652-5577 or 800-37-GRAND
Website: www.desymphony.org
Delaware's premier orchestra performs in the Grand Opera House from September through May. Wheelchair accessible.

Delaware Theatre Company
200 Water St.
Wilmington, DE 19801
Telephone: 302-594-1100
E-mail: tickets@delawaretheatre.org
Website: www.delawaretheatre.org
Located on the Wilmington Riverfront. The Brandywine Valley's only resident professional theater company's five-play season presents classic and contemporary works and brings noted professional actors, directors, and designers to the region. DTC is wheelchair accessible. Large-print programs are available on request. The theater is equipped with an infrared listening system. Sign language interpretation is offered for selected performances.

DuPont Theatre
DuPont Building
Tenth and Market Streets
Wilmington, DE 19801
Telephone: 302-656-4401 or 800-338-0881
Fax: 302-594-1437

Website: www.duponttheatre.com
In continuous operation sine 1913. Six-show
season and children's series. Group, senior,
and student rates. Listening devices available.
Wheelchair accessible.

First State Ballet Theatre
641 W. Newport Pike
Wilmington, DE 19804
Telephone: 302-636-1577
Website: www.FirstStateBallet.com
Provides performing opportunities for aspiring
dancers and presents professional-quality
dance to audiences throughout the state. Contact the Ballet Theatre for schedule. Wheelchair accessible.

The Grand Opera House
818 N. Market St.
Wilmington, DE 19801
Telephone: 302-652-5577 or 800-37-GRAND
Website: www.grandopera.org
Restored 1871 opera house hosts a variety
of programs. Wheelchair accessible.

OperaDelaware
818 N. Market St.
Wilmington, DE 19801
Telephone: 302-658-8063
Fax: 302-658-4991
Website: www.operade.org
Nationally recognized company presents pro-
fessional opera at its best. Productions in the
Grand Opera House with full orchestra. Family
opera theater, lectures, and opera dinners.
Wheelchair accessible.

Theatre N at Nemours
Entrance at 11th and Tatnall Streets
Parking garage on 11th Street between West
  and Tatnall
Wilmington, DE 19801
Telephone: 302-658-6070

The beautiful ceiling in Wilmington's Grand Opera
House draws the eye upward before actors and
musicians take their places on stage. GREATER WILM-
INGTON CONVENTION AND VISITORS BUREAU

Website: www.theatreN.org
Art-house and foreign movies. Wheelchair
accessible.

Three Little Bakers Dinner Theatre
3540 Three Little Bakers Blvd.
Pike Creek Valley
Wilmington, DE 19808
Telephone: 302-368-1616 or 800-368-3303
Fax: 302-452-2535
Website: www.tlbinc.com
See listing in Food section of this chapter.

Wilmington Drama League
10 W. Lea Blvd.
Wilmington, DE 19802
Telephone: 302-764-1172
Website: www.wdl.org
Community theatre presents a wide variety
of plays and musicals.

RECREATION AND LEISURE

Bicycling

Alan's Bicycles
4723 Concord Pike
Wilmington, DE 19803
Telephone: 302-478-0990

Sells bicycles and related equipment. Has
brochures on local clubs, trails, and events.
If you're new to the area, this is a good place
to get advice about road and mountain biking.

Brandywine Creek State Park

Adams Dam Road just east of the intersection
   of DE Routes 92 and 100
Greenville, DE 19807
Telephone: 302-577-3534
   (nature center 302-655-5740)
Website: www.destateparks.com
The Creek Run Trail is open for bicycling.

Delaware Tourism Office

99 Kings Highway
P.O. Box 1401
Dover, DE 19903
Telephone: 800-441-8846
Free maps.

White Clay Bicycle Club

Website: www.whiteclaybicycleclub.org.
Information about road and mountain biking.

Canoeing, Kayaking, and Tubing

Brandywine Creek State Park

Adams Dam Road just east of the intersection
   of DE Routes 92 and 100
Greenville, DE 19807
Telephone: 302-577-3534
   (nature center 302-655-5740)
Website: www.destateparks.com
Visitors with their own boats should use the
parking area near Thompson's Bridge (on DE
Route 92). Canoeing is also offered through the
park's interpretive programs for $14 per person.

Wilderness Canoe Trips

Fairfax Shopping Center
(Mailing address: P.O. Box 7125)
On U.S. Route 202 just north of DE Route 141
Wilmington, DE 19803
Telephone: 302-654-2227 or 800-494-CANOE
Fax: 302-654-1711
E-mail: wildernesscanoe@aol.com
www.wildernesscanoetrips.com
Store hours: Summer, 9 A.M. to 5 P.M.; winter,
   10 A.M. to 4 P.M.
Trips: Family canoe, kayak, and tubing trips on
   the Brandywine depart from the shop behind
   Bennigan's restaurant in Fairfax Shopping
   Center. Paddlers watch a safety video before
   getting outfitted and transported to the put-
   in spot. Canoe or kayak: Two- or four-hour
   trips. Four-hour trips depart from the shop
   at 9:30 or 10:30 A.M. and put in at Brandy-

wine Picnic Park. Two-hour trips depart from
   the shop at 1 or 2 P.M. and put in near the
   Brandywine River Museum. Tubing: Two-
   hour trips depart from the shop at noon
   or 2 P.M. and put in at Smith's Bridge.
Prices: Per tube or per boat, from $12 for a
   single tube for two hours to $51 for a canoe
   for four hours.
Other: Reservations strongly recommended.
   Arrive at the shop a half hour before departure time. Wilderness Canoe Trips can haul
   your privately owned canoe or kayak to any
   of their access points and return for $25.

Fishing

Brandywine Creek State Park

Adams Dam Road just east of the intersection
   of DE Routes 92 and 100
Greenville, DE 19807
Telephone: 302-577-3534
   (nature center 302-655-5740)
Website: www.destateparks.com
Anglers can fish for smallmouth bass, bluegill,
and crappie in Brandywine Creek and for trout
in Wilson's Run. A fishing license and trout
stamp are required. These can be purchased
at the park office.

Golf

Delcastle Golf Club

801 McKennan's Church Rd.
Wilmington, DE 19808
Telephone: 302-995-1990
Website: www.delcastlegolfclub.com
A par-seventy-two championship course with
rolling hills, wide fairways, and large bend
greens, designed by Ed Ault. Reserved starting
times. Walk-on golfers and golf outings welcome.

Ed Oliver Golf Club

800 N. DuPont Rd.
Wilmington, DE 19807
Telephone: 302-571-9041
Website: www.edolivergolfclub.com
Par sixty-nine, beautifully landscaped,
tree-lined fairways.

Rock Manor Golf Club

1319 Carruthers Ln.
Wilmington, DE 19803
Telephone: 302-652-4083

Fax: 302-652-7059
Eighteen-hole course with small, well-bunkered greens and tree-lined back nine.

Three Little Bakers Country Club
3540 Foxcroft Dr.
Wilmington, DE 19808
Telephone: 302-737-1877 (pro shop)
Website: www.TLBINC.com
Eighteen-hole, par-seventy-one, semiprivate golf course. Features all bent grass on tees, greens, and fairways.

Hiking

Alapocas Woods Natural Area
Alapocas Drive off DE Route 141, about .5
    mile west of U.S. Route 202
Website: www.destateparks.com
Located along the Brandywine River, Alapocas Woods is an oasis at the edge of Wilmington. It's a forested retreat, home to native plants and abundant wildlife. Situated between the piedmont and coastal plain zones, the park has spectacular geological formations.

Ashland Nature Center
Brackenville and Barley Mill Roads
Hockessin, DE 19707
Telephone: 302-239-2334
Fax: 302-239-2473
Website: www.delawarenaturesociety.org
Hours: Monday through Friday, 8:30 A.M. to
    4:30 P.M.; Saturday, 9 A.M. to 3 P.M.; Sunday
    1 to 4 P.M.
Four self-guiding nature trails on two hundred acres of meadow, marsh, pond, and forest, plus habitat exhibits. Seasonal butterfly house.

Brandywine Creek State Park
Adams Dam Road just east of the intersection
    of DE Routes 92 and 100
Greenville, DE 19807
Telephone: 302-577-3534
    (nature center 302-655-5740)
Website: www.destateparks.com
This 933-acre park with fourteen miles of trails is divided by gray stone walls built of local stone by Italian masons in the late 1800s, when it was a dairy farm owned by the du Pont family. The Creek Run Trail is open for bicycling. Other activities include canoeing, fishing, interpretive programs at the Brandywine

Creek Nature Center, and sledding and cross-country skiing in winter.

Brandywine Park
1001 N. Park Dr.
Wilmington, DE 19802
Telephone: 302-577-7020
Website: www.destateparks.com
This picturesque park is in the heart of Wilmington State Parks and runs along both sides of the Brandywine River. For visually impaired visitors, a Sensory Trail is available.

Rockford Park and Rockford Tower
1021 W. 8th St.
Wilmington, DE 19802
Telephone: 302-577-7020
Website: www.destateparks.com
Hours: Park hours 8 A.M. to sunset year-round.
    Hours for observation deck near top of
    tower: May 1 through October 31, Saturday
    and Sunday, 10 A.M. to 4 P.M.
The centerpiece of this park is historic Rockford Tower, a century-old water tower. Surrounded by large, open spaces, this is a good place for hiking and jogging.

Rockwood Park
Just south of Shipley Road on Washington
    Street Extension
Telephone: 302-761-4340
Website: www.rockwood.org
Hours: Sunrise to 10 P.M.
Has a 1.2-mile trail and many shorter trails. On the grounds of Rockwood Mansion.

Wilmington Trail Club
Website: www.wilmingtontrailclub.org
Weekly and special events.

Valley Green Park
Centreville Rd. at DE Route 82 (Campbell Rd.)
Telephone: 302-576-3810
Streamside trail.

Ice Skating

Skating Club of Wilmington
1301 Carruthers Lane, off Foulk Road near
    U.S. Route 202
Wilmington, DE 19803-4601
Telephone: 302-656-5005
Fax: 302-658-8889
Website: www.wilmicesk8.com

Observatory

Mt. Cuba Astronomical Observatory
Off Hillside Mill Road
Greenville, DE 19806
Telephone: 302-654-6407
Website: www.physics.udel.edu/MCAO/
Occasional public programs. Admission fee.
Reservations required. Age restrictions apply.

Playgrounds

Brandywine Park
1001 N. Park Dr.
Wilmington, DE 19802
Telephone: 302-577-7020
Website: www.destateparks.com

Talley-Day Park
1300 Foulk Rd., just north of Shipley Rd.
Wilmington, DE 19803
Playground, tennis courts, basketball courts,
walking paths, and picnic pavillion.

River Tours/Taxi

Christina River Boat Company, Inc.
P.O. Box 2061
Wilmington, DE 19899
Telephone: 302-984-2722
Fax: 302-984-0107
A riverfront boat service providing taxi service,
history tours, murder mystery dinners, charter
rentals, and entertainment.

There's no better place for baseball on a fine
summer evening than Frawley Stadium in Wilmington, home of the Single-A minor-league
Wilmington Blue Rocks. Watch out for antlers:
the mascot is Rocky Bluewinkle, a big blue
moose. WILMINGTON BLUE ROCKS

Spectator Sports

Delaware Smash
1007 Market St., D-1083
Wilmington, DE 19898
Telephone: 302-774-4238
Fax: 302-774-4240
Website: www.delawaresmash.com
Billie Jean King's World Team Tennis profes-
sional team plays teams from across the coun-
try at the DuPont Country Club in July.

McDonald's LPGA Championship
DuPont Country Club
P.O. Box 394
Rockland, DE 19372
Telephone: 302-428-1681 or 877-776-5742
Fax: 302-428-1007
Website: www.mcdslpgachampionship.com
One of four majors on the LPGA Tour; attracts
top international women golfers.

Wilmington Blue Rocks Baseball Club
Frawley Stadium
801 S. Madison St.
Wilmington, DE 19803
Telephone: 302-888-2583
Fax: 302-888-2032
Website: www.bluerocks.com
Professional minor-league baseball club affili-
ated with the Kansas City Royals. Single-A
Carolina league. Season runs April through
September. Wheelchair accessible. Excellent
family fun, free parking. Mascot is a large blue
moose, Rocky Bluewinkle.

Tennis Courts

Brandywine Park
1001 N. Park Dr.
Wilmington, DE 19802
Telephone: 302-577-7020
Website: www.destateparks.com

Rockford Park
Park Drive off Riverview Avenue near DE
  Route 52
Wilmington, DE 19806
Telephone: 302-577-7020
Website: www.destateparks.com

Talley-Day Park
1300 Foulk Rd., just north of Shipley Road
Wilmington, DE 19803

Train Excursions

Wilmington & Western Railroad
Greenbank Station off DE Route 41, one block
   north of Kirkwood Highway
1601 Railroad Avenue
(Mailing address: P.O. Box 5787)
Wilmington, DE 19808
Telephone: 302-998-1930
Fax: 302-998-7408
E-mail: schedule@wwrr.com
Website: www.wwrr.com
Steam-diesel-powered train tours through the
scenic Red Clay Valley. *Note:* Railroad was
damaged during severe storms in September
2003. Call first to verify that trains are running.

All aboard! The Wilmington & Western Railroad
steam train takes riders through Red Clay Valley.
GREATER WILMINGTON CONVENTION AND VISITORS BUREAU

ACCOMMODATIONS

Hotel du Pont

The Hotel du Pont inspires an abundance of adjectives. Breathtaking, historic, romantic, exceptional–take your pick, all of these terms are appropriate for Delaware's premier hotel. Savvy travelers have one additional way to describe this landmark property: They call it a bargain. The Hotel du Pont offers the luxury, appointments, and service you'd expect at a top establishment in New York or Washington, D.C., at about a third of the price.

Pierre S. du Pont, founder of Longwood Gardens, wanted to bring a little prestige to Wilmington, so he commissioned a twelve-story Italian Renaissance hotel. Eighteen French and Italian craftsmen labored for more than two years carving, gilding, inlaying, and painting the hotel before it opened in 1913. It was immediately proclaimed a rival to the finest European hotels. Since its inception, the Hotel du Pont has been owned and operated by DuPont.

The hotel proved to be a magnet for the rich and famous. Charles Lindbergh, Ingrid Bergman, Eleanor Roosevelt, and Joe DiMaggio are just some of the many luminaries who have stayed here. They must have enjoyed the ornate Gold Ballroom. The 4,295-square-foot room was built in 1918 and has a vaulted 27-foot ceiling. Classical scenes done in the rare sgraffito technique adorn the walls. This art form involves applying layers of plaster in different hues, then carving them to varying depths to expose the color. Inspired by the French Louis XVI style, the murals in the Ballroom extend almost from floor to ceiling.

Bas-relief medallions of twenty famous women in history–from the queen of Sheba to Helen of Troy to Pocahontas–encircle the French Neoclassical ceiling. Two huge chandeliers, large mirrors, and gold draperies add to the room's elegance. Today the Ballroom hosts functions for two hundred to five hundred people. If you're not lucky enough to be invited to an event there, ask the concierge whether you can sneak a peek.

Guest rooms and suites at the Hotel du Pont are luxuriously appointed and meticulously maintained. Furniture and flower arrangements create the feel of a fine home. HOTEL DU PONT

All of the hotel's 206 guest rooms and 11 suites, plus most of the public areas, were renovated in 1992 at a cost of $40 million. The spectacular results earned the Hotel du Pont the coveted International Gold Key Award for design. Management can proudly display this prize next to the many others the hotel has won: AAA Four Diamond Award, Mobil Four Star Award, and a spot on *Condé Nast Traveler*'s Gold List, to name a few. The Hotel du Pont is a member of Preferred Hotels & Resorts Worldwide and Historic Hotels of America.

Guest rooms range from about 550 to 650 square feet, with suites a spacious 1,200 square feet. No matter what room type you choose, you'll find the comforts of a fine residence, from the Queen Anne and Chippendale furnishings to the doorbell. All rooms have two incoming phone lines (voice mail in three languages), robes and slippers, servi-bar, color television, large leather-inlaid desk, an iron and ironing board, a safe, and a makeup mirror. Oversize bathrooms include a deep soaking tub and separate shower.

Suites are located in the hotel's corners. The additional space is ample for a powder room, plus a dining area with full-size dining/conference table. The bedroom area and bath can be closed off with a key so the private area of the suite stays that way, a feature especially valued by business travelers who may meet with colleagues in the evening. Marble-floored bathrooms have Jacuzzi, shower, and separate area for toilet and bidet. Everything is maintained impeccably.

The hotel's amenities include twenty-four-hour room service, afternoon tea served in the lobby lounge, a breakfast-type café, and a fine restaurant (see the Food section of this chapter). A shopping arcade is on the lower level.

Another mark of distinction is the Hotel du Pont's magnificent art collection, which is displayed throughout the building. More than seven hundred original works by N. C. Wyeth, Andrew Wyeth, Jamie Wyeth, Frank Schoonover, John McCoy, and other Brandywine Valley painters make the hotel's collection more impressive than what you'd find at many museums. To continue this support of the arts, the hotel showcases one new painting by a local artist each week and offers it for sale.

Not many hotels can boast of having an on-site theater, but the Hotel du Pont has one: the DuPont Theatre, a 1,252-seat venue that features Broadway touring shows as well as a children's theater season, lectures, and corporate and nonprofit functions. The splendor and intimacy are reminiscent of theaters in the heyday of American drama.

Its history, appointments, service, food, proximity to Brandywine Valley attractions, and money-saving getaway packages all add up to make the Hotel du Pont a special place to stay.

Visiting Hotel du Pont

Eleventh and Market Streets, Wilmington, DE 19801
Telephone: 302-594-3100 or 800-441-9019
Fax: 302-594-3108 • Website: www.hoteldupont.com
Rooms: 217 rooms, 18 with two double beds, the rest with king-size beds; all have a separate soaking tub and shower. There also are 9 one-bedroom suites and 2 two-bedroom suites.
Rates: Rooms $159 to $319; suites $450 to $650. Contact the hotel or consult the website for details on packages.
Credit cards: Visa, MasterCard, American Express, Discover, and Diner's Club.
Personal checks: Not accepted.
Check-in: 3 P.M.
Check-out: Noon.
Smoking policy: 80 percent of the rooms are designated nonsmoking. Smoking not permitted in public areas or restaurant.
Wheelchair accessible: Yes.
Children: Welcome. Cribs available. Babysitting can be arranged.
Pets: Pets that weigh less than thirty pounds are accepted with a $100 nonrefundable deposit.
Parking: Valet parking available. Several parking lots and garages across 11th Street. Overnight parking costs $14.
Other: Fitness club. Extensive meeting and banquet facilities. For banquet information and reservations, call 800-853-6378.

The Inn at Montchanin Village

Montchanin Village is reminiscent of Brigadoon, the fictional town in the Lerner and Loewe musical that reawakened for one day every hundred years; anyone lucky enough to fall under its spell would enter a long-ago world of beauty and fantasy.

The restored settlement at Montchanin Village is real, not mythical, but otherwise it's as magical as its invented counterpart. The *Mobil Travel Guide* four-star inn offers charming, luxurious accommodations in a countryside setting, where the buildings, pathways, and cottage gardens create a harmonious whole. Krazy Kat's restaurant, also rated four stars, is worth a trip in itself.

The settlement at the crossroads was begun in 1799 to house laborers from the nearby Du Pont powder mills. By 1859, the site had tenant houses, a blacksmith shop, and a school. The village's importance increased when the railroad came through. In 1889, a railroad station and a post office were established. This was also the year the village was named in honor of Anne Alexandrine de Montchanin, grandmother of Du Pont company founder Eleuthère Irénée du Pont.

By the 1950s, the structures were being rented out. Things remained pretty much stagnant for the next forty years. When the current owners, Missy and Dan Lickle, took over the property in 1991, they decided to do renovations and convert it to a country inn. Like many people who enter the innkeeping business, the couple thought it would take only a few months to spruce things up for guests. Five years later, the Lickles opened the Inn at Montchanin Village and Krazy Kat's restaurant.

It was worth the wait. The painstaking restorations and renovations are evident, as is the Lickles' creativity in adapting the existing structures for new uses. The inn is listed on the National Register of Historic Places and is a member of the Historic Hotels of America and Small Luxury Hotels of the World organizations.

The Inn at Montchanin Village has twenty-eight luxury rooms and suites in several buildings around the property. Your visit will begin in the Dilwyne Barn, an 1850 structure that now houses the reception area. Within seconds, you'll understand exactly what makes this place so special. Meticulous restoration maintains historical integrity. The decorating is luxurious and creative. Service and cleanliness are unimpeachable. And the inn has something that's all too rare at top-notch hotels: a sense of humor that starts with their cow and crow logo.

The bedroom of the du Pont Suite at the Inn at Montchanin Village has a wooden bed with coffered canopy. A separate seating area and kitchenette are part of the suite. THE INN AT MONTCHANIN VILLAGE

The Jefferson Suite at the Inn at Montchanin Village has a bathroom you could spend a whole weekend in. THE INN AT MONTCHANIN VILLAGE

The barn also houses the gathering room, where guests are welcome to read, play games, have something to drink, or get cozy near the huge fireplace. The furniture arrangement creates different conversation areas so the large space doesn't feel cavernous. A fitness center is another reason to spend some time in this building.

There's nothing cookie-cutter about the guest rooms here. Each has its own character; no two floor plans are identical. The decorating varies from room to room as well. Missy chose antique and reproduction furniture, sumptuous fabrics, and interesting accessories. One room has a massive mahogany bed; another boasts a whimsical bed with painted animals. Some rooms have gas fireplaces. One- and two-bedroom suites are available.

All the accommodations have the same service and amenities. No matter what the room size, each has extra seating; Frette linens; a minikitchen with coffeemaker, microwave, and Portmeirion china; and lots of books to read. There's even an umbrella by each door in case of inclement weather. Twice-a-day housekeeping service keeps everything immaculate.

The bathrooms are all different, too, with unique colors and styles of marble and stone and a variety of residential-grade cabinetry. Some bathrooms have a shower only, others have a soaking tub and a shower, but they're all marvelously equipped. From the lit makeup mirror to the signature line of toiletries to the heated towel bar to the fresh-cut flowers, luxury is the norm. There's also a scale in every bathroom, but nobody will force you to use it if you don't want to.

It's delightful to stroll around the grounds. The Inn at Montchanin Village has four thousand square feet of greenhouses and a staff of three horticulturists, so it's no surprise that the landscaping is exquisite. Plantings help define spaces and create private garden nooks. The scent of the flowers is heavenly in spring and summer as you walk past the picturesque stone structures along the cobblestone pedestrian path.

Visiting The Inn at Montchanin Village

Route 100 and Kirk Road, (Mailing address: P.O. Box 130)
Montchanin, DE 19710
Telephone: 302-888-2133 or 800-COWBIRD
Fax: 302-888-0389 • Website: www.montchanin.com
General manager: Blake Peery.
Rates: Rooms, $150 to $185; suites, $225 to $375.
Credit cards: MasterCard, Visa, American Express, Discover, and Diner's Club. A credit card is required for a stay at the property.
Personal checks: Accepted for advance deposits only.

Check-in: 3 P.M.
Check-out: 11 A.M.
Smoking policy: Nonsmoking.
Wheelchair accessible: No. The site has steep, uneven topography and cobblestone paths. Rooms are in separate buildings and often include interior and exterior stairs. The restaurant on-site, Krazy Kat's, is fully accessible.
Children: Well-mannered children are welcome.
Pets: No.
Food: See Krazy Kat's in the Food section of this chapter.
Other: Meeting space and equipment are available. Contact the inn for details.

Other Recommended Accommodations

Best Western Brandywine Valley Inn
1807 Concord Pike
Wilmington, DE 19803
Telephone: 302-656-9436 or 800-537-7772
Fax: 302-656-8564
Website: www.brandywineinn.com
Rooms: 96 guest rooms, all with microwave, refrigerator, television, iron and ironing board, and coffeemaker. Business Plus guest rooms have a queen bed, lounge chair with footrest, oversize desk with ergonomic seating, unlimited high-speed Internet access, separate telephone voice line with cordless phone, flat-screen stereo television, DVD player, and printer. Winterthur Chambers and suites are appointed with Winterthur reproduction furniture and fabrics.
Rates: Rooms range from $99 to $165; suites, from $129 to $385. Deluxe Continental breakfast included. Contact the hotel or consult the website for details on packages, some of which include admission to local attractions.
Credit cards: Visa, MasterCard, American Express, Discover, Diner's Club, Amoco Multi, Amoco Torch, and Carte Blanche.
Personal checks: Not accepted.
Check-in: 3 P.M.
Check-out: Noon.
Smoking policy: 88 percent of the guest rooms designated nonsmoking. Smoking not permitted in the hotel's public areas.
Wheelchair accessible: Yes.
Children: Under age twelve stay free with parents. Cribs available.
Pets: Allowed with some restrictions; prior arrangements necessary.

Food: No restaurant on site. Bennigan's Restaurant within walking distance. Dozens of restaurants nearby in both directions on U.S. Route 202.
Parking: Free on-site.
Other: Fitness center, outdoor pool, children's pool, and Jacuzzi. Shuttle service to local businesses. Video conference center.

Brandywine Suites Hotel
707 N. King St.
Wilmington, DE 19801
Telephone: 302-656-9300 or 800-756-0070
Fax: 302-656-2459
Website: www.brandywinesuites.com
Rooms: 49 two-room suites. King or queen rooms with sleeper sofa and computer hookups.
Rates: $79 to $169, including Continental breakfast.
Credit cards: Visa, MasterCard, American Express, Discover, and Diner's Club.
Personal checks: Accepted for advance deposits only; must clear before visit.
Check-in: 3 P.M. If rooms are ready, check-in can be earlier; call to verify.
Check-out: Noon.
Smoking policy: 39 suites designated nonsmoking; 10 suites on the fourth floor permit smoking. Smoking not permitted in hotel's public areas.
Wheelchair accessible: Yes.
Children: Ages twelve and under stay free in parents' room. Rollaway beds available for $15 per night. Cribs available.
Pets: No.

Food: The Brandywine Bistro serves lunch and dinner.

Parking: Garage parking across the street for $8.50 per day, which can be paid through the hotel bill.

Other: Two blocks from the Wilmington train station and bus station. One block from the Federal Courthouse. Meeting rooms and business center.

Courtyard by Marriott Wilmington/Brandywine

320 Rocky Run Parkway
Talleyville, DE 19803
Telephone: 302-477-9500 or 800-321-2211
Fax: 302-477-0929
Website: www.marriott.com

Rooms: 75 rooms and 3 suites. Standard rooms have king-size or double beds, two-line phone, speaker phone, data port, voice mail, cable/satellite television, in-room movies, hair dryer, iron and ironing board, in-room coffee service.

Rates: Standard rooms, $89 to $144; suites $164. Contact the hotel or consult the website for details on packages.

Credit cards: Visa, MasterCard, American Express, Discover, and Diner's Club.

Personal checks: Accepted with proper identification.

Check-in: 3 P.M.

Check-out: Noon.

Smoking policy: 6 rooms designated smoking, all in one area of the hotel. Smoking prohibited in hotel's public areas.

Wheelchair accessible: Yes. One room has roll-in shower.

Children: Stay free with parents. Portable cribs available.

Pets: No.

Food: Breakfast served only, not included in room rate. Several restaurants within walking distance, and dozens of others close by in both directions along U.S. Route 202.

Parking: Free on-site.

Other: Indoor pool. Printer and fax available. Self-service laundry facilities. Free coffee in lobby. Meeting rooms for up to twenty-five.

Courtyard by Marriott Wilmington/Downtown

1102 West St.
Wilmington, DE 19801
Telephone: 302-429-7600 or 888-LODGING
Fax: 302-429-9167
Website: www.marriott.com/courtyard/ilgcy/

Rooms: 125 rooms. Jacuzzi rooms available.

Rates: Fluctuate, but average $74 to $149. Contact the hotel or consult the website for details on packages.

Credit cards: Visa, MasterCard, American Express, Discover, and Diner's Club.

Personal checks: Accepted with proper identification.

Check-in: 3 P.M.

Check-out: Noon.

Smoking policy: Smoking and nonsmoking rooms available.

Wheelchair accessible: Yes.

Children: Under 17 stay free with parents. Rollaway beds and cribs available at no charge.

Pets: No.

Food: Courtyard Cafe serves breakfast, not included in room rate. Cocktail lounge open Monday through Thursday, 4:30 to 10:30 P.M.; Friday through Sunday, 5 to 10 P.M. Many restaurants nearby in downtown Wilmington.

Parking: Across West Street, $8.50 per day (free overnight on Friday and Saturday).

Other: Fitness center. Laundry and valet service. Copy service and fax available.

Days Inn Wilmington

5209 Concord Pike
Wilmington, DE 19803
Telephone: 302-478-0300 or 800-DAYSINN
Fax: 302-478-2401
Website: www.daysinn.com

Rooms: 100 rooms with one king bed, one queen bed, or two double beds. All have in-room safe, voice mail, cable television with HBO, data port, iron and ironing board, coffeemaker, and hair dryer. Most have refrigerator and microwave.

Rates: $50 to $75, including Continental breakfast with waffle bar. Contact the hotel or consult the website for details on packages.

Credit cards: Visa, MasterCard, American Express, Discover, and Diner's Club.

Personal checks: Not accepted.

Check-in: 2 P.M.

Check-out: Noon.

Smoking policy: Smoking and nonsmoking rooms available.

Wheelchair accessible: Yes.

Children: Under twelve stay free with parents. Cots available for $10.

Pets: Yes, with a $10 fee per pet per day; prior arrangements necessary.

Food: None on-site. Dozens of restaurants in both directions on U.S. Route 202.

Parking: Free on-site. Truck parking available.

Other: Guest laundry. Dry cleaning available weekdays. Fax and copy service. Pool and fitness center planned.

Doubletree Hotel Wilmington

4727 Concord Pike
Wilmington, DE 19803
Telephone: 302-478-6000 or 800-222-TREE
Fax: 302-477-1492
Website: www.doubletreehotels.com

Rooms: 236 rooms and 8 suites. All deluxe rooms and suites have two dual-line telephones with voice mail, data port, cable television with HBO, iron and ironing board, hair dryer, coffeemaker, and same-day valet service. Refrigerator available for small fee.

Rates: $79 to $189 for rooms, $199 to $250 for suites. Freshly baked chocolate chip cookies included. Contact the hotel or consult the website for details on packages.

Credit cards: Visa, MasterCard, American Express, Discover, and Diner's Club.

Personal checks: Accepted.

Check-in: 3 P.M.

Check-out: Noon

Smoking policy: One floor of guest rooms is set aside for smoking. Smoking not permitted in hotel's public areas.

Wheelchair accessible: Yes.

Children: Welcome. Portable cribs available. Rollaway beds available for $10.

Pets: No.

Food: Palette's Restaurant and Lounge serves breakfast, lunch, and dinner. There is also a bar.

Parking: Free on-site.

Other: Fitness center and indoor pool. Twenty-four-hour fax and copy service. Meeting rooms available. The hotel is adjacent to Concord Mall.

Holiday Inn Wilmington North

4000 Concord Pike
Wilmington, DE 19803-1783
Telephone: 302-478-2222
Fax: 302-479-0850
Website: www.holiday-inn.com/wilmington-n

Rooms: 138 rooms and 1 suite with king-size or two double beds, data port, complimentary in-room coffee, clock radio, iron and ironing board, hair dryer, cable television with HBO, pay-per-view movies, Nintendo, and Web TV. Refrigerators available. Same-day valet service weekdays.

Rates: $75 to $105. With rollaways cots, a family of four or five can stay in the same room at no extra charge. Contact the hotel or consult the website for details on packages; some include discount tickets to local attractions. Kids 18 and under free in parents' room.

Credit cards: Visa, MasterCard, American Express, Discover, and Diner's Club.

Personal checks: Not accepted.

Check-in: 2 P.M.

Check-out: Noon.

Smoking policy: 85 percent of the guest rooms are designated nonsmoking. Smoking not permitted in restaurant or other public areas of hotel.

Wheelchair accessible: Yes.

Children: Cribs available; rollaways $6.

Pets: No.

Food: Damon's Restaurant features barbecue ribs, steaks, seafood, and salads. The Clubhouse in the restaurant has large television screens for sports and news. Dozens of other restaurants are nearby on U.S. Route 202 in both directions.

Parking: Free on-site.

Other: Outdoor pool, fitness center and pool in adjoining building. Meeting space, twenty-four-hour fax and copy service. Room service available. Rental car desk on-site. Laundry facilities, laundry service and dry cleaning service. Staff speaks English, Spanish, and Hebrew.

**Homewood Suites by Hilton
at Wilmington Brandywine Valley**
350 Rocky Run Parkway
Wilmington, DE 19803
Telephone: 302-479-2000 or 800-CALL-HOME
Fax: 302-479-0770
Website: www.homewood-suites.com
Rooms: 113 suites. Kitchen areas have a refrigerator, coffeemaker, microwave, and utensils and dishes for four. Rooms also have data port, voice mail, iron, and ironing board.
Rates: One-bedroom suites start at $165; two-bedroom suites are $250. Includes breakfast daily, and all-you-can-eat buffet in the Social Room Monday through Thursday, 5 to 7 P.M. Weekend packages available.
Credit cards: Visa, MasterCard, American Express, Discover, and Diner's Club.
Personal checks: Not accepted.
Check-in: 4 P.M.
Check-out: Noon.
Smoking policy: 95 percent of the rooms are designated nonsmoking. Smoking not permitted in public areas.
Wheelchair accessible: Yes.
Children: Cribs and rollaway beds available with advance notice.
Pets: No.
Food: Several restaurants are within a three-minute walk.
Parking: Free on-site.
Other: Fitness center, outdoor heated pool. A shuttle is available for destinations within a five-mile radius, Monday through Thursday, 7 A.M. to 7 P.M., and Friday, 7 A.M. to 3 P.M. Meeting rooms and a business center. Laundry facilities. A walking trail and bike trail are easily accessible.

McIntosh Inn
300 Rocky Run Parkway
Wilmington, DE 19803
Telephone: 302-479-7900
Fax: 302-479-5098
Website: No.
Rooms: 72 double, queen, and king rooms.
Rates: $65 to $95, including Continental breakfast.
Credit cards: Visa, MasterCard, American Express, and Diner's Club.

Personal checks: Not accepted.
Check-in: 3 P.M.
Check-out: 11 A.M.
Smoking policy: 90 percent of the guest rooms are designated nonsmoking. Smoking is not permitted in public areas.
Wheelchair accessible: Yes.
Children: Seventeen and under stay free with parents.
Pets: No.
Food: Several restaurants are within a three-minute walk.
Parking: Free on-site.
Other: Fitness center.

Sheraton Suites Wilmington
422 Delaware Ave.
Wilmington, DE 19801
Telephone: 302-654-8300 or 800-325-3535
Fax: 302-654-6036
Website: www.sheraton.com
Rooms: 223 suites have wet bar with refrigerator and coffeemaker, two telephones, computer port, iron and ironing board, hair dryer, separate living room with sofabed. SMART guest rooms have added features such as Hewlett-Packard printer/fax/copier, two-line phones, free local calls, and oversize desk.
Rates: $99 to $245, including Continental breakfast and evening hors d'oeuvres. Contact hotel for details on packages.
Credit cards: Visa, MasterCard, American Express, Discover, Diner's Club, Carte Blanche, and Japanese BA.
Personal checks: Accepted with proper identification.
Check-in: 3 P.M.
Check-out: 12 noon.
Smoking policy: One floor of guest rooms is set aside for smoking. Smoking not permitted in public areas.
Wheelchair accessible: Yes.
Children: Cribs available.
Pets: No.
Food: Basil restaurant, The Bar lounge, and room service.
Parking: Garage parking underground. There is an extra charge.

Other: Fitness center with sauna, indoor pool. Meeting facilities can accommodate up to three hundred.

Wyndham Hotel
700 King St.
Wilmington, DE 19801
Telephone: 302-655-0400 or 888-LODGING
Fax: 302-429-5979
Website: www.wyndham.com
Rooms: 219 rooms with one king-size bed, two double beds, or a king-size bed and a sitting area with a pull-out sofa. $89 to $209. Includes clock radio, hair dryer, coffeemaker, cable television with in-room movies, iron and ironing board, telephone with data port and voice mail.
Rates: Contact the hotel or consult the website for details on packages.

Credit cards: Visa, MasterCard, American Express, Discover, and Diner's Club.
Personal checks: Accepted with proper identification.
Check-in: 3 P.M.
Check-out: 12 noon
Smoking policy: 83 percent of guest rooms are designated nonsmoking. Smoking not permitted in hotel's public areas.
Wheelchair accessible: Yes.
Children: Under twelve stay free with parents. Cribs available.
Pets: No.
Food: Terranova Café & Grill serves breakfast, lunch, and dinner. Room service available.
Parking: Garage parking under hotel for $8 per night.
Other: Fitness center and indoor pool. Business center. Meeting and banquet facilities.

FOOD

Bistro 1717
1717 Delaware Ave. (Trolley Square)
Wilmington, DE 19806
Telephone: 302-777-0464
Hours: Dinner Tuesday through Saturday, 5 to 9 P.M.
Prices: Appetizers $7 to $16, entrees $16 to $24.
Take-out: Yes.
Wheelchair accessible: Yes, including restrooms.
Smoking policy: All nonsmoking.
Dress: Upscale casual.
Credit cards: Visa, MasterCard, and American Express.
Personal checks: Not accepted.
Other: French Asian bistro. Culinary Institute of America–trained chef.

Bon Appetit Gourmet Food Shoppe
3629 Silverside Rd.
Wilmington, DE 19810
Telephone: 302-478-4344
Hours: Monday through Friday, 9 A.M. to 6 P.M.; Saturday, 10 A.M. to 3 P.M.
Prices: Sandwiches with side salad average $5.95.
Take-out: Yes.

Wheelchair accessible: Yes, but not restroom.
Smoking policy: All nonsmoking.
Dress: Casual.
Credit cards: Not accepted.
Personal checks: Accepted with proper identification.
Other: This gourmet shop is a slice of France in the Talleyville Shopping Center. Salads, sandwiches, pâtés, cheeses, coffees, soups, and fresh baked goods are some of the many foods available. Little round tables are cozy and comfortable; lots of magazines available if you want something to read while you're waiting. Large selection of gourmet items to go.

Brandywine Brewing Co.
3801 Kennett Pike (DE Route 52 at Route 141) in the Greenville Center
Greenville, DE 19807
Telephone: 302-655-8000
Fax: 302-655-8144
Website: www.brandywinebrewing.com
Hours: Daily, 11:30 A.M. to 1 A.M.
Prices: Sandwiches $7 to $11, dinner entrees $11 to $23.
Take-out: Yes.

Wheelchair accessible: Yes, including restrooms.

Smoking policy: All nonsmoking.

Dress: Casual.

Credit cards: Visa, MasterCard, American Express, Discover, and Diner's Club.

Personal checks: Not accepted.

Other: Daily specials and a wide range of menu items available. On-site award-winning microbrewery. Special dinner selections in spring and summer. Singer-guitar combo Thursday at 10 P.M. Jazz band Friday at lunchtime.

Buckley's Tavern

Rt. 52, 5812 Kennett Pike
Centreville, DE 19807
Telephone: 302-656-9776
Fax: 302-656-9752
Website: www.buckleystavern.net

Hours: Lunch Monday through Friday, 11:30 A.M. to 2:30 P.M.; Sunday brunch, 10 A.M. to 3 P.M. Dinner Monday through Thursday, 5:30 to 9:30 P.M.; Friday, 5:30 to 11 P.M.; Saturday, 5 to 11 P.M.; Bar open daily until 1 A.M. Tavern menu offered until 11 P.M. Monday through Saturday, until 10 P.M. on Sunday.

Prices: Lunch entrees $6.95 to $12.95, dinner entrees $10.95 to $21.95. Salads, pasta, and sandwiches also available at lunch and dinner.

Take-out: Yes.

Wheelchair accessible: Yes, but not restrooms.

Smoking policy: All nonsmoking.

Dress: Upscale casual.

Credit cards: Visa, MasterCard, American Express, and Diner's Club.

Personal checks: Not accepted.

Other: Eclectic, frequently changing menu highlights fresh, regional ingredients. Extensive wine and beer list. An institution along the Kennett Pike, sought out by locals and visitors alike.

Café Mezzanote

11th and Tatnall Sts. in the Nemours Building
Wilmington, DE 19801
Telephone: 302-658-7050
Fax: 302-658-7237

Hours: Lunch Monday through Friday, 11 A.M. to 2:30 P.M. Dinner Sunday through Thursday, 5 to 10 P.M.; Friday and Saturday, 5 to 10:30 P.M. Bar open Friday and Saturday until 1 A.M. Sunday brunch, 11 A.M. to 3 P.M.

Prices: Lunch averages $12; dinner averages $22. Brunch is $20 for adults, $10 for under age 12.

Take-out: Yes.

Wheelchair accessible: Yes, including restrooms.

Smoking policy: All nonsmoking.

Dress: Business casual.

Credit cards: Visa, MasterCard, American Express, and Discover.

Personal checks: Accepted with proper identification.

Other: Authentic Italian cuisine. Happy hour from 5 to 7 P.M.

Catherine Rooney's Irish Pub and Restaurant

1616 Delaware Ave.
Wilmington, DE 19806
Telephone: 302-654-9700
Website: www.catherinerooneys.com

Hours: Monday through Saturday, 11 A.M. to 1 A.M.; Sunday, 11 A.M. to 10 P.M.

Prices: Lunch averages $8, dinner averages $13.

Take-out: Yes.

Wheelchair accessible: Yes. There is a step up to the restrooms.

Smoking policy: All nonsmoking.

Dress: Casual.

Credit cards: Visa, MasterCard, and American Express.

Personal checks: Not accepted.

Other: Traditional Irish food and pub food. Sing-along Thursday, 8 to 11 P.M.; live entertainment Friday and Saturday, 10 P.M. to 1 A.M.

Celebrity Kitchens

1601 Concord Pike (Independence Mall)
Wilmington, DE 19803
Telephone: 302-427-2665
Fax: 302-427-9060
Website: www.celebritykitchens.com
Hours: Dinner by advance reservation only.

Prices: $35 to $65.
Take-out: No.
Wheelchair accessible: Yes, including restrooms.
Smoking policy: All nonsmoking.
Dress: Sophisticated casual.
Credit cards: Visa, MasterCard, and American Express.
Personal checks: Accepted with proper identification.
Other: Recreational cooking school operates at same time. Amateurs learn to cook from "celebrity" chefs. Interactive, entertaining, and social. Chef cooks tableside either as demonstration or with hands-on help from guests; guests eat the results and take home the recipes. Call Celebrity Kitchens or consult the website for details.

Charcoal House

1836 Lovering Ave.
Wilmington, DE 19806
Telephone: 302-652-9093
Hours: Monday through Friday, 8 A.M. to 3 P.M. Breakfast menu available all day; there's also a lunch menu.
Prices: Breakfast $2.25 to $6.25, lunch $2.25 to $8.50.
Take-out: Yes.
Wheelchair accessible: No.
Smoking policy: All nonsmoking.
Dress: Casual.
Credit cards: Not accepted.
Personal checks: Not accepted.
Other: Fun environment.

Columbus Inn

2216 Pennsylvania Ave.
Wilmington, DE 19806
Telephone: 302-571-1492
Fax: 302-571-1111
Website: www.columbusinn.com
Hours: Monday through Friday, 11 A.M. to 1 A.M.; Saturday, 5 P.M. to 1 A.M.; Sunday brunch 10 A.M. to 3 P.M. No brunch in summer.
Prices: Lunch sandwiches average $8.95, entrees $10.95 to $17.95; dinner entrees average $24.95; brunch buffet $20.95 for adults, $10.95 for ages 2 to 10.
Take-out: Yes.

Wheelchair accessible: First floor is accessible; restrooms may be difficult.
Smoking policy: Nonsmoking.
Dress: Upscale casual.
Credit cards: Visa, MasterCard, American Express, and Discover.
Personal checks: Not accepted.
Other: Sophisticated casual dining with American cuisine, award-winning wine list, and largest single malt scotch selection in Wilmington. Live music Thursday and Friday evenings. Reservations recommended.

Dead President's Pub and Restaurant

618 N. Union St.
Wilmington, DE 19805
Telephone: 302-652-7737
Hours: Monday through Friday, 11 A.M. to 1 A.M.; Saturday and Sunday, noon to 1 A.M.
Prices: Entrees $12 to $16.50, sandwiches less.
Take-out: Yes.
Wheelchair accessible: Yes, including restrooms.
Smoking policy: All nonsmoking.
Dress: Casual.
Credit cards: Visa, MasterCard, American Express, and Discover.
Personal checks: No.
Other: Classic old tavern atmosphere with American fare. Fish, soups, steaks. Daily specials.

Deep Blue Bar and Grill

111 W. 11th St.
Wilmington, DE 19801
Telephone: 302-777-2040
Fax: 302-777-1012
Website: www.DeepBlueBarandGrill.com
Hours: Lunch Monday through Friday, 11:30 A.M. to 2 P.M. Dinner Monday, Tuesday, and Wednesday, 5:30 to 10 P.M.; Thursday and Friday, 5:30 to 11 P.M.; Saturday, 5 to 11 P.M. Closed Sunday.
Prices: Lunch averages $13, dinner averages $24.
Take-out: Yes.
Wheelchair accessible: Yes, including restrooms.
Smoking policy: All nonsmoking.
Dress: Business casual.

Hotel du Pont:
The Green Room

The Green Room in the Hotel du Pont is the epitome of elegance. No wonder it has won awards for its extensive menu and experienced, professional service.

More marriage proposals may have been tendered in the Green Room than anywhere else in the state of Delaware. The setting is ultraromantic with arched windows, velvet draperies, towering ceiling, and gold chandeliers. There's even a harpist who plays from the musicians' gallery, enough to inspire any suitor to get down on one knee.

The Green Room in the Hotel du Pont is the most elegant restaurant in the city. HOTEL DU PONT

(continued on page 232)

(continued from page 231)

French-Continental cuisine includes entrees like roast duck with hazelnut mashed potatoes, herb-roasted Maine lobster with sweet corn timbale and truffled butter sauce, and grilled porterhouse steak with Merlot-chili preserves. Wild game like boar or venison is often on the menu. Food items are complemented by a twenty-eight-page wine list, an indication why the restaurant has received the Award of Excellence from *Wine Spectator*.

Weekday lunches are the setting for Wilmington's movers and shakers to discuss business and politics.

Sunday brunch in the Green Room includes a buffet with everything you'd expect at an elegant meal: salads, breads, cheeses, and artistic pastries like a lavender-and-white-checked cake. Cooked entrees can also be ordered. While evenings at the Green Room are adult occasions, brunch is a family-friendly experience.

Fortunately, you don't have to be contemplating marriage or about to finalize a merger to eat in the Green Room. All you need to do is make a reservation.

**VISITING THE GREEN ROOM AND THE BRANDYWINE ROOM
AT THE HOTEL DU PONT**

**Eleventh and Market Streets, Wilmington, DE 19801
Telephone for reservations: 302-594-3154 or 800-338-3404
Website: www.dupont.com/hotel/dining.htm**

Hours: Breakfast Monday through Saturday, 6:30 to 11 A.M. Lunch Monday through Saturday, 11:30 A.M. to 2 P.M. Dinner Monday through Saturday, 5:30 to 10:30 P.M.; Sunday, 5 to 10 P.M. Sunday brunch, 10 A.M. to 2 P.M.
Prices: Lunch entrees $9 to $20; dinner entrees $25 to $34; brunch costs $32.
Reservations: Recommended.
Smoking policy: Nonsmoking.
Credit cards: Visa, MasterCard, American Express, Discover, and Diner's Club.
Wheelchair accessible: Yes, including restrooms.
Dress: Jackets required for dinner Friday and Saturday. Brunch in the Green Room is more casual but still has a sophisticated, elegant feel. If you bring the kids to brunch, it's a good excuse to get them dressed up.
Other: Complimentary valet parking Sunday through Thursday.

Credit cards: Visa, MasterCard, American Express, Discover, and Diner's Club.
Personal checks: Accepted with proper identification.
Other: Bar menu available between lunch and dinner. Live jazz Friday and Saturday evenings, except in June, July, and August.

Del Rose Cafe
1707 Delaware Ave.
Wilmington, DE 19806
Telephone: 302-656-3015

Fax: 302-656-4503
Hours: Monday and Tuesday, 11 A.M. to 9 P.M.; Wednesday through Saturday, 11 A.M. to 1 A.M. Late-night menu served Wednesday and Thursday starting at 9 P.M., Friday and Saturday starting at 10 P.M.
Prices: Lunch $4.95 to $7.95, dinner $7.95 to $14.95.
Take-out: Yes.
Wheelchair accessible: No.
Smoking policy: All nonsmoking.

Dress: Casual.
Credit cards: Visa, MasterCard, American Express, and Discover.
Personal checks: Not accepted.
Other: Live late-night entertainment Wednesday through Saturday, 10 P.M. to 1 A.M.

Eclipse
1020 N. Union St.
Wilmington, DE 19805
Telephone: 302-658-1588
Fax: 302-661-1080
Hours: Lunch Monday through Friday, 11:30 A.M. to 2 P.M. Dinner Monday through Saturday, 5:30 to 10 P.M.; Sunday, 5 to 9 P.M.
Prices: Lunch entrees $9 to $15, dinner entrees $18 to $25.
Take-out: Yes.
Wheelchair accessible: Yes, including restrooms.
Smoking policy: All nonsmoking.
Dress: Upscale casual.
Credit cards: Visa, MasterCard, American Express, Discover, and Diner's Club.
Personal checks: Not accepted.
Other: Specializes in impeccably fresh fish. Manhattan-esque decor with an urban, fast-paced feel. Intimate setting. Full-service bar.

821 Market Street Bistro
821 N. Market St.
Wilmington, DE 19801
Telephone: 302-652-8821
Fax: 302-652-4481
Website: www.restaurant821.com
Hours: Lunch Monday through Friday, 11:30 A.M. to 2 P.M. Dinner Monday through Saturday starting at 5 P.M.
Prices: Lunch $6 to $15. Dinner appetizers average $9, entrees average $23.
Take-out: Yes.
Wheelchair accessible: Yes, including restrooms.
Smoking policy: All nonsmoking.
Dress: Smart casual.
Credit cards: Visa, MasterCard, American Express, Discover, and Diner's Club.
Personal checks: Not accepted.
Other: Meals served tapas-style in main dining room. Dinner can be arranged in the candlelit cedar wine cellar for a party of up to eight, who sit at an antique farmhouse table. The chef prepares a six-course degustation (tasting menu). Extensive wine list. Food is French-Italian influenced, focusing on fresh, organic, seasonal ingredients. Private dining room available. The restaurant has won many awards, including *ZAGAT Survey*'s "Favorite Restaurant in Delaware." Located in the heart of Wilmington's downtown across from the Grand Opera House. Reservations strongly suggested. Offers "Shopping with the Chef" trips Saturday morning. For $175 per person (four-person minimum), you may accompany the chef to the markets in the morning and eat what he prepares in the evening. Call 302-652-0410.

Galluccios Restaurant & Pub
1709 Lovering Ave.
Wilmington, DE 19806
Telephone: 302-655-3689
Fax: 302-655-9120
Hours: Daily, 11 A.M. to 1 A.M.
Prices: Lunch $5 to $8, dinner $7 to $14.
Take-out: Yes.
Wheelchair accessible: Yes, but not restrooms.
Smoking policy: All nonsmoking indoors. Smoking permitted on patios.
Dress: Casual.
Credit cards: Visa, MasterCard, American Express, Discover, and Diner's Club.
Personal checks: Not accepted.
Other: Neighborhood restaurant. Two outdoor patios where smoking is permitted.

Harry's Savoy Grill
2020 Naamans Rd.
Wilmington, DE 19810
Telephone: 302-475-3000
Fax: 302-475-9990
Website: www.harrys-savoy.com
Hours: Lunch Monday through Friday, 11:30 A.M. to 2:30 P.M. Dinner Monday through Thursday, 4:30 to 10 P.M.; Friday and Saturday, 4:30 to 11 P.M.; Sunday, 12 noon to 9 P.M.
Prices: Lunch averages $10, dinner averages $20.
Take-out: Yes.
Wheelchair accessible: Yes, including restrooms.
Smoking policy: All nonsmoking.
Dress: Business/upscale casual.

Credit cards: All major cards accepted.

Personal checks: Accepted with proper identification.

Other: Broad range of culinary offerings from award-wining prime rib to fresh seafood. *Wine Spectator* award-winning wine list, in-house sommelier. Named "Best Restaurant in Wilmington" by *Main Line Today* in 2000, and "Best Place for a First Date" by *Delaware Today* in 2001. Live entertainment on Friday and Saturday evenings in the bar/grill. Children's menu and high chairs available; magician performs on Tuesday. Seasonal patio.

Harry's Seafood Grill
at the Riverfront Market
101 S. Market St.
Wilmington, DE 19801
Telephone: 302-777-1500
Hours: Open for lunch and dinner; call for hours.
Prices: Lunch averages $12, dinner averages $27.
Take-out: Yes.
Wheelchair accessible: Yes, including restrooms.
Smoking policy: All nonsmoking.
Dress: Upscale casual.
Credit cards: All major cards.
Personal checks: Not accepted.
Other: Outdoor dining in season. Raw bar and sushi bar. Also serves Harry's famous prime rib.

Iron Hill Brewery
710 St. Madison St.
Wilmington, DE 19801
Telephone: 302-472-BREW
Website: www.ironhillbrewery.com
Hours: Monday through Saturday, 11:30 A.M. to 1 A.M. Sunday brunch, 11:30 A.M. to 2 P.M.
Prices: Lunch $6 to $10, dinner $12 to $18.
Take-out: Yes.
Wheelchair accessible: Yes, including restrooms.
Smoking policy: Nonsmoking.
Dress: Casual.
Credit cards: Visa, MasterCard, American Express, Discover, and Diner's Club.
Personal checks: Not accepted.
Other: First level is restaurant. Upstairs is billiard room with five billiards tables and a full bar. Outdoor areas on both levels. Entertainment and deck parties.

Jammin Jesse's
1836 N. Lincoln St.
Wilmington, DE 19806
Telephone: 302-778-2310
Fax: 302-778-2766
Hours: Monday through Friday, 8 A.M. to 8 P.M.; Saturday, 9 A.M. to 3 P.M. Closed Sunday.
Prices: Breakfast averages $3.25, lunch averages $5.
Take-out: Yes.
Wheelchair accessible: No.
Smoking policy: All nonsmoking.
Dress: Casual.
Credit cards: Visa, MasterCard, American Express, and Discover.
Personal checks: Accepted with proper identification
Other: All home cooking in an old row house in a residential area. Soups, turkey dishes, and roast beef are specialties.

Joe's Crab Shack
600 S. Madison St. along the Wilmington Riverfront
Wilmington, DE 19801
Telephone: 302-777-1803
Website: www.joescrabshack.com
Hours: Friday and Saturday, 11 A.M. to 11:15 P.M.; Sunday through Thursday, 11 A.M. to 10:15 P.M.
Prices: Appetizers start at $1.99; sandwiches and entrees range from $5.99 to $24.99.
Take-out: Yes.
Wheelchair accessible: Yes, including restrooms.
Smoking policy: Nonsmoking.
Dress: Casual.
Credit cards: Visa, MasterCard, American Express, Discover, and Diner's Club.
Personal checks: Not accepted.
Other: Energetic environment; servers dance in the aisles and urge patrons to do the same. Crabs a specialty.

Krazy Kat's Restaurant

The menu at Krazy Kat's is the only place I've ever seen a salad listed as a Panache of Field Greens. The description fits the food—and the restaurant—perfectly. One definition of *panache* is "an ornamental tuft," an apt analogy for the restaurant that's a figurative feather in the cap of Montchanin Village. The better-known meaning, "dash or flamboyance," suits Krazy Kat's decor and food to a tee.

The restaurant's name will probably clue you in: You're not going to find anything stodgy or standard here. What you will discover behind the huge wooden door of the renovated blacksmith's shop is a *Mobil Travel Guide* four-star restaurant. Animal-striped upholstered chairs, faux-finish walls, and portraits of cats and dogs in military uniforms are startling at first, but after you've spent a few minutes in the comfortable seats, enjoying the fireplace and the soft music, the overall effect is charmingly eclectic.

The best news for patrons is that there's substance to go with the style. The menu, which changes quarterly, features the finest, freshest ingredients, prepared exquisitely. Sauces and side dishes are chosen because their textures and flavors complement the main dishes. Creative food pairings provide new and interesting dishes but are never overly complicated or contrived. The crispy salmon lunch entree is served with creamy herb risotto and white truffle-leek sauce. A pan-roasted Muscovy duck dish at dinner is accompanied by pomme puree, choucroute, and foie gras sauce. The appetizers and soups receive as much attention as the entrees; fans of crab bisque will be in heaven. An extensive wine list includes many selections available by the glass.

Krazy Kat's is named for an eccentric woman who used to live on the property. Owner Missy Lickle recalls that her grandmother referred to the woman as "one crazy cat." The restaurant's sense of humor is evident in the decor.

Forty guests can be seated in the Main Dining Room, twenty in the Annex. Krazy Kat's is open for breakfast and dinner seven days a week, and for lunch Monday through Friday.

Montchanin Village was originally inhabited by laborers from the nearby Du Pont powder mills. Today its several buildings have been restored with the restaurant, luxury accommodations, and an exuberant garden. Weather permitting, take some time to enjoy the grounds before or after your meal.

If you're lucky enough to be staying at the Inn at Montchanin Village (see the Accommodations section of this chapter), you'll have the opportunity to dine at Krazy Kat's more than once.

(continued on page 236)

At Krazy Kat's Restaurant the decor is distinctive and the dining is divine. THE INN AT MONTCHANIN VILLAGE

(continued from page 235)

KRAZY KAT'S RESTAURANT

Montchanin Village, Delaware Route 100 and Kirk Road, Montchanin, DE 19710
Telephone: 302-888-4200 • Website: www.montchanin.com

Hours: Breakfast Monday through Friday, 7 to 10 A.M.; Saturday, Sunday, and holidays, 8 to 11 A.M. Lunch Monday through Friday, 11 A.M. to 2 P.M. Dinner Monday through Saturday, 5:30 to 10 P.M.; Sunday, 5:30 to 9 P.M.
Prices: Lunch appetizers average $8, entrees $9 to $14, dinner appetizers average $10, entrees $28.
Take-out: No.
Smoking policy: Nonsmoking.
Wheelchair access: Yes.
Dress: At lunch, business or luncheon attire is appropriate. At dinner, jackets are strongly encouraged for gentlemen; ties are optional.
Children: The atmosphere is adult and sophisticated; children who are comfortable in that situation are welcome.
Credit cards: Visa, MasterCard, American Express, Discover, and Diner's Club.
Personal checks: Not accepted.
Other: Meeting rooms with catered food from Krazy Kat's are available.

Just Desserts Cafe
1831 Delaware Ave.
Wilmington, DE 19806
Telephone: 302-658-1477
Website: www.justdessertscafe.com
Hours: Monday through Friday, 9:30 A.M. to 8 P.M.; Saturday and Sunday, 8 A.M. to 8 P.M. Winter and summer hours may differ.
Prices: Average lunch entree $6.50, average dinner entree $10.
Take-out: Yes.
Wheelchair accessible: Yes, including restrooms.
Smoking policy: All nonsmoking.
Dress: Casual.
Credit cards: Visa, MasterCard, and American Express.
Personal checks: Not accepted.
Other: Cozy atmosphere. Extensive menu items and homemade desserts. Acoustic brunch series on Sunday, 11 A.M. to 2 P.M., is $13.95 for buffet. Sometimes a $3 cover is charged, which is waived if you order the buffet. Antiques and jewelry for sale.

Kahunaville, and the Deck at Kahunaville
550 S. Madison St.
Wilmington, DE 19801
Telephone: 302-571-8401
Fax: 302-571-6212
Website: www.kahunaville.com
Hours: Monday through Thursday, 11:30 A.M. to 10 P.M. with bar open until 11 P.M.; Friday and Saturday, 11 A.M. to 11 P.M., bar open until 1 A.M.; Sunday, 11:30 A.M. to 9 P.M., bar open until 11 P.M.
Prices: $7 to $17.
Take-out: Yes.
Wheelchair accessible: Yes, including restrooms.
Smoking policy: All nonsmoking.
Dress: Casual.
Credit cards: Visa, MasterCard, American Express, and Discover.
Personal checks: No.
Other: An entire warehouse converted to tropical island atmosphere along the Wilmington riverfront across from Frawley Stadium. Large arcade area. Children's menu. Fancy drinks, both alcoholic and nonalcoholic, a

specialty; "flair" bartenders prepare them. In summer, the outdoor deck hosts live performances. Check the website for concert information.

Kelly's Logan House
1701 Delaware Ave.
Wilmington, DE 19803
Telephone: 302-655-6426
Website: www.loganhouse.com
Hours: Bar open 11 A.M. to 1 A.M. Restaurant open Monday through Saturday, 11:30 A.M. to midnight. Happy hour Monday through Friday, 3 to 6 P.M. Late-night menu, 10 P.M. until midnight. Closed Sunday.
Prices: Average $8. Same menu for lunch and dinner.
Take-out: Yes.
Wheelchair accessible: Yes, including first-floor restrooms.
Smoking policy: All nonsmoking indoors. In winter, an outdoor area with propane heater is a designated smoking area.
Dress: Casual.
Credit cards: Visa, MasterCard, American Express, and Discover.
Personal checks: Not accepted.
Other: Oldest operating tavern in Wilmington, since 1864. Food includes wraps, sandwiches, and burgers. Live music: Tuesday, authentic Irish music; Wednesday, acoustic music; Thursday, Friday, and Saturday, full band upstairs. Friday and Saturday, a DJ is downstairs at the dance floor. Two patios open in summer.

Luigi Vitrone's Pastabilities Restaurant
415 N. Lincoln St.
Wilmington, DE 19805
Telephone: 302-656-9822
Website: www.ljv-pastabilities.com
Hours: Tuesday through Thursday, 5 to 9 P.M.; Friday and Saturday, 5 to 10 P.M.; Sunday, 5 to 8:30 P.M.
Prices: Entrees $12.95 to $26.
Take-out: Yes.
Wheelchair accessible: Yes, but not to the restrooms.
Smoking policy: All nonsmoking.
Dress: Upscale casual.
Credit cards: Visa, MasterCard, American Express, Discover, and Carte Blanche.

Personal checks: Not accepted.
Other: Authentic regional Italian cuisine in a cosmopolitan, romantic atmosphere.

Madeline's Restaurant
531 N. DuPont St.
Wilmington, DE 19805
Telephone: 302-656-4505
Hours: Monday through Friday, 11 A.M. to 9 P.M.; Saturday, 4 to 9:30 P.M.; Sunday, 12 noon to 8 P.M.
Prices: Lunch $4 and up, dinner $8.25 to $19.
Take-out: Yes.
Wheelchair accessible: Yes. A tight fit for wheelchairs in ladies' room; easier access in men's room.
Smoking policy: All nonsmoking.
Dress: Casual.
Credit cards: Visa, MasterCard, and American Express.
Personal checks: Not accepted.
Other: Friendly atmosphere. Italian cuisine. Also do catering.

Mikimotos Restaurant/Asian Grill and Sushi Bar
1212 Washington St.
Wilmington, DE 19801
Telephone: 302-656-TOFU
Fax: 302-656-RICE
Website: www.mikimotos.com
Hours: Monday through Thursday, 11 A.M. to 11 P.M.; Friday, 11 A.M. to midnight; Saturday, 4 P.M. to midnight; Sunday, 4 to 10 P.M.
Prices: Lunch $8 to $15, dinner $8 to $25.
Take-out: Yes.
Wheelchair accessible: Yes, including restrooms.
Smoking policy: All nonsmoking.
Dress: Upscale casual.
Credit cards: Visa, MasterCard, American Express, Discover, and Diner's Club.
Personal checks: Accepted with proper identification.
Other: Exciting, contemporary decor with food selections to match. Large selection of sake. Excellent sushi and Asian-inspired cuisine. Sushi classes. Small outdoor patio. Reservations recommended for parties of six or more and for any size party on weekends.

moro restaurant
1307 North Scott St.
Wilmington, DE 19806
Telephone: 302-777-1800
Fax: 302-777-2350
Website: www.mororestaurant.net
Hours: Tuesday through Saturday, 5 to 11 P.M.
Prices: Appetizers average $9, entrees $25.
Take-out: No.
Wheelchair accessible: Yes, including restrooms.
Smoking policy: All nonsmoking.
Dress: Upscale casual.
Credit cards: Visa, MasterCard, American Express, and Discover.
Personal checks: Not accepted.
Other: Sleek design, warm contemporary decor. Spaces feel private, so guests don't feel like they're on display. Menu changes twice weekly. Food and wine prices offer a good value. Chef's tasting dinner available with advance reservations.

Mrs. Robino's Restaurant
520 N. Union St.
Wilmington, DE 19805
Telephone: 302-652-9223
Fax: 302-658-8124
Website: www.mrsrobinos.com
Hours: Monday through Thursday, 11 A.M. to 9 P.M.; Friday and Saturday, 11 A.M. to 10 P.M.; Sunday, noon to 9 P.M.
Prices: $4.95 to $11.95. Lunch and dinner menus are the same, with dinner specials available.
Take-out: Yes.
Wheelchair accessible: Yes, but call first for back entrance. Restroom accessible.
Smoking policy: All nonsmoking.
Dress: Casual.
Credit cards: Visa and MasterCard.
Personal checks: No.
Other: Children's menu. Fourth-generation Italian restaurant with homemade pasta and other dishes. Reservations accepted.

Pan Tai
837 Union St.
Wilmington, DE 19805
Telephone: 302-652-6633
Hours: Lunch Monday through Friday, 11:30 A.M. to 2:30 P.M. Dinner Monday through Thursday, 5 to 10 P.M.; Friday and Saturday, 5 to 10:30 P.M. Closed Sunday.
Prices: Wide range up to $23.
Take-out: Yes.
Wheelchair accessible: Yes, including restrooms.
Smoking policy: All nonsmoking.
Dress: Casual.
Credit cards: Visa and MasterCard.
Personal checks: Not accepted.
Other: Unique southeast Asian cuisine. High chairs available.

Red Room
550 S. Madison St.
Wilmington, DE 19801
Telephone: 302-571-8440
Hours: Thursday and Friday, 5 P.M. to 2 A.M.; Saturday, 7 P.M. to 2 A.M.
Prices: Tapas menu items from $8 to $32.
Take-out: No.
Wheelchair accessible: Yes, including restrooms.
Smoking policy: Nonsmoking.
Dress: Upscale casual.
Credit cards: Visa, MasterCard, American Express, Discover, and Diner's Club.
Personal checks: Not accepted.
Other: Live entertainment Thursday and Friday, 7 to 9 P.M., then a DJ takes over. European bottle service available in the super lounge: buy a bottle for the table, and mix your own drinks. Juices and drink mixes are provided.

Ristorante Mona Lisa
607 N. Lincoln St.
Wilmington, DE 19805
Telephone: 302-888-2201
Fax: 302-888-2294
Hours: Lunch Tuesday through Friday, 11 A.M. to 2:30 P.M; dinner Monday through Saturday, 4 to 10 P.M.
Prices: Lunch averages $11, dinner averages $16.
Take-out: Yes.
Wheelchair accessible: Yes, including restrooms.
Smoking policy: All nonsmoking.
Dress: Casual.
Credit cards: Visa, MasterCard, and American Express.
Personal checks: Not accepted.

Sugarfoot Fine Food
1014 N. Lincoln St.
Wilmington, DE 19805
Telephone: 302-655-4800
Fax: 302-655-4809
Hours: Monday through Friday, 9 A.M. to 4 P.M.
Prices: $5.50 to $12.
Take-out: Yes.
Wheelchair accessible: No.
Smoking policy: All nonsmoking.
Dress: Casual.
Credit cards: Visa and MasterCard.
Personal checks: Not accepted.

Sugarfoot Fine Food
1007 N. Orange St.
Wilmington, DE 19801
Telephone: 302-654-1600
Fax: 302-655-4809
Hours: Monday through Friday, 7 A.M. to 3 P.M.
Prices: $5.50 to $12.
Take-out: Yes.
Wheelchair accessible: Yes, including restrooms.
Smoking policy: All nonsmoking.
Dress: Casual.
Credit cards: Visa, MasterCard, and American Express.
Personal checks: Not accepted.
Other: Also sells flowers.

Temptations
11A Trolley Square
Wilmington, DE 19806
Telephone: 302-429-9162
Hours: June through October, open Monday through Saturday, 10 A.M. to 10 P.M. Rest of year, open Monday through Thursday, 10 A.M. to 9 P.M.; Friday and Saturday, 10 A.M. to 10 P.M.
Food: Ice cream parlor, candy store, luncheonette.
Take-out: Yes.
Wheelchair accessible: No.
Smoking policy: All nonsmoking.
Dress: Casual.
Credit cards: Visa, MasterCard American Express, Discover, and Diner's Club.
Personal checks: Accepted with proper identification.

Other: More than thirty-five flavors of Bassett's and own make ice cream. Full lunch menu with salads, soups, and sandwiches. In business since 1979. Friendly, wholesome atmosphere.

The Terrace at Greenhill
Ed Oliver Golf Course
800 DuPont Rd.
Wilmington, DE 19807
Telephone: 302-575-1990
Fax: 302-575-1349
Hours: Lunch Monday through Saturday, 11:30 A.M. to 2:30 P.M. Dinner Monday through Thursday, 4:30 to 8:30 P.M.; Friday and Saturday, 4:30 to 9 P.M.; Sunday 4 to 7:30 P.M. Sunday brunch, 10 A.M. to 2:30 P.M.
Prices: Lunch averages $8, dinner averages $14, Sunday brunch is $5.
Take-out: Yes.
Wheelchair accessible: Yes, including restrooms.
Smoking policy: All nonsmoking.
Dress: Casual.
Credit cards: Visa, MasterCard, American Express, and Diner's Club.
Personal checks: Accepted with proper identification.
Other: On a public golf course overlooking the city of Wilmington.

Three Little Bakers (dinner theater)
3540 Three Little Bakers Blvd.
Pike Creek, DE 19808
Telephone: 302-368-1616 or 800-368-3003
Fax: 302-452-2535
Website: www.tlbinc.com
Hours: Thursday and Sunday, buffet opens at 11:30 A.M., matinee shows start at 2 P.M.; Wednesday, Friday, and Saturday evenings, doors open at 5 P.M., buffet opens at 5:30 P.M., and shows start at 8 P.M.
Prices: Dinner and show tickets run from $30 to $50.
Take-out: No.
Wheelchair accessible: Yes, including restrooms.
Smoking policy: All nonsmoking.
Dress: Upscale casual.
Credit cards: Visa, MasterCard, American Express, and Discover.

Personal checks: Accepted with proper identification.

Other: Reservations required. Contact the theater or consult the website for details. Price depends on time of show and where you sit. Group tours can be accommodated.

Timothy's Restaurant

930 Pettinaro Park Dr., in Shipyard Shops along Christina Riverfront
Wilmington, DE 19801
Telephone: 302-429-7427
Fax: 302-429-7440
Website: www.timothyrestaurants.com
Hours: Daily, 11 A.M. to 1 A.M.
Prices: Sandwiches $7.99 to $8.99; diner entrees with soup or salad and two side dishes, $13 to $20.
Take-out: Yes.
Wheelchair accessible: Yes, including restrooms.
Smoking policy: Nonsmoking.
Dress: Casual.
Credit cards: Visa, MasterCard, American Express, and Discover.
Personal checks: Not accepted.
Other: Convenient riverfront location in outlet center.

Toscana Kitchen & Bar

1412 N. DuPont St.
Wilmington, DE 19806
Telephone: 302-654-8001
Fax: 302-654-8250
Website: www.bigchefguy.com
Hours: Lunch Monday through Friday, 11:30 A.M. to 2 P.M. Lunch served in bar 2 to 5 P.M. Dinner Monday through Wednesday, 5 to 10 P.M.; Thursday through Saturday, 5 to 11 P.M.; Sunday, 5 to 9 P.M.
Prices: Lunch entrees average $10, dinner entrees average $18. Salads and individual pizzas available, $7 to $9.
Take-out: Yes.
Wheelchair accessible: Yes, including restrooms.
Smoking policy: All nonsmoking.
Dress: Upscale casual.
Credit cards: Visa, MasterCard, American Express, Discover, and Diner's Club.

Personal checks: No.
Other: Live music Wednesday evening. Italian cuisine.

Walter's Steak House & Saloon

802 N. Union St.
Wilmington, DE 19805
Telephone: 302-652-6780
Fax: 302-652-6785
Website: Listed on umbrella site, www.restaurants.com
Hours: Monday through Saturday, 5 to 11 P.M.; Sunday, 4 to 10 P.M.
Prices: $15.95 to $33.95, average $20.
Take-out: Yes.
Wheelchair accessible: No.
Smoking policy: All nonsmoking.
Dress: Upscale casual.
Credit cards: Visa, MasterCard, American Express, and Discover.
Personal checks: Not accepted.
Other: Third generation in business. Award-winning beef. Complimentary raw bar included with entree on Sunday, Monday, and Thursday. Call for take-out, don't use fax.

Washington Street Ale House

1206 Washington St.
Wilmington, DE 19801
Telephone: 302-658-2537
Fax: 302-658-2755
Website: www.wsalehouse.com
Hours: Daily, 11 A.M. to 1 A.M. Saturday and Sunday brunch, 10 A.M. to 2 P.M.
Prices: Lunch and dinner $8 to $17, brunch $7 to $12.
Take-out: Yes.
Wheelchair accessible: Yes, including restrooms.
Smoking policy: All nonsmoking.
Dress: Casual.
Credit cards: Visa, MasterCard, American Express, Discover, and Diner's Club.
Personal checks: Accepted with proper identification.
Other: Fireside dining. Twenty handcrafted microbrews on tap. Extensive menu of soups, salads, burgers, pizza, entrees, and desserts. Reservations recommended for parties of eight or more.

Waterworks Cafe
16th and French Streets
Wilmington, DE 19801
Telephone: 302-652-6022
Fax: 302-429-0993
Hours: Lunch Wednesday through Sunday, 11:30 A.M. to 2 P.M. Dinner Wednesday and Thursday, 5 to 8 P.M.; Friday and Saturday, 5 to 9 P.M.
Prices: Lunch $8 to $14, dinner $17 to $29.
Take-out: Yes, call ahead.
Wheelchair accessible: Yes, including restrooms.
Smoking policy: All nonsmoking.
Dress: Upscale casual.
Credit cards: Visa, MasterCard, American Express, and Discover.
Personal checks: Not accepted.
Other: Historic area along waterfront. Originally a mill known for innovations to the milling process. Later became the Wilmington pumping station.

Zanzibar Blue
1000 West St. (at Delaware Avenue)
Wilmington, DE 19801
Telephone: 302-472-7001
Fax: 302-472-7002
Website: www.zanzibarblue.com
Hours: Lunch Monday through Friday, 11 A.M. to 2 P.M. Dinner Sunday through Thursday, 5 to 10 P.M.; Friday and Saturday, 5 to 11 P.M. Sunday brunch has two seatings: noon and 2 P.M.
Prices: Lunch $9 to $14, dinner $17 to $24, brunch $22.95.
Take-out: No.
Wheelchair accessible: Yes, including restrooms.
Credit cards: Visa, MasterCard, American Express, Discover, and Diner's Club.
Personal checks: Not accepted.
Smoking policy: All nonsmoking.
Dress: Upscale casual.
Other: Live jazz nightly in the café area, first set starting at 7 P.M. Sunday through Thursday and at 8 P.M. on Friday and Saturday. Café patrons may order from the dining room menu or from a café menu. Café seating is first-come, first-served. Reservations are accepted for the dining room. Happy hour nightly from 5 to 7 P.M., $1 off drinks. Live jazz at Sunday brunch.

CALENDAR OF EVENTS

For up-to-the-minute information about events, contact the sites and organizations by phone or consult their websites or www.brandywineguide.com.

Ongoing

Sundays and Mondays: Make-It-Take-It, Delaware Museum of Natural History
Wednesdays through Saturdays: Helicopter rides, American Helicopter Museum & Education Center
Wednesdays: Art After Hours, Delaware Art Museum
Thursdays: Read and Explore, Delaware Museum of Natural History
Monthly, last Monday: Meet an Animal, Delaware Museum of Natural History
Monthly except January, July, and August, first Friday: Art on the Town, Wilmington
Monthly, first Friday: Art Stroll, Kennett Square
Monthly, third Saturday: Family helicopter rides, American Helicopter Museum & Education Center
Monthly, Saturdays: Family Saturday, Delaware History Museum
Bimonthly: Featured Artist of the Month, Delaware Art Museum
Occasional Saturdays: People to People Workshop, Delaware Center for the Contemporary Arts
Every six to eight weeks: Doll appraisals, Delaware Toy & Miniature Museum
Occasionally: "Meet a Hero from History," Brandywine Battlefield Park
Spring and fall: Sleep under the Stars Campout, Rockwood Mansion Park
Every other year: Regional "Biennial," Delaware Art Museum

Scheduled Events

Early January through Late March: Welcome Spring, Longwood Gardens
January, the Saturday, Sunday, and Monday including Martin Luther King Jr. Day: Invention Convention, Hagley Museum
January, Martin Luther King Jr. Day (third Monday): King Day programs, Delaware History Museum; Martin Luther King Jr. Day Celebration, Winterthur
February, Sunday before Valentine's Day: Victorine's Valentine Day, Hagley Museum
February, usually the Sunday before Washington's Birthday: Washington's Birthday Celebration, Brandywine Battlefield Park
February, Presidents' Day: Open House, American Helicopter Museum
February (resuming in 2005): Howard Pyle's Pirate Party, Delaware Art Museum
February and March: Kids' Art Exhibit, Chadds Ford Historical Society
March through June: Spring garden walks, Winterthur
March: Antiques show, Chester County Historical Society
March, second Sunday: Charter Day, Brandywine Battlefield Park
March, Saturday before St. Patrick's Day: St. Patrick's Day parade, Wilmington
March, one Sunday midmonth: St. Patrick's Day celebration, Hagley Museum
March, one weekend: Art and Antiques Show, Hagley Museum
Late March through early April: Easter display, Longwood Gardens
Easter Sunday: Easter in the Garden, Winterthur

April: Van tours of Brandywine Battlefield National Historic Landmark, Brandywine
    Battlefield Park
April through mid-November: N. C. Wyeth House and Studio Tours, Brandywine
    River Museum
April: Lecture series, Chadds Ford Historical Society
April and May: Community Open, Delaware Center for the Contemporary Arts
Early April through late May: Acres of Spring, Longwood Gardens
April, late in the month: Dr. Carothers' Day program, Delaware History Museum
April through October, second Sunday: Living-history demonstrations, Brandywine
    Battlefield Park
Spring: Lunchtime programs, Chester County Historical Society
Spring: History Day, Chester County Historical Society
May, first Saturday: Wilmington Garden Day, Wilmington
May, first Sunday: Point-to-Point races, Winterthur; May Day Festival, West Chester
May, one weekend early in month: Wilmington Flower Market, Wilmington
May, early in month: Polish Festival, Wilmington
May, the Sunday closest to May 5: Cinco de Mayo, Kennett Square
May, one weekend midmonth: May Festival, West Chester
May, Mother's Day: Willowdale Steeplechase, Unionville (Kennett Square)
May, Mother's Day weekend: Wildflower, plant, and seed sale, Brandywine
    River Museum
May: Golf outing, Chadds Ford Historical Society
May through August, Thursday evenings: Swingin' Summer Thursdays, West Chester
May through September, weekends: John Chads House and Barns-Brinton House
    open, Chadds Ford Historical Society
May through October, Saturday mornings: Growers Market, West Chester
Mid-May through mid-October, Fridays: Farmers' Market, Kennett Square
May, Memorial Day weekend: Antiques show, Brandywine River Museum;
    Brandywine River Blues Fest, Chaddsford Winery
Late May through late August or early September: Festival of Fountains, Longwood
    Gardens
Late May through mid-September: Summer Nights under the Stars Outdoor Concert
    Series, Chaddsford Winery
Summer: Trolleybus tours, Kennett Underground Railroad Center
June through August, usually Saturdays: Summer concert series, Kennett Square
June, first Friday: Gallery Walk, West Chester
June, a Saturday early in month: Blues & Brews, and Cruise Night, Kennett Square
June, first or second Sunday: Super Sunday street fair, West Chester
June, one weekend early in month: Greek Festival, Wilmington
June, one Sunday early in month: Taste of Wilmington Festival, Wilmington
June (resuming in 2005): Craft Fair, Delaware Art Museum
June, one weekend midmonth: St. Anthony's Italian Festival, Wilmington; Clifford
    Brown Jazz Festival, Wilmington
June, Friday and Saturday the week before Father's Day: Greenville Summer Art
    Show, Wilmington
June, Father's Day: Fatherfest, American Helicopter Museum
June: Concert Series, Rockwood Mansion Park
July, Tuesdays: The Creek Kids, Hagley Museum
July, Thursday mornings: Sights and Sounds workshops for children, Brandywine
    River Museum

July and August, Tuesdays: Terrific Tuesdays for children, Winterthur

July and August, Saturdays: Summer Dollar Days, Hagley Museum

July Fourth: Independence Day Celebration along Christina Waterfront, Wilmington

July, date varies: Turk's Head Music Festival, West Chester

July, second weekend: Ice Cream Festival, Rockwood Mansion Park

July, one Saturday late in the month: Antique Car Show, Chadds Ford Historical Society

Late July through early September: Summer Concert Series, Wilmington

August, some Sundays: Summer Science Sundays, Hagley Museum

August, Wednesdays: Bike and Hike, Hagley Museum

August, one weekend midmonth: Cool Blues, Brews, and BBQs, Wilmington

August or September: Caribbean Festival, Wilmington

September, Labor Day weekend: Jazz Festival, Chaddsford Winery

September, weekend after Labor Day: Mushroom Festival, Kennett Square; Chadds Ford Days, Chadds Ford Historical Society

September, Sunday after Labor Day: Carriage House Attic Sale, Brinton 1704 House

September: GardenFest, Longwood Gardens

September and October, most weekends: Fall Harvest Market, Brandywine River Museum

September, one weekend midmonth: Pennsbury Land Trust Hot Air Balloon Festival (Chadds Ford)

September, third Sunday: Downtown Restaurant Festival, West Chester

September, one Sunday midmonth: Hagley Car Show, Hagley Museum

September through May: Wednesday evening lectures, Chester County Historical Society

September, one Saturday late in month: DuPont Riverfest & Delaware Transportation Festival, Wilmington

September, one Sunday late in month: Revolutionary Times Battle Reenactment, Brandywine Battlefield Park

Fall: Lunch 'n' Learn, Chester County Historical Society

Fall, three Sundays: Concert Series at the Soda House, Hagley Museum

October, first Friday: Gallery Walk, West Chester

October, first Saturday: Chester County Day, West Chester

October, first week: Wilmington Independent Film Festival, Wilmington

Early October through mid-October: Autumn's Colors, Longwood Gardens

Early October through late November: Hayrides for groups, Rockwood Mansion Park

October, one day; African-American art exhibit, Chester County Historical Society

October, one weekend midmonth: All-Helicopter Air Show–Rotorfest, American Helicopter Museum

October, one weekend midmonth: Craft Fair, Hagley Museum

October, Thursday before Halloween: Halloween Parade, West Chester

October, Thursday through Sunday before Halloween: Great Pumpkin Carve, Chadds Ford Historical Society

Late October through the Sunday before Thanksgiving: Chrysanthemum Festival, Longwood Gardens

October, one Sunday late in month: Pennsylvania Hunt Cup Races, Unionville (Kennett Square)

November: Fall conference, Chester County Historical Society

November, one weekend early in the month: Delaware Antiques Show, Winterthur

November, Friday, Saturday, and Sunday early in month: Festival of Museum Shopping, Hagley Museum

Early November through early January: Yuletide, Winterthur

November: Van tours of Brandywine Battlefield National Historic Landmark, Brandywine Battlefield Park

November and December, most weekends: Holiday Shops, Brandywine River Museum

November and December, selected evenings: Night of Enchanted Lights for families, Winterthur

Late November and early December: Visit with Santa Claus, American Helicopter Museum

Late November through Sunday after Christmas: Holiday tree exhibit, Chadds Ford Historical Society

November, Thanksgiving Day through early January: A Longwood Gardens Christmas, Longwood Gardens

November, day after Thanksgiving through early January: A Brandywine Christmas, Brandywine River Museum

November, Friday after Thanksgiving: Tree lighting, holiday parade, and open house, Kennett Square

November, day after Thanksgiving through early January: Christmas at Hagley, Hagley Museum

December, Fridays, Saturdays, and Sundays until Christmas: Holiday Open House Weekends with Santa, Rockwood Mansion Park

December, Sundays: Horse-drawn carriage rides on State Street, Kennett Square

December, Friday through Monday early in month: Old-Fashioned Christmas, West Chester

December, first Saturday: Candlelight Christmas, Brandywine Battlefield Park in conjunction with Chadds Ford Historical Society; YWCA Holiday House Tour, West Chester

December, selected Saturdays before Christmas: Breakfast with Santa, Winterthur

December, first weekend: Critter Sale, Brandywine River Museum

Early December through mid-January: Winter Wonderland Festival of Lights, Rockwood Mansion Park

December, second Saturday: Holiday House Tour, Delaware Art Museum

December, second Sunday: Old Home Candlelight Tour, Kennett Square

December: Old-fashioned Christmas events, Chester County Historical Society

December 27 and 28: Dino Days, Delaware Museum of Natural History

SPECIALTY TOURS

To help you make the most of your time in the Brandywine Valley, here are attractions grouped by specific interests. Refer to the chapter in parentheses for detailed information.

Regional Highlights

If you only have a day or two in the Brandywine Valley, put Longwood Gardens (Kennett Square) at the top of your list. Then, depending on your interests, add Brandywine Battlefield Park (Chadds Ford), the Brandywine River Museum (Chadds Ford), the Chester County Historical Society (West Chester), or Winterthur, An American Country Estate (Wilmington).

For Antique Lovers

Antique shops along PA/DE Route 52 in Fairville and Centreville (Chadds Ford and Wilmington)
Antique shops along U.S. Route 1 from Chadds Ford to Kennett Square (Chadds Ford and Kennett Square)
Brandywine River Museum Antiques Show (Chadds Ford)
Chester County Historical Society Antiques Show (West Chester)
Delaware Antiques Show (Wilmington)
Delaware Toy and Miniature Museum (Wilmington)
Nemours Mansion and Gardens (Wilmington)
Winterthur, An American Country Estate (Wilmington)

For Art Lovers

Brandywine River Museum, including the N. C. Wyeth House and Studio (Chadds Ford)
Delaware Art Museum (Wilmington)
Delaware Center for the Contemporary Arts (Wilmington)
Galleries or an Art Stroll event in downtown Kennett Square (Kennett Square)
Galleries or an Art on the Town event in Wilmington (Wilmington)
Galleries or a Gallery Walk in downtown West Chester (West Chester)
Somerville Manning Gallery (Wilmington)

For Families

American Helicopter Museum and Education Center (West Chester)
Brandywine Zoo (Wilmington)
Delaware Museum of Natural History (Wilmington)
Delaware Toy and Miniature Museum (Wilmington)
Hagley Museum (Wilmington)
Historical Society of Delaware/Delaware History Museum (Wilmington)
Kalmar Nyckel tall ship (Wilmington)
Longwood Gardens (Kennett Square)

Rockford Park Tower (Wilmington)
Wilmington Blue Rocks baseball game (Wilmington)
Winterthur, An American Country Estate, especially Enchanted Woods (Wilmington)

For Garden Lovers

Brandywine River Museum wildflower garden (Chadds Ford)
Gibraltar Gardens (Wilmington)
Goodstay Gardens (Wilmington)
Longwood Gardens (Kennett Square)
Nemours Mansion and Gardens (Wilmington)
Winterthur, An American Country Estate (Wilmington)

For History Lovers

Brandywine Battlefield Park (Chadds Ford)
Chadds Ford Historical Society, including the John Chads House and Barns-Brinton
    House (Chadds Ford)
Chester County Historical Society (West Chester)
Hagley Museum (Wilmington)
Historical Society of Delaware/Delaware History Museum (Wilmington)
Kennett Underground Railroad Center/Kennett History Station (Kennett Square)
Rockwood Mansion Park (Wilmington)
William Brinton 1704 House (West Chester)

For Nature and Outdoor Recreation Lovers

Ashland Nature Center (Wilmington)
Brandywine Creek State Park, hiking (Wilmington)
Canoeing on the Brandywine with Wilderness Canoe Outfitters (Wilmington)
    or Northbrook Canoe Company (West Chester)
Golf (Kennett Square, West Chester, and Wilmington)
Horseback riding (West Chester and Kennett Square)
Ice skating (West Chester and Wilmington)
Mt. Cuba Astronomical Observatory, Observatory public night (Wilmington)

For Shoppers

Baldwin's Book Barn (West Chester)
Chadds Ford Barn Shoppes (Chadds Ford)
Holly Peters Oriental Rugs (Chadds Ford)
Olde Ridge Village Shoppes (Chadds Ford)
QVC Studio Tour (West Chester)
Shipyard Shops along the Christina Riverfront (Wilmington)
West Chester's boutiques, mainly on High, Gay, and Market Streets (West Chester)

Unique Festivals

Balloon Glow (Chadds Ford)
Chester County Day (West Chester)
Fireworks and Fountains at Longwood Gardens (Kennett Square)
Great Pumpkin Carve (Chadds Ford)
Mushroom Festival (Kennett Square)

FURTHER READING

Brandywine Conservancy, Inc. *An American Vision: Three Generations of Wyeth Art.* Boston: Bulfinch Press, an imprint of Little, Brown and Company, 1987.

Bryson, Lew. *Pennsylvania Breweries. 2nd ed.* Mechanicsburg, PA: Stackpole Books, 2000.

Carr, William H. A. *The du Ponts of Delaware.* New York: Dodd, Mead & Co., 1964.

Cope, Gilbert, and John Smith Futhey. *History of Chester County, Pennsylvania, with Genealogical and Biographical Sketches.* Bowie, MD: Heritage Books, 1995. (Originally published 1881 by Louis H. Everts, Philadelphia.)

Du Pont de Nemours (E. I.) and Co. *Du Pont, the Autobiography of an American Enterprise.* Wilmington, DE: E. I. du Pont de Nemours and Co., 1952.

Hagley Museum and Library, Jill Mackenzie, ed. *Impressions of Hagley.* Wilmington, DE: Hagley Museum and Library, 1991.

Harper, Douglas R. *West Chester to 1865: That Elegant & Notorious Place.* West Chester, PA: Chester County Historical Society, 1999.

Hoffecker, Carol E. *Delaware: The First State.* Wilmington, DE: Middle Atlantic Press, 1988.

James, Marquis. *Alfred I. du Pont, the Family Rebel.* Indianapolis: Bobbs-Merrill Co., 1941.

Kipp, Carol, ed. *Centreville: The History of a Delaware Village.* Centreville, DE: Centreville Civic Association, 2001.

McCoy, Anna B. *John W. McCoy: American Painter.* Camden, ME: Down East Books, 2001.

McGuire, Thomas J. *Brandywine Battlefield Park: Pennsylvania Trail of History Guide.* Mechanicsburg, PA: Stackpole Books, 2001.

Meryman, Richard. *Andrew Wyeth: A Secret Life.* New York: HarperCollins Publishers, 1996.

Michaelis, David. *N. C. Wyeth: A Biography.* New York: Alfred A. Knopf, 1998.

Munroe, John A. *History of Delaware.* Newark, DE: University of Delaware Press, 1984.

Swisher, Joe A. *The Complete Guide to Delaware Historic Markers.* Photographs by Roger Miller. Baltimore: Image Publishing, 2002.

Switala, William J. *Underground Railroad in Pennsylvania.* Mechanicsburg, PA: Stackpole Books, 2001.

Taylor, Frances Cloud. *The Trackless Trail Leads On: An Exploration of Conductors and Their Stations.* Kennett Square, PA: self-published, 1995.

Thompson, George E., Sr. *A Man and His Garden: The Story of Pierre S. du Pont's Development of Longwood Gardens.* Kennett Square, PA: Longwood Gardens, 1976.

Thompson, Thomas R. *Chris: A Biography of Christian C. Sanderson.* Philadelphia: Dorrance & Company, 1973.

Toohey, Jeanette M. *Pre-Raphaelites: The Samuel and Mary R. Bancroft Collection of the Delaware Art Museum.* Wilmington, DE: Delaware Art Museum, 1995.

Westerman, Carla. *Chadds Ford: History, Heroes and Landmarks.* Gettysburg: Thomas Publications, 2003.

Williams, William H. *The First State: An Illustrated History of Delaware.* Northridge, CA: C. A. Windsor Publications, 1985.

Winkler, John Kennedy. *The Du Pont Dynasty.* New York: Reynal & Hitchcock, 1935.

Wyeth, Andrew, with Thomas Hoving. *Andrew Wyeth: Autobiography.* Boston: Bulfinch Press, an imprint of Little, Brown and Company, 1995.

ACKNOWLEDGMENTS

This book owes its existence to the scores of people who offered many types of support. In particular, I am grateful to personnel at tourism promotion agencies, convention and visitors bureaus, and chambers of commerce throughout the region. Their help was invaluable in identifying likely candidates for inclusion.

A big thank-you goes to staff members at all of the sites covered. These people returned my calls, answered my e-mails, took me on tours, reviewed preliminary versions of the text for accuracy, and in some cases provided photographs. One of the nicest parts of this project was getting to meet many of these fine people.

The following people deserve my thanks. American Helicopter Museum: Kathleen Bratton; Brandywine Battlefield Park: Erin McDonald, Helen Mahnke, and Elizabeth Rump; Brandywine Conference and Visitors Bureau: Lisa Carnesi; Brandywine River Museum: Halsey Spruance; William Brinton 1704 House: Barbara Clough and Jacquie Roach; Chadds Ford Historical Society: Karen Smith and Lori Stoudt; Chaddsford Winery: Lee Miller; Chester County Conference and Visitors Bureau: Doug Harris; Chester County Historical Society: Michael Dolan, Otis Morse, Diane Rofini, and Roland Woodward; Delaware Art Museum: Lora Englehart and Lise Monty; Delaware Center for the Contemporary Arts: Jessi LaCosta.

Also, from the Delaware Historical Society: Jan Morrill; Delaware Sports Museum and Hall of Fame: Dave Kujala and Jon Rafal; Delaware Museum of Natural History: Joann Outten and Stephen Reynolds; Delaware Toy and Miniature Museum: Beverly Thomes; Greater Wilmington Convention and Visitors Bureau: J. Harry Feldman and Catherine Larkin; Hagley Museum: Suzanna Rogers; Kennett History Station/Kennett Underground Railroad Center: Mary L. Dugan; Kennett Square Borough: Mary Hutchins; Longwood Gardens: Colvin Randall and Elizabeth Sullivan; Nemours Mansion and Gardens: Francesca Biella Bonny, Paddy Dietz, Shirley S. Jelinek, and Susan Matsen; QVC: Brandon Hamm.

In addition, Rockwood Park Mansion: Anthony L. Carter and Philip Nord; Christian C. Sanderson Museum: Pat Koedding, Jim Nelson, Richard A. McLellan, and Thomas R. Thompson; West Chester Business Improvement District: Malcolm Johnstone and Elizabeth McGuire; Wilmington Blue Rocks: Ray Cotrufo; Winterthur, An American Country Estate: Joyce Gamble, Deborah Harper, Hillary Holland, Catherine Larkin, and Susan Newton.

These people at local accommodations were very helpful. Brandywine River Hotel: Stacey Walker; Broadlawns Bed and Breakfast: Dorene and Bill Winters; Fairville Inn Bed and Breakfast: Jane and Noel McStay; Faunbrook Bed and Breakfast: Pat Phillips; Harlan Log House Bed and Breakfast: Beverly McCausland and Laird McCausland; Hedgerow Bed and Breakfast Suites: Barbara and John Haedrich; Hotel du Pont: Carolyn F. Grubb; The Inn at Montchanin Village: Blake Peery; Kennett House Bed and Breakfast: Carol and Jeff Yetter; Pennsbury Inn: Cheryl and Chip Grono.

Many people provided information about restaurants. The Dilworthtown Inn: James Barnes and Robin Kraheck; Hotel du Pont Green Room: Carolyn F. Grubb; Kennett Square Inn: Stephen Warner; Krazy Kat's: Blake Peery; Simon Pearce on the Brandywine: Scott Evans, Michael Seznec, and P. J. Skehan; specialTeas Tea Room: Carole Bradley, Judith Finnigan, and Diane Nayman.

I am fortunate to have had assistance from shop owners, artists, and gallery staffers. DragonFly Gallery: Kathleen Cole; Holland Art House: Ben Gall and Tom Bromley; Anna Brelsford McCoy; Dennis Park; Holly Peters Oriental Rugs: Graham Cunningham, Holly Peters, and Jamie Wright; Peter Sculthorpe; Simple Pleasures: Joanne and Rick Sterlacci; Somerville Manning Gallery: Victoria Manning, Sarah Stevens, and Sadie Somerville; Van Tassel/Baumann American Antiques and Girlhood Embroidery: Ruth Van Tassel; Westtown Station Gallery: Ken Kazanjian.

A special thank-you goes to Rick Davis, of Rick Davis Photographic Communications (rickdavis@earthlink.net), who generously gave me permission to reproduce some of the beautiful photographs he took for West Chester's Business Improvement District.

For information about Amelia Earhart's vertical flight achievements in southeastern Pennsylvania, thanks to Walter Ellis of the Philadelphia Aero Club.

My eternal gratitude goes to the team at Stackpole Books: Joyce Bond, Amy Cooper, Kerry Jean Handel and Beth Oberholtzer, Donna Pope, Wendy Reynolds, and Caroline Stover. Every writer should have the opportunity to work with an editor like Stackpole's Kyle Weaver. Kyle is well organized, creative, supportive, knowledgeable, and professional, and also happens to be a nice person. Without his ongoing commitment, I never would have had the motivation to finish this book.

There is no way I could have accepted the obligation to take on this project, let alone fulfilled that obligation, without the support of my family and friends. My mother, Babe Hernes, took on the role of research assistant with enthusiasm and completed her duties with competence and style. I received priceless moral support from Seymour Hernes, Barry Silverman, Helene and Andy Silverman, and Shirley Silverman. My writerly friends Wanda McGlinchey-Ryan and Arlene Owen were my cheerleaders throughout this project. Others too numerous to mention offered ongoing encouragement for which I will always be grateful.

Jason and Steven Silverman are the two best assistants any mom could have. They toured sites with me, kept a running tally of my page count, helped proofread, gave their opinions on photographs, and were understanding when I said, "Just a minute, I'm working!" I look forward to spending more time exploring the Brandywine Valley with them.

My husband, Alan B. Silverman, supplied every kind of support possible, from moral to technical. He took photographs, did computer magic to read electronic photo files, took over my domestic and child-care responsibilities when I was working extra hours . . . and remained patient and loving every step of the way.

INDEX

ABOUT THE AUTHOR

Sharon Hernes Silverman is the author of several hundred articles and seven books, including *Pennsylvania Snacks: A Guide to Food Factory Tours* (2001), *Daniel Boone Homestead: Pennsylvania Trail of History Guide* (2000), and *Going Underground: Your Guide to Caves in the Mid-Atlantic* (1991). For three years she wrote "At the Inn," a column for *Maryland Magazine*. Her travel-writing assignments have taken her from Great Britain to Hawaii, but her favorite place to write about is her native Pennsylvania. In 1992, she won a Hawaii Visitors Bureau travel writing award for her *Denver Post* article about the island of Niihau. Silverman lives with her husband and two sons in West Chester, Pennsylvania.

Bedding Plants

Carolyn Jones

Whitecap Books Ltd.
Vancouver/Toronto

Copyright © 1990 by Carolyn Jones

Whitecap Books

Vancouver/Toronto

Edited by Elaine Jones

Cover photographs and interior photographs by David Jones

Cover design by Carolyn Deby

Typeset at The Vancouver Desktop Publishing Centre Ltd.

Printed and bound in Canada by Friesen Printers, Altona, Manitoba

Canadian Cataloguing in Publication Data

Jones, Carolyn, 1950–
Bedding plants

(Ontario gardening series)
ISBN 0-921061-93-5

Bedding Plants–Ontario. I. Title
II. Series

SB423.75.C2J65 1990   635.9'62'09713
C90-0911668-9

CONTENTS

Foreword

This book is intended for gardeners east of the Rockies—a region where rain is seldom more than adequate, where winters are cold and summers are hot—a region, in fact, where growing plants is a challenge and growing them well, an achievement.

Spring is always a chancy time, arriving on a different date each year and staying for only a brief visit. Frost is slow to thaw and just when it seems safe to plant out, another snowfall whitens the landscape. Summer arrives at last, and plants grow at a tremendous rate. Then, as day follows hot day, with never a hint of rain, plants start to droop in the heat and gradually stop growing. When rain finally comes, it may be a thunderstorm that threatens to wash the plants that were selected with such care out of the ground, or pound them into the mud. Yet, in spite of the setbacks and unforeseen tricks of nature, gardeners are ever optimistic. They share information with neighbors, read voraciously and continue to plan for the next growing season. And that is the beauty of bedding plants: each year brings a new opportunity to experiment with colorful new annuals.

This book describes and gives advice on growing just about every bedding plant you are ever likely to encounter—from the common varieties found in every garden center to plants carried by only a few specialty growers and those found only in seed catalogues.

Unfortunately, the majority of garden centers and small nurseries no longer grow their own bedding plants. With the high cost of heating greenhouses, it becomes uneconomical to grow comparatively small quantities of plants. Instead, large commercial operations, often many miles away where winters are less severe, grow the bedding plants and ship them in by transport truck. The customer is at the mercy of the supplier and has to take what is offered. If you are looking for something other than the "bread and butter" annuals, it is worth searching for the rare nursery that grows its own plants. Once the spring rush is over, some owners may even be willing to try something new for you.

Most growers won't try something they don't think will sell, and another solution for buyers wanting to experiment with new plants is to start their own plants from seed. If you are a novice at growing from seed, start with something easy, such as marigolds or zinnias. The seed is inexpensive and almost foolproof. With experience, you can move on to more exotic plants—those that you *won't* find in the local garden center but that *will* earn you a reputation for having a green thumb.

Most of all, enjoy experimenting with bedding plants, as each year brings a new crop of surprises.

—*Trevor Cole*
Curator, Dominion Arboretum
Ottawa, Ontario

Acknowledgments

Many people and organizations helped in preparing this book; to them all I offer my sincere thanks.

For allowing us to visit their display gardens and take photographs, thanks go to Minter Gardens, Chilliwack, and Butchart Gardens, near Victoria; and for answering horticultural questions concerning these two facilities, special thanks to Brian Minter and Daphne Fraser.

To Bob Kell, William Choukalos and Karl Chalupa for their patience in allowing strangers into their gardens to take photographs.

To the staff at Ball-Superior Seed Company, Mississauga; Ball Seed Company, West Chicago, Illinois; BC Greenhouse Builders, Burnaby; Eddi's Wholesale Garden Supply, Surrey; Fraser Nurseries, Richmond; Green Valley Fertilizer, Surrey; Skagit Nurseries, Mt. Vernon, Washington; and Van Noort Bulb Company, Surrey, for information concerning their products.

To Alex Downie, Vandusen Botanical Garden, Vancouver; Gunter

Edel, New Westminster Parks Board; and the gardeners at Stanley Park, Vancouver, for their help in naming cultivars used in photographs.

To Dr. Norma Senn, Fraser Valley Community College, Chilliwack, and All-America Selections Trial Ground Judge, UBC Department of Plant Science, Vancouver; Dr. Gerald Straley, UBC Botanical Gardens, Vancouver; Dr. Henry Gerber, BC Ministry of Agriculture and Food, Cloverdale; and the soil scientists at Soilcon Laboratories, Richmond, for help with taxonomic and technical details.

To Dr. Robert Armstrong, Longwood Gardens, Pennsylvania, for taking the time to share the story of New Guinea impatiens with me; and to Clive Innes, Holly Gate International, Sussex, England, for help with the taxonomy of Livingstone daisy and ice plant.

To George McLauchlan, foreman at Sunset Nursery, Vancouver Parks Board for answering many questions on propagation.

To Blythe Foottit, North Gower; Marjorie Mason Hogue, Pineridge Garden Gallery, Pickering; Mark Stephens, Westgro Sales; and John Valleau, ValleyBrook Gardens, St. Catherines—many thanks for information on gardening in Ontario. Special thanks to Trevor Cole, Curator, Dominion Arboretum, Ottawa, for his invaluable comments.

I am grateful to Colleen MacMillan, my publisher at Whitecap Books, for offering me the opportunity to write this book, and to the other staff at Whitecap for their help. To Elaine Jones, my editor, for her encouragement, patience and excellent advice.

To my friends Pat Logie and Douglas Justice go my deepest appreciation and admiration. Pat provided me with all the unusual bedding plants I had hoped to write about, giving me the opportunity for hands-on experience, and she answered endless questions about cultivars, propagation and care of bedding plants, particularly in a greenhouse situation. Douglas shared with me his extensive knowledge of all areas of horticulture and his deep love of plants. His generosity in reading the manuscript, his honesty and sense of humor made all the difference.

To my children, Gwyneth, Morgan and Evan, and to my husband, David, for his kind support and for all those early mornings in search of just the right shot before the sun got too bright—while I was fast asleep—I extend my love and gratitude.

Finally, I dedicate this book to the memory of my grandmother, Dorothy Hilda Myser, through whose eyes I first saw gardens as magical places.

1

What are Bedding Plants?

$\mathbf{M}$ost gardening book series have one volume about annuals, but the scope of this book is expanded to cover most of the plants you are likely to find in the "bedding plant" section of a garden shop and which you might see used in bedding schemes and hanging baskets in public display gardens. It groups together in one volume those plants that are used for the same purpose in the garden: that is, seasonal color. These plants are temporary on the garden scene, being planted with the intention of removing them at the end of the season. Included are annuals, biennials, perennials, a few plants that are shrubs in their native land, several vines and creepers and some plants that grow from bulbs or tubers.

Unusual annuals that you are not likely to find in shops are also described here. The commercial bedding plant industry is oriented to producing a plant which looks good, preferably in bloom, in May in a 4-inch (10-cm) pot at the largest. There is tremendous price competition, so most suppliers are not willing to grow an unusual crop which might be more expensive to produce or difficult to sell. You might find these unusual bedding plants at a specialty garden center, but, in most cases, they will have to be grown from seed.

Following are explanations of the various categories of bedding plant referred to in the encyclopedia part of the book. Knowing more about the origins of bedding plants and how they grow in the wild will give you a better understanding of their needs in your garden.

Hardy and half-hardy annuals

An annual is a plant that completes its life cycle in one growing season; that is, it grows, blooms, sets seed and dies all in one year. Examples are sweet alyssum, marigold, and lobelia. Annuals must be propagated from seed, but, unless you intend to save the seed, remove fading flowers to prevent seed from forming. Once annuals set seed, they will stop blooming.

Annuals fall into two groups: hardy and half-hardy. Most of the common hardy annuals are native to Europe, so it is not surprising that they were among the very first flowers cultivated in gardens. It would have been easy to save a bit of seed from a wild plant and throw it into some corner of the garden in the early spring. In their natural life cycle, these hardy annuals bloom in summer and set seed, which drops into the garden, overwinters and sprouts early in the spring. Some may sprout in the fall and the young seedlings will survive the winter and bloom the next spring. All hardy annuals are native to temperate zones and many are the popular "cottage garden flowers," such as cornflowers and love-in-a-mist.

Hardy annuals tend to be easy to grow from seed and do not require any bottom heat to germinate. They may be seeded directly in the garden in March or April and come into bloom quickly. Many will seed themselves in the garden, so watch for seedlings when you weed. Some bloom early and then fade out, whether you deadhead them or not. Cornflowers, candytuft, godetia and annual chrysanthemum tend to do this, but a second sowing will produce bloom later in the summer.

Most of the popular annuals are half-hardy annuals. They are native to the warmer parts of the world and were introduced to Europe by explorers, who brought them home from South Africa, South America, Asia and Australia. You can well imagine that these annuals need some extra care to adapt to our cool weather. Like the hardy annuals, they are grown from seed, but if the seeds are sown in soil which is too cold, they will not germinate. The seeds are generally sown indoors to get earlier bloom. Some require a very warm temperature, which can be provided by setting pots on a heating cable or other heat source. Plants should not be set out until the weather warms up at the end of May or early June. Once established in the garden, they put on a colorful display through the summer.

Half-hardy perennials

Another large group of plants that we use extensively for summer bedding also originates from hot climates, but these plants are actually perennials rather than annuals in their native homes. This means that either some leaves remain on the plant year-round and the plant lives for many years, but does not become woody as a shrub does, or that the leaves die back to ground level, but the roots remain alive (a herbaceous perennial). Unlike an annual, the plant is not "programmed" to set seed and die. They are referred to as half-hardy perennials because they cannot survive the frost.

The fact that they are perennial is not so critical in terms of their use as summer bedding, but knowing their natural inclination is useful in other ways. Many may be propagated from cuttings as well as seed. If a particular plant has some unique feature—for example, the dainty leaves of the geranium 'Distinction'—it may be kept alive indefinitely from cuttings. Named cultivars that are propagated from cuttings are actually clones of one original plant; that is, they have identical genes. (Plants grown from seed, although very similar in appearance, are usually variable genetically.) To keep these half-hardy perennials alive from year to year, they must be overwintered in a greenhouse. Those which will tolerate lower light levels, such as fibrous begonias or the polka dot plant, can even be taken indoors for use as houseplants.

Half-hardy shrubs and subshrubs

A handful of bedding plants are actually shrubs or subshrubs from warmer climates. Shrubs form woody branches, while subshrubs are woody just at the base. The interesting feature about the shrubby bedding plants is that because they form woody tissue they have the strength to be trained into tree form, called standards in the nursery trade. Flowering maple, fuchsia and lantana are often trained in this way, and you may see some plants that are over fifteen years old with thick trunks. They are valuable in bedding schemes because they bloom all summer and add height, but they are tricky for the home gardener to overwinter, requiring a cool greenhouse, a sunroom or extra lighting. Fuchsia trees are readily available and not so expensive that it prohibits planting them for one season only.

Biennials

Biennial bedding plants bloom in the second year after they are sown. Some examples are forget-me-nots, wallflowers and sweet williams; they are seeded in summer, planted out in the fall, and after a winter chill they bloom in the second year. Ornamental cabbage and kale fall into this category, but, being grown for foliage alone, the plants are removed before they bloom.

Tubers and rhizomes

Four of the bedding plants included are perennials that form tubers or rhizomes. Both are types of swollen roots or stems which function as underground storage organs. These plants may easily be kept from year to year, and some gardeners have tuberous begonias that are over twenty years old.

Using Bedding Plants in the Garden

The first priority when it comes to gardening is that you enjoy it. Whether you have a small balcony garden to dabble in or a large garden to tend, it should meet your personal needs and provide you with pleasure and enjoyment. Consider ideas you get from books and from visiting public and friends' gardens, but don't spoil your fun by imposing others' ideas on your own.

When it comes to designing with bedding plants, you can afford to experiment, because any scheme you don't like will be gone at the end of the season, while favorite arrangements can be repeated year after year. The consequences of planting shrubs or trees in the wrong location are much more serious, but with many bedding plants you can even dig them up and move them during the summer if you are so inclined.

There has been a revival of interest in herbaceous perennials in the past few years and a trend to abandoning traditional bedding plans in favor of more extensive use of perennials. The rationale is that perennials are less work and cost less than buying bedding plants each spring.

In fact, though, perennials do require plenty of work and most bloom for about one month, rather than the four or five months that most bedding plants bloom. A combination of both types of plants will offer greater variety, give color through most of the year, reduce cost and still allow experimentation from season to season.

Formal bedding schemes

With the rise of heated greenhouses in Britain in the 1850s, formal bedding-out schemes became the rage. Flower beds with complex outlines were laid out in lawns and filled with bright colors and patterns. These schemes have three components: dot plants for height, groundwork plants for filling in and edging plants to complete the picture. During the late 1800s, there was a movement to replace formal bedding schemes with huge herbaceous borders.

The legacy of these formal bedding schemes is still seen today in public gardens. For example, Figure 7-7 shows a standard lantana used as a dot plant, with groundwork plants of blue salvia, dwarf white marguerite daisies, and red geraniums. Three edging plants are used in neat rows: dwarf yellow marigolds, blue ageratum and white sweet alyssum.

In the home garden, the same orderly effect can be achieved on a smaller scale. Figure 6-10 shows parallel rows of red geraniums and silver dusty miller used to edge a mixed border. A mass of impatiens along a shady front path, a standard fuchsia centered in a circle of begonias, or a bed of snapdragons in a sunny lawn are all echoes of a bygone day.

With formal bedding schemes, it is important to group plants of the same cultivar. To avoid a spotty effect, use large numbers of a few cultivars, rather than a few plants each of many varieties. Formal flower beds are especially effective when situated in a well-tended lawn or with an evergreen hedge as a backdrop.

Bedding plants in the mixed border

The mixed border is an ideal way to use bedding plants in the garden, balanced with the permanent plant material available to Ontario gardeners. The mixed border consists of a framework of shrubs with spaces, or "bays," for hardy perennials and bedding plants. Shrubs are usually planted toward the back of beds, as most will become tall in time.

Combine broadleaf and needle evergreens for year-round texture and add flowering shrubs for summer, winter or fall color. Depending on the plant hardiness zone you live in, your local nursery can help select shrubs suitable for your area. This basic plan will give you an easy-to-care-for framework. In the bays between and at the front of shrubs, plant perennial flowers that flourish in your zone. Some bloom early in the spring, before bedding plants; some are unrivalled for flower form and color, lending an air of richness to the garden scene. Bedding plants are the final touch in a mixed border, adding a splash of color in the summer months. The effect of such a well-balanced border is calming and the garden becomes a retreat from the busy pace of daily life.

Bedding plants in a rock garden

A rock garden is really a special type of mixed border, which combines low-growing plants of many types in a sloping setting, accented with large rocks. Rock garden purists prefer plants from high elevations, which are naturally ground-hugging, and would look askance at a rock garden with bedding plants, but experiment and see what works for you. Some suggestions are made in the encyclopedia and any of the "under 1 foot (30 cm) in height" plants from the quick reference chart could be considered.

Specialty gardens

Few gardeners can allot space to a cutting garden as was done in estate gardens, but a row of asters in an out-of-the-way corner or in the vegetable garden will provide masses of cut flowers. Some species, such as zinnias, bloom even more if they are cut.

Providing a child's garden for youngsters is an excellent way to encourage an interest in living things. Children particularly enjoy sweet peas, which they can cut for gifts or set on the table. They like fuchsias because they can pop the flower buds which fill out like balloons, and common flowers such as marigolds, which they recognize in other gardens. Four-o'clocks have big seeds that would be easy for a toddler to handle. Easy-to-grow species with a long bloom time are the best bet for children.

Filling in the gaps in new shrub borders

Newly planted shrubs should be far enough apart that they will not become crowded in a few years, and bedding plants are useful for filling in the gaps in these new shrub plantings. From a design point of view, it is best to use only one or two types of plants for such a purpose. Low-growers such as lobelia, impatiens, alyssum and fibrous begonias are ideal. If taller growers are needed, consider plants such as snapdragons and cornflower, which have a narrow upright habit. One note of caution: leaves of some shrubs, especially coniferous plants such as false cypress and juniper, will turn brown and their shape will be permanently spoiled if they are crowded by neighboring plants. As summer progresses, trim bedding plants if necessary to prevent crowding.

Container gardens: on the ground or in the air

Bedding plants are sensational in containers, be it hanging baskets, window boxes, planters of cedar, concrete, plastic or terra cotta. An advantage of growing bedding plants in containers is that the scene may be changed with the season. A large Chinese egg pot full of flowers by the front door is dramatic-looking, easy and fairly inexpensive to arrange. For some balcony gardeners, growing bedding plants in containers has become an art. Spring is ushered in with pots of pansies, wallflowers and spring-flowering bulbs, which are replaced with masses of lobelia, marigolds, geraniums and ageratum for all-summer color. In fall, interest is created using ornamental cabbage, dusty miller and perhaps an evergreen shrub. Chapters 5 and 6 are devoted to containers and hanging baskets.

3

From the Plant's Point of View

An understanding of a plant's biological requirements can assist in getting the most out of your garden. The light a plant needs in order to produce its own food through photosynthesis and the soil in which it will secure its roots and take up water and nutrients are the two most important factors in its environment. Gardening is a combination of putting a plant in the right spot and at the same time modifying its situation through watering, fertilizing and improving the soil. As you work, keep a mental checklist of plant needs, and you will find that your skill and appreciation increases enormously.

Light

This is the most difficult aspect of plant culture to control in the garden, so it is really the factor limiting which plants you will be able to use in a specific setting.

Light

The amount of sun a location receives is usually defined in terms of full sun, part or half-shade, and shade. Full sun is defined as at least four hours of sun during the middle of the day, between about 10 a.m. and 4 p.m. Half-shade is sun during the early morning or late afternoon, or the light received under trees with small leaves, such as birch. Shade cast all day by a building or trees with large leaves is full shade.

However, other factors should be taken into consideration. Reflected light bouncing off a white wall, for example, will brighten an otherwise shady area or turn a sunny location into a baking hot spot, and plants that normally prefer some shade will tolerate more light if the soil is not overly dry or if the area is protected from drying winds.

As with many situations in gardening, often you won't know until you try. If the light factor is not right, your plants will soon let you know. Lack of light will cause the plant to become stretched; the leaves may become thin and the plant will not bloom well. If a plant gets too much sun, the leaves will look bleached or dry and burned-looking. Because they do not have extensive roots, most bedding plants will tolerate being moved, so if you feel the plant is unhappy with a particular sun situation, it is possible to dig it up, with an 8-inch (20-cm) ball of soil, and to replant it in a different location, watering it in well.

When planting under trees, remember that even though the light factor may be right for a shade-tolerant plant, the roots of a tree tend to steal all the moisture and nutrients from the soil. This is especially true of coniferous trees. If you are using bedding plants in such a setting, enrich the soil and be generous with fertilizer. Liberal amounts of mushroom manure or horse manure and a sprinkling of an all-purpose fertilizer such as 6-9-6 or 5-10-10 will give outstanding results.

To sum up, the first consideration when choosing the plants for any location is light. If you are planning your garden in winter or early spring, be sure to consider the light factor when the sun is higher in the sky and there are leaves on the trees.

Soil testing

Ontario has a wide range of soil types; it is not within the scope of this book to give more than a brief introduction to the complex subject of soil science. If you wish to get the most out of your garden, it is worthwhile having your soil tested commercially. For a surprisingly reasonable price, you can find out the pH, particle size and soil fertility. Soil-testing laboratories will also suggest ways you can improve your soil. As soil amendments and fertilizers can be expensive, having your soil tested can be well worth the cost. For a soil-testing lab near you, refer to the yellow pages of your telephone directory under laboratories—testing. Samples can also be sent to most labs through the mail, if you live out of town.

The following sections will introduce you to some of the facets of soil science.

Soil texture ✓

Soils have both a mineral and an organic component. The mineral component is derived from weathered rock. The size of mineral particles contributes to soil texture: many very fine particles result in a clay soil; as particle size increases the soil becomes sandy. This texture determines the rate of flow of water, with water moving slowly through a clay soil and more quickly through a sandy soil. Consequently, it takes a lot of watering to thoroughly wet a clay soil, and it doesn't dry out quickly. A sandy soil needs less water to be wet to the same depth, but it dries out very quickly. To get an idea of which type of soil you have, squeeze a damp handful of soil, then gently press on the ball. If it forms a firm, hard ball, you probably have clay soil—common in many parts of Ontario. If the soil ball crumbles easily, your soil is probably sandy.

Clay soil can be very difficult to manage. Coarse sand can improve the texture of the soil. However, in order to make a significant change, it is necessary to add about 50 percent sand to the soil—a considerable amount. This could be done by spreading an 8-inch (20-cm) layer of sand over your soil and digging it in to a depth of 16 inches (40 cm), incorporating the sand well into the soil. If you have a large area to treat, it is more economical to arrange for a truckload of sand to be delivered. Be sure to use only coarse sand.

The texture of clay soil can also be improved by adding organic matter. Well-rotted manure, compost, wood chips and peat moss are possibilities. If poor drainage is a problem in your soil, peat moss may not be the best choice because of its ability to hold moisture.

Note: When wood chips are added to the soil, soil organisms begin to break it down, which actually reduces the available soil nitrogen initially. Therefore, it is necessary to add extra nitrogen so your plants will not suffer. You can add 8 ounces (227 grams) by weight of bloodmeal to each 5 pounds (2.2 kg) of chips, or add an equivalent amount of nitrogen in another form—preferably a slow-release fertilizer such as a lawn fertilizer with sulfur-coated urea.

In addition to differing in the way they drain, clay and sandy soil differ in their ability to retain plant nutrients. Fertilizer molecules, particularly those of nitrogen and potassium, are easily washed out of sandy soils, but are held in clay soils more firmly, remaining available to plants. If you have a sandy soil, you will use more fertilizer to keep your plants healthy than if you have a clay soil. Adding organic matter to sandy soil will improve its ability to retain both moisture and nutrients.

Because it is 60 percent carbon, decomposed organic matter (humus) also darkens the soil, causing it to absorb heat and warm faster in the spring. The spongier texture of a soil with plenty of organic matter makes it easier for plant roots to penetrate, so plants will grow faster.

Poor drainage can result from a high water table. In this case, drainage tiles should be installed, or, easier for the home gardener, raised planters or beds can be contructed. Landscape ties or timbers make this an easy and relatively inexpensive job.

Soil pH

The pH is a measure of the acidity of a solution and is always expressed as a number from 0 to 14; 7 is a neutral pH. The lower the pH, the more acidic the solution; the higher the pH, the more alkaline. For example, lemon juice has a pH of 2; vinegar, pH 3; beer, pH 4. Milk has a pH of nearly 7; sea water, pH 8; and milk of magnesia, pH 10. Soil pH is determined by mixing the soil with water and measuring the pH of the resulting solution. Gardeners often refer to acidic soils as being sour and to neutral or slightly alkaline soils as being sweet. Depending on the pH of the soil, certain nutrients may exist in unavailable forms or may be present in toxic amounts.

In the province of Ontario, the soils range in pH from 5.5 (strongly acid) to 8.5 (moderately alkaline). Acid soils are more commonly associated with soils high in organic content, more common in the north of the province. Alkaline soils often consist of heavy clay, common in the southern part of the province—once part of an ancient seabed. The ideal pH range for growing most of the bedding plants covered in this book is 6 to 7. This is because at pH 6.5, there is the greatest availability of all soil nutrients.

If you do not have your soil tested professionally, keep an eye open for soil-testing clinics in local garden centers, or purchase a soil-testing kit to use at home. If your soil test shows that your soil is above pH 7, add generous amounts of organic matter. Most types of peat moss are acidic and will help to bring down the pH. Ideally, test the pH of any peat moss you add so you know what effect it will have.

Note: When adding peat moss to the soil, always make sure it is well-moistened. Put some peat moss in a wheelbarrow, add hot water and mix well until all of the peat moss has absorbed water.

If your soil test shows that your soil is below pH 6, it is necessary to make your soil sweeter by adding lime. There are three liming materials available to the home gardener. Hydrated lime (calcium hydroxide) is fast-acting and should only be used in preparing new beds before planting, never around existing plant material. Ground limestone (calcium carbonate) is sold as home and garden lime or agricultural lime. It takes from one to three months to act, depending on the particle size of the lime. Dolomite lime (calcium-magnesium carbonate) is ground from limestone high in magnesium, an important plant nutrient. Like calcium carbonate lime, it takes one to three months to act. Wood ashes also make the soil sweeter.

In general, adding 5 pounds of lime per 100 square feet (2.2 kg per 10m²) of soil will raise the pH one point. Do not use more lime than this in one application. If a greater change than one point is necessary, apply twice a year. For faster results, use hydrated lime at 3 pounds per 100 square feet (1.6 kg per 10m²), in new beds only, never near plants. Do not add lime and fertilizer to the soil at the same time; allow at least a week between the two.

Plant nutrients: N, P and K

The three major plant nutrients are nitrogen, phosphorus and potassium. N is the chemical symbol for nitrogen, P is for phosphorus and K is for potassium. The three numbers, which must appear on all fertilizers, represent the percentage of N, P and K in a standardized reference form. For example, 20-20-20 has the equivalent of 20 percent nitrogen, 20 percent phosphorus and 20 percent potassium.

Nitrogen is important for overall plant health, but especially for the leaves. As explained in the section on soil, some forms of nitrogen are readily washed out of some soils. A deficiency of nitrogen causes the older leaves to turn yellow and the new leaves to become quite small. Too much nitrogen results in dark green leaves, lots of soft leafy growth and few flowers. Excess nitrogen will also depress the amounts of phosphorus and potassium taken up.

Phosphorus, particularly important in root development, is often bound up in the soil in forms unavailable to plants. Availability is increased by adding well-rotted manure to the soil. Because phosphorus moves slowly through the soil, it is best added to the planting hole rather than scattered on the surface. Too little phosphorus will result in unusually dark green leaves and retarded growth. Leaves may be purplish and drop early. This symptom is often seen in a cold, wet spring. Adding phosphorus to the soil will help the plant cope with cool soil. Too much phosphorus is not usually a problem.

Potassium encourages general plant vigor and maturity. It increases a plant's resistance to disease and cold weather. A deficiency shows up as mottled lower leaves, yellowing beginning at the margin. Serious root injury may result from excessive amounts of potassium.

A professional soil test or a soil-testing kit can test for N, P and K. It is wise to know their availability in your soil before adding expensive fertilizers. Fertilizer run-off causes problems in our waterways.

Minor nutrients

Plants need other nutrients in smaller quantities. Calcium, magnesium, sulfur, iron, manganese, zinc, copper, boron, chlorine and molybdenum all play a role, but—with the exception of magnesium and iron—they are unlikely to be deficient in most garden soils. If using soilless potting mixes in containers, however, it is worth adding "fritted trace elements." This fertilizer has trace elements (all those listed above except calcium, magnesium, sulfur and chlorine) with finely ground glass (frit) as a carrier. In terms of liming materials, calcium is present in lime and magnesium in dolomite lime.

Fertilizer application types

There are basically two application types of fertilizer—dry and wet.

Granular fertilizers are mixtures of dry fertilizers. They are sprinkled on the soil surface, mixed into the top few inches (5–10 cm) and watered in well. They are easy to use and ideal for making up a flower bed. Adding a formula such as 6-9-6 or 5-10-10 will get plants off to a good start and last for about four to six weeks. The application should be repeated in the middle of July.

Soluble fertilizers are liquid or dry concentrates that must be diluted or dissolved in water. They are especially suitable for watering young transplants and container gardens, and take up less storage space than bulky granular fertilizers. Soluble fertilizers are fast-acting and give the gardener an opportunity to respond immediately to a plant's needs. At transplant time, use a fertilizer with plenty of phosphorus, such as 10-52-17, to promote root growth. If a plant has too much leafy growth and not enough bloom, use a fertilizer with less nitrogen, such as 15-30-15. If foliage is pale, use more nitrogen, for example, 20-20-20. (Check for spider mites first; they also cause pale foliage.)

Controlled release fertilizers such as Osmocote or Nutricote are the deluxe way to go. Nutrients are released according to the soil temperature, so plants get food when they are growing the fastest. The beauty of controlled release fertilizers is that they last from three months to one year, depending on the preparation. Most widely available to the home gardener is the three-month 14-14-14 formulation; applied in late May, it will feed plants through the summer.

Organic fertilizer

Some gardeners prefer to use natural products to provide plant nutrients. The following recipe is a general-purpose organic fertilizer. It may be used for vegetable and other garden plants. Omit lime if your soil is higher than pH 6 to 7. Mix together:

- four parts by volume seed meal or fish meal
- one part by volume rock phosphate or 1/2 part bone meal
- one part by volume dolomite lime
- one part by volume kelp meal

While organic fertilizers are a bit more expensive, they are much longer-lasting in the soil than chemical fertilizers. As the summer warms up and activity of soil microorganisms increases, more and more nutrients are released. If used each year, the soil will improve continually.

4

Planning
and
Planting

There are two basic approaches to planning a garden. In the first, the garden designer decides what picture he or she wishes to achieve and then systematically decides which plants to use. In terms of bedding, the procedure is as follows:

- Decide where in your garden you would like to use bedding plants.
- Make a note of the light and soil conditions, the heights required and the area of ground to be covered.
- Use the quick reference chart to determine possibilities based on height, suggested uses, light and soil.
- Refer to the photographs and read about each possible choice in the encyclopedia to find out more about cultivation, foliage, flower shape and color .
- Estimate the number of plants you need based on the suggested planting distances.

- If you prefer to buy as many plants as possible, buy seeds for only the hard-to-find varieties. (You may need to ask at your local garden center as to whether they plan to carry the plants you wish to buy.) If you like to grow all your plants from seed, order accordingly.

The second approach starts with the plants and works backwards. It is practiced by many plant collectors. If you would like to grow a certain bedding plant, wander around your garden (mentally or physically) looking for a spot that will meet its needs. This approach may not create such a fine effect in the garden, but it is ideal for the plant lover.

Buying bedding plants

There is a lot of competition in the bedding plant market these days, with grocery stores, hardware stores and even furniture stores getting into the act. If you like to get a good deal, shop carefully. There are advantages to buying in a garden center, even though the price may be higher. The plants are more likely to be labelled as to cultivar, the staff are more knowledgeable and the store should have a better selection. Garden shops are more likely to give their plants better care than grocery or hardware stores, because they have trained staff.

Choose plants which look compact, fresh and have good foliage color. If the plants are too tiny, they may have just been transplanted and will not be rooted yet. (If you do buy such young plants, allow them to grow in the packs for a few more weeks before planting out.) On the other hand, if the plants are too large and leggy in the packs, they may be stressed. Peek under the leaves for pests; yellow leaves may indicate hunger or spider mites.

Commercial bedding plant growers use a constant feeding program of soluble fertilizer in the irrigation system. Once in retail outlets, the plants are rarely fertilized. If the plants are being sold for a very low price (sometimes only a dime per pack over the wholesale price), a retailer is not going to spend money on expensive fertilizers and labor. Ideally, try to buy from a grower-retailer who sells directly to the public. If this is not possible, shop where there is a fast turnover of stock. If plants look like they have been in the store too long, they may be hungry and, with such a fast-growing crop as bedding plants, neglect might mean a permanent setback. Once purchased, plants should be fertilized immediately with half-strength 20-20-20.

While bedding plants have traditionally been sold several to a pack (sometimes called a basket), the trend is shifting to produce plants individually in 4-inch (10-cm) pots. These plants have been cared for in the greenhouse for up to a month longer than those in packs, and therefore sell for a higher price. If you have the budget or have a small garden, they are worth buying for the instant impact.

When to buy

The traditional date for planting bedding plants is the Victoria Day weekend. Even so, frosts can sometimes be expected after that date, especially in or north of the snow belt. It is often a good idea, before actually planting your bedding plants out in the garden, to leave them in your garage at night, bringing them out into the sun during the day, for a week or so after you buy them. This will allow them to "harden off," making the transition to a permanent place in the garden less abrupt. Fertilize plants with half-strength 20-20-20 every three or four days until they are planted in the garden.

Some bedding plants, such as snapdragons and marigolds, can take more cold weather than others. In the encyclopedia section those bedding plants that need really warm weather to thrive are noted—hold off planting these until well into June. Of course, the farther north you are in the province, the shorter your frost-free season; adjust planting dates accordingly. On the other hand, if you have an apartment balcony or covered patio that you intend to decorate with containers of flowers, the overhead protection may allow you to plant a bit sooner.

Soil preparation

As soon as the soil dries out enough, prepare the ground for planting. Test soil and adjust pH (see page 12). Using a short-handled fork, loosen soil around weeds and remove them, taking care to remove their roots as well. Spread 2–4 inches (5–10 cm) of organic matter over the soil using the flat side of a leveling rake. Broadcast a general fertilizer such as 6-9-6 or 5-10-10 over the soil at 24 lbs. per 100 square feet (12 kg per 10 m²). (If lime has been added, wait a week before adding fertilizer.) Dig fertilizer and organic matter well into the top 10 inches (25 cm) of soil, using a short-handled spade. Remove large stones and break up heavy clods as you dig. Avoid walking on and compacting freshly dug soil; lay a board over the surface to walk on if necessary. Finally, level soil surface with the flat side of your leveling rake again.

Planting

Although it runs contrary to our natures, the best day for transplanting bedding plants is an overcast day or one prior to a rainy spell. If the weather is sunny, transplant in the evening, so plants have a good 18 hours to adjust to the change before the sun blazes again.

Make sure plants are well watered before setting them out. Soak if necessary and let drain. Prepare a watering can with a solution of 10-52-17 or 20-20-20. Turn plants upside down to pop them out of their containers. If they do not just slip out, don't tug. Holding the pot upside-down, rap the rim of the pot on the edge of a table and the plant should loosen enough to slide out. With plants that are planted more than one to a pack, gently pull the soil apart into individual root balls.

This next step is a difficult one. Flowers on plants such as marigolds, snapdragons and zinnias should be removed when plants are set out. Although I had always heard this, I could never bring myself to do it. One year when I set out a bed of marigolds, I accidentally dropped my trowel on several of them, snapping off all the flowers. Those plants promptly doubled in size and produced many more blooms, while the others hardly grew at all. This is hard to do after you have waited months to see some color in the garden, but it makes a tremendous difference.

Using a small trowel, make a hole in the soil and set the plant in it. The plant should be at the same soil level as it was in the container. Fill the hole in and water the plant. Water with the prepared fertilizer solution after you have planted three or four plants, rather than waiting until all your planting is done, which may be several hours later.

Tall growers such as snapdragons, asters and salpiglossis need the support of thin bamboo stakes. Plants which have a floppy habit, such as Swan River daisy and wishbone flower, are best supported with twiggy branches. Use prunings about 8 inches (20 cm) long, placed in the soil around young plants, for them to grow through. (These supports stay in place all season, disappearing as the plants grow up around them.)

Care through the summer

Give lots of water during dry spells and some feeding, depending on what fertilizer you used when planting. If it was a granular fertilizer, sprinkle a little 6-9-6 or 5-10-10 on the beds in the first week of July and again in the first week of August. If you used a 3–4 month controlled release fertilizer, you shouldn't need to supplement it. Watch your plants closely and adjust fertilizer with a soluble plant food if necessary (see page 15).

Plants that tend to become leggy will need to have their growing tips pinched. Refer to the encyclopedia for instructions concerning specific plants and use your own judgement as well. The growing tip is not necessarily where the flower is, which can be confusing; look for new leaves unfurling. This tip is known by biologists as the "apical meristem," meristem being rapidly growing and dividing cells. Whereas animals grow all over, plants grow from meristem tips only. In the axil where a leaf meets a stem, there is usually a bud in waiting, an emergency backup if anything happens to the apical meristem. The apical meristem is "dominant," producing hormones that inhibit growth in the axillary buds, but if you pinch out the apical meristem, the side buds start to grow and the plant becomes very bushy. This is great for plants such as geraniums, because they become full and have many more blooms. This principle can be applied to all pruning practices.

"Deadheading," or removing dead flowers, is important to keep the plants well groomed and to prevent them from setting seed. Once annuals set seed, they will stop blooming.

5

Gardening in
Containers

Container gardening and bedding plants go hand in hand. For apartment dwellers, wonderful effects can be achieved in containers. For dressing up a patio or entrance, they are a natural. The container should be as large as possible, while keeping in scale with the setting.

Containers

The most popular wooden containers for garden use are western red cedar planters and oak whiskey barrels. Cedar planters tend to dry out quickly, so it is worth lining them with black plastic before filling with soil. Staple it down if you have access to a staple gun, and punch two or three holes in the bottom for drainage. Window boxes of less than a foot (30 cm) in width will be difficult to keep watered.

Terra cotta clay pots are very attractive but somewhat less practical.

Only the more expensive types are guaranteed to be frost-proof, so leaving them out all winter may be risky, particularly if water cannot drain away freely or if the pot is narrower at the top than at the base. Clay pots dry out very quickly; this is prevented by painting the inside of the pots with a tar emulsion or latex paint before filling them with soil.

Concrete planters are very effective, especially in a setting with contemporary architecture. The most popular glazed ceramic containers are the Chinese dragon pots imported from the Orient. Because they are glazed and very thick, they are generally frost-proof if they have drainage holes. Plastic pots make practical containers; they do not dry out quickly and are inexpensive and long lasting. The minimum size should be about 12 inches (30 cm) across.

Be creative when it come to choosing containers; an eclectic collection of containers can become the focal point of a patio garden.

Potting mix recipes

Never use ordinary garden soil alone in a container. It compacts, with poor results. Either use a packaged potting mix or make up your own. The advantages of making your own are that you know exactly what is in it, you can make it in large quantities and it is less expensive. Following are two recipes for homemade potting mix:

Soilless mix	Mix with some soil
27 quarts (27 L) peat moss	27 quarts (27 L) peat moss
9 quarts (9 L) sterilized sand	4 quarts (4 L) sterilized sand
4 oz. by weight (120 g) dolomite lime	4 quarts (4 L) pasteurized
3 oz. by weight (90 g) FTE*	garden soil
	4 oz. by weight (120 g) dolomite lime
	3 oz. by weight (90 g) FTE*

* FTE are fritted trace elements (see page 14)

The advantage of adding soil to a mix is that it holds the water and nutrients better than peat or sand, especially if it is a good soil. Sand can be sterilized by boiling, but soil should be pasteurized. The process is as follows. First shake soil through a 1/4 inch (.6 cm) screen to remove rocks. Place the soil in a pan to a depth of about 4 inches (10 cm), moisten and cover with aluminum foil. Insert a meat thermometer through the foil into the soil, but not touching the pan and set in the oven at 200°F (93°C) for half an hour. When the soil reaches 180°F (82°C), remove pan from oven. Do not allow soil to become hotter than this temperature, or beneficial bacteria will be destroyed. Pasteurization kills worms, slugs, disease-causing fungi and bacteria, soil insects, most viruses and weed seeds. Even more effective is a treatment in the microwave for ten minutes on full. Turn out onto clean newspapers and allow to cool.

Perlite or vermiculite can be substituted for the sand, especially for hanging baskets where lightness is an asset. Use sand when weight is required to prevent tall plants, such as standard fuchsias, from blowing over. Use coarse builders' sand, not beach sand.

Note: After measuring peat moss, thoroughly moisten with warm water, squeezing the water through the peat. Never use dry peat in the garden.

Adding fertilizer

The recipes above make a little over one bushel of potting mix (35 L). To this quantity, add one of the following fertilizers:

- 6 ounces by weight (180 g) 14-14-14 Osmocote or Nutricote
- 4 ounces by weight (120 g) granular fertilizer such as 6-9-6
- 1/2 cup (60 mL) of the organic fertilizer recipe given on page 15.

What, when and how to plant

Most bedding plants may be grown in containers. Refer to the quick reference chart under the heading "containers" and the encyclopedia section for suggested plant material.

Most summer-flowering bedding plants should be planted during the last week of May; exceptions are noted in the encyclopedia section. Containers can be planted several weeks earlier if they are under cover of a balcony or if you can move them indoors on nights that promise to be clear and cold.

Only in the very warmest parts can container gardens for early spring be planted the previous fall. In most areas they freeze too hard and even cold-tolerant plants like pansy are winter-killed.

If your container is very deep and you do not want the weight of a full depth of soil, a foot (30 cm) of vermiculite or perlite can be added to the bottom of the container. Fill the container up to within a few inches (5 cm) of the rim with potting mix. Planting techniques are described on page 19.

Care through the season

The smaller the container, the more care it requires in terms of watering and fertilizing. A small planter box will need water perhaps twice a day by the end of the summer. There are a number of crystals on the market made out of compounds that absorb many times their weight in water and hold it as a reservoir for the plant roots. Although they are still somewhat experimental, greenhouse growers report that the addition of these crystals to the potting mix cuts down on the frequency of watering, making them a useful addition to container plantings.

Fertilizer required through the summer will depend on what type was used in the mix. Controlled release and organic fertilizers will feed plants for several months and need not be repeated. If granular fertilizer was used in the mix, apply more the first week of July and the first week of August, sprinkling 1/3 ounce by weight over each square foot (or 100 g per m²) of soil surface. If you prefer, use a half-strength soluble fertilizer every week (see page 15). Remove faded blooms and pinch the tips of plants to encourage bushiness.

6

Hanging Baskets
and
Moss Baskets

A well-grown hanging basket enriches a setting in a way few other decorations can rival. The city of Victoria on Vancouver Island is famous for its magnificent moss baskets, which hang from blue and white lamp standards, and many other cities are also gracing their streets with these masses of bloom.

Hanging baskets are a specialized type of container garden, so all of the same considerations mentioned in Chapter 5 apply. The larger the container, the greater the ratio of soil volume to surface area. In terms of hanging baskets, this means many plants can be planted and there will still be an adequate volume of soil to ensure root health. It also means that the larger the container, the slower the rate of surface evaporation—less watering for you. So remember, bigger is better when it comes to hanging baskets.

Buying ready-made hanging baskets

In the spring, it seems like every retail outlet sells hanging baskets. Some are gorgeous, in full bloom in late May and packed with top-quality plants nurtured since January; these are a worthwhile investment.

Others are inexpensive, using small pots and few plants. For the same price you could make a larger hanging basket filled with interesting plants in your choice of colors. Baskets you make yourself may not be in full bloom until June, but are better in the long run than poor quality ready-made baskets.

When buying ready-made baskets, sprinkle 1 tablespoon (15 mL) of granular or slow-release fertilizer on the soil surface and water well.

Containers

Most hanging baskets are planted in containers of wood, plastic, clay, pulp or wire. Western red cedar is the best wood for hanging baskets. The standard cedar basket is 12 inches (30 cm) square at the top and the sides taper to form a 4-inch (10-cm) square at the bottom. If you are making your own, it would be much better to make them larger and not so sharply tapered, allowing for more soil volume. Holes are drilled in the side 1/2 inch (1 cm) from the rim to attach wires. Before you plant your cedar basket, line the inside with black plastic, stapling it down if you can, and punching two or three holes in the bottom for drainage. This way the soil will not dry out as quickly.

Plastic hanging baskets are most often available in green, white and terra cotta red. Fancier pots in a wider selection of colors are sold in large garden centers. The minimum size to buy is 10-inch (25-cm); 12-inch (30-cm) baskets are also manufactured—try asking your garden center (early in the season) to order some if they're not in stock.

Clay pots either have holes in the pot to attach rope or they can be hung in a rope holder. Clay pots dry out very quickly and should be coated inside with black tar emulsion or latex paint.

Pulp pots, made out of dark gray fiberboard, are the least expensive and yet many gardeners feel they are quite attractive, being more natural looking than plastic. They last two or three years, longer if the inside is coated with varathane or latex paint.

Hanging baskets with one type of plant

Plants such as impatiens, fuchsia, ivy geranium, browallia, calceolaria, lotus vine, petunia and hanging basket tuberous begonia are outstanding in hanging baskets when planted alone. In a 10-inch (25-cm) basket, it is best to use 5 or 6 plants, one in the middle and the others around it. If plants are purchased in 4-inch (10-cm) pots, they will fill the basket up faster.

Mixed baskets

When it comes to making a mixed basket, anything goes. A classic combination for a square cedar or pulp basket is as follows:

- Use an upright geranium in the center of the basket.
- Plant two ivy geraniums in opposite corners.
- Plant two trailing fuchsias in the two remaining opposite corners.
- In the four spaces left along the sides plant any of the other plants suggested in the encyclopedia or the quick reference chart. Favorites include trailing lobelia, nepeta and schizanthus.

The delight of planting your own hanging basket is that it may be customized to your light situation or your preferred color scheme. A hanging basket for a shady place in a pastel color scheme might be planted with the upright pink fuchsia 'Miss California', 2 'Pink Marshmallow' fuchsias, 2 schizanthus, 2 mauve ivy geraniums, a green and white variegated English ivy and a green and white wandering Jew. For a hanging basket in lots of sun, using a bright color scheme, the following combination would work well: an upright red geranium, 2 yellow calceolaria, 1 nasturtium, 1 creeping zinnia, 1 lotus vine, 1 trailing lobelia, and a black-eyed-susan vine.

Planting conventional hanging baskets

If you have a greenhouse or a sunroom, plant your hanging basket in March or April. If you will be placing the basket outdoors, but can leave it under cover for a month (a carport or covered patio for example), you could plant it up in early May. If it goes straight outdoors, don't plant until late May.

Information on buying bedding plants and recipes for potting mixes is given in chapters 4 and 5. To plant up the basket, first water all the plants well and allow them to drain. Fill the basket about two-thirds full of potting mix.

Remove the plants from their pots (see page 19) and gently place them where you wish them to go in the basket. Fill in the spaces between them with more potting mix, making sure that the plants are at the same soil level as they were in their pots. Firm the soil gently and water the basket with a solution of 10-52-17 starter fertilizer.

There is a trick to attaching the wires for hanging baskets, which makes leveling the basket a simple operation. Hold the wires together in your hand and give them one bend together, so they will all be the same length. Then attach each one to a side of the basket, making sure the sharp ends are tucked into the soil to prevent injuries.

Planting moss-lined wire baskets

Moss baskets are much more expensive to buy because of the labor involved, so this is where you can really benefit from making your own. They are easy to make once you know how. To begin, you need a wire basket and a bag of moss. Again, a larger basket is better. They are manufactured in 2-inch (5-cm) increments from 8 inches to 28 inches (20–71 cm). You may have to order the larger sizes through your garden center, but do so early in the season. They are manufactured with round bottoms and flat bottoms, but the latter are easier to work with.

The advantage of moss baskets over conventional hanging baskets is that they are "side-planted." This gives a much greater surface area over which to plant, and because the plants can be seen before they actually get long enough to trail, you can use plants that are less trailing in habit. Figure 1-4 shows a moss basket which is planted with upright tuberous begonias, and Figure 8-6 shows a mixed moss-lined wire basket. Dwarf marigolds, sweet alyssum, viscaria, fibrous begonias, ageratum—almost any dwarf bedding plant—may be used. Moss baskets give you a chance to be your most creative!

Many moss baskets used in public parks and gardens have a large saucer attached to the bottom, which keeps them from drying out as quickly. Wire baskets for home gardeners do not come with attached saucers, but you can easily attach one yourself. A 14-inch (36-cm) wire basket sits nicely in a 7-inch (18-cm) plastic saucer. Make 4 holes in the saucer by heating up a skewer on the stove and pushing it into the plastic 1/4 inch (.6 cm) down from the rim. The saucer may then be wired onto the basket after it is planted. If a green saucer is used it will not be very noticeable and will not be visible once the plants grow longer.

The first step is to line the basket half-way up with a layer of moss 1 inch (2.5 cm) thick. If a saucer will not be attached to the basket later, cut a circle of plastic about 12 inches (30 cm) across and press it into the bottom of the basket on top of the moss. This will serve the same purpose, but doesn't store as much water. Now fill the basket about half-full of soil. If the basket is round on the bottom, set it on an empty pot so it won't roll around.

A 14-inch (36-cm) wire basket is usually constructed with four vertical wires soldered to nine circular wires, making 32 openings in the basket. Because the basket tapers, the openings near the top are wider. In a 14-inch (36-cm) basket, plant approximately 16 plants on the sides and 8 in the top opening, spacing them evenly. (If 16 plants are used, only half of the holes will be planted.)

Start planting into the holes about two rows up from the bottom of the basket. To plant into the sides, pull apart two wires to enlarge the hole. Pull back the moss and poke the roots of the bedding plant through the hole. Push the moss back across the hole and bend the wires back the way they were. Clearly this only works with plants grown in packs; a plant in a 4-inch (10-cm) pot would have too large a root ball to side-plant.

As you work your way up the basket, add more moss lining and soil. At the top there is room to use some plants with larger root balls, such as fancy begonias grown from tubers or 4-inch (10-cm) pot plants.

Attach wires as described above under "Planting conventional hanging baskets" and water the basket well with a solution of 10-52-17 starter fertilizer.

Care of hanging baskets through the summer

Depending on what plants you use in your basket, you will have the best success hanging it in a spot that receives partial or full shade. Even sun-loving plants tend to do better with a bit of shade when grown in hanging baskets. Shade-loving plants such as fuchsias and hanging-basket tuberous begonias should definitely be given full shade.

Water your hanging baskets diligently during hot weather. Small baskets may need to be watered twice a day. If the basket is not too heavy, take it down and soak the whole basket in a tub of water for an hour or so.

Fertilizer required through the summer will depend on what type was used in the mix. Controlled release and organic fertilizers will feed plants for several months and need not be repeated. If granular fertilizer was used in the mix, apply more in late June and again in late July, sprinkling 1/3 ounce by weight over each square foot (or 100 g per m²) of soil surface. If you prefer, use a half-strength soluble fertilizer every week (see page 15). Remove faded blooms and pinch the tips of plants to encourage bushiness.

Propagation

Propagation refers to any technique that will increase the number of plants on hand (buying them doesn't count!). For some gardeners, especially those with greenhouses, starting a new plant from a seed or cutting is a source of great satisfaction. One of winter's pleasures is poring over seed catalogues and planning what new plants to try next season. Other gardeners prefer to leave propagation to someone else.

Seeding is the most common technique for starting the majority of bedding plants and is much more economical than buying plants, a consideration if large numbers are needed. Some cultivars are easy to start from seeds; others require bottom heat, extra light and up to six months to be ready to plant out in late May. There are some cultivars which resent transplanting and should be sown directly into the garden.

Propagation from cuttings is the best method for many bedding plants—a good-sized plant in bloom can be produced in less time than from seed. For named cultivars, such as the fuchsia 'Swingtime' or the geranium 'Distinction', propagation from cuttings is the only way to produce an exact replica of the original plant. Many gardeners, particularly in garden clubs, enjoy swapping cuttings.

Division is a technique of propagation that is suitable for several of the bedding plants included in this book: dahlias, canna lilies, tuberous begonias, ivy, wandering Jew (if taken indoors through the winter) and carnations, black-eyed susan and nepeta (if they overwinter).

Particular details for seeding, making cuttings and division are given with each entry in the encyclopedia section, but the basic techniques are outlined in this chapter.

Starting bedding plants indoors from seeds

Dates to sow are given under each entry in the encyclopedia section. Most bedding plants are sown indoors in March. Slow-growing plants such as begonias and geraniums are seeded in December or January. Start the following in February: snapdragons, canna lilies, cigar flower, carnations, gazanias, lantana and lobelia. You can wait until April for China asters, celosia, globe amaranth and nasturtiums. Ornamental cabbage and kale, wallflowers, forget-me-nots, pansies and primulas, used for late fall or early spring displays, are sown in June.

Seedlings are subject to attack by a number of damping-off fungi (see page 39). To prevent such attacks, hygiene is of the utmost importance. If reusing pots, disinfect them by soaking them in a solution of detergent and one part laundry bleach to ten parts hot water. Particularly sensitive plants should be watered with a fungicide after seeding.

Sowing the seeds. If many seeds are to be sown, use flats—rectangular boxes of wood or plastic. For smaller numbers of seeds, use 6- to 10-inch (15- to 25-cm) azalea pots (pots that are wider than they are deep). For large seeds or seedlings that will remain in their pots from sowing until they go into the garden, use individual 2- to 3-inch (5- to 7.5-cm) pots. Flats of 2401s—24 thin plastic pots joined as one unit—are also handy. Insert them into an ordinary plastic flat for strength and ease of carrying.

Use only sterilized potting mix, either purchased or homemade. If making your own mix, use the recipe on page 22, adding 3/4 ounce (21 g) by weight superphosphate. (Do not add other fertilizers to a seeding mix.)

Fill container with potting mix to within 1/4 inch (.6 cm) of the rim, gently pressing it down. Sow seeds as specified in the encyclopedia section under each entry. Water with lukewarm water using a watering can with a "seedling rose," which makes a very fine spray; start the flow of water over another container and move the watering can so it sprinkles on the seeded mix when it is flowing evenly. Or set the container in a pan of lukewarm water until the surface of the mix is wet. Allow to drain well and cover with glass or clear plastic if specified; if the containers are in direct sunlight, cover the glass with a sheet of paper to minimize temperature fluctuations. Do not overwater, as more seedlings damp off from overwatering than fail from too little water.

Soil temperature remains 10 degrees cooler than the temperature in a room and some crops need 70°F (21°C) to germinate, which is not possible in a normally heated home. One solution is to purchase a heating cable. The least expensive ones have a thermostat set at 70°F (21°C), which is perfect. (Commercial growers prefer a thermostat they can control, which is much more expensive.)

To use a heating cable, first make a wooden box out of cedar or all-weather wood. Lay the cable on the bottom, arranging it so that it snakes back and forth. Secure it with insulated staples. Put a 1-inch (2.5-cm) layer of perlite or vermiculite over the cable. Pots and flats may then be set directly into the box. Keep the containers close together to conserve heat when the cable is on. If directions in the encyclopedia state "germination at 60–70°F (15–21°C)," use of a heating cable is optional, but it will give better results. If only 70°F (21°C) is mentioned, that temperature is required for good results and a heating cable should be used. The top of some refrigerators are warm and may be used to germinate seeds. Another alternative for seeds which require dark and warm soil is to put them near the water heater. Hardy annuals normally germinate at cool temperatures and need no bottom heat.

If directions indicate flats should be covered with glass or plastic to conserve moisture and heat, be sure to remove it once seeds germinate.

The **first transplanting** of the seedlings from the seed tray to an individual pot (called pricking out by the British), gives each plant room to develop and access to a potting mix which includes more fertilizer. Seedlings are generally transplanted when the one or two sets of true leaves appear. The first leaves to appear on a seedling are actually not true leaves but are "seed leaves" which were in the seed and contain stored food. These seed leaves will shrivel up and fall off as the true leaves take over the job of providing the young plant with food through the process of photosynthesis. You will recognize the true leaves as they have the characteristic shape of the mature plant.

Seedlings may be transplanted into 1201s—12 thin plastic pots (packs) joined as one unit. Plant four to each pack, the way they are sold in shops. Better still, transplant into individual 2- to 4-inch (5- to 10-cm) pots. This way the intermingled roots won't be pulled apart when planting-out time comes. Use pasteurized potting mix but, whether it is your own mix or one from the store, add fertilizer as described on page 23. (Commercial mixes do not contain fertilizer unless stated on the label.) When transplanting, hold each seedling by its seed leaves and lift it from the soil with a dibber or fork. Make a hole in the potting mix and lower the roots into the hole, keeping the plant at the same level it was in the seed tray. Gently firm the soil around the roots and water gently.

Some plants stay in the same pots from the time they are sown until they are planted out into the garden. Remember to use a balanced soluble fertilizer with these seedlings once they have true leaves, as the seeding mix contained only phosphorus.

Hardening off is the process whereby the seedlings are gradually acclimatized to the weather outdoors. Two weeks before the planting-out dates, set them under a cloche or cold frame outdoors, or put plants out during the day and bring them in at night.

Starting bedding plants from seed outdoors

Seeds of many plants can be sown directly in the garden. The advantages are less fuss indoors and less expense; the main disadvantage is later bloom. Prepare soil as described on page 18. Cover the bed with 1 inch (2.5 cm) of soil that has been sifted through a 1/4 inch (.6 cm) sieve. Sow the seeds and cover with a layer of sifted soil that is approximately the thickness of the seeds. Water gently.

What are F_1 hybrids? These are plants which are the result of a careful cross between two parent plants. F_1 hybrid bedding plants are more uniform, vigorous and are generally superior plants. Due to extra handling, seeds are a bit more expensive. Seeds collected from F_1 hybrids will not be true to the parent; if you intend to save your own seeds, bear this in mind.

Making stem cuttings

Bedding plants that are half-hardy perennials, shrubs or subshrubs may be propagated by cuttings. New plants then become clones of the parents, that is, they have exactly the same genes and must be propagated from cuttings to be true. Some plants grow faster or bloom sooner from cuttings. Plants which are often grown from cuttings include fuchsia, geranium, marguerite daisy, flowering maple, coleus, felicia, nepeta, English ivy, heliotrope, silver nettle vine, lotus vine, ice plant, osteospermum, wandering Jew, New Guinea impatiens, trailing verbena, and lantana.

The ideal time of year to make cuttings is in August or September. Using a razor blade, cut below the fourth leaf joint on a shoot. Pinch off any flower buds and the bottom two leaves or sets of leaves. This will give two nodes (leaf joints) above the soil and two in the soil, where new roots will form. In late summer a rooting compound is not necessary.

Several cuttings can be rooted in a 6- to 10-inch (15- to 25-cm) azalea pot, or they may be rooted individually in 2- to 4-inch (5- to 10-cm) pots. Fill pots with a mixture of half peat and half perlite or vermiculite and press down gently. Water well and allow to drain. Make holes for the cuttings with a pencil; never use the cutting to make the hole.

Insert the cutting into the hole and water with a fungicide. Keep in a bright place but out of direct sunlight. Lightly mist the leaves twice a day and water when the soil surface becomes dry. Cuttings root in about ten days and, once rooted, should be fertilized with half-strength soluble 10-52-17 starter fertilizer. If several cuttings were made in one pot, they should be transplanted into individual pots after one month.

Growing under lights

It is difficult to grow sturdy seedlings indoors without extra light, unless you have a sunroom. Provide extra light by using two fluorescent tubes—one cool white and one warm white—4 to 6 inches (10–15 cm) from the plants. Such a light arrangement would also allow you to overwinter cuttings of suitable bedding plants without them becoming stretched and weak. If you do not have extra lights, consider delaying seeding for a few weeks from the recommended sowing time to reduce the amount of time seedlings spend indoors. There is also more light later in the spring, making even a window sill a brighter place to grow.

Pests
and
Diseases

The following are the most common pests and diseases that you are likely to encounter in the garden; only a few greenhouse pests and diseases have been included because there are so many. If a problem does not fit one of the following descriptions, take a sample (or a photo) into your favorite garden center and ask for help.

If you employ someone to spray for pests or diseases, he or she must be a licensed operator who has passed the provincial examination. The excellent reference book *Insect and Disease Control in the Home Garden* is available free of charge from the Ontario Ministry of Agriculture and Food, Consumer Information Branch, 801 Bay Street, Toronto, Ontario, M7A 2B2, or from your local office.

The current trend in gardening, however, is to turn away from chemical methods of pest control. Chemical controls are expensive, unpleasant to use and potentially dangerous to both the user and the environment. We often forget that the pesticides we use can also kill beneficial insects, such as ground beetles, butterflies and bees. Toxic chemicals produced during the manufacture of pesticides can also harm the environment. In addition, pesticides find their way into the food chain, threatening the health of animals right to the top of the chain, including such predatory birds as eagles, falcons and owls. For more information on alternative pest and disease controls, inquire at your local library.

If you are using pesticides, please remember the following:

- Only use an insecticide if damage is seen. Do not spray regularly to prevent insect pests.
- As a first choice, use an insecticidal soap or an organic pesticide.
- Always read the label very carefully and follow instructions exactly.
- Wear rubber gloves and long sleeves and trousers. Launder your clothing and take a shower after spraying.
- Do not spray when the bees are out foraging. The best time of day is just before the sun sets.
- Do not spray unless the air is still.
- Do not spray if you have any health problems or are pregnant.
- Store all chemicals and fertilizers out of the reach of children and pets in a locked box or cupboard.
- Do not spray with chemicals indoors; always take the plants outdoors.
- Always store pesticides in their original containers to prevent accidental consumption.

APHIDS are insects with soft, pear-shaped bodies, which cluster in large numbers near the ends of new shoots and under leaves, causing them to curl. Usually green, gray or pink, they suck the sap of plants and produce a sweet substance called "honeydew." Ants often "farm" aphids, carrying them to infest new plants and collecting the honeydew. If you see an army of ants marching up and down a plant's stems, look for aphids. Because aphids suck the sap, they may transmit viral diseases from plant to plant. If there are only a few aphids, they may easily be rubbed off the plant by hand. Or use an insecticidal soap (except on nasturtiums or sweet peas), rotenone or an all-purpose insecticide such as malathion.

Aphids have many natural predators that may keep things under control without your intervention. Ladybird beetles and their young, which look like little blackish-green dragons, prey on aphids. Parasitic wasps lay their eggs in the aphids, which are eaten by the larvae when they hatch. If you see a beige aphid "mummy" on the leaves, this is what has happened. Avoid spraying any pesticides if biological controls are working.

ASTER WILT is caused by the pink fungus (*Fusarium* sp.), which clogs up the water-conducting vessels in the plant. Young plants may suddenly collapse and die. On more mature plants, the leaves may turn yellow and wilt, beginning with the lower leaves. A thin coating of pink spores may be seen on the lower stem. There is no treatment and the plant should be removed. The disease persists in the soil and may be transmitted on shoes or tools. Do not throw diseased plants in the compost and do not plant China asters in the same place twice.

BACTERIAL BUD ROT is a disease that affects the leaves and flowers of canna lilies before they unfurl. It can spread into the stems and kill the whole plant. The disease is spread by water and on tools and hands. If the disease is present, remove and destroy infected plant parts. Keep the plants as dry as possible by encouraging good air circulation and watering only in the morning.

CABBAGE BUTTERFLY is dainty and white or pale yellow. It flutters around ornamental cabbages and kale, where it lays eggs that hatch into green caterpillars up to 2 inches (5 cm) long. They are hard to spot because they lie along the midrib of the leaf, but they can munch a lot of cabbage in a short time. Hand pick if possible. A spray containing B.T. (*Bacillus thurengiensis*) is harmless to other creatures but contains a bacterium which infects and kills the caterpillars. Some books recommend Sevin, but it is extremely toxic to bees.

CATERPILLARS There are numerous caterpillars found in the garden. They are all the larval stage of moths and butterflies and most feed on leaves. B.T. (*Bacillus thurengiensis*) is the pesticide of choice. See also cabbage butterfly caterpillars, above, and cutworms, below.

CLUB ROOT is a disease caused by a fungus in the soil. It infects many members of the family Brassicaceae: broccoli, Brussels sprouts, cauliflower, kale, cabbage, stocks and wallflowers, and is more prevalent on acid, poorly drained soil. Diseased plants have large or small club-like swellings on their roots. Lime well where these crops are to be grown. Some gardeners advise never to buy young plants of these crops to avoid bringing the fungus in with the soil. Once the fungus is in the garden, there is little to be done to get rid of it, except to wait it out. Do not grow plants from this family for up to five years if your soil has club root.

COLORADO POTATO BEETLE is 3/8 inch (1 cm) long, yellow-orange with black stripes. Its larvae are red and round, to 1/4 inch (.6 cm) long, sometimes with two rows of black dots along their sides. Both eat holes in the leaves of many members of the potato family, including flowering tobacco. Handpick beetles, or lay a board over the soil surface to attract them as a hiding place. They can then be collected and flushed down the toilet.

CUCUMBER BEETLES of several species feed on many different vegetables and ornamental plants. They are 3/8-inch (1-cm) long, yellow-green beetles with small black spots and they eat small holes in leaves and petals. They are prevalent in late summer and are attracted to plants with light-colored flowers. Adults hibernate through the winter—a thorough clean-up of weeds and dead vegetation in the fall will help control populations. The female beetle lays its eggs in or on the soil around the base of plants—cultivation of the soil as soon as temperatures reach 70°F (21°C) in the spring will kill some of the larvae. Handpick beetles or collect under a board as with the Colorado potato beetle.

CUTWORMS are large, to 2 inches (5 cm), hairless caterpillars that curl up when disturbed. They are the larval stage of many species of dark, night-flying moths. Some cutworms climb plants to feed on stems and fruit, some feed at surface level and some feed underground. Scratch the soil around the plants to expose cutworms and dispose of them. You can handpick climbing cutworms at night, using a flashlight to see. Deter surface-feeding cutworms by making 3-inch-high (8-cm-high) collars for plants from old paper milk cartons or toilet paper tubes and pushing these 1 inch (2.5 cm) into the ground around each plant. A mulch of wood ashes or pine sawdust around the base of each plant also discourages cutworms. A spray of *Bacillus thurengiensis* on the plant parts the cutworms are consuming will also help.

DAMPING-OFF refers to a fungal attack which results in seeds failing to emerge or in the collapse of young seedlings. Always sow seeds in sterilized soil and do not sow too thickly. Once seedlings emerge, grow on at the recommended temperature and provide good air circulation. If noted in the encyclopedia that damping-off is a particular problem, a suitable fungicide should be used. Ask at your garden center, as recommendations for fungicides are changing.

DRY BROWN PATCHES on the leaves are most often caused by too little water, although chemical damage must be considered if plants have been sprayed.

EARWIGS are dark brown insects about 1 inch (2.5 cm) long with forceps-like pincers at the rear. They are most often found hiding in dahlias, where they sometimes eat the flowers and leaves. To trap earwigs, stuff newspaper into the bottom of a clay flower pot and invert over a wooden stake near the damaged plants. The paper can then be burned each day.

FLEA BEETLES are tiny, 1/8-inch (.3-cm), black beetles that are hard to spot because they jump like fleas. Damage—tiny holes in the leaves—can be devastating. A bad attack can strip all the foliage and kill certain plants in a couple of days. Nasturtiums are particular favorites. If flea beetles are present, use rotenone dust or spray.

GRAY MOLD (*Botrytis*) is one of the most common of all fungal diseases, partly because spores are carried in the air. The disease may affect any plant part, but the grey fuzz it causes is most often seen on old flowers and leaves in humid conditions. Keeping the garden well groomed will help control the disease. Treating with a fungicide may help.

LEAFHOPPERS are small insects related to aphids and, like them, suck the plant sap. Unlike aphids, they jump and fly off the plants when disturbed. They feed on the undersides of leaves and shed their cast skins, a sign that they are present. While direct damage to plants is slight, they may transmit serious viral diseases. Spray with Ambush.

LEAF REDDENING is a sign of too-cold temperatures in the spring. It often indicates a deficiency of phosphorus, which is taken up poorly in cold weather. With the onset of warmer weather, leaf color will improve.

MEALY BUGS may infest flowering maples indoors or in the greenhouse. They are tiny, white, wooly insects which look like bits of fluff. They are usually found at the axil of stem and leaf and, like aphids, suck the plant sap. Kill them by dabbing them with a cotton swab dipped in rubbing alcohol, or spray with insecticidal soap.

OEDEMA is a fluid imbalance within a plant; it happens most often in late winter to greenhouse geraniums. The plants are given more water than they can get rid of, which results in blisters forming on the underside of the leaves. These rupture and form reddish, corky scabs.

Generally this is of little concern, but it is best to maintain good air circulation and water only in the morning and not too much, especially in overcast weather.

PHYSIOLOGICAL DISORDERS are not caused by disease organisms, but instead indicate less than ideal conditions of water, fertilizer or light. (LEAF REDDENING and OEDEMA are examples.) Refer to the cultural instructions to determine the problem and possible changes in plant care to alleviate it.

POWDERY MILDEW is a fungus disease which leaves a white, powdery coating on leaves and shoots. It appears most often during warm, muggy summer weather. Plants are also more susceptible if the soil is allowed to dry out. Try not to wet foliage when watering. Spray every two weeks with sulfur.

ROOT WEEVIL adults are dull, gray-black beetles with a distinctive long snout. (Do not confuse them with shiny, black ground beetles which are very beneficial in the garden.) They eat the margins of primula leaves and, unfortunately, are hard to eliminate. Generally primulas tolerate a moderate amount of weevil damage. Of serious concern is damage to rhododendrons and other woody plants. The weevil larvae eat the roots and girdle plant stems, eating around them at the base. This will easily kill a large shrub. In fact, some gardeners recommend planting primroses under rhododendrons to give the weevils something else to eat. When fresh leaf-notching is noticed, go out at night with a flashlight and handpick the adults. A board laid over the surface of the soil will attract weevils as a hiding place; they can then be collected and flushed down the toilet. Sprays are expensive and not very effective.

ROTS include root rots, stem rots and basal rots. It is a general term used for fungal diseases which cause plant tissue to become black and soggy. In seed trays, it may be prevented by using pasteurized potting mix and not overwatering. In the garden, rots are due to planting out too early and there is no practical cure.

RUST is a fungal disease that appears most often on snapdragons and sweet williams. As with many plant diseases, healthy plants are most resistant. The symptoms are reddish brown spots on the underside of the leaves. Plants which look healthy and are in full bloom may reveal a coating of rust spots under their leaves if one peeks. Although snapdragons usually bloom until the frost, infected plants will be ruined by about August and need to be removed. If desired, spray with sulfur.

SCALE insects are sometimes difficult to spot. On bedding plants, they are most common indoors or in the greenhouse. They appear as brown, yellow or white bumps on the stems. Poked with a fingernail, they will pop off the stem. These "bumps" hide mature scale insects; eggs are laid and the young crawl around and settle down in a new location. If the infestation is serious, the time to spray with rotenone or malathion is at this "crawler" stage, which you will have to look for. For most infestations, hand picking or dabbing each scale with rubbing alcohol will be just as easy as spraying, and much safer and less expensive.

SLUGS and **SNAILS** are mollusks, related to clams, limpets, moon snails and other aquatic animals bearing shells. Slugs have rudimentary shells and are certainly not as handsome as their cousins. They both do a tremendous amount of damage in gardens, eating seedlings right off at ground level and eating leaves all summer. Look for the glistening trails to be sure the damage is from slugs and not cutworms or caterpillars. Slug fences made of salt-impregnated plastic are safe, effective and nontoxic. A container of beer sunk into the ground will attract them and they will drown. A half-full beer bottle works well for this purpose and is inconspicuous. (One study showed that nonalcoholic beer was the most popular with these pests!) A board laid over the surface of the soil will attract them as a hiding place; they can then be collected and flushed down the toilet.

The most common metaldehyde slug and snail baits are bran-based and thus are very attractive to pets and toddlers, especially the pellet types. They have been the cause of many pet poisonings, sometimes resulting in death.

SPIDER MITES are a serious pest in the garden and indoors. They are difficult to spot because they are minute. A telltale sign is the yellowing of older (bottom) leaves or a pale dusty look to the foliage. Often leaves fall without even looking unhealthy. If you look under leaves, you may be able to see fine webbing, but it is best to use a magnifying glass to detect the mites themselves. If you watch carefully you can see them walking around. If you see tiny specks on the leaves, poke them to see if they run away—a sure sign they aren't dust! Control is difficult. Try insecticidal soap weekly for several weeks or use a miticide which contains dicofol.

THRIPS feed on the flowers of a number of garden plants and are an especially serious problem during hot, dry weather. Adult thrips are tiny, yellow to gray, about $1/10$ inch (2 mm) long and have two pairs of fringed wings. They are fond of pollen and enter flower buds before they are even open, causing the flower to abort. In addition to eating pollen, they will eat petals and, as a last choice, leaves. Thrips breed in nearby weeds, so keep the garden well-weeded if thrips are a problem.

VIRUS organisms are made up of genetic material and are not organized into cells as are other living organisms. There is debate as to whether they are "life" as we usually think of it, but they certainly have the ability to affect normal cell functions. There is presently no way to kill them without killing the plant. A plant that shows symptoms of a virus disease should be destroyed. Virus particles are spread from plant to plant by insects, nematodes and on pruning tools. Symptoms include abnormal growth, such as stunting, deformed leaves, yellow streaks or rings on the leaves, or streaks in the flowers. Interestingly, the attractive variegation of the flowering maple, *Abutilon thompsonii* 'Pictum', is caused by a virus that does not harm the plant.

WHITEFLY is a serious pest in the greenhouse, and may be introduced into your garden with plants grown in a greenhouse. They are tiny delicate white flies which hide under leaves and flutter about when the plants are moved. In the greenhouse, try one of the following:

- Trap flies with automotive STP oil painted onto an 8-inch (20-cm) square of cardboard hung near plants.
- Spray with permethrin or insecticidal soap weekly for several weeks.
- Burn an insect coil.

In the garden, spray with an insecticide containing permethrin, such as Ambush.

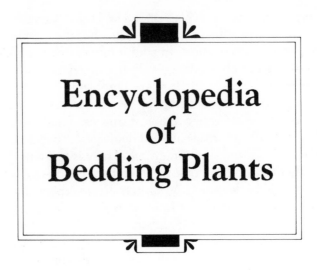

Encyclopedia
of
Bedding Plants

The following encyclopedia gives information on 122 bedding plants, with a description including height and bloomtime; origin and history; cultural details regarding light and soil and how to grow; and suggested uses in the garden. It is organized alphabetically according to botanical names and cross-referenced with common names. Only instructions specific to each entry are given; for general information, please refer to the opening chapters.

How plants are named

The international organization for plant nomenclature—Taxon—assigns plants their botanical names and makes changes as required. Although often referred to as Latin names, many have Greek roots. Botanical names seem intimidating at first, but with practice they become more comfortable to use. The following example explains the meaning of the various names and how they are distinguished.

Glechoma hederacea 'Variegata' (*Nepeta hederacea*) "nepeta"
LAMIACEAE

The first name (*Glechoma*) is the name of the genus to which this plant belongs (the generic name). A genus (plural genera) is a group of plants which are closely related. In some cases, as the above example illustrates, the generic name has also become the common name. Other examples are begonia, chrysanthemum, coleus, dahlia and fuchsia.

The second name (*hederacea*) is the name of the species to which the plant belongs (the specific name). Names of both genus and species are either italicized or underlined (unless being used as a common name). A multiplication sign (×) at the beginning of the species name indicates that it is not in fact a true species, but a hybrid between two or more species. The × is neither italicized nor pronounced.

Some plant species have naturally occurring subgroups which are consistently distinct enough to warrant an additional designation—subspecies, variety or forma. For example, *Amaranthus hybridus* var. *erythrostachys* is a variety found in the wild.

In the above example, 'Variegata' is the cultivar name and is not underlined or italicized, but is enclosed in single quotation marks. A cultivar is a variety originated and maintained by humans, and of botanical or horticultural importance, requiring a name. Such a plant would not usually be found in the wild. Many of these names are well known: 'Twinkles' impatiens, 'Bicentennial' fuchsia and 'Vodka' fibrous begonia are examples. Since 1959, new cultivar names have been distinct from Latin names, to avoid confusion.

Often, as plant breeders have made so many changes, the original species name is not applicable and is dropped completely, as with *Calceolaria* 'Sunshine'.

Names in parentheses, such as the above *Nepeta hederacea*, are synonyms that are in common usage, but are incorrect. Many books and catalogues still use these names, so they are included here for reference. Incorrect botanical names are not cross-referenced in the encyclopedia section, but they are listed in the index, followed by the correct botanical name.

The name shown in double quotation marks is the common name. One plant may have dozens of common names. In most areas of horticulture, growers use only botanical names, but in the bedding plant industry, common names are often used, even in commercial seed catalogues. Catalogues for home gardeners are set out either by botanical name or by common name, so it is best to know both.

The last name, shown in capitals, is the name of the plant family, which includes closely related genera. (It may or may not be capitalized in normal use and is not italicized.) The family name can usually be recognized by the ending *aceae* attached to the stem of the name of a genus within the family. Thus, LAMIACEAE, the name for the mint family, is composed of the stem *Lami*, from the name of a genus in the family, with *aceae* attached. Four old family names, with which you may have been familiar, have changed in accordance with these rules. COMPOSITAE has been changed to ASTERACEAE, CRUCIFERAE to BRASSICACEAE, LABIATAE to LAMIACEAE and LEGUMINOSAE to FABACEAE.

One note regarding ASTERACEAE, the huge family which includes chrysanthemum, marguerite daisy, sunflower and black-eyed susan: what most people think of as the flower is actually made up of many small flowers of two types. The outer "petals" are themselves individual flowers (ray florets), which are open and flattened. The central disk is composed of many tiny flowers (disk florets) pressed closely together. In the text, the familiar term petal is sometimes used to refer to the ray florets; although technically incorrect, it is easier to understand.

All-America Selections and Fleuroselect winners

Two international organizations select outstanding bedding plants. All-America Selections (AAS) has 33 trial grounds in Canada and the United States; judging results from all trial grounds are compiled to determine the winners. Fleuroselect has 22 trial grounds from Finland to southern Italy. Each year, trial ground nurseries receive seed of new plants, which are identified by number only, with no reference to breeder, to discourage prejudice. They also receive seed of the best corresponding bedding plants of each type on the market, for comparison. Old and new are grown side by side and notes on performance are made through the season. Awards are given to those new cultivars which are outstanding. In the Fleuroselect trials, scoring is heavily weighted towards plants that are a breakthrough in breeding, whether or not they are top-notch for the home garden.

AAS trial grounds are located at W.H. Perron & Co. in Bois Briand, Quebec, and at Stokes Seeds Ltd. in St. Catharines, Ontario. There are also 14 display gardens showing the latest AAS winners in these two provinces. AAS winners are noted in Canadian and American seed catalogues; Fleuroselect winners are more often seen in British catalogues.

Abutilon hybridum and *Abutilon pictum* 'Thompsonii' (A. *strictum* 'Thompsonii') "flowering maple" MALVACEAE
(Figure 1-1)

Flowering maple is a specialty bedding plant. It is used outdoors in bedding schemes in summer and is often trained as a standard. It must be overwintered in a greenhouse or indoors in a sunny window. A shrub in its native South America, it has maple-shaped leaves and nodding bell-like flowers in shades of white, yellow, orange or red. There are many named cultivars, some of which have variegated foliage. 'Thompsonii' has orange flowers and leaves that are mottled yellow due to the presence of a harmless virus.

Bloomtime: May to October.

Height: 2–4 feet (61–122 cm) in a pot, taller if trained as a standard.

Light and soil: Flowering maples prefer full sun but will tolerate some shade in a warm, sheltered place. Plant in a well-drained soil to which some organic matter has been added.

How to grow: Young plants are sometimes available from shops in spring if you look in the houseplant section. They may also be started from seeds or cuttings. Sow seeds indoors in March or April. Germination, at 60°F (15°C) soil temperature, takes about 20 days. Pinch out the growing tips when about 8 inches (20 cm) high to get a bushy plant, or train the plant as a standard. Refer to directions under *Fuchsia*, but train only one trunk. Set hardened-off plants out in late May, spacing them 18 inches (46 cm) apart. Water freely during spring and summer and give a half- strength liquid fertilizer recommended in Chapter 3 every second week from May to August. Before frost, bring plants into the greenhouse, or into a cool room indoors, giving them at least four hours of direct sunlight each day. Extra lighting may be required to keep plants bushy.

Pests and diseases: Watch for SCALE, WHITEFLY and MEALY BUGS indoors.

Uses: Grown as a bush, flowering maples are delightful in hanging baskets and window boxes because their flowers are easier to see than if they were planted in the ground. As standards, they are striking as a centerpiece to a formal bedding scheme or a large planter.

Ageratum houstonianum "ageratum" "flossflower" ASTERACEAE
(Figures 5-1 and 7-7)

A half-hardy annual, this native of Central America gets top marks for all-season bloom with a minimum of effort. Ageratum is usually just coming into bloom in packs in late May and continues blooming until the temperature dips below freezing. It prefers warm weather, so wait until June to plant ageratum.

The leaves of ageratum are up to 2 inches (5 cm) across and are roughly triangular in shape. The deep vein pattern and tiny hairs give them a textured appearance. The leaves, however, are almost completely hidden by the small fuzzy flowers which cover the plant.

There are many good cultivars of blue ageratum, but 'Blue Danube' and 'Blue Mink' stand up to the heat very well and bloom all summer. The white cultivars look messy because the flowers become brownish as they fade. There are mixed colors and tall types for cut and dried flowers available from seed companies.

Bloomtime: June to frost.

Height: 6–24 inches (23–61 cm), depending on the cultivar.

Light and soil: Full sun or part shade and a well-drained soil to which some organic matter has been added.

How to Grow: Young plants are readily available from shops in spring, or they may be grown from seeds. Sow in late February or early March on the surface of the potting soil and leave the pots uncovered, as light aids in germination. This, at 60–70°F (15–21°C) soil temperature, takes up to 8 days. Grow on at a soil temperature of 60–65°F (15–18°C). Young plants develop slowly.

When the weather has stabilized in June, set out young plants, spacing dwarf varieties 6–9 inches (15–23 cm) apart, tall types 12 inches (30 cm) apart.

Pests and diseases: Foot and root ROTS sometimes cause plants to collapse at ground level, a good reason not to plant too early.

Uses: Edging, pattern plantings and planter boxes for dwarf cultivars; border and cutting for taller cultivars.

"Alyssum, sweet" see *Lobularia*

Amaranthus caudatus "love-lies-bleeding" "tasselflower"
Amaranthus hybridus var. *erythrostachys* (A. *hypochondriachus*)
"prince's feather"
Amaranthus tricolor "Joseph's coat" AMARANTHACEAE
(Figures 6-1 and 1-2)

Loves-lies-bleeding is an unusual tropical native that has been popular since the 16th century. Although it is not readily available in shops, it is easy to grow from seed. It grows to about 4 feet (1.2 m) and produces striking 18-inch (46-cm) red tassels. Leaves are rounded at the base, taper to a point and are rather coarse. The cultivar 'Viridis' has green tassels and is popular with flower arrangers.

Prince's feather has upright flowers in red ('Pigmy Torch') or green ('Green Thumb') which are excellent cut. Joseph's coat is noted for its brilliant leaves; once established it grows rapidly to form a large bush.

Bloomtime: July to September, looking best in July and August.

Height: Love-lies-bleeding grows to 3–4 feet (.9–1.2 m); prince's feather and Joseph's coat grow to 2 feet (61 cm).

Light and soil: Prefers full sun and any well-drained soil to which some organic matter has been added.

How to grow: Although young plants are not generally available from shops, they are easily grown from seed. In March to April, sow and cover very lightly. Germination, at 60–70°F (15–21°C) soil temperature, takes 8–10 days. Grow seedlings on at 70°F (21°C). Set hardened-off plants out in late May, spacing them 18 inches (46 cm) apart. Alternatively, sow seeds in the garden in April, thinning to 18 inches (46 cm) apart in May. Light staking may be required. Joseph's coat needs more room than this in rich soils.

Pests and diseases: APHIDS sometimes infest plants.

Uses: Love-lies-bleeding is an unusual and fascinating annual. It makes an effective dot plant in formal bedding schemes or the center of a large planter. Plant prince's feather for cutting and Joseph's coat for foliage.

"Amethyst flower" see *Browallia*
"Animated oat" see *Avena*

Antirrhinum majus "snapdragon" SCROPHULARIACEAE
(Figure 1-3)

This popular flower from the Mediterranean has fascinated people for centuries and has picked up some interesting names along the way. Its common name, snapdragon, refers to the fact that if the sides of the flowers are pinched, the flower opens and snaps shut. It is also called dog-head, lion-mouth and wolf-muzzle in Greek, Latin and French respectively. In the Middle Ages, however, it was known as the caprice flower, for if a girl wore a spray of snapdragons it meant that she refused her lover's suit.

The fragrant blooms are red, bronze, rose, pink, yellow, white and bicolored. The flowers appear atop the stems in spikes, set off by simple bright green leaves.

Breeders have produced many cultivars. The 'Rocket' series is 3 feet (.9 m) tall and perfect for cutting. Dwarf bedding cultivars under 12 inches (30 cm) include 'Kolibri', 'Minaret' and 'Floral Carpet'. Some no longer "snap": 'Madame Butterfly', 24 inches (61 cm), and 'Sweetheart', 12 inches (30 cm), have double flowers that resemble azaleas. 'Bright Butterflies', 30 inches (76 cm), and 'Little Darling', 12 inches (30 cm), have trumpet-shaped blooms. Because of their expanded blooms, these last four show more color than traditional snapdragons. The 1987 AAS winner 'Princess White with a Purple Eye' is a striking bicolor which grows to 14–16 inches (35–40 cm) and does well in our area.

In the wild, snapdragons are perennial and they may survive over winter in very sheltered gardens in the Niagara region. They are generally grown as half-hardy annuals.

Bloomtime: May or June to frost, if old flowers are removed.

Height: 12–36 inches (30–91 cm), depending on the cultivar.

Light and Soil: Snapdragons bloom best in full sun, but will tolerate light shade. A well-drained soil to which some organic matter has been added is ideal. They will also tolerate slightly akaline and stony soil. Water well during dry spells.

How to grow: Young plants of many cultivars are readily available from shops in spring, or they may be started from seed in February. Pre-chill seeds at 40°F (4°C) for 5 days. Sow, gently pressing the seeds into the surface of the soil, but do not cover, as the seeds need light for germination. Cover the pots or flats with clear glass or plastic to maintain constant humidity. Germination, at 60–70°F (15–21°C) soil temperature, takes about 7 days. When true leaves appear, transplant and lower the temperature to 50°F (10°C), which keeps plants short and compact. Taller cultivars may require pinching. Set the hardened-off plants out in mid-May, spacing them 12–20 inches (30–50 cm) apart, depending on the cultivar. Pinch the tips when planting, and stake tall cultivars if they are in a windy location. Snapdragons may be planted out earlier than most bedding plants as they will tolerate some cold weather. If plants purchased from shops have flowers on them, pinch them off when planting out. Remove old flower spikes to encourage continued bloom.

Pests and diseases: APHIDS may infest growing tips. In some areas and years, RUST is a serious problem. If it infects your snapdragons, look in seed catalogues for rust-resistant cultivars. If plants show any signs of rust, do not allow them to overwinter; dig them up and put them in the garbage. Planting snapdragons in heavy, waterlogged soil may result in stem and root ROTS. SPIDER MITES can infect the undersides of the leaves.

Uses: Use at the front, middle or back of the border or mixed bed depending on height. Shorter types are also suitable for container cultivation.

"Aster, China or annual", see *Callistephus*

Avena sterilis "animated oat"
Briza maxima "quaking grass"
Lagurus ovatus "hare's tail" POACEAE

These are only three of a number of hardy annual ornamental grasses which are fun to grow. Although in different genera, they are grouped together here because of their similarity in cultivation and use. They are unusual and attractive in the garden and fresh in flower arrangements. All may be dried to be used in flower arrangements or for decorating wreaths. Animated oat comes from the north coast of Africa and has long "beards" from the seed capsules that twist and turn depending on how much moisture there is in the air. Quaking grass has seed heads that droop from wiry stems and tremble with the slightest breeze. Hare's tail has erect seed heads that are fluffy like a rabbit's tail. The last two species are native to the Mediterranean.

Bloomtime: Seed heads appear in late summer.

Height: Animated oats reach 36 inches (91 cm), quaking grass and hare's tail reach 18 inches (46 cm).

Light and soil: Full sun and well-drained soil.

How to grow: Sow seeds in the garden in April. Germination takes about three weeks. Space plants about 6 inches (15 cm) apart.

Pests and diseases: Generally trouble-free.

Uses: Annual ornamental grasses add movement to the garden and a soft texture to mixed plantings. Throw a few seeds into a mixed planter for contrast. Fresh and dried seed heads are great for arrangements and crafts.

"Baby blue eyes" see *Nemophila*
"Bachelor's button" see *Centaurea*

Begonia × *semperflorens-cultorum* "fibrous begonia" "wax begonia"
BEGONIACEAE
(Figure 2-1)

These simple and delightful bedding plants have a remarkably complex parentage made up of six species of begonias from Central and South America and Jamaica. The name fibrous refers to their roots, to separate them from their cousins, the tuberous begonias, which form a bulb-like tuber.

Fibrous begonias have shiny heart-shaped leaves up to 2 inches (5 cm) across. Leaf color may be bright green or bronze. There are dozens of the small pink, red or white flowers on the plant all season, making a colorful contribution to the garden whether the summer is wet or dry. These begonias are also very easy to grow.

Bloomtime: May to frost. (Pot them up and bring indoors for all-winter bloom.)

Height: 6–9 inches (15–23 cm).

Light and soil: Plant begonias in half or full shade and any well-drained soil, preferably enriched with moist peat moss or other organic matter.

How to grow: Fibrous begonias are readily available from shops in spring and are very slow to grow from seed, so most gardeners prefer to buy them. If you would like to try growing your own, seeds must be sown in January. The seeds are dust-like, with about 2 million seeds per ounce (28 g). To make sowing easier, mix seeds with a tablespoon (15 ml) of granulated sugar and sow on the surface of the potting mix, pressing it down gently. Do not cover it with soil, as light is required for germination. To maintain humidity, cover flats or pots with clear plastic or glass. Germination, at 70°F (21°C) soil temperature, takes 14–21 days. When seedlings emerge, fertilize with quarter-strength 20-20-20 and maintain soil temperature at 70°F (21°C) until April, then grow at 60°F (15°C).

Set hardened-off plants out in late May, spacing them 8 inches (20 cm) apart. Plants may be taken into the house before the frost, where they will bloom all winter, given a bright, sunny window. They may be planted out again the following spring. Cuttings can be taken from overwintered plants in spring, which is easier than growing them from seeds.

Pests and diseases: In some years, CUTWORMS may eat stems at ground level. Watch young plants carefully for any sign of damage in the first weeks after planting them out. Planting begonias in heavy, waterlogged soil may result in stem and root ROTS.

Uses: Edging, pattern plantings, rock gardens, planter boxes and the front of flower beds or mixed borders.

Begonia × *tuberhybrida* "tuberous begonia" BEGONIACEAE
(Figure 1-4)

From eight Andean species, begonia hybridizers have developed a dazzling array of flower types in this group. Most popular are the cultivars with double blooms up to 6 inches (15 cm) across in shades of pink, white, rose, red, yellow and orange. (The showy blooms are actually the male flowers; the two smaller female flowers are alongside.) The excellent seed series 'Nonstop' is available in ten separate colors or as a mixture.

Fancy cultivars have ruffled, frilled, picotee and two-toned flowers. These must be grown from tubers, which are available from shops in March. Leaves, up to 8 inches (20 cm) long, are rounded at the base and taper to a long point. They are dark green and have deep ridges and teeth along the edges, giving them a rich texture. Although they are referred to as tuberous-rooted begonias, a tuber is actually a modified stem rather than a thickened root. Begonia societies offer much specialty information and a chance to purchase unusual begonias.

Often sold as 'Pendula' begonias, hanging basket begonias are part of this group of hybrids. They have smaller flowers and more tapered, pointed leaves. Their trailing habit makes them excellent additions to any type of container.

Bloomtime: May to frost.

Height: 8–18 inches (20–46 cm) depending on the cultivar. The 'Pendula' cultivars have a trailing habit that makes them excellent for hanging baskets.

Light and soil: Tuberous begonias need shade or part shade and a well-drained soil that does not dry out, preferably enriched with moist peat moss.

How to grow: Like fibrous begonias, it is easier for home gardeners to purchase tuberous begonias as tubers or as young plants in spring, rather than to grow them from seed. Both are readily available in shops. Tubers should be planted in March, concave side up, with the top edge level with the soil surface. Use a peaty potting mix, setting the tubers in individual pots or one inch (2.5 cm) apart in a sturdy flat. Do not overwater. Grow indoors in a bright window until hardening off and setting out in late May.

Young plants of cultivars such as 'Nonstop' are available in spring and may be planted out in late May 12–15 inches (30–38 cm) apart. If you wish to try growing them from seed, follow the instructions for fibrous begonias. Tall-growing cultivars may need light staking. After the very first frost, dig the tubers and let the stems dry back. Pack them in a box of dry peat and store in a cool, dry, frost-free place until February or March. Tubers can be kept for over twenty years.

After a year or so, tubers will be large enough to divide if desired. To do this, set tubers out on a bright window sill in March, concave side up (without soil or pots), until the new shoots appear. Divide the tubers with a clean sharp knife, making sure each section has at least one shoot. Dust with a fungicide and plant as with whole tubers.

Pests and diseases: POWDERY MILDEW causes white powdery patches or spots on leaves and stems.

Uses: Bedding, planter boxes and tubs, and hanging baskets. Moss baskets planted with a single cultivar of tuberous begonia are lovely.

"Bells of Ireland" see *Molucella*
"Black-eyed susan" see *Rudbeckia*
"Black-eyed-susan vine" see *Thunbergia*

Brachycome iberidifolia "Swan River daisy" ASTERACEAE
(Figure 2-2)

This half-hardy annual from Australia has 3/4-inch (2-cm) daisy-like flowers of pink, violet and white. They are lightly fragrant, although the fragrance is not noticeable unless they are close at hand. The foliage is fine, giving an airy quality to the plant. The plants have a floppy habit, so they need the support of twigs, or they can be grown in containers and allowed to trail. Some seed catalogues list selected strains with more intense color, such as 'Purple Splendor' and 'Blue Splendor'.

Bloomtime: June to September.

Height: Up to 18 inches (46 cm) if staked.

Light and soil: Full sun and rich soil to which some moist peat or well-rotted manure has been added.

How to grow: Although young plants are not generally available from shops, they are easily grown from seed. Sow in March, just covering them with soil. Germinate at 70°F (21°C) until seedlings are established, then transplant and reduce temperature to 60°F (15°C). Set out hardened-off plants in late May, adding small twiggy branches to give support. Pinch the growing tip to encourage bushiness. Plants may be cut back by one-half if they become too floppy.

Pests and diseases: Generally trouble-free.

Uses: Best used in planter boxes and hanging baskets. In the flower border, be sure to support them and plant with other annuals for more impact.

Brassica oleracea "ornamental cabbage" "ornamental kale" "flowering cabbage" "flowering kale" BRASSICACEAE
(Figure 5-2)

Vegetables grown for their decorative rather than nutritive value, these plants have been developed by the Japanese from a European kale. The common name ornamental kale is more accurate than flowering kale, because the decorative part of the plant is the leaves rather than a flower. Color variations include purple, green and white. Some cultivars have tight rosettes of leaves (usually referred to as cabbages) while some have deeply cut feathery leaves (referred to as kale). In a wet autumn, the more open plants perform best because the rain can drain away more easily.

Bloomtime: Grown for foliage rather than the flowers. Plants set out in the late summer will give a most colorful display until hidden by snow or killed by hard frost. They are best left in place until the following spring, when they should be dug out before they start to give off the characteristic rotten eggs smell.

Height: 1–2 feet (30–61 cm).

Light and soil: Full sun or light shade. As the plants will not be doing much growing, soil need not be rich as long as it is well-drained.

How to grow: Plants are seldom available at garden centers and even the seed is usually only found in the larger seed catalogues. Sow indoors in late June and transplant the seedlings into individual small pots or cell packs. They are ideal for planting out in mid-August to replace plants that have finished flowering. Plant when they have about eight leaves, spacing the plants about 15–18 inches (38–45 cm) apart. They will look a little silly at first, but if you feed heavily with 20-20-20 liquid feed, applied once a week, they will grow at a tremendous rate and the leaves will soon touch. They color most brilliantly as the weather cools off.

Pests and diseases: The CABBAGE BUTTERFLY, white with pale green spots on its wings, will flutter daintily around your cabbage and kale and lay eggs, soon to be followed by hard-to-spot green CATERPILLARS that will rapidly eat all the leaves if not stopped. They often lie along a leaf midrib and are easy to hand pick.

Uses: Fall and winter bedding plants in borders or containers.

Briza see *Avena*

Browallia speciosa and *B. viscosa* "browallia" "amethyst flower"
SOLANACEAE
(Figure 5-3)

Good habit, foliage and flowers make browallia a welcome addition to any planter, hanging basket or border. Its flowers of white, blue or violet have five petals and resemble stars. The simple, bright green leaves taper to a point at each end. Most cultivars are well-branched and bushy. This South American native is a half-hardy perennial and will continue blooming in a greenhouse or sunny window indoors in winter. It doesn't like cold weather, so you probably won't see it in shops in April or early May, but it is worth waiting for.

'Sapphire' is deep blue, 'Heavenly Bells' is light Cambridge blue, 'Marine Bells' is indigo, 'Silver Bells' is white and 'Jingle Bells' is a mixture. All are bushy and compact.

Bloomtime: June to first cold weather, September or October.

Height: 10–12 inches (25–30cm).

Light and soil: Sun or partial shade and a well-drained soil. Add organic matter if possible, but browallia tolerates even poor, dry soil.

How to grow: Young plants are rarely available from garden centers, so they must be started from seed. Sow indoors in March, but do not cover, as light is required for germination. Germination, at 70°F (21°C) soil temperature, takes about 14 days. After transplanting, grow on at 60°F (15°C). When weather has warmed up in late May or early June, set out young plants 8–10 inches (20–25 cm) apart. Pinch growing tips to encourage branching.

Pests and diseases: Watch for WHITEFLY under leaves.

Uses: Edging, pattern plantings and at the front of beds and mixed borders. Excellent in containers and hanging baskets. Try blue browallia with yellow dwarf French marigolds; white browallia with peach tuberous begonias looks quite elegant.

"Burning bush" see *Kochia*
"Butterfly flower" see *Schizanthus*
"Cabbage, flowering or ornamental" see *Brassica*
"Cabbage tree" see *Cordyline*

Calceolaria **'Sunshine'** "pocketbook flower" "slipper flower" "pouch flower" "calceolaria" SCROPHULARIACEAE
(Figures 7-1 and 8-6)

Many calceolaria are sold in florists' shops for indoor decoration, but 'Sunshine' is the best one to grow in the garden. ('Goldri' is also excellent and very similar, but it is not readily available.) 'Sunshine' is a hybrid of *Calceolaria integrifolia* (formerly *C. rugosa*) and an unknown parent. It has a most unusual yellow flower, which is shaped like a pouch. Its leaves are mat green, crinkled and tapering to a point. A subshrub in its native Chile, calceolaria is grown as a half-hardy annual.

Bloomtime: May or June to September.

Height: 8–10 inches (20–25 cm).

Light and soil: Full sun or part shade and a well-drained soil. They like a warm spot protected from the wind.

How to grow: Young plants are sometimes available from shops in spring, or they may be started from seed. Sow seeds indoors in March, but do not cover as light is required for germination, which, at 70°F (21°C) soil temperature, takes about 14–16 days. After transplanting, grow on at 50–55°F (10–13°C). Set hardened-off plants out in late May, spacing them 8 inches (20 cm) apart. Plants dug up at the end of the season can be overwintered in a bright, cool, frost-free place.

Pests and diseases: In the garden, SLUGS and APHIDS may bother these plants. In the greenhouse they may get WHITEFLY and root or basal ROTS.
Uses: For edging and the front of beds and borders. *Calceolaria* 'Sunshine' also makes an outstanding moss basket or may be added to a mixed basket.

Calendula officinalis "Scotch marigold" "pot marigold" ASTERACEAE (Figure 8-1)

This easy-to-grow hardy annual was the "marigold" of the Elizabethans, who used it for cooking and decorating food. The specific name *officinalis* indicates that it was used by apothecaries for medicinal purposes. The wild species, native to southern Europe, grows up to 2 feet (61 cm) tall and has single daisy-like blooms of yellow or orange. Plant breeders have developed strains with double blooms in the same color range with the addition of apricot. 'Fiesta Gitana' (a Fleuroselect winner) and 'Bon Bon' grow to 12 inches (30 cm); 'Pacific Beauty', 18–24 inches (46–61 cm). 'Apricot Sherbet' is a lovely peach shade and grows to 15 inches (38 cm). While pot marigolds thrive even in poor soil with neglect, they will have more fully double blooms and bloom for a longer period if the soil is better and old flowers are removed. If flowers go to seed or if the weather is exceptionally hot, plants tend to look untidy by late July. Calendula will reseed itself, which is a blessing or a nuisance, depending on the plant's location and your point of view. It is easy to start another crop in June for flowers in the fall, if desired. Calendula is an excellent cut flower, particularly the taller varieties.
Bloomtime: May to late summer, fall for a second crop.
Height: 12–24 inches (30–61 cm) depending on the cultivar.
Light and soil: Prefer full sun and any well-drained soil. They will tolerate amazingly dry and poor soil, but may not bloom as heavily or have as many double blooms.
How to grow: Young plants are generally available from shops in spring, or they may be started easily from seed. Sow seeds indoors in March and cover lightly as seeds germinate best in darkness. Germination, at 60°F (15°C) soil temperature, takes about 10 days. After transplanting, grow on at 50°F (10°C). Set young plants out in May, pinching growing tips to encourage bushiness.
Pests and diseases: Pot marigolds are generally not bothered by problems, but POWDERY MILDEW may cause white powder on leaves if spring

weather is cool. Watch for APHIDS; CUTWORMS may eat stems.

Uses: Use dwarf cultivars at the front of beds and the taller ones in mixed borders for a "cottage garden look." Good for cutting.

"Calliopsis" see *Coreopsis*

Callistephus chinensis "China aster" "annual aster" ASTERACEAE (Figure 3-1)

In the 1730s, a Jesuit priest in China first sent seeds of a dark purple half-hardy annual to Europe. Although his name has been forgotten, his contribution to western horticulture has not. That original species had single flowers and was thought to be in the same genus as the perennial aster (*Aster*). More recently it has been appointed its own genus, *Callistephus*, meaning beautiful crown. Over the years, many colors have been developed from this one species, including red, pink, blue, violet, white, pale yellow and bicolors. Breeders have produced a dazzling array of flower forms—some like pompons, some with long needle-like petals, some like daisies and some with large, shaggy blooms. Unfortunately, China asters don't bloom until August or September, and they are prone to the serious disease aster wilt, which may kill plants completely. But do try a few, especially in an out-of-the-way corner of the garden where problems might go unnoticed if they develop. Even one row of asters will give dozens of stunning cut flowers.

Plant hybridizers have developed a number of seed strains that have increased resistance to aster wilt. 'Dwarf Queen' reaches 8 inches (20 cm) and is covered with double 2¹/₂-inch (6-cm) blooms of red, scarlet, light blue, rose pink, white, yellow and mixed colors. 'Pompon Mixed' reaches 20 inches (51 cm) as tall, upright, well-branched bushes with very tight button-like blooms 2 inches (5 cm) across; the whole plant may be cut at once as a long-lasting bouquet. 'Powderpuff' grows to 36 inches (91 cm) tall and only 12 inches (30 cm) wide; they are very upright plants with blooms 2¹/₂ inches (6 cm) across. The whole plant may be cut at once. 'Giant Princess Mixed' has crested centers and quill-like guard petals in a range of 17 different colors and grows to 30 inches (76 cm). 'Ostrich Plume' has recurved petals on double flowers in a wide range of colors, grows to 18 inches (46 cm) and is among the first to bloom.

Bloomtime: Late summer and autumn.

Height: 10–36 inches (25–76 cm), depending on the cultivar.
Light: Full sun and any well-drained soil to which some lime has been added.
How to grow: Young plants are generally available from shops in late spring or early summer. They may also be started from seed sown indoors in April. Cover seeds lightly. Germination, at 60–70°F (15–21°C) soil temperature, takes 8–10 days. Later sowings will extend the season of bloom. Set hardened-off plants out in early June, spacing them 12 inches (30 cm) apart. Seeds may also be sown directly into the garden in April or May. Stake tall cultivars for straighter stems if desired. Insects spread diseases, so keep plants insect-free.
Pests and diseases: ASTER WILT may attack plants. APHIDS and LEAFHOPPERS may infest plants, transmitting disease from one to another.
Uses: For an excellent cut flower and beautiful late-summer color, try some asters. But don't plant them as the focal point of your garden, because they can be unreliable.

Campanula isophylla "star-of-Bethlehem" CAMPANULACEAE
Although sold in shops in spring, star-of-Bethlehem is a tricky plant to grow outdoors. It is daylength-sensitive and does not bloom until August and September. Plants that are in bloom in May have been forced under lights. The stems are brittle and break easily and the flowers turn brown and yet do not fall off the plant. They are not a good choice for summer bedding; they are more suitable perhaps to bloom in pots in the greenhouse or hanging baskets which can be attended to frequently.

"Candytuft" see *Iberis*

Canna × *generalis* "canna lily" CANNACEAE
(Figure 1-5)
This group of hybrids brings the exotic look of tropical America to the home garden with very little effort. Canna lilies have huge leaves with rounded tips that vary in color from light to dark green, and from brownish to dark red. The flowers, which are up to 4 inches (10 cm) across, grow in spectacular clusters at the top of stems. Depending on the cultivar, they are yellow, orange, red, cream, salmon, or rose, and some are variegated and speckled with two colors. Canna lilies are usually used

as a centerpiece in large planters or beds, surrounded by other bedding plants. Use smaller canna cultivars in scale with a home garden. Because cannas form rhizomes (thickened underground stems), they may be dug before the first frost and kept over winter for next year. Look for them with bulbs, rather than with the annuals, in shops and catalogues.

'Seven Dwarfs Mixed' is a seed strain of cannas that grows to only 18 inches (46 cm) high, more in scale with a small garden than some of the taller types. 'Pfitzer's' named cultivars may be purchased as rhizomes; they grow up to 30 inches (76 cm). The giant canna with bronze leaves and red flowers seen in parks is usually 'Red King Humbert', which reaches 7 feet (2.1 m) in height—not for the small garden!

Bloomtime: July to frost.

Height: 1¹/₂–7 feet (.5–2.1 m), depending on the cultivar.

Light and soil: Plant in full sun. Canna lilies thrive in a rich moist soil. Add lots of well-decomposed organic matter or moist peat. In the wild, they grow in swampy areas, so they like lots of water.

How to grow: Buy rhizomes of named cultivars and start them indoors in March, barely covered with soil. Fertilize with 20-20-20 and grow on at 60°F (15°C) until planting out in late May. Rhizomes may be set directly in the garden in late May, but will take longer to bloom. In subsequent years, old rhizomes may be divided when new shoots appear, taking care to leave one shoot on each section of rhizome.

Cannas are also easily grown from seed, but may not bloom the first year. Start them in January or February by soaking the seeds in warm water for 24 hours, or nick the seed coats with a file before sowing. Keep the soil temperature at 70°F (21°C). Germination may take several months. When roots of the young plants are filling the pots, pot on into individual containers.

In the garden, remove faded flowers constantly. After frost, cut the stems back to 6–8 inches (15–20 cm) and dig the rhizomes. Shake off the soil, partially dry them and store in a cool, frost-free place in a box of dry peat. Check for signs of shriveling (sprinkle with water) or rot (remove affected rhizomes).

Pests and diseases: SLUGS and CUTWORMS may eat the rhizomes. The CATERPILLAR corn earworm eats canna lilies and a BACTERIAL BUD ROT may infect the flower buds.

Uses: For a touch of the exotic, plant cannas at the back or center of beds or the center of large planters.

"Carnation" see *Dianthus*

Catharanthus roseus (*Vinca rosea*) "Madagascar periwinkle"
APOCYNACEAE
(Figure 5-4)

The Madagascar periwinkle is becoming increasingly popular as a plant for use in hot, dry situations and for roadside planting, since it is very tolerant of air pollution. It is generally listed in both seed catalogues and garden centers by its old name, *Vinca*. The glossy dark green leaves make a good foil for the light-colored flowers, many of which have a contrasting eye zone. The plants have a spreading habit of growth, making them ideal for low planters. 'Bright Eye' is white with a red eye, 'Linda' is deep rose and 'Delicata' is pink with a rose eye.

Bloomtime: Late June to frost.

Height: 10–15 inches (25–38 cm).

Light and soil: Full sun in light, sandy soils. Will grow in most soils but flowers best if the soil is not too rich.

How to grow: Plants are generally available in limited amounts at garden centers, so early shopping is advisable. They are slow growing from seed and should be sown about 12 weeks before the last frost date. Cover the seed thinly and germinate in total darkness at 80° F (27° C). Take care not to overwater the seedlings. Plant out 15 inches (38 cm) apart.

Pests and Diseases: Generally trouble-free.

Uses: Good for edging planters and in any hot, dry situation.

Celosia cristata "celosia" "cockscomb" AMARANTHACEAE
(Figure 1-6)

Cultivars of this striking half-hardy annual fall into two groups: flowers in the Plumosa Group are fluffy and feathery, while those in the Crested Group are dense and sculpted, somewhat resembling a cock's comb. The flowers, in shades of red, orange, yellow, pink and cream, seem to glow. Leaves are up to 4 inches (10 cm) long and taper to a point at each end. The Plumosa cultivars are most popular and give the best display. 'New Look' has bronze foliage and scarlet plumes on 12-inch (30-cm) plants. 'Apricot Brandy' has golden plumes set off by brandy-colored leaves. An AAS winner in 1985, 'Century Mixed' grows to 28 inches (71 cm) in a wide selection of colors. Celosia is native to the tropics of Asia and does best in a warm, dry summer.

Bloomtime: June to frost. Purchased in shops, celosia generally have one large plume that will last all season with a few smaller plumes developing on side shoots. If the central flower is pinched out when planting, a bushier plant will develop with many very small plumes. If, however, celosia can be planted "green," that is, before plants begin to bloom, the maximum number of blooms will result. This is an advantage of growing them from seed yourself.

Height: 10–24 inches (25–61 cm) depending on the cultivar. Plant taller ones for good cut flowers.

Light and soil: Full sun and rich, well-drained soil are ideal, but celosia will also tolerate poor, dry soil.

How to grow: Young plants are generally available from shops in spring, or they can be grown easily from seed. Sow in April and cover seeds very lightly to prevent them from drying out. Germination, at 70°F (21°C) soil temperature, takes about 14 days. Continue growing plants at the same temperature after transplanting. Harden off in late May and plant outdoors in early June. Space 8–12 inches (20–30 cm) apart. (They don't grow a lot in width, so plant dwarf cultivars closer together, especially in poor soils.)

Pests and diseases: Root ROT may occur if soil is too cold or damp.

Uses: Edging, bedding and pattern plantings; containers; cut and dried flowers. Some gardeners find cockscomb too gaudy; some like their festive colors.

Centaurea cyanus "cornflower" "bachelor's button" ASTERACEAE
(Figure 5-5)

Loved since ancient times, cornflower was named *cyanus* by the Romans in honor of its heavenly blue color. In Britain and Europe, this hardy annual grows wild with red field poppies (*Papaver rhoeas*) in wheat fields. Because the British refer to wheat as corn, these flowers were called cornflowers. Growing to 30 inches (76 cm), cornflowers are slender and airy, with long narrow leaves and 1- to 2-inch (2.5- to 5-cm) flowers with many ragged petals. 'Blue Diadem' has fully double flowers 2$1/2$ inches (6 cm) across; 'Polka Dot Mixed' grows to a bushy 16 inches

(41 cm) and blooms in shades of blue, maroon, red, rose-pink, lavender and white.

Bloomtime: If deadheaded constantly, cornflowers will bloom all summer. Otherwise, they tend to stop flowering, although self-sown seedlings grow quickly and often bloom the same season.

Height: 16–30 inches (41–76 cm), depending on the cultivar.

Light and soil: Plants are healthiest in a spot with good air circulation and full sun. Any soil is satisfactory.

How to grow: Although young plants are not generally available from shops, they are easily grown from seed. Sow seeds directly in the garden, 1/2 inch (1 cm) deep, in September or late April; plants will bloom early in the spring from a fall or early spring sowing. Thin seedlings to stand 6–10 inches (15–25 cm) apart. Sow at several different times to extend the season of bloom. If sown indoors in March, use individual pots, as cornflowers resent transplanting. No bottom heat is required. Harden off plants and set out in mid-May. Staking of tall varieties is not always necessary as stems are wiry and quite strong.

Pests and diseases: Cornflowers are vulnerable to POWDERY MILDEW, which causes white fuzzy patches on the foliage. Plant in full sun with good air circulation and avoid overhead watering.

Uses: Because they have a softening effect, both in texture and color, cornflowers do not look out of place in an "English country" style of garden. They make excellent cut flowers and may be grown in the middle of a mixed border.

Cheiranthus cheiri "English wallflower"
Erysimum hieraciifolium (*Cheiranthus allioni*) "Siberian wallflower"
BRASSICACEAE
(Figure 7-4)

Although these two wallflowers are now assigned to separate genera, they are grouped together here because of their similar appearance, cultivation and use in the garden. Both are perennials grown as winter annuals, blooming very early in the spring. They are only hardy in sheltered gardens in the mildest regions, unfortunately. Fragrant flower spikes of gold, yellow, cream, bronze or rich red are set off by slender green leaves. Both species are native to Europe.

Bloomtime: English wallflowers, April to June; Siberian wallflowers, May to July.

Height: 9–24 inches (23–61 cm), depending on the cultivar.

Light and soil: Full sun or part shade in well-drained soil with a neutral or slightly sweet pH.

How to grow: Because of their limited useful growing range, you will have to grow them from seed. Sow in an open nursery bed in May or June (or in the vegetable garden after the early peas have come out). Thin or transplant to 8 inches (20 cm) apart. When they are 6 inches (15 cm) tall, pinch out the growing tips so they will become bushy. In September, move the plants to where they are to bloom. (Winter pansies like the same routine, so they can be done at the same time.) If you wish, leave wallflowers in the garden to naturalize in a wild corner with good sun. They will bloom every spring.

Pests and diseases: Generally trouble-free.

Uses: Plants add green to the winter garden. Use for spring bedding with flowering bulbs such as tulips and daffodils. Use dwarf cultivars for rock gardens and niches on a rock wall, tall ones for cutting.

"Cherry pie" see *Heliotropium*
"China pink" see *Dianthus*

Chrysanthemum carinatum (*C. tricolor*) "annual chrysanthemum"
ASTERACEAE
(Figure 8-2)

Annual chrysanthemum is a hardy annual from North Africa. It grows quickly, making a 2-foot (61-cm) bush that is covered in blooms by late June from a May planting. The daisy-like flowers are 2¹/₂ inches (6 cm) across, the petals having concentric rings of white, yellow, red and bronze. They are set off by the finely cut, bright green, almost succulent foliage. Handsome in the garden, they are a long-lasting cut flower as well.

Bloomtime: June to September, looking best in July and August.

Height: 18–24 inches (46–61 cm).

Light and soil: Best in full sun in a rich, well-drained soil.

How to grow: Although young plants are not generally available from shops, they are easily grown from seed. Sow directly in the garden or indoors in late March. No bottom heat is required. Set out young plants or thin seedlings to 12 inches (30 cm) apart. Give light support with bamboo stakes. Pinch the tips to encourage more side shoots. Remove old flowers to extend the season of bloom and then keep well-watered or the plants will flag in hot weather.

Pests and diseases: Generally trouble-free.

Uses: A fast filler for mid-summer color, annual chrysanthemums make good cut flowers also. Use in the middle of a mixed border.

Chrysanthemum frutescens "marguerite daisy" ASTERACEAE
(Figures 6-2 and 7-7)

Marguerites are the troupers of the bedding plant set, blooming tirelessly with little care until frost. In their Canary Island home they are perennials, but here they are grown as annuals in the garden. The most common marguerite has yellow or white daisy flowers up to 2 inches (5 cm) across; both colors have a yellow center. They make excellent cut flowers. There are several fancy cultivars on the market. 'Silver Lace' is a charming cultivar which is very bushy and compact, and has thread-like gray-green foliage. Smothered with 1-inch (2.5-cm) white daisies, it is delightful for any border or large planter, or in small bouquets. 'June Bride' has enlarged, shaggy looking disk florets (anemone-flowered). There is also a single pink that has a lovely flower but is a tall and slightly floppy plant, needing light staking.

Bloomtime: Starts blooming late May and looks great right up to the frost.

Height: 18–24 inches (46–61 cm), depending on the cultivar.

Light and soil: Full sun. Rich, well-drained soil that does not dry out gives the best looking plants.

How to grow: Young plants are occasionally available, or they may be started from cuttings taken in September. Take 2- to 3-inch (5- to 7.5-cm) cuttings of non-flowering side-shoots and overwinter indoors under lights. Cuttings may also be taken of overwintered plants in February, but fall cuttings will make larger plants. Set plants out in May. Removal of old flowers makes the plant tidier, but plants will bloom well even if not deadheaded.

Pests and diseases: Generally trouble-free.

Uses: Middle or back of beds and borders; large planters; cut flowers.

Chrysanthemum parthenium "feverfew" "matricaria" ASTERACEAE
(Figure 7-2)

Feverfew is technically a perennial, but it is short-lived and comes so quickly from seed that it is usually treated as an annual. The deeply cut, bright green leaves are soft and aromatic. Many delightful cultivars have been developed from the original species. 'Aureum' is primarily grown for its golden foliage; 'Golden Ball', 10 inches (25 cm) tall, has clusters of yellow pompons; 'White Bonnet', at 30 inches (76 cm), is fine for cutting. A new cultivar, 'Santana', is said to bloom all summer. Look for feverfew in the perennial section or grow it easily from seed. Although matricaria is not a correct common name, seed is offered under that name in some catalogues. Feverfew is native to Europe.

Bloomtime: On and off throughout the summer until fall. Although each plant blooms for only a month or so, feverfew seeds itself. In a group of plants, new plants will provide fresh flowers through the season. Old plants may be cut out after blooming to make room for new ones.

Height: It forms stiff bushes 6–18 inches (15–46 cm) in height depending on the cultivar.

Light and soil: Full sun is best, average soil.

How to grow: Although young plants are not generally available from shops, they are easily grown from seed. Sow seeds indoors in March or directly in the garden in April. Space 9 inches (23 cm) apart for dwarf cultivars; 18 inches (46 cm) for taller ones. Feverfew seeds itself. Young plants will provide fresh flowers through the season.

Pests and diseases: POWDERY MILDEW may be a problem.

Uses: Beds and borders, planters and pattern plantings (especially short cultivars); taller cultivars add airiness to bouquets; use them to set off roses and other larger flowers.

Chrysanthemum ptarmiciflorum see *Senecio*
"Cigar flower" see *Cuphea*

Clarkia amoena (*Godetia grandiflora*) "godetia" "satin flower"
ONAGRACEAE
(Figure 4-1)

This charmer, native to the Pacific coast, was named to commemorate Captain William Clark of the Lewis and Clark expedition of 1804–1806. Even in patches of flowers in the wild, no two flowers are identical. Each flower has four satiny petals in shades of lavender, pink, red, white or rose, with contrasting spots and edging on the petals. The leaves are oblong, up to 2 inches (5 cm) long; the flower buds and seed capsules are held erect at the ends of the stems.

Bloomtime: June to August. Bloomtime may be extended into fall by making later sowings.

Height: 12–24 inches (30–61 cm), depending on the cultivar.

Light and Soil: A light moist soil and full sun give the most blooms. Do not use too much fertilizer.

How to grow: Although young plants are not generally available from shops, they are easily grown from seed. A hardy annual, godetia may be seeded in the garden 1/4 inch (.6 cm) deep, in March or April (or start seeds indoors in March). To extend season of bloom, sow again in April and May. Space young plants 12 inches (30 cm) apart. Provide light support for tall cultivars or let them spread and make a clump; they look fine either way. Save seed capsules in August if you want to sow your own seeds.

Pests and diseases: Godetia are generally trouble-free, but APHIDS may appear in early spring and plants may be vulnerable to root ROT if drainage is poor.

Uses: Very showy in a border and long-lasting cut flowers.

Cleome hasslerana "cleome" "spider flower" CAPPARACEAE
(Figure 2-3)

Cleome (clee-oh-mee), an annual from Brazil and Argentina, likes warm weather, so it takes a while to get going, but it makes a striking plant. Growing to a large bush, it has 5-inch (13-cm) leaves divided into 5 to 7 pointed leaflets. At the top of each flower stem is a cluster of flowers, each having four long petals and six 2-inch (5-cm) stamens (the thin flower part which produces the pollen). The flowers farther down the stem develop long, narrow seed pods, which sit out from the stem on wiry stalks. Altogether, it is very unusual. Seed is available, both for separate colors—white ('Helen Campbell'), pink ('Rose Queen'), or violet ('Purple Queen')—and in mixed colors.

Bloomtime: July to frost.

Height: 3–4 feet (.9–1.2 cm) if grown in rich soil.

Light and soil: Full sun is essential. Cleome should be encouraged to grow quickly. Add organic matter to the soil and an all-purpose fertilizer. Soil should be well drained but not dry.

How to grow: Young plants are sometimes available from shops in spring, or they may be started from seed indoors in March. Pot into individual pots when large enough to handle and water weekly with a solution of 20-20-20. Harden off and set out in late May, June in a cold spring, spacing them 18 inches (46 cm) apart. Pinch the growing tips to encourage bushiness. The foliage of cleome has a strong odor, so plants should be set at the back of a bed where they won't be touched. Fertilize throughout the season.

Pests and diseases: CUTWORMS may eat the stem at the soil line. Watch carefully for damage after planting out. APHIDS may infest new growths.

Uses: Background planting at the back of a flower bed or mixed border; centerpiece to a large formal bed.

Cleretum bellidiformis (*Dorotheanthus bellidiformis*, *Mesembryanthemum criniflorum*) "Livingstone daisy" AIZOACEAE
(Figure 3-2)

Livingstone daisy is an annual from South Africa and is named for the famous African explorer, Dr. Livingstone. The narrow, tapering, spoon-shaped leaves are succulent and covered with a glistening coating that gives them a sugar-coated look. Flower colors include white, yellow, orange, pink, and shades of red to purplish-red, often with a contrasting white ring at the center of the flower. The flowers are daisy-like, but they are not true daisies (ASTERACEAE). Flowers close on rainy days. The name *Cleretum bellidiformis* has recently been given to this species.

Bloomtime: June to August.

Height: 2 inches high by 12 inches across (5 cm by 30 cm).

Light and soil: Well-drained soil but with some shelter from the mid-day sun or the plants will burn out.

How to grow: Not one of the popular annuals, it is seldom seen and you will have to grow it from seed. Sow in early March and cover seeds lightly, as darkness aids germination. At 60–70°F (15–21°C), this takes about 14 days. Set hardened-off plants out in late May, spaced 8 inches (20 cm) apart. They may also be sown directly in the garden in April.

Pests and diseases: If the ground is too wet, plants may collapse due to foot ROT. SLUGS will eat the leaves.

Uses: Excellent for color in a rock garden or a hot, sunny corner.

"Cockscomb" see *Celosia*

Coleus × hybridus "coleus" LAMIACEAE
(Figure 2-4)

The exotic leaf shapes and colors of coleus can add interest to a shady corner. There have been over 200 named cultivars developed from the Javan parent, *Coleus blumei*. The leaf color range includes red, orange, yellow, cream, bronze and every possible shade of green. Most cultivars have two or three colors on each leaf, with interesting borders and markings. Leaves are velvety and taper to a point, but some cultivars have added ruffles and frills. Although grown as annuals here, coleus are really perennials, and therefore make excellent houseplants in a sunny location. The 'Wizard' series is better in the garden than the 'Carefree' series. The 'Saber' series has very long leaves.

Bloomtime: Flowers should be pinched out before they develop. You will notice them as long spikes that start at the end of the stems. Pinch them off to keep the plant bushy.

Height: 6–18 inches (15–46 cm), depending on the cultivar.

Light and soil: Leaf color is best if plants have bright light, but not hot afternoon sun. Plant in light shade or on the east side of the house. Coleus like a moist, well-drained soil with some organic matter.

How to grow: Young plants are readily available from shops in spring, or they may be started from seed sown indoors in March. Sow at any time of year for houseplants. Do not cover seeds with potting mixture, but cover flats with clear plastic, to maintain humidity, until the seeds have germinated. Germination, at 60–70°F (15–21°C) takes 12–14 days. After transplanting, apply a fungicide drench to control damping-off. Cuttings may be taken in summer from favorite plants and rooted in water or vermiculite. Set young plants 8–12 inches (20–30 cm) apart and pinch out the growing tips to encourage bushiness.

Pests and diseases: Seedlings may DAMP OFF. In the garden, coleus is generally trouble-free.

Uses: An interesting addition to a shady container or corner of the garden. Try adding coleus to a planter with orange tuberous begonias or growing it with the cigar flower in a tub. Coleus also looks handsome in a brick planter in the shade.

Cordyline australis "dracaena palm" "spike" AGAVACEAE
(Figure 6-3)

A New Zealand native that doesn't normally bloom outdoors in this area, dracaena palm is grown for the decorative effect of the 1/2-inch-wide (1-cm) leaves, which arch to 3 feet (.9 m) long. Dracaena contrasts well with other bedding plants, and it makes a striking centerpiece for a bed or planter. They can be lifted in the fall and grown indoors for the winter.

Bloomtime: Grown for its foliage rather than its flowers.

Height: In a container, 34 feet (.91.3 m).

Light and soil: Full sun or part shade in a fertile, well-drained soil. Dracaenas are drought-resistant and tolerate winds.

How to grow: Young plants are generally available from shops in spring, or they can easily be grown from seed, although they take a year to reach a good size. They are good houseplants and can be grown in the house until they're large enough to make an impact in a planter outdoors. Germination at 70°F (21°C) takes about 2 months. Do not cover the seeds, but press them firmly into the soil surface.

They may also be propagated by removing leaves from mature stems and cutting the stems into 2- to 4-inch (5- to 10-cm) pieces. Place stems vertically in a sand and peat mixture, just buried, on bottom heat. Each eye on the stem will develop a shoot with about six leaves. When top growth appears, pot cutting individually into a 4-inch (10-cm) pot. Grow them in a sunny window indoors.

Plant out dracaenas in late May and bring them back indoors before the first frost. Check under the leaves for insect pests—you may need a magnifying glass to see spider mites.

Pests and diseases: SPIDER MITES sometimes infest the underside of the leaves.

Uses: As a centerpiece to a formal bed or planter.

Coreopsis tinctoria "calliopsis" "tickseed" ASTERACEAE
(Figure 1-7)

In 1737, Linnaeus gave the name *Coreopsis* to this genus because its seed resembled lice—from the Greek *koris* (lice) and *opsis* (similarity). Later there was a movement to change it to *Calliopsis*, that is, "beautiful to see" and although this generic name was never formally adopted, it is often used as a common name for the annual species of the genus.

An extremely easy, hardy annual to grow, calliopsis has wiry stems bearing yellow daisies with red and maroon markings. It is native to North America. *Coreopsis* 'Sunray' won a Fleuroselect medal.

Bloomtime: July to frost, if old flowers are removed, an onerous task, as the flowers are small and numerous. If they stop blooming, cut the plants back by one-third for a second bloom.

Height: 9–36 inches (23–91 cm), depending on the cultivar.

Light and soil: Full sun, a light well-drained soil (do not add too much organic matter).

How to grow: Although young plants are not generally available from shops, they are easily grown from seed sown directly in the garden or indoors in March. Space 6–9 inches (15–23 cm) apart. Stake tall cultivars with twiggy branches or bamboo canes.

Pests and diseases: Generally trouble-free.

Uses: Beds and borders; tall cultivars for cutting; dwarfs in mixed containers.

"Cornflower" see *Centaurea*

Cosmos bipinnatus "cosmos"
Cosmos sulphureus "yellow cosmos" ASTERACEAE
(Figure 4-2)

Cosmos and yellow cosmos are half-hardy annuals from Mexico bearing daisy-like flowers. They are not early bloomers, but are outstanding in late summer and fall when many bedding plants look tired. **Cosmos** forms a large bushy plant with feathery, bright green foliage and flowers up to 4 inches (10 cm) across in shades of white, pink, rose or purple-red. The best-known cultivar is 'Sensation Mixed', which makes excellent cut flowers. The cultivar 'Sea Shells' has petals rolled like fluted sea shells.

Yellow cosmos is smaller-growing and has darker green, less finely cut foliage. Flower colors include the yellows, orange-reds and flame colors. Look for 'Bright Lights Mixed', 'Diablo' and 'Sunny Red', a 1986 AAS winner.

Bloomtime: August to frost.

Height: Cosmos, to 3–4 feet (.9–1.2 m), depending on the cultivar. Yellow cosmos, to 2–3 feet (.6–.9 m), with some dwarf types 18 inches (46 cm) high.

Light and soil: Blooms best in full sun with light soil that is not too rich. Add organic matter but no fertilizer. Give plenty of water.

How to grow: Easy to grow. Young plants are generally available from shops in spring, or start from seed sown indoors in March. Germination, at 60–70°F (15–21°C) soil temperature, takes about 7 days. Plant out hardened-off plants in late May, spacing 12–18 inches (30–46 cm) apart. Pinch the growing tip to encourage bushiness and, in windy locations, stake plants. Remove faded flowers to encourage blooming.

Pests and diseases: APHIDS may infest young plants.

Uses: Cosmos have a soft effect in the garden and may be used in a mixed border to add texture and color. Plant near perennials such as bleeding heart and oriental poppies that die back in late summer; the cosmos will fill in the spaces. They are also excellent for cutting.

"Cupflower" see *Nierembergia*

Cuphea ignea "cigar flower" "firecracker plant" LYTHRACEAE
(Figure 1-8)

A shrub in its native Mexico and Jamaica, cigar flower makes a delightful annual that stands up well to summer heat and flowers profusely. Bushy and compact, cigar flower has dark green 1¹/₂-inch (4-cm) leaves that taper to a point at each end. It bears dozens of ³/₄-inch (2-cm) orange tubes with white and purple markings at the tip, which do resemble tiny cigars. It is not as showy as some bedding plants (that might be considered an advantage by some gardeners), but is so easy to grow that it should be grown more.

Bloomtime: June to frost.

Height: 12 inches (30 cm).

Light and soil: It is happy in sun or shade, but prefers a rich, well-drained soil that does not dry out.

How to grow: Although young plants are not generally available from shops, they are easily grown from seed sown indoors in mid-February. Germination, at 60–70°F (15–21°C) soil temperature, takes about 14–21 days. Set hardened-off plants out in late May, spacing them 12 inches (30 cm) apart. After checking for spider mites, plants may be brought indoors for the winter and set on a sunny window sill.

Pests and diseases: Cigar flower may get SPIDER MITES, especially in the greenhouse or indoors.

Uses: Containers, either alone or with other plants (such as dwarf marigolds, white or blue browallia); side planted in moss baskets; edging in beds or borders.

Dahlia **hybrids** "dahlia" ASTERACEAE
(Figure 4-3)

There are thousands of dahlia cultivars, and there seem to be almost as many stories about who discovered them in Mexico and how they were brought to Europe. They were certainly being grown in Europe by the early 1800s, and a dahlia craze was launched. In 1826, there were 62 cultivars in England; by 1841 the number had jumped to 1,200. In 1864 the Caledonian Horticultural Society offered a prize of 50,000 francs for anyone who could produce a blue dahlia. The money has yet to be claimed.

The universal popularity of dahlias can be attributed to the ease with which they are grown and the vast array of sizes, shapes and colors available (all except blue!). The leaves are variable in shape, but are generally divided into three leaflets with small teeth and pointed tips.

Only a dozen or so dahlia cultivars are sold as bedding plants. These bloom quickly from seed and are a dwarf 12–15 inches (30–38 cm). Flowers are single, semi-double or double and come in yellow, red, orange, pink or white. Most cultivars are sold as color mixtures, but those in the 'Sunny' series are sold as separate colors and are fully double. 'Redskin' (an AAS winner in 1975) has bronze foliage that sets off the bright double blooms. Seed is available for the "cactus" and "ball" type flowers as well, but these do not bloom as quickly as the bedding types.

Most fancy dahlias are named cultivars and consequently must be propagated by tuber division. Look for named cultivars with the summer-flowering bulbs in shops in March, or mail-order them from a specialist. Although only bedding dahlias are covered in detail here, the fancy dahlias can certainly be used in summer bedding schemes.

Because dahlias are named after Andreas Dahl (a pupil of Linnaeus), the correct pronunciation should be "doll-ia".

Bloomtime: May to frost.

Height: 12–24 inches (30–60 cm) for bedding cultivars.

Light and soil: Dahlias require full sun and rich, well-drained, fertile soil that does not dry out. Do not use a high-nitrogen fertilizer.

How to grow: Bedding plants are available in garden shops in spring. To grow them from seed, sow in early March and cover seeds lightly with soil. At 60–70°F (15–21°C), germination takes 10 days. Grow on at 55°F (13°C). Set plants out 12 inches (30 cm) apart in May. Remove dead flowers to encourage bloom and to tidy plants. (Take care when dead-heading, as the old and new flower buds look alike. The old buds are more pointed and softer when gently squeezed). Bedding dahlias form tuberous roots during the growing season and may be overwintered. Cut stems to 4 inches (10 cm) and dig roots. Allow them to dry, then store them in boxes covered with peat in a cool, dry, frost-free place. In March, bring them out into the light and allow growth to begin. Divide if desired, ensuring that each section has one shoot and a piece of the original stem. Plant out in April. Dahlias can survive a mild winter if left in the ground, but they should be dug and divided in spring.

Pests and diseases: APHIDS sometimes infest new growth, and EARWIGS hide in the flowers and eat holes in the leaves and petals.

Uses: Beds and borders; mixed planter boxes; long-lasting cut flowers.

"Daisy, African" see *Dimorphotheca, Gazania* and *Osteospermum*
"Daisy, blue" see *Felicia*
"Daisy, gloriosa" see *Rudbeckia*
"Daisy, Livingstone" see *Cleretum*
"Daisy, marguerite" see *Chrysanthemum frutescens*
"Daisy, Swan River" see *Brachycome*
"Daisy, Transvaal" see *Gerbera*

Dianthus barbatus "sweet william"
Dianthus chinensis "China pink"
Dianthus caryophyllus "carnation" CARYOPHYLLACEAE
(Figures 3-3, 4-4 and 4-5)

I have always found this genus to be a bit confusing, so I felt heartened to read the following quotation of an ancient scholar in the delightful book *Flowers, A Guide for Your Garden,* by Pizzetti and Cocker: "If I had the memory of Themistocles, who greeted every citizen by name; of Cyrus and of Scipio, who knew the names of all their soldiers; if I could, like Cineas, ambassador of Pyrrhus, name every senator and every citizen of Rome; it would still be impossible for me, entering a garden, to know all the dianthus by name."

There is confusion regarding the exact number of species in the genus *Dianthus* due to the variability of species and the ease with which they hybridize. Botanists generally set the number at 300. In the area of bedding plants there are mainly three types on the market.

Sweet williams have a variable life-cycle, being annuals, biennials or short-lived perennials from southern Europe. They can be started from seed in the summer and planted out into their flowering positions in the fall, where they will bloom in spring. Seeds may be started indoors in March, for bloom the same year. 'Double Flowered Mixed' grows to 18 inches (46 cm) and has about 60 percent double blooms. 'Indian Carpet' is a mix of single flowers in scarlet, crimson, pink, or white, often with a contrasting eye; they grow to 6 inches (15 cm). 'Wee Willie' blooms the first year from seed in June and July and is a very dwarf 4 inches (10 cm). It is usually available in shops in spring with the bedding plants. 'Double Flowered Mixed' and 'Indian Carpet' are often sold with the perennials.

Cultivars of *Dianthus chinensis*, **China pinks**, also bloom the first year from seed. 'Snowfire' makes a very eye-catching display in early summer with showy white $1^{1}/2$- to 2-inch (4- to 5-cm) blooms with red centers. Plants grow to 8 inches (20 cm) high. 'Telstar' (a Fleuroselect winner with scarlet blooms) and 'Princess Mixed' bloom all summer. They are half-hardy and, as the name suggests, the species is native to China.

Young **carnation** plants, *Dianthus caryophyllus*, are available in spring with the bedding plants or with perennials. Bedding cultivars (often referred to as annual carnations) bloom from July on from a February sowing, are excellent cut flowers and have attractive silver foliage. 'Giant Chabaud Mixed' grows to 24 inches (61 cm) high; staking is required. 'Knight Series Mixed' has very strong stems and a wide range of colors. The most outstanding annual carnation in the bedding plant trials is 'Scarlet Luminette' (a 1982 AAS winner), which is deeply fragrant and makes a wonderful cut flower. Carnations are native to Europe.

Bloomtime: Refer to each type above.

Height: 4–24 inches (10–61 cm), depending on the cultivar.

Light and soil: Full sun and well-drained soil to which some organic matter has been added. All dianthus like a sweet soil; add lime if the pH is below 6.5.

How to grow: Young plants of many cultivars are generally available from shops in spring, or they may be started from seed. See notes above for each type, but generally they should be sown in February or March. Germination, at 70°F (21°C) soil temperature, takes about 21 days.

Planting distance: Sweet williams: 9–15 inches (22–38 cm); Indian

pinks: 9–12 inches (22–30 cm); bedding carnations: 15 inches (38 cm).
Pests and diseases: APHIDS and CATERPILLARS may attack the leaves and new shoots.
Uses: Dwarf sweet william might be used at the front of a border, in a rock garden or in containers. Taller sweet william is suitable for a mixed border or larger container. (In a container on its own, it might be moved to a resting place when not in bloom.) Plant China pinks in mixed borders and in containers. Carnations look attractive in a mixed border, or, if you plan to cut them heavily, use a cutting garden or part of the vegetable garden.

Dimorphotheca **hybrids** "African daisy" "star-of-the-veldt" "Cape marigold" "dimorphotheca" ASTERACEAE
(Figure 7-3)
African daisies form a mat of 12-inch (30-cm) stems topped by blooms in shades of orange, yellow and cream, each with a dark disk at the center. The leaves, to 3¹/₂ inches (9 cm) long, have several small teeth along the edge. The dimorphothecas listed in seed catalogues and sold in shops are hybrids of two annuals from South Africa, *D. pluvialis* and *D. sinuata* (*D. aurantiaca*). Both love full sun and hot, dry locations, making them excellent additions to a rock garden. Some gardeners report dimorphothecas surviving a mild winter unprotected, but because they are annual, it is more likely that they have reseeded themselves.

The seed mixture 'Tetra Goliath' is an early bloomer with dense plants and 3¹/₂-inch (9-cm) blooms. 'Starshine' has 2- to 3-inch (5- to 8-cm) blooms in shades of carmine, pink, rose and white on plants which can spread up to 18 inches (46 cm) across. If you have the space to start them from seed, these would be worth a try, as the more commonly available 'Aurantiaca Mixed' have small flowers that are not as showy.

The name comes from the Greek and means "two shapes of seeds" (*di-morpho-theca*). This refers to the curious nature of this plant: the outer ray florets (see page 46) develop into seeds that look like minute sticks, while the central disk florets develop into larger flattened seeds.

Plants of another African daisy, osteospermum, are often sold as dimorphotheca. See that entry also for further information.
Bloomtime: June to frost, flowers opening on sunny days only. They don't hold up well in the rain, so in a very wet summer they may not look their best.

Height: 12–16 inches (30–41 cm).
Light and soil: Full sun with well-drained, sandy soil. Tolerate dry soil.
How to grow: Sometimes available in shops in May, they are also easily grown from seed. Sow outdoors in mid-April, spacing seeds 8 inches (20 cm) apart (or sow indoors in March). Cover the seeds with a very thin layer of sand. Although some books say seedlings are not easy to transplant, I know of several gardeners who have had no problems with transplanting. Set out plants in late May.
Planting distance: 8 inches (20 cm).
Pests and diseases: Leaves may be affected by GRAY MOLD in very wet weather.
Uses: Front of border, rock garden, dry places in the garden.

"Dracaena palm" see *Cordyline*
"Dusty miller" see *Senecio*
Erysimum hieraciifolium see *Cheiranthus*

Felicia amelloides "blue marguerite" "blue daisy" "felicia" ASTERACEAE
(Figure 2-5)
   In its native South Africa, the blue marguerite is a subshrub, but in this part of the world it doesn't overwinter. The plant is well-branched with attractive, rounded, 1-inch (2.5-cm) leaves that are slightly rough to the touch. The small blue flowers are 1 inch (2.5 cm) across with a yellow center. Because the flowers are small, they are not showy, but they have a delicate beauty that adds much to the garden.
Bloomtime: June until the frost, flowers open on sunny days.
Height: 12–24 inches (30–61 cm).
Light and soil: Full sun and well-drained soil to which some organic matter has been added.
How to grow: Rarely available from shops in May, blue marguerites are best grown from seed started indoors in March or April at 60°F (15°C). Pinch out the growing tips when the plants are about four inches (10 cm) high to encourage branching and more flowers. Plant out at the end of May, 9 inches (23 cm) apart. New plants can also be started from cuttings made from June to September. Plants can be dug and over-wintered in a greenhouse or sunroom.
Pests and diseases: Generally trouble-free.
Uses: At the front of beds and mixed borders; in sunny spots in rock

1-1 *Abutilon hybridum*
flowering maple

1-2 *Amaranthus tricolor*
Joseph's coat

1-3 *Antirrhinum majus*
'Kolibri Mixed'
dwarf snapdragon

1-4 *Begonia × tuberhybrida*
'Nonstop', upright
tuberous begonias

1-5 *Canna × generalis*
'The President'
canna lily

1-6 *Celosia cristata*
'Apricot Brandy'
cockscomb

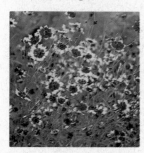

1-7 *Coreopsis tinctoria*
'Single Dwarf Mixed'
calliopsis

1-8 *Cuphea ignea*
cigar flower

1-9 *Mimulus* hybrids
'Calypso Mixed'
monkey flower

1-10 *Nemesia strumosa*
'Carnival Blend'
nemesia

1-11 *Tropaeolum majus*
'Glorious Gleam Mixture'
nasturtium

2-1 *Begonia* × *semp.-cultorum*
     'Prelude Pink'
     fibrous begonia

2-2 *Brachycome iberidifolia*
     Swan River daisy

2-3 *Cleome hasslerana*
     'Rose Queen'
     spider flower

2-4 *Coleus* × *hybridus*
     'Carefree Mixed'
     coleus

2-5 *Felicia amelloides*
     blue marguerite

2-6 *Impatiens wallerana*
     'Super Elfin Blush'
     common impatiens

2-7 *Limonium sinuatum*
     'Pacific Mixed'
     statice

2-8 *Lychnis coeli-rosa*
     viscaria

2-9 *Nemophila menziesii*
     baby blue eyes

2-10 *Nigella damascena*
      love-in-a-mist

2-11 *Torenia fournieri*
      'Compacta'
      wishbone flower

3-1 *Callistephus chinensis*
'Pinocchio Mix'
China aster

3-2 *Cleretum bellidiformis*
Livingstone daisy

3-3 *Dianthus chinensis*
'Telstar'
China pink

3-4 *Helichrysum bracteatum*
'Semidwarf Mixed'
strawflower

3-5 *Lathyrus odoratus*
'Bolton's Old Fashioned'
sweet pea

3-6 *Lavatera trimestris*
'Silver Cup'
mallow

3-7 *Matthiola incana*
'East Lothian Mixed'
stock

3-8 *Pelargonium peltatum*
ivy geraniums

3-9 *Phlox drummondii*
'Dwarf Beauty Mix'
annual phlox

3-10 *Viola* × *wittrockiana*
'Universal Red'
pansy

3-11 *Xeranthemum annuum*
common immortelle

4-1 *Clarkia amoena*
'Dwarf Azalea Flowered'
godetia

4-2 *Cosmos bipinnatus*
'Sensation Mixed'
cosmos

4-3 *Dahlia* 'Rigoletto'
dahlia

4-4 *Dianthus barbatus*
sweet william

4-5 *Dianthus caryophyllus*
'Grenadin Mixed'
carnation

4-6 *Fuchsia* × *hybrida*
'Empress of Prussia'
fuchsia

4-7 *Portulaca grandiflora*
'Calypso Mixed'
moss rose

4-8 *Salvia splendens*
'St. John's Fire'
red salvia

4-9 *Schizanthus* hybrids
'Hit Parade Mixed'
butterfly flower

4-10 *Verbena canadensis*
trailing verbena

4-11 *Zinnia elegans*
'Peter Pan Mixed'
zinnia

5-1 *Ageratum houstonianum* 'Blue Blazer' flossflower

5-2 *Brassica oleracea* 'Snow Prince' (l) and purple kale (r),

5-3 *Browallia speciosa* 'Marine Bells' browallia

5-4 *Catharanthus roseus* Madagascar periwinkle

5-5 *Centaurea cyanus* bachelor's button

5-6 *Gomphrena globosa* 'Mixed' globe amaranth

Morgan Jones

5-7 *Impatiens* 'Gemini' New Guinea impatiens

5-8 *Nierembergia hipp.* var. *violacea* 'Purple Robe' cupflower

5-9 *Petunia × hybrida* 'Falcon Blue' multiflora petunia

5-10 *Salpiglossis sinuata* 'Bolero Mixed' salpiglossis

5-11 *Salvia farinacea* 'Victoria' blue salvia

6-1 *Amaranthus caudatus*
love-lies-bleeding

6-2 *Chrysanthemum
frutescens*
marguerite daisy

6-3 *Cordyline australis*
dracaena palm
in center of barrel

6-4 *Glechoma hederacea*
'Variegata'
nepeta

6-5 *Hedera helix*
'Glacier'
English ivy

6-6 *Hypoestes phyllostachya*
'Pink Splash'
polka dot plant

6-7 *Kochia scoparia*
forma *trichophylla*
summer cypress

6-8 *Lobelia erinus*
trailing lobelia (l);
Sanvitalia procumbens (r)

6-9 *Lotus berthelotii*
lotus vine

6-10 *Senecio cineraria*
'Diamond' dusty miller
with 'Matador' geraniums

6-11 *Thunbergia alata*
black-eyed-susan vine

7-1 *Calceolaria* 'Goldri'
pocketbook flower

7-2 *Chrysanthemum
parthenium* 'Gold Ball'
feverfew or matricaria

7-3 *Dimorphotheca* hybrids
African daisy or
star-of-the-veldt

7-4 *Erysimum hieraciifolium*
Siberian wallflower

7-5 *Gazania* × *hybrida*
'Chansonette'
gazania

7-6 *Helianthus annuus*
'Teddy Bear'
sunflower

7-7 *Lantana camara* with
blue salvia, marguerites
and geraniums

7-8 *Papaver nudicaule*
'Champagne Bubbles'
Iceland poppy

7-9 *Primula* × *polyantha*
polyanthus

7-10 *Rudbeckia hirta*
'Marmalade'
black-eyed susan

7-11 *Tagetes erecta*
'Gold Lady'
African marigold

7-12 *Tagetes tenuifolia*
'Tangerine Gem'
signet marigold

8-1 *Calendula officinalis* 'Fiesta Gitana' Scotch marigold

8-2 *Chrysanthemum carinatum* annual chrysanthemum

8-3 *Heliotropium arborescens* fragrant heliotrope with geraniums

8-4 *Lobularia maritima* 'New Carpet of Snow' sweet alyssum

8-5 *Molucella laevis* bells of Ireland

8-6 Moss basket, 'Lemon Gem' marigolds, lobelia & geraniums

8-7 *Nicotiana alata* 'Domino Mix' flowering tobacco

8-8 *Osteospermum ecklonis* African daisy

8-9 *Pelargonium × domesticum* regal pelargonium

8-10 *Pelargonium × hortorum* 'Petals' fancy leaf geranium

8-11 *Verbena × hybrida* 'Sandy White' garden verbena

gardens; in planters and hanging baskets, alone or with other bedding plants.

"Feverfew" see *Chrysanthemum parthenium*
"Firecracker plant" see *Cuphea*
"Flossflower" see *Ageratum*
"Flowering tobacco" see *Nicotiana*
"Forget-me-not" see *Myosotis*
"Four-o'clock" see *Mirabilis*

Fuchsia × *hybrida* "fuchsia" ONAGRACEAE
(Figure 4-6)

Fuchsias are so popular that, like geraniums and begonias, there are special clubs devoted to their cultivation. The flowers, which hang from the tips of the stems, have a long tube that opens out into four sepals. These enclose the bud like a balloon until it opens, then extend sideways or curve backwards above the flower. There are four petals in single species and cultivars, but more in double cultivars; these petals are sometimes referred to as the corolla or "skirt." The stamens and style extend below the petals, adding a delicate touch. The color range includes combinations of white, pink, red, rose, violet and purple. Cultivars have been developed from many species, the main three being *Fuchsia fulgens*, *F. magellanica* and *F. triphylla*.

Fuchsias are half-hardy shrubs from the mountain woodlands of Central and South America, and they enjoy semi-shade with protection from the mid-day sun. Most fuchsias need protection from the frost and must be overwintered in a greenhouse or sunroom. Some cultivars, indicated on the following table, may be root-hardy in very sheltered sites. (The tops die down, but the roots send up new shoots in spring.) These cultivars also seem to be more sun-tolerant. Hardy fuchsias grow up to 3 feet (1 m) tall.

Some fuchsias grow upright, while others have a trailing habit. The trailing cultivars are perfect for growing in hanging baskets, where their flowers may be more fully appreciated. Cultivars marked both upright and trailing have a wide-growing habit and are suitable for bushy plants or for container planting. They will not trail straight down, but will grow over the edges. Following are some popular fuchsia cultivars.

Name	sepals	petals	single	dougle	trailing	upright	hardy	standards
Bicentennial	orange	dark orange		•	•			•
Dark Eyes	red	dark blue		•	•			•
Display	rosy-red	cerise	•			•		
Dollar Princess	cerise	purple		•		•	•	
Double Otto	red	purple		•		•	•	
Empress of Prussia	scarlet	magenta	•			•	•	
Gartenmeister Bonstedt*	orange-red	orange-red	•			•		
Indian Maid	red recurving	purple		•	•			•
Jack Shahan	pink	pink	•		•	•		•
Lena	pale pink	magenta		•	•	•		•
Lisa	blue	pink		•	•			•**
Marinka	red	red	•		•			•
Miss California	pink recurving	pale pink	•			•		•
Mrs. Popple	red	navy blue	•			•	•	•
Papoose	red	dark purple	•			•	•	
Peppermint Stick	carmine recurving	violet		•		•		
Pink Galore	pink	pink		•	•			
Pink Marshmallow	white recurving	white flushed pink		•				•
Riccartoni	scarlet	violet	•			•	•	
Snowcap	red	white		•		•		•
Swingtime	red	white		•	•			•
Winston Churchill	red recurving	magenta wavy		•		•		

Cultivars marked under standard are suitable for training as standards.
* dark olive green foliage takes more sun
** very slow-growing, thus taking longer to make a standard than some cultivars

Training standard fuchsias. Fuchsia trees—standard fuchsias—are fuchsias that have been trained to form a trunk by staking and pruning. An elegant addition to a bed or planter, they are seldom seen in nurseries. You can train a fuchsia quite easily provided you have a place to overwinter it, as it takes a full year. Start with a soft plastic pot (the kind used in nurseries) 8 inches wide by 12 inches deep (20 cm by 30 cm). Secure a 4-foot (1.2 m) cedar stake to the pot by nailing the stake to a cross-piece and nailing the cross-piece to the pot. To make a fuller crown on the tree, two fuchsia plants of the same cultivar are used. (Branches and roots of the two plants will intermingle.)

Use a potting mix that is rich in organic matter, but has some sand to add weight, otherwise plants will easily tip over when full-grown. Plant one fuchsia on either side of the cedar stake. As the plants grow, gently secure the tip of each fuchsia to its own side of the stake with a piece of soft green plastic sold for tying plants. The object of this training is to get two straight stems, with the stake between them for support. This will form the trunk for the fuchsia tree. As the plants grow, they will send out side shoots, which should be shortened to two leaf nodes. Do not remove the large leaves that grow along the main stems.

When the plants have grown to within 2 inches (5 cm) of the top of the stake, pinch out the growing tips to encourage branching. Do not let the main stems grow taller than the stake, because then they can no longer be tied to it for support. When the crown develops and becomes heavy with bloom, the whole crown could snap off. As the crown develops, keep pinching the growing tips to encourage branching. It takes about six months to train the trunks up the stake and another six months for a well-branched crown to develop.

Cultivars suitable for training as standards are indicated in the table above. 'Miss California' is particularly attractive as a standard, but 'Lena' requires a lot of fussing and 'Lisa' is slow growing.

Bloomtime: May to frost, looking great in the fall if well cared for.

Height: 12–24 inches (30–61 cm), upright or trailing, depending on the cultivar.

Light and soil: Although some cultivars will take sun, most prefer filtered or afternoon shade. Plant in a well-drained soil to which some moist peat has been added.

How to grow: Plants are frequently available in shops in spring. For fancy cultivars, contact your local fuchsia society; they usually have annual sales. Set plants out at the end of May or early June. Keep them moist or the flower buds may drop. Remove old flowers and fertilize weekly with a liquid fertilizer. Early in the season, a balanced fertilizer such as 20-20-20 may be used to encourage growth, but by July use a formulation with more phosphorus to encourage bloom.

Fuchsia plants which are several years old produce an abundance of bloom, so overwinter plants if possible. To do this, gradually withhold water from plants in mid-October to force them into dormancy. All the leaves will fall, and the plants should not be watered again until spring. Store them in a cool, 55°F (13°C), but not necessarily bright, place. Check the plants from time to time; if the stems start to wither, spray them with tepid water. In March, soak the pots in water. This will cause the buds to swell and you may then prune the plants. Cut each stem back to just above the sixth node, approximately. After pruning, remove the plants from the pot, shaking off all old soil. Rinse roots and repot with fresh potting mix. Water well and place them in a bright window or greenhouse. On warm days, put the plants outside, out of direct sunlight, to harden off. Set them out in late May. After three years, the plants should be thrown away.

Fuchsias can also be grown from seed, or from cuttings taken in August or September and kept over winter. Seedlings won't be true to the parent, but it can be fun. To grow fuchsias from seed, allow some flowers to develop berries. (Not all cultivars will set berries.) Break up very ripe, soft berries into a bowl of water and clean the seeds, dry them on paper towels and store in a cool, dry place. Plant in spring or fall in soil 55°F (13°C) or warmer. The germination rate is normally very good.

For suggestions on using fuchsias in hanging baskets, see Chapter 6.

Pests and diseases: APHIDS sometimes suck the sap of leaves and stems. SLUGS eat the new shoots of hardy fuchsias. SPIDER MITES can infest the underside of the leaves. WHITEFLY may be a problem in the greenhouse. A PHYSIOLOGICAL DISORDER causes yellow and purple spots and the leaves later fall off.

Uses: Fuchsia is a classic for hanging baskets, either alone or mixed with other bedding plants. Use in planters and use upright cultivars in borders.

Gazania × hybrida "gazania" "African daisy" ASTERACEAE
(Figures 6-3 and 7-5)

Gazanias are another daisy-like flower from South African and, like the two other African daisies, they like a warm spot in full sun, and the flowers open only on sunny days. Gazanias come in shades of yellow, mahogany, tangerine, red, white, pink and orange, and often have rings of contrasting color. The leaves form a rosette around the base of the short stems. They are surprisingly frost-tolerant and will continue to flower well into fall.

The 'Mini-Star' series is available in separate colors, the 'Tangerine Mini-Star' won AAS and Fleuroselect awards; 'Mini-star Yellow' was a Fleuroselect winner. 'Sundance' has flowers of mixed colors, including one that has red and yellow striped petals; it grows quickly from seed. 'Carnival' has stunningly marked and colored flowers and silvery foliage.

Bloomtime: May to frost.

Height: 6–8 inches (15–20 cm).

Light and soil: Full sun and a well-drained soil to which some organic matter has been added. Gazanias tolerate dry soil.

How to grow: Young plants are generally available from shops in spring, or they may be started from seed. Sow in February. Germination is erratic, and it is essential to use only fresh seeds. Set young plants out in late May, 15 inches (38 cm) apart. Remove faded flowers. Plants may be started from cuttings taken in August or September and inserted into very sandy soil. Plants may also be increased by division.

Pests and diseases: In very wet weather, GRAY MOLD may be a problem.

Uses: Its low-growing, almost trailing habit makes gazania a perfect candidate for rock gardens, pockets in a rock wall or the edge of an informal mixed border. Use in containers or hanging baskets, alone or with other bedding plants.

"Geranium, ivy or trailing" see *Pelargonium peltatum*

"Geranium, Martha Washington or pansy" see *Pelargonium* × *domesticum*

"Geranium, zonal" see *Pelargonium* × *hortorum*

Gerbera jamesonii "gerbera daisy" "Transvaal daisy" ASTERACEAE

Gerbera daisies are often sold in stores in spring and are very tempting, but they are a tricky plant to grow—particularly to water correctly—and for that reason are not recommended as good bedding plants in this area. They are best suited to a cool greenhouse or container under cover, where their watering and care can be more easily controlled.

Glechoma hederacea 'Variegata' (*Nepeta hederacea*) "nepeta" "creeping charlie" LAMIACEAE
(Figures 6-4 and 8-6)

Nepeta is a creeping evergreen perennial native to Europe and Asia. It is a "must" for hanging baskets, with its long, trailing stems covered with round, green and white leaves. The fine stems are very effective as they move in the breeze. Nepeta also works well trailing from window boxes and planters.

Bloomtime: Although grown for its foliage, it has small, lilac, pea-like flowers.

Height: Trailing stems as long as 4 feet (1.2 m) by the end of summer.

Light and soil: Full sun or light shade and any well-drained soil.

How to grow: This is the variegated form of the pernicious lawn weed. It roots easily from cuttings or may be divided in the fall. Watch for shoots reverting to the plain form since this will out-grow the variegated parts.

Pests and diseases: MILDEW is occasionally a problem.

Uses: Hanging baskets; containers; trailing over retaining walls.

"Globe amaranth" see *Gomphrena*
"Godetia" see *Clarkia*

Gomphrena globosa "globe amaranth"
Gomphrena haageana AMARANTHACEAE
(Figure 5-6)

Gomphrena globosa is a half-hardy annual native to India. In Thailand, its flowers are used in dried arrangements for weddings. Wreaths are made with a circle of wet clay into which the flower heads are stuck. When the clay dries, the flowers retain their rich color indefinitely. The cultivar 'Buddy' has flowers of a vivid royal purple, one of those colors people seem to either love or hate. It grows to a uniform height of 9 inches (23 cm) and makes a good edging plant. There are also seed strains of mixed colors, but the white is not a pure white and is not as striking as the purple.

Gomphrena haageana is a perennial native to Texas and Mexico. Its cultivar 'Strawberry Fields' is grown as an annual for its dried heads. Flowers are bright red and the plant grows to 2 feet (.6 m).

Bloomtime: July to September.

Height: 9–24 inches (23–61 cm), depending on the cultivar.

Light and soil: Full sun and well-drained soil that is not too rich.

How to grow: Although young plants are not generally available from shops, they are easily grown from seed. In April, soak the seeds in water for 3 days and then spread them thinly over the top of the soil. Germinate at 70°F (21°C) for 14 days in total darkness. Grow on at 70°F (21°C). Set hardened-off plants out in late May or early June, 6–9 inches (15–23 cm) apart, farther for 'Strawberry Fields'.

Pests and diseases: APHIDS may infest new shoots.

Uses: Use 'Buddy' to edge beds and borders, 'Strawberry Fields' in mixed borders and for flower arrangements, fresh or dried. All flowers dry very well with no special treatment; the flowers of 'Buddy' do not have long stems but can be used to decorate wreaths. Children enjoy them in various crafts.

"Grasses" see *Avena*

"Hare's tail" see *Avena*

Hedera helix "English ivy" ARALIACEAE
(Figure 6-5)

An all-purpose plant for the garden, ivy is included here because it is an excellent addition to a hanging basket or planter. There are several cultivars with small leaves that are often sold with the bedding plants in shops in spring. You may also find them with the ground covers or with the houseplants. English ivy, a native of Britain and Europe, is evergreen and survives the winter outdoors. Three of the many cultivars are 'Baltica', with dark green leaves and distinctive white veins; 'Glacier', with gray-green leaves and a white margin, and 'Gold Heart', which has a yellow heart-shaped blotch in the middle of each leaf.

Bloomtime: Grown for its foliage, ivy doesn't flower until it is many years of age. The flowers look like green pompons 1 inch (2.5 cm) across.

Height: Growing as a creeper or vine, ivy grows 1–2 feet (30–61 cm) each year.

Light and soil: Full sun to heavy shade. Ivy will grow in any soil, but grows faster in a rich soil.

How to grow: Young plants are generally available from shops in spring, or they may be started from cuttings taken at any time of the year. It is possible to take them in March and stick them right in the soil in the garden, where they will root if the weather is wet.

Pests and diseases: Generally trouble-free.
Uses: Trailing out of planters and hanging baskets, with summer or winter bedding.

Helianthus annuus "sunflower" ASTERACEAE
(Figure 7-6)

Helianthus translates from the Greek into "sunflower," a name given to these huge plants because the flowers of some cultivars turn toward the sun. Once seeds begin to form, the flowers stop moving, usually all facing in an easterly direction. Commercial sunflower growers take advantage of this, planting sunflowers in north/south rows—it makes harvesting easier when almost all the heads are facing into the row.

It is thought that the first *Helianthus* seeds were imported from Mexico and grown in the Madrid Royal Gardens in 1562. Many parts of the plants have economic importance: the seeds are delicious, both to people and birds, and cooking oil is produced from the seed. The leaves may be used as animal forage and the Chinese make a textile from the plant fibers. In the garden, sunflowers are a tremendous hit with children because they grow to 8 feet (2½ m) or more in height, their huge blooms facing downward. The leaves are heart shaped, up to 15 inches (38 cm) long and hairy on both surfaces. Sunflowers are hardy annuals native to the United States, Canada and Mexico. In 1910, a Mrs. Cockerell found a chestnut-colored sunflower growing on the roadside in Boulder, Colorado. From this, she developed many variously colored cultivars.

'Italian White' has cream petals with a black center; it reaches 4 feet (1.2 m) and blooms are 4 inches (10 cm) across. 'Large Flowered Mixed' has 6-inch (15-cm) blooms of many colors on 5-foot (1.5-m) plants. 'Teddy Bear' grows to only 2 feet (61 cm) and has double blooms. There are also a number of giant cultivars.
Bloomtime: July to October.
Height: 2–10 feet (.6–3 m), depending on the cultivar.
Light and soil: Prefers full sun and any well-drained soil. It has surprisingly small roots for such a tall plant, so staking is a good idea, especially in windy places.
How to grow: Although young plants are not generally available from shops, they are easily grown from seed. Sow seeds directly in the garden in April, or indoors in March. Plants should be spaced 12–36 inches (30–90 cm) apart.

Pests and diseases: Generally trouble-free.

Uses: Sunflowers are popular with children and fun for gardeners of all ages. 'Teddy Bear' makes an interesting centerpiece to a large planter.

Helichrysum bracteatum "strawflower" ASTERACEAE
(Figure 3-4)

Native to Australia, strawflowers "have the dubious distinction of being equally attractive dead or alive," write Pizzetti and Cocker. This is certainly true: the plants themselves are an attractive addition to a mixed border in the garden and they are everlasting when dried. The leaves are long, narrow and bright green. Blooms come in soft shades of pink, gold, yellow or cream, as well as more brightly colored cultivars. Seed is available as separate colors or in mixtures. 'Hot Bikinis' won a Fleuroselect award. Watch for a new cultivar of dwarf strawflower that can be used as an edging and still be dried.

Bloomtime: June to frost.

Height: 3–4 feet (.9–1.2 m).

Light and soil: Prefers full sun and any well-drained soil that is neutral or slightly sweet.

How to grow: Although young plants are not generally available from shops, they are easily grown from seed. Sow seeds indoors in March, but do not cover, as light is required for germination. Germination, at 70°F (21°C) soil temperature, takes 10–14 days. Grow plants on at 70°F (21°C). Set hardened-off plants out in late May, spacing them 12 inches (30 cm) apart. Alternatively, seeds may be sown directly in the garden in May. Pick the flowers before the colored bracts open to reveal the disk. If picked when the bracts are fully open, the disk florets will form seeds and the flower will fall apart. The stems become quite dry and brittle, so it is worthwhile removing the stems after picking and inserting thin florist's wire from the back up through the flowers before letting them dry. Using pliers, bend the end of the wire over and gently pull it back into the flower. The flowers may then be used on the wires instead of stems.

Pests and diseases: Generally trouble-free.

Uses: Attractive in a mixed border or in a large planter. If you plan to cut them constantly, you may wish to plant strawflowers in the cutting or vegetable garden. Popular with children, they are lovely for decorating wreaths and other craft projects.

Heliotropium arborescens "heliotrope" "cherry pie" BORAGINACEAE
(Figure 8-3)

Heliotrope was first discovered in Peru, where it is a perennial, in 1740. It was sent to Paris, where it was popular for flower arrangements and was dubbed the herbe d'amour (plant of love). Commonly grown by the British during Queen Victoria's time, it was popular for its rich fragrance. The Victorians called it "cherry pie" because it smells as sweet as a freshly baked cherry pie. The fragrance is also reminiscent of vanilla. Heliotrope was once planted in fields of tomatoes and cucumbers to attract bees for pollination. It has an open, spreading habit and mid-green leaves. The light violet flowers are arranged on a curved spike.

Strangely enough, heliotrope went out of style and virtually disappeared from the bedding plant market. Although grown in Butchart Gardens on Vancouver Island and in Stanley Park in Vancouver, BC, from cuttings for over forty years, the only cultivars available to home gardeners were those which could be grown from seed. 'Marine', for example, develops into good-looking plants with deep purple broccoli-like flower heads and deep purplish-green leaves, but the blooms are generally not fragrant. With the current interest in fragrant plants, the type of heliotrope grown from cuttings should become more available.

Bloomtime: June to October.

Height: 12–24 inches (30–61 cm), depending on the cultivar.

Light and soil: Full sun or light shade. They need a very rich soil to flourish, so add lots of organic matter and some general fertilizer.

How to grow: Although young plants are not generally available from shops, some types may be grown from seed (see above). There are several seed strains on the market which claim to be fragrant. Sow seeds in February at 70°F (21°C).Germination is not always good and may take up to three weeks. Pinch back young plants to encourage branching. Set plants out 12 inches (30 cm) apart into the garden or into containers in late May or early June. Fertilize regularly. If you get a seedling which is particularly fragrant, keep it through the winter indoors. Although hard to find, try a specialty nursery for cuttings of the fragrant heliotrope.

Pests and diseases: Generally trouble-free in the garden. In the greenhouse, plants may get WHITEFLY.

Uses: Cultivars such as 'Marine' look good in mixed planters with other bedding plants. Try it with dwarf marigolds and ageratum, or with white browallia and orange gazanias. The very fragrant type is good in hanging baskets and in beds with plants such as geraniums and French marigolds. Heliotrope may also be trained as a standard. See instructions under *Fuchsia.*

Hypoestes phyllostachya (*H. sanguinolenta*) "polka dot plant"
ACANTHACEAE
(Figure 6-6)

A perennial from Madagascar, the polka dot plant is usually grown and sold as a houseplant, but it is possible to grow it as a bedding plant. In the garden it makes a bushy plant, its rich olive green leaves spotted and splashed with pink. At the end of September, it looks as fresh as in June. In my experience, it received virtually no attention except for watering and had no diseases or pests. 'Pink Splash' has the largest pink spots of available cultivars.

Bloomtime: Although grown for its decorative foliage, polka dot plant develops tiny purple tubular flowers in late summer.

Height: To 16 inches (41 cm).

Light and soil: Full sun, partial shade or shade, in well-drained soil.

How to grow: Young plants are generally available from shops with houseplants. It is also easy to grow from seed sown indoors in early April. Set out hardened-off plants in late May or June, depending on the season. Plants may be dug up and brought back indoors before the frost and grown in a sunny window.

Pests and diseases: Generally trouble-free.

Uses: Edging plant for beds and borders. Pots and planter boxes, alone or with other bedding plants. *Hypoestes* and pink tuberous or fibrous begonias make a striking combination.

Iberis amara "hyacinth-flowered candytuft" "rocket candytuft"
Iberis umbellata "globe candytuft" BRASSICACEAE

These two candytufts bloom from May to July and, if allowed to seed themselves, reappear each year. Both are hardy annuals from Europe and rocket candytuft has been grown as a garden plant since the sixteenth century. It is a striking plant; the tiny white flowers form along a tall spike that resembles a hyacinth. It is also fragrant. Globe candytuft bears its tiny flowers in flat-topped clusters over a neat mound-shaped plant. Most seed mixtures include white, maroon, lilac and rose flowers. Globe candytuft has no fragrance. The leaves are narrow and midgreen.

Bloomtime: May to July, unless later sowings are made to extend the season of bloom.
Height: Rocket candytuft, 12–24 inches (30–61 cm); globe candytuft 12–15 inches (30–38 cm).
Light and soil: Full sun and any well-drained soil. They will tolerate dry soil, but not "wet feet."
How to grow: The best way to grow these is to seed them in October where they are to flower. Throw more seeds out in March, April and June to have blooms until fall. They may also be started indoors from March on and set out from May on. Thin seedlings or space young plants 6 to 9 inches (15–23 cm) apart.
Pests and diseases: Generally trouble-free.
Uses: Use rocket candytuft in mixed flower borders and for cutting. Globe candytuft is good for edging and at the front of mixed borders. Use with plants such as browallia and geraniums, which will fill in the gap they leave later in the summer.

"Ice plant" see *Lampranthus*
"Immortelle, common" see *Xeranthemum*

Impatiens **hybrids** "New Guinea impatiens" BALSAMINACEAE
(Figure 5-7)
Quite different in many ways from common impatiens (see below), these exotic plants not only have beautiful flowers, but also decorative leaves. They like full sun or part shade, but do not bloom well in full shade. The flowers are up to 3 inches (7.5 cm) across and the leaves are long and pointed at the tip. They are dark green, often with a yellow center to the leaf and a dark red midrib.
New Guinea impatiens are a relatively recent arrival on the bedding plant market. In the winter of 1969–70, a team of American plant collectors went to New Guinea, looking for orchids, rhododendrons and pitcher plants. The trip was sponsored jointly by the US Department of Agriculture and Longwood Gardens in Pennsylvania. In the damp cool forests of New Guinea, about 3,300 feet (1,000 m) above sea level, they found 25 interesting types of impatiens. They sent cuttings back to Dr. Robert Armstrong, a horticultural researcher at Longwood Gardens, who made crosses between several of the species. This first generation of crosses, known as F1 hybrids, were outstanding and inspired the breeding

program which has produced the dozens of New Guinea impatiens now available.

Most New Guinea impatiens are grown from cuttings. 'Gemini' is an excellent cultivar with pink flowers and green and yellow foliage. New Guinea impatiens may also be grown from seed and the AAS winner 'Tango' is the first of these to receive an award. It needs direct sunlight for best results and will produce masses of bright orange blooms.

Bloomtime: June to frost.

Height: To 18 inches (46 cm).

Light and soil: Full sun to light shade; in full shade they will grow but will be leggier and have fewer blooms. New Guinea impatiens prefer a light soil to which moist peat or well-rotted manure has been added. Keep them well fertilized and watered.

How to grow: The easiest way to grow New Guinea impatiens is to buy young plants, generally available from shops in spring. They may also be started from 3–4 inch (7.5–10 cm) tip cuttings taken April to September and rooted in peat and perlite at 60°F (15°C) soil temperature, but it is not easy to keep them healthy without extra light.

Pests and diseases: Generally trouble-free in the garden; susceptible to SPIDER MITES and VIRUS disease in the greenhouse.

Uses: Striking in beds and containers, alone or with other bedding plants. They combine well with browallia, sweet alyssum or lobelia.

Impatiens wallerana "common impatiens" BALSAMINACEAE
(Figure 2-6)

It is hard to find fault with impatiens, as they have so much to recommend them. They bloom from May to frost, even in heavy shade; they're easy to care for and are bothered by few pests and diseases; and they have attractive foliage and a compact habit of growth. The flowers are not spoiled by rain; there is no need to stake or deadhead; and they come in a wide (sometimes wild) color range and are adaptable to many uses in the garden. They will even pinch-hit on a sunny window sill for temporary color indoors. Not a bad repertoire!

The slightly iridescent, 2-inch (5-cm) flowers have five petals that overlap with the characteristic spur at the back of the flower. They come in shades of red, orange, rose, pale pink, white, mauve and striped combinations. The 2-inch (5-cm) leaves are dark green with scalloped edges.

Impatiens is a perennial in its native East Africa, but will not survive the frost. The seeds of impatiens, especially the excellent F1 hybrid cultivars, are very expensive and the seedlings are slow-growing, which is why the price is often higher than that of other bedding plants. In recent years, there has been downward pressure on the price of bedding plants and some growers have stopped growing impatiens altogether. Some growers will cut corners by selling impatiens grown from cuttings, but such plants do not usually perform as well in the garden. You may be able to see the difference when shopping, because plants grown from cuttings tend to be thick at the base where they join the soil. Impatiens are not difficult to grow from seed; consider growing your own to take advantage of the wide selection in seed catalogues. Try the 'Super Elfin' series, 8–10 inches (20–25 cm); the 'Futura' series, 10–12 inches (25–30 cm); or the 'Twinkles' series if you like bicolors. The 'Blitz' series tolerates heat and sun.

Bloomtime: May to frost.

Height: 8–12 inches (20–30 cm), depending on the cultivar.

Light and soil: Light or full shade. They will take some sun, but not blazing hot sun all day. Impatiens like a light soil to which moist peat has been added, and benefit from a bit of bark mulch around their roots to keep them cool and moist.

How to grow: In mid-March, sow seeds and cover lightly with fine sterile sand. The seeds are as fine as dust, so you may find it easier to mix them with a spoonful of clean sand or sugar before sowing. Keep the soil temperature at 70°F (21°C) and cover the pots or flat with clear plastic until the seeds have germinated, about 16 days. Light and moisture are required for germination. When the seedlings are up, remove the plastic and grow on at 60–65°F (15–18°C). Do not overwater or overfertilize. Keep plants on the dry side for more compactness and bloom. Set plants out, 12 inches (30 cm) apart, at the end of May or early June. Fertilize with 20-20-20 monthly.

Pests and diseases: Generally trouble-free, although they may get APHIDS, MITES or a PHYSIOLOGICAL CONDITION that causes premature leaf drop.

Uses: At the front of beds and mixed borders; in hanging baskets and planters, alone or with other bedding plants.

"Irish lace" see *Tagetes*
"Ivy, English" see *Hedera*

"Johnny-jump-up" see *Viola*
"Joseph's coat" see *Amaranthus*
"Kale, flowering or ornamental" see *Brassica*

Kochia scoparia forma trichophylla (*K. scoparia* var. *culta*) "summer cypress" "burning bush" CHENOPODIACEAE
(Figure 6-7)
Burning bush is so-named because it turns purplish-red at the first touch of frost. In most years, this red color persists throughout an Indian summer. A half-hardy annual from southern Europe, it becomes a slender column of feathery bright green with tiny flowers in the summer. 'Childsii' has a more compact habit.
Bloomtime: Not grown for its blooms.
Height: 'Childsii' grows to 2 feet high by 1 foot wide (61 cm by 30 cm).
Light and soil: Full sun and a well-drained soil is best, but summer cypress will grow in all soils and light situations.
How to grow: Although young plants are not generally available from garden shops, they may be grown from seed sown indoors in March. Germinate at 60°F (15°C), harden off and set plants out in late May. Seeds can also be sown directly in the garden in April. In some areas it has become a serious weed from overwintering seed.
Pests and diseases: Generally trouble-free.
Uses: Summer cypress makes an excellent dot plant for formal bedding, in the garden or in the center of a large container. It looks like a hedging plant and would make an effective temporary low hedge, to screen a part of the garden or set off a patio.

Lagurus see *Avena*

Lamiastrum galeobdolon 'Variegatum' "silver nettle vine" LAMIACEAE
Like ivy and nepeta, silver nettle vine is added to hanging baskets for foliage interest. The creeping stems are square in cross-section and have a pair of leaves at 4-inch (10-cm) intervals. The leaves have scalloped edges, with silver markings, flushed bronze in cold weather. It is hardy in the garden as a ground cover, but is quite invasive. Silver nettle vine is native to Europe.

Bloomtime: Grown for foliage rather than flowers, silver nettle vine may produce spikes of yellow flowers in June and July.
Height: Trailing to several feet (1 m).
Light and soil: Prefers some shade, but any soil will do.
How to grow: It is rarely available in garden centers with the bedding plants but is often sold with the perennials. As a perennial it grows best in part shade. Plants lifted in early spring, as soon as the frost is out of the ground, can be forced into growth indoors and will give a supply of cuttings which can be rooted for use in baskets or planters. Afterwards, replant the stock plant in the border ready for next spring.
Pests and diseases: Generally trouble-free.
Uses: Trailing out of containers and from hanging baskets.

Lampranthus multiradiatus (*L. roseus, Mesembryanthemum multi-radiatum, M. roseum*) "ice plant" "mesembryanthemum" AIZOACEAE
There are many plants which go by the common name ice plant, however this is the best known and the most commonly grown, especially on the west coast. It has silky, shocking pink (rarely white), daisy-like flowers, to 1½ inches (4 cm) in diameter. Flowers usually open only on sunny days. The succulent gray-green leaves, to 1 inch (2.5 cm) long, are triangular in cross-section. Ice plant is a subshrub in its native South Africa, and may be overwintered indoors.

Just for information, the plant that grows along the highways in California, which is also called "ice plant," is *Carpobrotus* and is not grown here. The British refer to *Mesembryanthemum cristallinum* as ice plant because the leaves are covered with a sparkling coating which glistens in the sun. It is a South African plant which is rarely seen here.
Bloomtime: June to frost.
Height: Creeping plants, reaching up to 12 inches (30 cm) in height and spread.
Light and soil: Grow in a spot shaded from the midday sun. Ice plant requires well-drained, even dry, sandy soil. Too rich a soil will cause a lush growth of leaves but only a few flowers.
How to grow: Young plants are seldom sold, so it is necessary to grown them yourself from seed, available from Thompson and Morgan. (T&M sell a mixture of *Lampranthus* species and hybrids, including orange and white.) Sow seeds at any time in the spring at a temperature of 70°F (21°C) and keep in the dark until seeds germinate (15–30 days).

Transplant seedlings into individual pots when they are 1 inch (2.5 cm) high. Alternatively, take cuttings 2 inches (5 cm) long in late summer or early autumn. Remove lower leaves and leave cuttings to dry for a day before inserting them in pots of pure sand.

Pests and diseases: New shoots may be infested with APHIDS.

Uses: Dry places with light shade or north-facing slopes in the rock garden.

Lantana camara "lantana" VERBENACEAE
(Figure 7-7)

Lantana are somewhat of a specialty item. They really require a greenhouse for overwintering, but they are included here for general information. Lantana are usually seen in park plantings, where they are trained as standards, and can be up to 15 years old. The small flowers cluster in a rounded head at the end of the stems. With some cultivars, the flowers change color as they age, giving a fascinating rainbow effect. Shades include white, lilac, yellow, pink, rose and red, depending on the cultivar.

A shrub native to tropical America, lantana is a serious weed in some parts of the world. It has contaminated fields in South Africa and makes cattle ill. The foliage has quite a strong scent when touched, which some find offensive.

Bloomtime: May to October.

Height: 18–48 inches (46–122 cm) high by 36 inches (91 cm) wide. Trained as a standard, the trunk may be 5–6 feet (1.5–1.8 m) high.

Light and soil: Full sun and any rich, well-drained soil. Plants can either be grown in pots, which are easily moved in and out with the season, or they can be planted out in the spring and dug and brought into the greenhouse at the end of September.

How to grow: Young plants are sometimes available from shops in spring, or they can be started from 3-inch (7.5-cm) cuttings taken in August. Root in half peat/half sand with bottom heat. If plants are to be grown for bedding, pinch the tips to encourage bushiness. For standards, see instructions under *Fuchsia*, but train only one trunk up the stake. Lantana may also be grown from seed. Soak seeds 24 hours in warm water. Germination, at 70°F (21°C) soil temperature, takes about 1–3 months. Set hardened-off plants out in late May, spacing them 12 inches (30 cm) apart for bedding. At the end of September, bring them into the greenhouse and overwinter at 45°F (7°C), increasing temperature to 50–55°F (10–13°C) during March and April. Plants will normally drop all their leaves. Keep them barely moist in winter and water them freely in spring and summer.

Pests and diseases: WHITEFLY is a pest in the greenhouse.

Uses: Standards make a lovely centerpiece to a formal bedding scheme. Used as bedding plants, lantana blooms tirelessly all summer and fall.

Lathyrus odoratus "sweet pea" FABACEAE
(Figure 3-5)

A hardy annual native to Italy, this sweet scented flower with its graceful blooms and soft colors has won many a gardener's heart. Most gardeners can find a corner in which to grow sweet peas; they are always welcome in a vase on the table or given in a bouquet.

The original sweet pea, which was deliciously fragrant, was a vine bearing small red and purple flowers. In 1699, a few seeds were sent from Father Francisco Cupani of Palermo to his friend Dr. Uvedale near London, England. Over the next two hundred years, English gardeners zealously selected sweet peas for flower size, ruffled petals and range of color, but unfortunately the scent was almost lost. Pizzetti and Cocker tell this story:

> "Charles Unwin, one of the major sweet pea hybridists of our time, wrote that some years ago he received the gift of some Sweet Pea seeds from an almost forgotten English village. The flowers were small and not very attractive in color, but their fragrance was marvelous and, after an entire lifetime dedicated to Sweet Peas, Unwin admitted that, 'until that moment I never fully realized why Sweet Peas were so named'. Unfortunately, neither in England nor on the continent is it now possible to find seed of the original fragrant sweet peas. Possibly they *do* exist in some hidden out-of-the-way garden, and it would be a fascinating occupation to seek them out."

Seed of some very fragrant sweet peas may be acquired from the two English firms, Bolton and Unwin. Other seed catalogues also sell fragrant strains—look for names such as 'Old-fashioned' or 'Antique'. Sow a showy sweet pea and a fragrant sweet pea together, to get the best of both worlds.

There are hundreds of cultivars of sweet peas available in Britain, where there are sweet pea societies and shows devoted exclusively to sweet peas. If started early, sweet peas will perform well. Dwarf cultivars that do not need staking are also available.

Bloomtime: June to frost if old flowers are removed and plants are well cared for.

Height: 1–6 feet (.3–1.8m), depending on the cultivar.

Light and soil: Bloom best in full sun with rich, well-drained soil that is neutral or slightly sweet. Add well-rotted manure or moist peat and some dolomite lime if necessary and dig well, preferably in autumn.

How to grow: This is one plant that pays big dividends for an early start when grown from seed. As with most bedding plants, there is a much greater choice of cultivars when started from seed. In March, soak seeds for 24 hours to soften the seed coat, then sow and cover with $1/2$ inch (1 cm) of potting mix. Germination, at 60°F (15°C) soil temperature, takes about 14 days. (Higher temperatures will inhibit germination.) Seeds may be sown directly in the garden in March, but they sometimes rot in a cold spring and are very easy to start indoors. In very mild districts it may be worth trying a fall sowing, protecting the seedlings with a cloche or a wooden A-frame covered with insulation material. While this seems like a lot of work, it results in much stronger plants with larger flowers.

Indoors, pinch the tips of seedlings when they are 4 inches (10 cm) high. Set hardened-off plants out in early May, spacing them 6–10 inches (15–25 cm) apart. Train tall-growing cultivars up canes or netting. Remove spent flowers and seed pods if any set. Feed every week with a half-strength 15-30-15 or similar fertilizer for best results.

Pests and diseases: SLUGS, APHIDS and SPIDER MITES may infest sweet peas. A number of fungi may cause problems, including root ROT (if seeded in a very cold, wet spring), POWDERY MILDEW, and GRAY MOLD. Mottling of the leaves and stunting may be caused by a VIRUS. That sounds frightening but, with the exception of root rot, these diseases are not common.

Uses: Use short types in the flower border, grow tall types at the back of the border on a trellis or in the middle of the border up a tripod of stakes. They can even be grown on a sunny balcony in a large container if the soil is rich and well watered. Sweet peas make excellent cut flowers.

Lavatera trimestris "lavatera" "mallow" MALVACEAE
(Figure 3-6)

The lavatera in public gardens always attracts attention and inspires creative guesswork as to its identity. Many people think it is some kind of petunia because of its trumpet-shaped flower. Others guess hollyhock (to which it is related) because of its upright growth habit. Lavatera is a very elegant hardy annual from the Mediterranean region, which deserves to be more widely grown. The 3-inch (7.5-cm) flowers have a distinctive pompon in the center of each trumpet. Plants are well-branched, with handsome rounded leaves that turn red in the fall.

The cultivar 'Mont Blanc' is glistening white and reaches 21 inches (53 cm) in height; 'Mont Rose' is pink and the same height; 'Loveliness' is pink but not as compact, reaching 3–4 feet (.9–1.2 m); 'Silver Cup', so named for winning the Fleuroselect Silver Cup, never before awarded to an annual, grows to 2 feet (.6 m) and has glowing, pink, 4-inch (10-cm) blooms.

Bloomtime: July to September.

Height: 21–48 inches (53–122 cm), depending on the cultivar.

Light and soil: Best in full sun and average, rather than rich, soil.

How to grow: In spring, when the ground has dried, sow seeds where they are to bloom, just covering them with soil. Thin the seedlings to stand 12–18 inches (30–46 cm) apart. Alternatively, they may be started indoors in March in individual pots. Set hardened- off plants out in late May, spacing them 12–18 inches (30–46 cm) apart.

Pests and diseases: RUST may affect the leaves.

Uses: Use toward the center of a mixed border. May also be used for cutting.

Limonium sinuatum "statice" "sea lavender"
Psylliostachys suworowii (*Limonium suworowii*, *Statice suworowii*)
"Russian statice" "rat-tail statice" PLUMBAGINACEAE
(Figure 2-7)

Although these two species are now in different genera, they are grouped together here because of their similarity, cultivation and use in the garden.

Common statice is a delightful plant from the Mediterranean that is easy to grow, attractive in the garden and provides everlasting flowers for arranging and art projects. The actual flowers are tiny and white, but each is surrounded by a tissue-paper-like calyx that keeps its bright color indefinitely. Colors include cream, rose, purple, blue and yellow. The flowers cluster at the top of long stems that have papery wings along them. The leaves, which are about 16 inches (41 cm) long, with deeply wavy margins, form a rosette around the base of the flower stem. Although statice is perennial in the wild, it is usually grown as an annual because it will not survive the frost. It is easy to grow from seed, which is available in separate colors or mixed colors.

Russian statice (closely related to common statice) is an annual native to southern USSR, Afghanistan and Iran. It has long pink flower spikes that stick up above the plant like pokers or twist around in corkscrew shapes. These striking flowers are excellent for fresh floral arrangements. The plants are similar in height and cultivation to the common statice.

Bloomtime: June to September.

Height: Most types grow 18–24 inches (46–61 cm); the dwarf cultivar of common statice, 'Petite Bouquet', reaches only 12 inches (30 cm).

Light and soil: Prefers full sun and any well-drained soil.

How to grow: Although young plants are not generally available from shops, they are easily grown from seed. In March, germinate at 60°F (15°C) soil temperature. Seeds of Russian statice may be slow to germinate. Set young plants out in May, spacing them 12 inches (30 cm) apart, closer for dwarf cultivars. Seeds may also be sown directly in the garden in May.

Pests and diseases: Generally trouble-free unless the summer is exceptionally damp, when the stems and flowers may get GRAY MOLD or POWDERY MILDEW.

Uses: Mixed borders, bedding schemes. Try dwarf types in mixed planters. Excellent dried (just hang in a cool dry place) for decorating wreaths and for arranging.

Lobelia erinus "edging lobelia" LOBELIACEAE
(Figures 6-8 and 8-6)

Lobelia is well-loved by gardeners for its deep rich shade of blue. This very dwarf spreader is native to South Africa, where it is a half-hardy annual or perennial, but it is generally grown as an annual in our climate. Lobelia has tiny flowers with three lower petals and two upper petals; some have a tiny spot of white at the throat. The flowers cover the plant in a mass of color, hiding the thin stems and small leaves. It was first introduced into European gardens in 1752, and now there are many beautiful cultivars. 'Mrs. Clibran' is blue with a white eye, 'White Lady' is white, 'Rosamund' is wine-red, 'Cambridge Blue' is light blue. All four have bright green leaves and reach about 8 inches (20 cm) in height. 'Crystal Palace' has dark blue flowers and bronzy foliage that intensifies the flower color. There are a number of cultivars that have a more trailing habit and are recommended for hanging baskets, but the dwarf types just mentioned trail enough to look good in hanging baskets. In fact, they often look better trailing out of mixed planters because they are neater than the trailing types.

Bloomtime: May to frost.

Height: 8 inches (20 cm), longer for trailing cultivars.

Light and soil: Lobelia will tolerate some sun if well watered, but it thrives in light shade. For best results, add some organic matter to the soil to retain moisture. If allowed to dry out, lobelia will turn brown and look wretched. I know more than one gardener (myself included) who has had to remove lobelia from hanging baskets after a lapse in watering.

How to grow: Young plants are available from shops in spring, or they may be started from seed in late February. Sow several seeds in the center of a 3-inch (7.5-cm) pot, but do not cover. Germinate at 70°F (21°C) soil temperature for 21 days. Seedlings grow slowly. Plant the whole clump of seedlings out in late May, 4–8 inches (10–20 cm) apart. Because it is a perennial, rooted cuttings may be kept through winter in a sunny spot indoors. Stems usually root themselves along the ground as they grow; these rooted pieces can then be potted into sterilized soil.

Pests and diseases: Generally trouble-free, although seedlings may DAMP OFF.

Uses: Pattern plantings, edging of formal or mixed borders. Attractive in a more informal setting—under rhododendrons, for example. Outstanding in containers, either alone or with other bedding plants, and in hanging baskets with other bedding plants.

Lobularia maritima "sweet alyssum" "alyssum" BRASSICACEAE
(Figure 8-4)

Sweet alyssum, like ageratum, fibrous begonia, lobelia and marigold, is a most reliable and easy to grow summer bedding plant. From May to frost, it is a carpet of bloom, with dozens of tiny four-petalled flowers clustered at the tip of each spreading stem. Alyssum is available in white as 'Snow Crystals' (with larger, heat-tolerant flowers), 'Wonderland White' which blooms earlier, 'Carpet of Snow' and 'Snow Cloth'. The

Thompson and Morgan catalogue lists 'Sweet White', notable for its rich honey fragrance. There are a number of deep purple cultivars: 'Royal Carpet', 'Wonderland Deep Purple' and 'Navy Blue'. 'Wonderland Rosy-Red' and 'Rosie O'Day' are both rosy purple. Sweet alyssum is a perennial in its native Mediterranean region, but is grown as an annual here.

True alyssum, *Aurinia saxatilis* (formerly *Alyssum saxatilis*) is a winter-hardy perennial. It blooms earlier than the annual sweet alyssum, its cascading stems and sheets of bright yellow flowers a common sight in many home rock gardens. True alyssum is often seen growing with two other April-blooming perennials, *Iberis sempervirens* (the white evergreen candytuft) and *Aubrietia deltoidea* (purple rock cress). These two species are often confused with purple and white sweet alyssum because of the similarity of their spreading habits.

Bloomtime: May to frost.

Height: 4 inches (10 cm) high.

Light and soil: More compact in full sun but tolerates some shade. Any well-drained soil. Tolerates drought and heat also.

How to grow: Young plants are generally available from shops in spring, or they may be started from seed sown in late March. Do not cover seeds, as light aids germination. Germinate at 60–70°F (15–21°C) soil temperature for 8 days. Grow on at 55–60°F (13–15°C). Set out hardened-off plants in May, spacing them 8 inches (20 cm) apart. Sweet alyssum will often seed itself in the garden; watch for the seedlings with their oval olive-green leaves when weeding in the spring. Plants may also be started by seeding them directly in the garden in April.

Pests and diseases: Indoors, seedlings may be susceptible to DAMPING-OFF. SLUGS like sweet alyssum and FLEA BEETLES may eat holes in the leaves of seedlings.

Uses: Pattern plantings and edging formal beds; at the front of mixed borders; in rock gardens and at the top of walls; in hanging baskets and in containers.

Lotus berthelotii "lotus vine" FABACEAE
(Figure 6-9)

Having just appeared on the market in the early eighties, lotus vine is fast gaining popularity for use in hanging baskets and containers. Its fine silvery foliage on long trailing branches sets off the blooms of other bedding plants. It is also striking in a hanging basket on its own. It blooms occasionally with red, 1-inch (2.5-cm), pea-like flowers.

Originally from the Canary Islands, it grows there as a shrub with trailing branches. It is not related to either the Egyptian water lotus (*Nymphaea lotus*) or the sacred lotus (*Nelumbo nucifera*), both water plants.

Bloomtime: Grown mainly for its foliage, but it does bloom occasionally.

Height: Trailing stems to 2 feet (.6 m) in length.

Light and soil: Full sun or part shade and any well-drained soil.

How to grow: Look for plants in the larger nurseries that specialize in unusual plants. It can also be grown from cuttings.

Pests and diseases: Watch for SPIDER MITES.

Uses: Trailing from hanging baskets and planters; cascading down a bank or in a rock garden. It can be pruned to keep it more compact.

"Love-in-a-mist" see *Nigella*
"Love-lies-bleeding" see *Amaranthus*

Lychnis coeli-rosa (*Silene coeli-rosa, Viscaria elegans*) "viscaria"
CARYOPHYLLACEAE
(Figure 2-8)

A confusion of botanical names exists around viscaria. There are many other species of *Silene* and *Lychnis*, so one must be careful to get the right one when ordering seeds or buying plants.

Viscaria has an airy quality, with 1-inch (2.5-cm) blooms atop wiry stems. Flowers come in shades of white, pink, mauve or rosy red. The leaves are long, narrow and gray-green. Long popular in England where it is a hardy annual, viscaria is being seen more often in our area, making a nice change in typical bedding plant arrangements.

Bloomtime: June to September.

Height: 6–18 inches (15–46 cm), depending on the cultivar.

Light and soil: Full sun or part shade and a well-drained soil.

How to grow: Although young plants are not generally available from shops, they are easily grown from seed. It is available from Thompson and Morgan, either through the catalogue, or from their seed racks in larger garden shops. Sow seeds indoors in March, germinating at a 60°F (15°C) soil temperature. Set out hardened-off plants in late May, spacing them 6 inches (15 cm) apart.

Pests and diseases: Generally trouble-free.

Uses: An elegant addition to the mixed border. Also attractive in containers and side-planted in moss baskets.

"Madagascar periwinkle" see *Catharanthus*
"Mallow" see *Lavatera*
"Maple, flowering" see *Abutilon*
"Marguerite, blue" see *Felicia*
"Marguerite daisy" see *Chrysanthemum frutescens*
"Marigold, African, French or signet" see *Tagetes*
"Marigold, Cape" see *Dimorphotheca*
"Marigold, English or pot" see *Calendula*
"Marvel-of-Peru" see *Mirabilis*
"Matricaria" see *Chrysanthemum parthenium*

Matthiola incana "stock" "common stock" BRASSICACEAE
(Figure 3-7)

A native of Europe, *Matthiola incana* was called "gillyflower" in the sixteenth century. In Shakespeare's *A Winter's Tale*, the shepherdess Perdita argues with the young Polixenes over the merits of the striped gillyflowers. She says "of streak'd gillyvors . . . our rustic garden's barren, and I care not to get slips of them," explaining that she objects to man interfering with "great creating nature." This scene shows us that even in the 1500s, gardeners were tinkering with plant selecting and knew how to propagate plants from cuttings (slips).

Although truly a hardy biennial, some stocks have been selected to bloom the first season from seed. 'Trisomic 7-Week' or '10-Week Mixed' are most commonly available in shops in spring. They produce bushy plants with upright stems bearing mostly double fragrant blooms. The color range includes white, pink, rose, crimson, dark blue and purple.

Some cultivars are "selectable" for doubleness. If seedlings are grown at 55–60°F (13–15°C), they will be two shades of green when at the two-leaf stage. Discard the dark green seedlings, because they will bear single flowers. This procedure is important to the British growers, who are very serious about stocks and have many tall cultivars suitable for exhibition and cutting. The latest development in selectable stocks—'Stockpot'—comes from Japan. They have bred stock seedlings to have a notch on the leaf if they are going to be double. Seedlings without the notch can be thrown out.

I'm sure commercial bedding plant growers don't select for double-ness, but you certainly could if you grew your own seedlings. Double stocks are formal in style, single stocks are more informal—perfect for a natural setting where they can be allowed to seed themselves. Figure 3-7 shows both double and single flowers.

Bloomtime: June and July from March sowings, August and September from May sowings.

Height: 1–3 feet (.3–.9 m), depending on the cultivar.

Light and soil: Prefers full sun, but will tolerate some shade. A rich, well-drained soil to which some dolomite lime and organic matter has been added is best.

How to grow: Young plants are sometimes available from shops in spring, or they may be started from seed sown March to May. Germinate for 14 days at 70°F (21°C). Grow on at 50–55°F (10–13°C). (See note about selecting for doubles above.) Do not allow seedlings to be damaged or dry out, as they will bloom poorly. Handle seedlings by their leaves rather than their stems and do not overwater, to reduce the possibility of infection by damping-off fungi. Plant out from late April on, 12 inches (30 cm) apart. For a later bloom, sow directly in the garden.

Pests and diseases: In the insect department, watch for FLEA BEETLES, CATERPILLARS and APHIDS. Like other members of the cabbage family, stocks may be afflicted by CLUB ROOT. Other fungal diseases include DAMPING-OFF, basal and root ROTS and MOLDS. Although this sounds discouraging, stocks are easy to grow.

Uses: A fragrant addition to beds, borders, bouquets and floral decorations.

Matthiola longipetala subsp. *bicornis* "evening scented stock" "night scented stock" BRASSICACEAE

Evening scented stock is not much to look at, with narrow gray-green leaves, up to 2 inches (5 cm) long, and tiny pink or mauve flowers spaced along thin flower stalks. It will hardly be noticed among the other plants except for its fragrance filling the air in the evening and on dull days. It is easy to grow—a packet of seeds scattered into a flower bed or planter near a door or window is an inspired addition to the garden.

Evening scented stock is native to Greece. The name *bicornis* means "two-horns," and refers to the two horn-like structures at the end of the 3/4-inch (2-cm) seed capsules.

Bloomtime: Evening scented stock begins blooming about two months after sowing, continuing for two months.

Height: 12 inches (30 cm).

Light and soil: Prefers full sun but will tolerate some shade. Plant in any well-drained soil to which some organic matter has been added.

How to grow: Rarely available as plants in shops, but easy to grow from seed. Sow seeds directly in the garden in April and again mid-May and late June to get flowers all summer.

Pests and diseases: Generally trouble-free.

Uses: To add fragrance to the garden or hanging baskets.

"Mesembryanthemum" see *Cleretum* and *Lampranthus*

Mimulus **hybrids** "monkey flower" "mimulus" SCROPHULARIACEAE
(Figure 1-9)

Monkey flowers are one of the few annuals that do well in shade and wet soil. There are several parent species of monkey flower, native to swampy areas of North and South America; some are perennials and some annuals. Monkey flowers are generally grown as annuals, as they will not survive the frost.

The showy, 1- to 2-inch (2.5- to 5-cm) flowers, in bright yellow, orange and red shades, often have spots on the petals. They aren't easy to combine with other flowers, but are certainly colorful enough to make a show on their own.

Bloomtime: May to August.

Height: 12 inches (30 cm).

Light and soil: Full to semi-shade, with a moist soil.

How to grow: Young plants are occasionally available from shops in spring, or they may be started from seed. Sow seeds indoors in March, but do not cover with soil, as light is required for germination. Cover flats or pots with clear plastic or glass to maintain humidity. Germination, at 60–70°F (15–21°C) soil temperature, takes about 10 days. Set out hardened-off plants in late May, spacing them 8 inches (20 cm) apart.

Pests and diseases: Generally trouble-free.

Uses: So showy they may be best on their own, or with yellow or rust-colored flowers. Use in beds and containers.

Mirabilis jalapa "four-o'clock" "marvel-of- Peru" NYCTAGINACEAE

A bushy plant with large coarse leaves, *Mirabilis* bears dozens of trumpet-shaped blooms about 1 inch (2.5 cm) in diameter. They can be red, yellow, orange, rose or white; they are sometimes striped and often have more than one flower color on a single plant, making a very pretty effect. The only drawback to four-o'clocks is that the flowers are only open early in the morning, on dull days and late in the day—hence the name. (Actually, they should be called five o'clocks due to daylight saving time.) They have large seeds that germinate quickly and produce large seedlings, making them an ideal plant for a child's garden. The other common name refers to their origin, Peru, where they are perennial. They form a tuberous root that can be taken up and stored through the winter, like a dahlia, to be set out again in spring.

Bloomtime: July to frost.

Height: 2 feet (.6 m).

Light and soil: Prefers full sun and any well-drained soil, but might be worth trying afternoon shade to see more bloom. They will do well in very sandy soil and in hot windy places, but like an abundance of water in the summer.

How to grow: Sow seeds in the garden in April, or indoors in March. The big seeds are easy for a young child to handle. Plant seedlings outdoors in May, 12 inches (30 cm) apart. Before the first frost, dig up the tuberous roots, let them dry and store them in a box of peat in a cool, dark place. Plant them out again in April.

Pests and diseases: APHIDS may infest growing tips.

Uses: In mixed borders and in large containers. Best in an informal setting, rather than formal bedding schemes.

Moluccella laevis "bells of Ireland" LAMIACEAE
(Figure 8-5)

This unusual plant, a half-hardy annual native to Asia Minor, is fun to grow. Each node on the stem produces two scalloped leaves and a cluster of seven or eight lime-green "bells" that encircle the stem, facing outward. Each bell is actually the calyx of a flower and a single stem will bear flowers at various stages. Near the top of the stem, the bells will contain a fuzzy white unopened flower bud, further down a tiny white flower and below that the flowers will have fallen off, leaving just the calyx. As the plant grows, the stems full of bells become over 1 foot (30

106

cm) long and make an interesting addition to a flower border and outstanding cut flowers, lasting well over a week. (Pick off the two leaves at each node, as they detract from the bells.)

Bloomtime: Grown for the green, bell-like calyces, which appear with the flowers from June to September.

Height: To 3 feet (.9 m). Stake bells of Ireland to produce long straight stems or use the curving stems in asymmetrical flower arrangements.

Light and soil: Prefer full sun and any well-drained soil. They will give even better results if some organic matter is added to the soil.

How to grow: Although young plants are not generally available from shops, they may be grown from seed. In March, refrigerate seeds for 5 days before sowing indoors in sandy soil. Germination is irregular, occurring over a 5-week period. Alternating soil temperature between 50°F (10°C) at night and 70°F (21°C) in the day encourages germination. Harden off and plant out 9 inches (23 cm) apart in May. Seeds may also be sown directly in the garden in April and thinned. Many books say the seedlings are difficult to transplant into the garden, but this has not been my experience. Stake plants with light bamboo canes.

Pests and diseases: Generally trouble-free.

Uses: In a mixed border or large planter; excellent for cut flowers. They may be dried (most successfully with silica gel).

"Monkey flower" see *Mimulus*
"Moss rose" see *Portulaca*

Myosotis sylvatica "forget-me-not" BORAGINACEAE

Forget-me-nots are low-growing, spreading plants with small, sky blue flowers, each with a white eye. Biennials by nature, young forget-me-nots are planted in the fall, along with bulbs, to bloom the following spring. Once in the garden, they seed themselves and may easily be moved. The seedlings are simple to identify because they have hairy, bright green leaves that are broad across the middle and taper to each end. The leaves grow in a rosette shape, joined at the base. It is not until their second year that the flowering stems are produced and their ultimate height is reached.

The name *Myosotis* comes from the Greek meaning "mouse ear," no doubt because of the fuzziness of the leaves rather than their shape. There is some confusion of the names in this genus. Seed catalogues often list forget-me-nots as *Myosotis alpestris*, a name correctly applied to a perennial that is rarely known in cultivation. *Myosotis scorpioides* (or M. *palustris*) is the water forget-me-not, a creeping bog plant.

There are many sentimental stories about the origin of the common name. In their marvelous book *Flowers: A Guide for Your Garden*, Pizzetti and Cocker tell us:

> "The most pleasing and simplest story has for its protagonists the forget-me-not and God, who, according to the German tradition of this legend, is an old, very dignified, melancholy figure. After much work distributing names among all the animals, plants, flowers and objects, a small voice cried out 'Forget me not, O Lord,' and God replied, 'Forget-me-not shall be your name.' And so it has been."

Forget-me-nots are also available in pink and white.

Bloomtime: March to May.

Height: 8–24 inches (20–61 cm), depending on the cultivar. Most garden cultivars are under 12 inches (30 cm).

Light and soil: Sun or shade and any well-drained soil, preferably one to which some organic matter has been added.

How to grow: Young plants are generally available from shops in spring or fall; sometimes they are in the perennial section. However, they are easy to grow from seed. During summer, sow seeds where they are to bloom or in an out-of-the-way bed for transplanting in autumn. Space seedlings 6 inches (15 cm) apart. Plants will bloom the following spring.

Pests and diseases: In very wet weather, plants may get MILDEW or MOLD.

Uses: Use as a "winter bedding plant": planted in fall to bloom in early spring. Attractive planted at the front of a mixed border or under roses. Use in containers with spring bloomers.

"Nasturtium" see *Tropaeolum*

Nemesia strumosa "nemesia" SCROPHULARIACEAE
(Figure 1-10)

A charming half-hardy annual from South Africa, nemesia is hard to grow in our climate since it doesn't like hot, humid weather. The flowers, to 1 inch (2.5 cm) across, are white, orange, yellow, pink or lilac, some with spots on the outer petals or in the bearded throat. The colors are fresh, but not too intense. The plants are erect and well-branched, with long, narrow, light green leaves.

Bloomtime: June to August, when they can be cut back to flower a second time. Bloomtime can also be extended by making a second sowing.

Height: 8–12 inches (20–30 cm), depending on the cultivar.

Light and soil: Light, dappled shade in a soil with lots of organic matter. Any stress will result in spindly plants, so keep them well-fertilized and watered.

How to grow: Young plants are never seen in garden centers so they must be started from seed in March. Germinate in the dark at 60°F (15°C) for 7–14 days. Set out hardened-off plants, 4–6 inches (10–15 cm) apart, in May. A second sowing can be made in May for later summer bloom.

Pests and diseases: If soil is too cold or wet, plants can suffer root ROT.

Uses: Lovely in hanging baskets, beds and containers for early summer color. Try planting with browallia or cupflower, which are slow to get going but have a strong finish. They can take over from the nemesia.

Nemophila menziesii (*N. insignis*) "baby blue eyes" HYDROPHYLLACEAE (Figure 2-9)

This hardy annual from California has a bright and cheerful effect in the garden. The sky blue flowers have five overlapping petals and a white center, set off by fresh green leaves. The habit is open and sprawling, which makes baby blue eyes more suited to a rockery, or trailing out of a container with other bedding plants, than a formal bedding plant scheme. The specific name honors Archibald Menzies, a British Royal Navy surgeon. He joined Captain George Vancouver's voyage to the Pacific coast in 1792 in order to collect botanical specimens for King George III's "very valuable collection of exotics at Kew [gardens]"—Vancouver's own words.

Bloomtime: June to September.

Height: 6–8 inches (15–20 cm), spreading to over 12 inches (30 cm) across.

Light and soil: Full sun or light shade, well-drained soil, preferably with added organic matter. Water well in summer.

How to grow: Sow seeds in March, either indoors or in their garden locations. Many books say the seedlings are difficult to transplant into the garden, but this has not been my experience. Plants should be spaced about 9 inches (23 cm) apart. Stems are quite brittle, so take care when weeding around baby blue eyes. They do not seem to mind a bit of bark mulch around their roots to keep them cool and moist.

Pests and diseases: APHIDS may infest new shoots.

Uses: Rock gardens, informal woodland settings, trailing out of containers.

"Nepeta" see *Glechoma*

Nicotiana alata "flowering tobacco" "nicotiana" SOLANACEAE (Figure 8-7)

Although related to the tobacco plant, *Nicotiana alata* is grown only for decorative value. Like its cousin, it has large handsome leaves that grow up to 12 inches (30 cm) long and are diamond-shaped in outline. The flowers consist of a long tube opening out into a star shape 2 inches (5 cm) across. They are very elegant, in shades of white, pink, rose, red or dusky purple, and, in some cultivars, are fragrant. Flowers of the parent species close during the day, but those of the cultivars remain open all day. Plants can grow up to 5 feet (1.5 m) tall, making the dwarf cultivars more suitable to most gardens. The 'Nicki' series, most common in shops, reach 16–18 inches (41–46 cm) and are not fragrant. 'Lime Green' reaches 30 inches (76 cm) and has an unusual flower color that is striking in floral arrangements. The 'Domino' series grows to 12–14 inches (30–36 cm) and plants are bushier, producing more flowers. They come in separate colors or a mix, which, depending on the seed house, includes lime green. Native to South America where it is perennial, flowering tobacco likes warmth and will not survive winters outdoors, but they will self-seed.

Bloomtime: June to frost.

Height: 1–5 feet (.3–1.5 m), depending on the cultivar.

Light and soil: Full sun to full shade and a rich, well-drained soil to which much organic matter has been added.

How to grow: Young plants are generally available from shops in spring, or they can easily be grown from seed. Sow seeds indoors in March, but do not cover with soil, as light is required for germination, which, at 70°F (21°C) soil temperature, takes about 14 days. Set out hardened off plants 12 inches (30 cm) apart when the weather has warmed up, late May or early June.

110

Pests and diseases: Young plants may be infested with APHIDS. COLORADO POTATO BEETLES attack older plants.

Uses: Dwarf cultivars in containers, mixed beds and borders, and for cutting.

Nierembergia hippomanica var. *violacea (N. caerulea)* "cupflower"
SOLANACEAE
(Figure 5-8)

Cupflower belongs to the same family as flowering tobacco and petunias and is also native to South America. Perennial in its homeland, it is grown as a half-hardy annual here and will not overwinter. The foliage is attractive: finely cut, dark green and feathery. The plant forms a mound about 1 foot (30 cm) high and wide. In June there is a scattering of bloom, but by later in the summer the plants are almost covered with 1-inch (2.5-cm), violet-purple, cup-shaped flowers. Plants grown from cuttings may bloom more heavily earlier in the summer.

Bloomtime: June to frost.

Height: 12 inches (30 cm).

Light and soil: Prefers full sun and any well-drained soil.

How to grow: Young plants are not generally available from shops, but they are easily grown from seed. Sow seeds indoors in March, germinating at 60°F (15°C). Set young plants out, spaced 8 inches (20 cm) apart, in late May or June. Plants can also be started from cuttings taken in late summer, rooted in a sandy soil mix, and overwintered in the greenhouse, or on a sunny windowsill. If grown under fluorescent lights with long day length, they will flower in the winter and make a cheerful antidote to the winter blues.

Pests and diseases: Generally trouble-free.

Uses: Excellent as an edging to a flower bed or mixed border, particularly from August on when the bloom is most abundant. Also suitable for rock gardens, containers and hanging baskets.

Nigella damascena "love-in-a-mist" "nigella" RANUNCULACEAE
(Figure 2-10)

Love-in-a-mist is an oddball annual like bells of Ireland, and just as easy to grow. The finely cut leaves create a green "mist" that surrounds the delicate white or blue flowers. The flowers of most cultivars have a double row of papery petals and resemble cornflowers. They are excellent cut flowers and produce an interesting round seed capsule that dries well and can be used for flower arrangements.

Love-in-a-mist gets its botanical name from the Latin *niger*, meaning black. This refers to its tiny jet-black seeds, which look like chips of coal. They can be saved and will be viable for up to two years.

Love-in-a-mist has been known since ancient times, when it was valued for its medicinal properties. Native to Asia Minor, it also grows wild in the Mediterranean.

Bloomtime: June to August, longer if a second sowing is made.

Height: 18 inches (46 cm) or more.

Light and soil: Prefers full sun and any well-drained soil with added organic matter.

How to grow: Although young plants are not generally available from shops, they are easily grown from seed. Many books say the seedlings are difficult to transplant into the garden, but this has not been my experience. Sow seeds in the garden or indoors in March, just covering them with soil. Young plants should be spaced 9 inches (23 cm) apart. Dry seed pods by hanging them upside-down in a cool, dry place. Love-in-a-mist self-seeds readily.

Pests and diseases: Generally trouble-free.

Uses: Wonderful for a soft textural effect in a mixed border. Good for cutting and drying.

Osteospermum ecklonis (*Dimorphotheca ecklonis*) "African daisy" "osteospermum" ASTERACEAE
(Figure 8-8)

This particular African daisy—as other plants go by the same name— is a subshrub from southern Africa. It has daisy-like flowers up to 3 inches (7.5 cm) with white petals and a striking navy blue disk at the center. The plant has a bushy habit, similar to that of a marguerite, and handsome dark green foliage. There are many more species of osteospermum growing in South Africa which may find their way into gardens in years to come. Young plants of *Osteospermum ecklonis* are sometimes sold as Spanish marguerite, which is strange since they are from Africa.

Bloomtime: June to frost. Remove old flowers to encourage continued bloom.

Height: To 24 inches (61 cm) high.

Light and soil: Prefers full sun, a hot spot and any well-drained soil.

How to grow: Young plants grown from cuttings are sometimes available from shops in spring, or make cuttings yourself if you have access to a plant. Set plants out in late May, 12 inches (30 cm) apart. Remove old flowers for continued bloom.

Pests and diseases: In a very wet, cold summer, GRAY MOLD may develop on the leaves.

Uses: Very striking in a mixed border or in a large planter with other bedding plants. Try them combined with lavender and felicia.

"Painted-tongue" see *Salpiglossis*
"Pansy," "tufted pansy" see *Viola*

Papaver nudicaule "Iceland poppy" PAPAVERACEAE
(Figure 7-8)

This native of the subarctic is a short-lived perennial, usually grown as a biennial or hardy annual. The leaves form a rosette around the base of the plant, which throws up 18- to 24-inch (46- to 61-cm) stems with 2- to 4-inch (5- to 10-cm) fragrant blooms of orange, yellow, apricot, white, pink, scarlet or rose. 'Champagne Bubbles' has pastel blooms on 24-inch (61-cm) stems, making excellent cut flowers; 'Sparkling Bubbles' has deeper shades; 'Garden Gnome' and 'Wonderland' are dwarf cultivars, suitable for bedding or rockery schemes.

Bloomtime: June to September.

Height: 10–24 inches (25–61 cm), depending on the cultivar.

Light and soil: Prefers full sun and any well-drained soil. Poor, dry soils are more suitable than rich, damp soils.

How to grow: Young plants are sometimes available from shops in spring, or they can easily be grown from seed. Sow indoors in March or April, transplanting them when young into individual pots. (Plants develop a tap root and resent root disturbance.) Another method, as they are hardy annuals, is to sow them directly in the garden in March, just covering them with soil. Plants should be spaced to stand 8–10 inches (20–25 cm) apart. Remove faded flowers.

Pests and diseases: In wet, cold summers the leaves may get POWDERY MILDEW.

Uses: In addition to bedding, borders and rock gardens, Iceland poppies make excellent cut flowers. Cut stems in the morning, just as the nodding buds are lifting but before the flowers open. Sear stems in boiling water or with a flame.

Papaver rhoeas selections "Shirley poppy" PAPAVERACEAE

"In Flanders' fields the poppies blow,
Between the crosses, row on row "

These lines, written by John McRae in 1915, have immortalized the humble weed *Papaver rhoeas*, the corn or field poppy and inspired the small, felt poppies worn around the world on Remembrance Day.

A hardy annual native to vast areas of Europe and Asia, field poppies have erect, slender stems covered with minute, silky hairs. The nodding bud opens to reveal a blood-red flower, 2 inches (5 cm) in diameter, like crushed silk. The leaves are about 6 inches (15 cm) long, covered with small hairs and divided. This species, with *Papaver somniferum* (opium poppy), produce the commercial poppy seed used in cooking.

Pizzetti and Cocker relate the story of the creation of Shirley poppies from an account written by their originator, the Reverend W. Wilks:

"In 1880 I noticed in an abandoned corner of my garden a group of the common red poppy, *Papaver rhoeas*, among which was a solitary flower with petals slightly margined in white. I marked the flower and saved the seed, which the following year produced about two hundred plants, four or five of which had white edged petals. The best of these were marked, their seed saved, and the same process of selection and elimination was repeated for several years; with the subsequent flowers having an increasingly large area of white on the petals and correspondingly smaller areas of red until a pale pink form was obtained, followed by a plant with white flowers. Next I began the long process of changing the centers of the flowers from black to yellow, and then to white, until I succeeded in obtaining a group of plants with petals ranging in color from brilliant red to pure white, with all the intermediate shades of pink plus an extensive selection with margined and suffused petals; all the flowers having yellow or white stamens, anthers and pollen, and a white center . . . . It is interesting to note that all the gardens of the world, whether they be rich or poor, are ornamented by direct descendants of the single seed capsule cultivated in the vicarage garden at Shirley [England] during the August of 1880."

Reverend Wilks had reason to be proud of his creation, as they are exquisite flowers. There are also double Shirley poppies available and Thompson and Morgan list 'Rev. Wilks Mixed' as having many fancy types such as bicolors and picotees. 'Allegro' is a dwarf field poppy of the original type; the Stokes catalogue suggests planting them near graves for remembrance as well as borders and rock gardens.

Bloomtime: June to August.

Height: 12–36 inches (30–91 cm), depending on the cultivar.

Light and soil: The same as *Papaver nudicaule*.

How to grow: See *Papaver nudicaule*.

Pests and diseases: See *Papaver nudicaule*.

Uses: In mixed borders and informal gardens. Good in containers with other bedding plants so that their delicate flowers can be viewed at close range.

Pelargonium × *domesticum* "regal pelargonium" "Martha Washington geranium" "pansy geranium" "pelargonium" GERANIACEAE
(Figure 8-9)

Like the zonal geraniums, regal pelargoniums are the result of complex plant breeding, mainly derived from three species: *P. cucullatum*, *P. fulgidum*, and *P. grandiflorum*, all half-hardy perennials from South Africa. The flowers are more delicate than those of the zonals; in shades of peach, pink, bronze, lavender, white and red, they often have petal edges or throats of a contrasting color. The foliage is a brighter green and has pointed teeth along the leaf margin, rather than the more scalloped edges of the zonals. The leaves do not have the dark rings that characterize the zonal geraniums. All four common names are in use, but pelargonium is preferred by Europeans and Martha Washington geranium is used more by Americans.

Bloomtime: May to October.

Height: 15–24 inches (38–61 cm), depending on the cultivar.

Light and soil: The same as zonal geraniums (*Pelargonium* × *hortorum*).

How to grow: Regal pelargoniums are always grown from cuttings of named cultivars and sold in bloom in shops in spring. The flowers are damaged by rain, so they are best grown on a covered patio or on an apartment balcony, for example. Cuttings can be taken from plants in September, but whitefly is a problem, particularly for regal pelargoniums indoors.

115

Pests and diseases: WHITEFLY.
Uses: Best in containers on a covered balcony or patio.

Pelargonium × *hortorum* "geranium" "zonal geranium" "zonal pelargonium" GERANIACEAE
(Figures 6-3, 6-10, 7-7, 8-3, 8-6 and 8-10)

To the home gardener, there is no doubt that the summer bedding plants with vivid red flowers, large rounded leaves and a characteristic pungent odor are geraniums. Correctly, however, they are in the genus *Pelargonium*, and there is a movement in gardening circles to use pelargonium as a common name to distinguish them from true geraniums. True geraniums (in the genus *Geranium*) are frost-hardy perennials with small flowers in pastel shades.

Because the name geranium has been used so extensively for the past two hundred years to describe *Pelargonium* × *hortorum*, there is something to be said for continuing to use it. Even the color "geranium red" is commonly used.

Most gardening magazines and catalogues use geranium. A number of gardening books, particularly those from Britain, prefer pelargonium. Most gardeners continue to use geranium to refer to the summer bedding plant, using true geranium or hardy geranium when meaning plants in the genus *Geranium*. Unlike use of botanical names, there is no one correct common name. In this book, the popular use of geranium is retained.

The first zonal geraniums were sent to Holland from South Africa in 1609 by the governor of the Cape colony. During the late 1700s and the early 1800s, the Cape colony passed into British hands and at the same time there was a boom in greenhouse growing in Britain. Many species of *Pelargonium* were imported into Britain and their popularity peaked in the Victorian era. During World War I, growing ornamental plants in greenhouses in Britain was banned due to fuel shortages, and geranium numbers fell.

In the 1950s and '60s in America, disease was a tremendous problem with geraniums, wiping out vast crops. The culprits were the fungal disease verticillium wilt, bacterial blight and a number of viral diseases. The advent of Culture-Virus-Indexing has completely changed the situation, allowing disease-free plants to be grown. This is a technique whereby plants are grown in a laboratory until they are free of disease organisms and new plants are raised from this "clean" stock. In addition, from years of patient breeding, the British, Dutch and Americans have developed thousands of cultivars, including all the "fancy leaf geraniums."

In addition to the typical red, geranium flower colors include pale pink, hot pink, salmon, white and orange. Leaves often have a circle of darker green on them, the "zone" for which they are named. Fancy leaf cultivars include green and white or green and gold leaves, or solid yellow leaves and hundreds of other combinations. Many of these fancy cultivars are named clones, and must be propagated by cuttings and overwintered. Plants are available from specialty growers or clubs.

Initially, these were rather poor and did not flower very profusely or with such large flower heads. Modern hybrids, however, are just as good as those grown from cuttings in nearly all respects. Most of the geraniums that you will find on sale in garden centers, nurseries and corner lots have been raised from seed.

By sowing the seed in late January or early February, the commercial grower can produce a good-sized plant in a 4-inch (19-cm) pot, in flower, by mid-May. This eliminates the need to heat a large area of greenhouse for several months, resulting in lower prices for the finished plant. Later-sown seedlings are occasionally sold in packs, rather than in individual pots, but these will not give the same display and may not come into flower for several weeks.

There are four main advantages to the seed-grown geraniums: plants are usually disease-free (diseases can be transferred when cuttings are taken), they develop a symmetrical growth habit, they produce more flowers and they are less expensive. Outstanding seed cultivars include the Fleuroselect-winning 'Sprinter Series', AAS winner 'Rose Diamond', Fleuroselect winner 'Cherry Diamond' and 'Scarlet Diamond'.

Bloomtime: May until frost, especially if old flower heads are picked off.
Height: Usually 1–3 feet (.3–.9 m), but if they are trained up a stake and overwintered in a greenhouse, they may reach up to 6 feet (1.8 m).
Light and soil: Although most zonal geraniums prefer full sun, some of the cultivars with golden leaves may burn in full sun. Zonal geraniums may also burn in a very hot place, such as a hot greenhouse or a spot that has a lot of reflected light and trapped heat. Any well-drained soil is fine; they tolerate dry soil.

How to grow: Young plants are always available from shops in spring or they can be started from seed, but it is a slow process. They take six months from sowing to blooming. In mid to late February, soak seeds between two wet paper towels for 48 hours, then sow 1/4 inch (.6 cm) apart and cover with 1/8 inch (.3 cm) of fine potting soil. Cover flat with clear plastic for 5 days and maintain 70°F (21°C) soil temperature; germination takes 12–25 days. Transplant when the first true leaves appear and keep soil temperature at 70°F (21°C) during the day, but 60°F (15°C) during the night, to keep plants compact. Use artificial lights for 18 hours each day, beginning when seeds germinate and continuing for six weeks to produce bloom in May or early June.

The following technique is used with good results in Britain and reduces energy consumption in the greenhouse. Seeds are sown at the beginning of October, and soil temperature is kept at least 70°F (21°C) until seeds germinate. The temperature is then reduced to 65°F (18°C) until transplanting, when it is further reduced to 45°F (7°C). Using this technique, plants bloom about the last week of May.

Set hardened-off plants out in late May, 18 inches (45 cm) apart. Best long-term results will be obtained by removing flowers and buds when setting the plants out. Flower stalks snap off easily from where they join the main stem. Through the summer, remove old flowers and dead or yellow leaves and pinch back the growing tip from time to time. (The growing tip is where the new leaves are unfurling. Often you will see a tiny flower bud just beside them. If you are careful, it is possible to pinch just the leaves, not disturbing the flower bud.)

In September, cuttings can be taken to be overwintered indoors. Using a razor blade, take 3- to 4-inch (7.5- to 10-cm) cuttings from healthy plants. Carefully remove all leaves from the bottom inch (2.5 cm) of the cutting. Fill 2 1/4-inch (6-cm) pots (or styrofoam cups with a hole in the bottom) with a moist rooting mix of perlite and peat, and make a hole in the mix with a dibble or pencil. Insert one cutting to each pot. Roots should appear in 7–10 days, at which time cuttings should be potted into 4-inch (10-cm) pots with a good potting mix. Fertilize with half-strength 20-20-20 once a month until March. If plants are in a warm greenhouse and are growing quickly, they can be fertilized more often. Pinch tips when about 6 inches (15 cm) high.

Zonal geraniums bloom best with a restricted root zone, so do not plant them into a too large container. In Europe, some gardeners prefer to keep plants in their pots all summer, plunging the pots into the soil. This also has the advantage of keeping the roots drier and more compact, a benefit in wet soils. Eight-inch (20-cm) pots are adequate for this technique.

Various techniques are used for overwintering geranium plants. Some gardeners dig plants up, shake the soil off, and hang them upside down.

Other gardeners dig plants up and pot them into boxes of soil. In both cases they should be placed in a basement for cold storage if possible. The ideal temperature is about 50°F (10°C). A third method is to pot plants up in sterilized potting mix, cut them back by one-third and keep them in a sunny window in the house through the winter.

Pests and diseases: GRAY MOLD causes gray fuzzy patches on stems and leaves. In the greenhouse, WHITEFLIES and LEAFHOPPERS may be a problem. VIRUS diseases can be carried between plants by APHIDS and LEAFHOPPERS; they can be spread by tools when cuttings are made. Whether you buy seedlings or rooted cuttings, do not buy plants with leaves that are puckered or crinkled or with round yellow rings on them, signs of viral disease.

There are a few PHYSIOLOGICAL DISORDERS which indicate a cultural problem. In general, these disorders are temporary and when the weather warms up, the symptoms disappear. If plants appear to be healthy otherwise, they are not cause for concern. OEDEMA is caused in the greenhouse by moist soil in combination with cool, cloudy spring weather. The plants take up too much water and "water blisters" form on the undersides of the leaves. They burst and then form cork-like spots. Although unsightly, this condition disappears when the weather warms. LEAF REDDENING occurs if the nights are too cool in the greenhouse; again, it's not a problem once the plants are set out. Dry soil will cause DRY BROWN PATCHES on the leaves. In itself this is not a problem on one or two leaves, but it can indicate that the plants have not been properly cared for.

Uses: Excellent for bedding schemes and edging and a must for containers, zonal geraniums combine well with many other bedding plants. Consider them behind sweet alyssum or dusty miller, interplanted with heliotrope or felicia, or with marigolds or calendula, if you are partial to bright colors. They work well with marguerite daisies, especially 'Silver Lace'. Zonal geraniums look great with blue lobelia and silvery lotus vine, trailing from a large planter. A classic is a large zonal geranium (or several) in a heavy terra cotta pot.

Pelargonium peltatum "ivy geranium" "trailing geranium" GERANIACEAE
(Figure 3-8)

Ivy geraniums are beautifully suited to hanging basket and container cultivation. Blooms, some double, are in shades of pink, white, crimson and mauve. The leaves, as the common name suggests, resemble ivy leaves in shape, but are bright green. Like the other pelargoniums, ivy geraniums are native to South Africa, but they do not like full sun and burn easily. The vast majority of the plants sold in shops are named cultivars grown from cuttings, but there is a new seed mixture, 'Summer Showers', which has gotten excellent comments by gardeners. An interesting group of cultivars, the Swiss balcony geraniums or mini-cascade geraniums, are much more floriferous than the common ivy geraniums. Although they begin to bloom a bit later and have smaller flowers, they become a mass of bloom trailing 2 feet (1.2 m) from a window box, even on the north side of a house. Flowers are "self-cleaning," and do not need to be deadheaded.

Bloomtime: May to frost.

Height: Trailing to 18–24 inches (46–61 cm), depending on the cultivar.

Light and soil: Full or partial shade and well-drained soil with added organic matter. Too much sun will result in small, cup-shaped leaves and small blooms with some burning.

How to grow: Young plants are almost always available from shops in spring, or they can be started from cuttings or seed as for zonal geraniums, except that plants must be kept more shaded.

Pests and diseases: See *Pelargonium* × *domesticum*. Ivy geraniums are most susceptible to OEDEMA, so water only in the morning and on sunny days. Keep well fertilized.

Uses: Hanging baskets, either alone or with other bedding plants; trailing over the edge of containers or walls.

Petunia* × *hybrida "petunia" SOLANACEAE
(Figure 5-9)

For all-summer and autumn bloom in the widest range of colors imaginable, it is hard to beat petunias. Some gardeners have favorite cultivars, which they plant faithfully year after year for a beautiful display. Some prefer to try something new each season. If you get hooked on petunias, you will never be bored.

Like their cousins, flowering tobacco, tobacco, potatoes and tomatoes, the two species that are the parents of our garden petunias come from South America. In the wild, *Petunia violacea* and *P. nyctaginiflora* are perennial, and while they can be overwintered, they are so inexpensive and readily available that we grow them as annuals.

The most popular category of petunia is the **single grandiflora**. These have large single blooms in a dazzling array of shapes and colors. Some of the most popular single grandifloras are:

BICOLOR:	'Blue Frost'	blue center with white ruffled edges
	'Penny Candy'	red and white striped with ruffled edges
	'Red Picotee'	red and white, Fleuroselect winner
	'Ultra Crimson Star'	red and white, All-America Selection 1988
WHITE:	'Supermagic White'	compact and weather tolerant, non-stretching
	'Ultra White'	base branching, dwarf, good for containers
	'White Cascade'	good for containers
	'White Flash'	early large pure white, rain resistant
YELLOW:	'Yellow Magic'	ruffled butter yellow, less fading than some
PURPLE AND BLUE:	'Blue Cloud'	velvety violet, compact habit
	'Royal Cascade'	deep velvety purple
	'Sky Cascade'	clear sky blue
	'Sugar Daddy'	a popular favorite; bright reddish-purple with deeper wine-red veins; great in containers
	'Supercascade Lilac'	smooth lavender with white throat

RED:	'Red Cascade'	bright red for beds or pots
	'Red Flash'	very compact and weather resistant
	'Ultra Red'	very dwarf base-branching plants
PINK:	'Appleblossom'	compact habit and weather resistant
	'Blush Supercascade'	pale pink with a rose throat

In general, all of the 'Ultra' series are very good. They come in 11 separate colors. The 'Cascade' or 'Supercascade' series are outstanding in containers because they will trail over the edge, but they can also be used in beds.

Single multiflora petunias have smaller flowers, but more of them. They are more widely used for massed bedding in the garden or in parks. Popular cultivars include:

BICOLOR:	'Starfire'	deep scarlet with a white star
WHITE:	'Paleface'	white with a cream throat
YELLOW:	'Summer Sun'	the best yellow petunia to date
PURPLE:	'Sugar Plum'	reddish-purple with wine-red veins

The 'Resisto' series of single multifloras was developed in Europe to withstand cool wet summer conditions; they grow equally well here. They also perform well in hot, dry summers. There are six separate colors available: 'Red Star' (red and white bicolor), 'Blue Star' (blue and white bicolor), 'Blue', 'Scarlet', 'White' and 'Rose', as well as a mix.

There are **double grandiflora** and **double multiflora** petunias available that resemble carnations. They are not as weather resistant as the singles, but would do well under cover of a south-facing balcony. The 1987 AAS winner 'Purple Pirouette' has large, deep purple blooms with white edges.

Bloomtime: May to frost.

Height: 6–10 inches (15–25 cm), depending on the cultivar.

Light and soil: Full or half-day sun and any well-drained soil. Fertilize and water well in summer.

How to grow: Young plants are always available from shops in spring, or they can be grown from seed. Sow in early March and cover seeds very lightly, as light aids germination. At 70°F (21°C) soil temperature, this takes 10–12 days. Use bottom heat if possible. Set hardened-off plants out in late May, spacing them 15 inches (37 cm) apart. Pinch the growing tips often during the season to encourage bushiness. Removing old flowers keeps plants looking top-notch, but it's a chore because plants are sticky.

Pests and diseases: Petunias are generally trouble-free, but APHIDS may infest new growth on young plants. Occasionally, VIRUS diseases attack petunias, causing the plants to be stunted. Basal and root ROTS may cause plants to collapse in cold, wet soil, a good reason not to set out plants too early. CUTWORMS can attack petunias.

In areas with heavy industry and automobile exhaust, petunias can be damaged by SMOG, causing bleached and dead bands on the upper and lower leaf surfaces. White- and light-flowered cultivars are particularly susceptible. If smog is a problem, plant darker-flowered cultivars or choose resistant annuals such as snapdragons.

Uses: Massed in flower beds, used for edging, in containers and window boxes. In hanging baskets, petunias are best on their own.

Phlox drummondii "annual phlox" POLEMONIACEAE
(Figure 3-9)

The delicate annual phlox is related to two fine perennials, border phlox (*Phlox paniculata*) and rockery phlox (*P. subulata*). They all are native to North America; the annual, from Texas, is half-hardy and does not overwinter. The stems are somewhat trailing and each ends in a cluster of 5-petalled flowers. Leaves are bright green. Flower colors include soft shades of white, red, pink, maroon and lavender. Phlox have an old-fashioned look and are easy to grow.

The cultivar 'Twinkle' has star-shaped blooms and is only 6 inches (15 cm) high. 'Cecily' grows to 8 inches (20 cm) high and many flowers have a contrasting eye. 'Petticoat Mixed' is generally available as young plants in shops in spring; it has good sun and drought tolerance. There are also taller types suitable for cutting that are not generally sold in shops.

Bloomtime: July to September.

Height: 6–14 inches (15–36 cm), depending on the cultivar.

Light and soil: Prefers full sun and a moist soil to which some organic matter has been added. Water well in dry weather.

How to grow: Young plants are generally available from shops in spring; if possible, buy plants that are "green," that is, not in bloom yet. Phlox can easily be started from seed. Sow indoors in March, 1/8 inch (.3 cm) deep, directly into individual pots (they do not like to be transplanted). Seeds need 60°F (15°C) soil temperature and total darkness to germinate. When the seedlings are up, grow them on at 55°F (13°C). Plant out in late May, spacing them 9 inches (23 cm) apart. Or sow directly in the garden in April for late June bloom. The weakest seedlings often have the brightest colors, so bear this in mind when thinning. Removing old flowers extends the flowering period.

Pests and diseases: SLUGS like young plants.

Uses: Beds, borders, window boxes and planters.

"Pocketbook flower" see *Calceolaria*
"Polka dot plant" see *Hypoestes*
"Polyanthus" see *Primula*
"Poor-man's orchid" see *Schizanthus*
"Poppy, Iceland" see *Papaver nudicaule*
"Poppy, Shirley" see *Papaver rhoeas*

Portulaca grandiflora "moss rose" "portulaca" PORTULACACEAE
(Figure 4-7)

Portulaca is an annual sun lover from Brazil and Argentina with 1-inch (2.5-cm) rose-like single or double flowers. Colors include white, pink, rose, red and yellow in shades that look festive planted as a mixed group. The trailing stems bear ½-inch (1.3-cm), sausage-shaped, fleshy leaves. While most portulacas close their blooms on a cloudy day, two cultivars, 'Afternoon Delight' and 'Cloudbeater Mixed', stay open all day.

Bloomtime: June to September.

Height: To 6 inches (15 cm) high by 12 inches (30 cm) across for most cultivars.

Light and soil: A hot, sunny spot with very well-drained (even dry) sandy soil.

How to grow: Young plants are generally available from shops in spring,

or they can easily be grown from seed. Sow seeds indoors in March, directly into small pots to avoid transplanting. Press seeds into soil but do not cover, as light is required for germination. Germination, at 70°F (21°C) soil temperature, takes about 10 days. Grow on at 60–65°F (15–18°C) with lots of light and not too much water. Plant out at the end of May, spacing 6 inches (15 cm) apart.

Pests and diseases: If planted out too early, plants can DAMP OFF. APHIDS can occasionally be a problem.

Uses: Edging for paths and at the front of sunny borders, trailing over the top of a wall or planted in a rock garden.

"Pouch flower" see *Calceolaria*

Primula × *polyantha* "polyanthus" "primrose" "primula" PRIMULACEAE (Figure 7-9)

Polyanthus are hybrids of three species: *Primula vulgaris* (also called *P. acaulis*), English primrose; *P. veris*, cowslip; and a third species over which there is some disagreement. At any rate, all parents are native to Europe and polyanthus have been in gardens for as long as there have been gardens in Europe. *P. veris* was thought to have many curative properties. There is an old French saying, "Qui a du bugle et du sanicle fait au chirurgien le nicle." (Who possesses ajuga and primulas has no need of a doctor.) In 1768, a small book devoted to the primulas indicated them for curing blemishes, headaches, weeping, gallstones, red eyes, fever, coughing and wounds.

An ideal plant for shaded parts of the garden, look for polyanthus in the supermarkets and garden centers in early spring. Use them to brighten the home until the blooms fade, then harden them off and plant outdoors. They will probably bloom again next spring. The dazzling array of colors includes white, yellow, orange, peach, pink, rose, red, lavender, purple and maroon, often with a contrasting eye or edge to the petals. The five-petalled flowers cluster above the rosette of bright green basal leaves. In a group of seedlings, some plants will be fragrant.

Bloomtime: Early spring.

Height: 6–10 inches (15–25 cm) , depending on the cultivar.

Light and soil: Part shade or shade and a moist, well-drained soil to which some organic matter has been added. They do not like to dry out.

How to grow: Young plants are generally available from shops in spring,

which is the easiest way to get them. Because the seeds need cool temperatures to germinate, they are germinated commercially in bulb companies' coolers that are empty in the summer. Seedlings are shipped to growers in August for potting on and sale in bloom in the fall. Home growers can germinate the seeds in a sunny window sill in February for bloom the following spring; air temperature of about 70°F (21°C) is perfect. Seeds take up to 4 weeks to germinate; fresh seeds germinate best. Press seeds gently into the potting mix, but do not cover with mix. Keep moist. Set young plants out in May. Mature plants can also be propagated by division in July; dig up the whole plant and gently pull apart the separate clumps.

Pests and diseases: Polyanthus are popular with ROOT WEEVILS, SLUGS, SNAILS, and CUTWORMS. There are a number of viruses and fungi that may attack polyanthus, but they are generally healthy in the garden.

Uses: To provide early spring color, polyanthus are perfect for an informal or woodland setting, at the front of a mixed border, as an edging, or in containers.

"Prince's feather" see *Amaranthus*
Psylliostachys suworowii see *Limonium*
"Quaking grass" see *Avena*

Rudbeckia hirta "black-eyed susan" "gloriosa daisy" ASTERACEAE
(Figure 7-10)

Although black-eyed susans are short-lived perennials, they bloom the first year from seed and make colorful bedding plants and cut flowers. Native to eastern North America, daisy-like blooms up to 3 inches (7.5 cm) across have brown centers and petals in shades of orange. The leaves are long and hairy, and taper to a point. 'Marmalade' grows to 22 inches (56 cm) and has bright gold petals; 'Rustic Dwarf Mixed' is the same height but its blooms are yellow, orange, gold, bronze or mahogany, with contrasting rings of color. Both are excellent. 'Goldilocks' won a Fleuroselect medal for its compact height of 10 inches (25 cm), double blooms that look like golden petticoats and the fact that the masses of new flowers hide the old flowers. For something different, 'Irish Eyes' has 4¹/₂-inch (11-cm) flowers with gold petals and green centers on 30-inch (76-cm) plants.

Bloomtime: August to October.

Height: 1–3 feet (.9–1.2 m), depending on the cultivar.

Light and soil: Prefers full sun and any well-drained soil to which some organic matter has been added.

How to grow: Young plants are not usually available with the bedding plants, but try looking for them with the perennials. They are easily grown from seed sown in March. Germination, at 70°F (21°C) soil temperature, takes about 20 days. Set young plants out from April on, spacing them 12–18 inches (30–46 cm) apart, depending on the cultivar.

Pests and diseases: Watch for SLUGS and SNAILS.

Uses: Bedding and cut flowers, in borders and in large containers.

"Sage, mealy-cup" see *Salvia farinacea*

"Sage, scarlet" see *Salvia splendens*

Salpiglossis sinuata "salpiglossis" "painted-tongue" SOLANACEAE
(Figure 5-10)

Salpiglossis is a delightful change for gardeners who find that some annuals are too bright and hard to work into a garden scheme. In the same family as the petunia, salpiglossis also produces trumpet-shaped flowers all summer and has sticky stems. There the similarity ends. Salpiglossis is an elegant upright plant with wiry stems. Blooms are in shades of yellow, purple and red, with delicate veining and markings in contrasting colors, reminiscent of a stained glass window. Salpiglossis is native to Chile.

'Splash' blooms profusely, and 'Bolero' has huge blooms veined in gold; both reach 24 inches (61 cm). 'Dwarf Friendship Mixed' is early-blooming and compact. 'Diablo' is also to be recommended.

Bloomtime: July to frost.

Height: 15–24 inches (38–61 cm), depending on the cultivar.

Light and soil: Prefers full sun and a rich well-drained soil. Add some organic matter if possible. On poorer soil 'Splash' does better than other cultivars.

How to grow: Although young plants are not generally available from shops, they can be grown from seed. Sow indoors in March, gently pressing seeds into the soil, but do not cover. Complete darkness is required for germination, which, at 70°F (21°C) soil temperature, takes about 20 days. Set young plants out in late May, spacing them 12 inches (30 cm) apart. Tall types can be staked with small twigs. Remove old flowers to encourage more bloom.

Pests and diseases: APHIDS may infest new growth and root ROT may cause plants to collapse in wet soils. Delay planting until late June if weather is very cold.

Uses: Mid-height planting in a mixed border. Salpiglossis is useful for filling in between new shrub plantings as it has an upright habit. Try several plants in a large planter with shorter annuals such as purple alyssum, 'Cambridge Blue' lobelia or dimorphotheca. They make excellent cut flowers if you don't mind the sticky stems.

Salvia farinacea "blue salvia" "mealy-cup sage" LAMIACEAE
(Figures 5-11 and 7-7)

For many years seen mainly in park plantings, this lovely, half-hardy perennial is now showing up in many garden centers. Originally from New Mexico and Texas, blue salvia makes a great addition to a bedding scheme or mixed border. It is an elegant plant, with small, blue, pea-like flowers on tall spikes above gray-green foliage. Blue is always a welcome color in any garden, and this plant also offers an attractive bushy habit. The most widely grown cultivar is 'Victoria', which is a Fleuroselect winner.

Bloomtime: June or July to October. Plants look fresh right up to the frost.

Height: 18 inches (46 cm).

Light and soil: Prefers full sun and any well-drained soil.

How to grow: Young plants are becoming more widely available from shops in spring, or they can be started from seed. Sow in small individual pots in March. Do not cover, as light is required for germination. At 70°F (21°C) soil temperature, germination takes about 14 days. Set young plants out in late May, spacing them 12 inches (30 cm) apart.

Pests and diseases: Generally trouble-free.

Uses: Pattern plantings, edging and bedding. Excellent in containers and window boxes. Long lasting cut or dried flower.

Salvia splendens "red salvia" "scarlet sage" LAMIACEAE
(Figure 4-8)

One of the most widely planted of summer bedding plants, red salvia must be used with care in the home garden due to its vibrant red color—if over-used it certainly does not create a restful atmosphere. The bright green leaves are rounded at the base and taper to a long point, with teeth along the edges. The individual red flowers, each surrounded by a red bract that makes them appear even larger, form a tall spike.

In its native Brazil, *Salvia splendens* is a subshrub, but it will not survive our winters. It blooms quickly from seed and is grown here as a half-hardy annual. Purple and white cultivars of this species of salvia have also been developed, but the white flowers often fade to brown and are untidy looking.

Bloomtime: Dwarf cultivars begin to bloom in late May or June; taller ones begin in early June. Both continue to the frost.

Height: 10–30 inches (25–76 cm), depending on the cultivar.

Light and soil: Full sun or very light shade and fertile, well-drained soil.

How to grow: Young plants are readily available from shops in spring, or they can be started from seed. Sow seeds indoors in March, but do not cover, as light is required for germination, which, at 70°F (21°C) soil temperature, takes about 14 days. Grow on at 60°F (15°C) soil temperature. Feed lightly when transplanted with one of the liquid fertilizers (see page 15). Do not overfertilize seedlings or they will burn. Set young plants out in late May, spacing them 12 inches (30 cm) apart, closer for dwarf cultivars.

Pests and diseases: Generally trouble-free.

Uses: Pattern plantings, edging or borders. Best with white, yellow or blue flowers or silver dusty miller.

Sanvitalia procumbens "creeping zinnia" ASTERACEAE
(Figures 6-3 and 6-8)

Creeping zinnia is covered with ¹/₂-inch (1-cm) flowers with yellow petals and black disks, resembling tiny sunflowers. The leaves are simple, tapering to a gentle point. As the name suggests, the habit is creeping, which makes this Mexican native a good addition to a sunny planter or hanging basket. The cultivar 'Flore Pleno' has double flowers, giving it an extra row of petals, but the attractive black center still shows. 'Mandarin Orange' is the first orange-flowered creeping zinnia and an AAS winner.

Bloomtime: June if started indoors, July if started outdoors. Continues blooming well right to the frost, even in rainy weather.

Height: 6 inches (15 cm), spreading to a foot (30 cm) or so across.

Light and soil: Prefers full sun or partial shade and any well-drained soil to which some organic matter has been added. It tolerates heat and drought.

How to grow: Although young plants are not generally available from shops, they are easily grown from seed. Sow in March indoors for earlier bloom. Germination, at 60°F (15°C) soil temperature, takes about 10 days. Set hardened-off plants out in late May, spacing them 3 inches (7.5 cm) apart, or sow directly in the garden in May.

Pests and diseases: Generally trouble-free.

Uses: Trailing over the edge of containers or retaining walls, in hanging baskets, either alone or with other bedding plants.

"Satin flower" see *Clarkia*

Schizanthus **hybrids** "schizanthus" "butterfly flower" "poor-man's orchid" SOLANACEAE
(Figure 4-9)

Schizanthus is a lovely annual which is very popular with those who know it. Many gardeners first see it in the mixed hanging baskets that are sold for Mother's Day. It trails and is covered with dozens of small, orchid-like flowers in shades of pink, rose, red, white, yellow or mauve, attractively marked and spotted. The foliage is bright green and finely cut, almost fern-like. As seedlings are rarely in bloom in packs in garden centers in spring and may not be labelled, it is not always easy to spot. You may need to ask shop staff to point it out.

In its native Chile, the butterfly flower grows on the cool slopes of the Andes, but it is not winter-hardy in this region.

Bloomtime: June to August or September, depending on the season. Make a second sowing to extend the season of bloom.

Height: 10–24 inches (25–61 cm) in height or trailing, depending on the cultivar.

Light and soil: Full sun or light shade and rich, moist soil with added organic matter.

How to grow: You may find this at one of the larger garden centers, as it is not very commonly grown. They can also be started from seed sown in late March. Press seeds into soil but do not cover. Set pots or flats in total darkness. Germination, at 60°F (15°C) soil temperature, takes about 15 days. Do not set out young plants until late May. Seedlings can be started again in May for autumn bloom.

Pests and diseases: APHIDS may infest new growths. Overwatering may result in root ROT.

Uses: Lovely in hanging baskets and trailing over the edge of containers, Schizanthus can also be used right in the garden, planted near bedding plants, such as browallia and China asters, which are at their best late in the summer.

"Sea lavender" see *Limonium*

Senecio cineraria (*Cineraria maritima*, *Centaurea maritima*) "dusty miller"
Chrysanthemum ptarmiciflorum (*Pyrethrum ptarmiciflorum*) "silver lace dusty miller" ASTERACEAE
(Figure 6-10)

Although they are in different genera, dusty miller and silver lace dusty miller are grouped together here because of their similar appearance, uses and cultivation. There is much confusion over their botanical names. Dusty miller is sold in seed catalogues as *Centaurea* and *Cineraria*. Silver lace dusty miller is never listed under its botanical name, but is thrown in with the other dusty millers or sometimes called *Pyrethrum*. In this case, it's probably best to look for the plants by common name and read the description carefully, as there are other plants which are less often called dusty miller.

Dusty miller is a member of one of the largest genera of flowering plants. There are 2,000–3,000 species of *Senecio* in all parts of the world. It is an evergreen subshrub in its Mediterranean home, but it is not winter-hardy in this region. It is grown for its decorative foliage, rather than its yellow daisy-like blooms. The leaves are covered with a matting of fine, white hair which gives them a silvery appearance. There are three excellent cultivars on the market. 'Diamond' is the most finely cut, with indentations right into the midrib of the leaf. 'Silverdust' somewhat resembles an oak leaf, with indentations about halfway into the leaf. 'Cirrus' has leaves with scallops around the edges, rather than indentations. They all grow to 12–18 inches (30–46 cm) in the garden. Park seed catalogue lists 'Silver Queen', which grows to only 8 inches (20 cm).

Silverlace dusty miller has aromatic foliage and seldom gets enough heat in our climate to produce its white daisy-like blooms. It also seems a bit slower to get going in a cool spring and has a more upright growth habit than dusty miller. Pinch the growing tips often when young to encourage bushiness. The leaves are more finely cut than the most finely cut dusty miller, hence the common name. It will reach 24 inches (61 cm).

Bloomtime: Neither of these two plants are grown for their blooms. Dusty miller will bloom late summer some years, if the first frost is very late, but it is best to pinch off the long flower stalks to keep the plants compact. Silverlace dusty miller seldom blooms outdoors, however long the season.

Height: 8–24 inches (20–61 cm), depending on the cultivar.

Light and soil: Prefers full sun and any well-drained soil. Both types of dusty miller will tolerate poor dry soil.

How to grow: Young plants are readily available from shops in spring, or they can be started from seed. Sow seeds indoors in early March and cover only lightly, as light aids germination. At 70°F (21°C) soil temperature, this takes about 14 days. Maintain humidity and even soil temperature. Set hardened-off plants out in late May, spacing them 12 inches (30 cm) apart. Pinch growing tips to encourage branching. If flower shoots develop in late summer, it is best to cut them off. Because it is really a perennial, plants can be lifted in the fall and overwintered in the home. They do, however, need bright light to remain compact and should only be grown if you have a very bright window or fluorescent lights. New plants can be grown from cuttings taken from the soft new growth in early spring, but since they are so easy to grow from seed, this is only worthwhile if you find a different, improved form.

Pests and diseases: Generally trouble-free.

Uses: Dusty miller looks neat separating various low bedding plants in formal pattern plantings. Use it as an edging for flower beds or rose gardens. Silverlace dusty miller is less dense, so it gives a less formal effect. Use it in a mixed border. It also cuts well, adding softness to bouquets.

Setcreasea pallida 'Purple Heart', *Tradescantia albiflora*, *T. fluminensis*, and *Zebrina pendula* "wandering Jew" COMMELINACEAE

Although they are in different genera, these four species are grouped together here because of their similar appearance, uses and cultivation. Like ivy, nepeta and silver nettle vine, they are grown for the contribution their foliage makes to a mixed container planting. They are often sold as houseplants and are easily recognized by the fact that the base of their leaves wrap around the creeping stems. All are native to Texas, Mexico or South America, where they are perennial, but they do not survive frost.

Setcreasea pallida 'Purple Heart' has deep purple leaves up to 6 inches (15 cm), which are covered with soft hair. It produces small violet flowers with three petals.

The two species of *Tradescantia* have shimmering leaves to 3 inches (7.5 cm) long produced along zig-zag stems. Leaves may be green or striped with white, purple or yellow, depending on the cultivar. The small three-petalled flowers are white. The species of this genus hybridize easily, and there are many hybrids available.

Zebrina pendula is similar to *Tradescantia albiflora*, except that it has rose-purple flowers.

Bloomtime: Although grown for foliage rather than bloom, wandering Jew produces small flowers during summer (or winter if grown as a houseplant).

Height: Trails to 18 inches (46 cm).

Light and soil: Part shade or shade and rich, moist soil.

How to grow: Young plants are generally available from shops in spring. Look in the houseplants section in supermarkets. They are easily propagated from cuttings taken at any time of year. Because they do not tolerate frost, do not set plants out until the danger of frost is past, in late May or June.

Pests and diseases: Leaves may be eaten by SLUGS. A PHYSIOLOGICAL DISORDER causes leaves to turn brown and fall off; this is not a disease.

Uses: Trailing from planters and hanging baskets, with other bedding plants.

"Silver lace dusty miller" see *Senecio*
"Silver nettle vine" see *Lamiastrum*
"Slipper flower" see *Calceolaria*
"Snapdragon" see *Antirrhinum*
"Spider flower" see *Cleome*
"Star-of-Bethlehem" see *Campanula isophylla*
"Star-of-the-veldt" see *Dimorphotheca*
"Statice, common, Russian and rat-tail" see *Limonium*
"Stock, common" see *Matthiola incana*

"Stock, evening or night scented" see *Matthiola longipetala*
"Strawflower" see *Helichrysum*
"Summer cypress" see *Kochia*
"Sunflower" see *Helianthus*
"Sweet pea" see *Lathyrus*
"Sweet william" see *Dianthus barbatus*

Tagetes erecta "African marigold"
Tagetes filifolia "Irish lace"
Tagetes patula "French marigold"
Tagetes tenuifolia (*T. signata pumila*) "signet marigold" ASTERACEAE
(Figures 7-7, 7-11, 7-12 and 8-6)

One of the mainstays of our summer gardens, marigolds provide the yellow shades that give contrast to the pinks and reds of geraniums and petunias. Providing the old flowers are removed, they will bloom all summer. There are hundreds of cultivars of marigold on the market, derived from four species of half-hardy annuals native to Mexico. Despite the fact that marigolds originally came from Mexico, they tolerate wet weather quite well, especially the French marigolds. (I have not seen an explanation of why the terms "French" and "African" are used when they are all from Mexico). Marigolds have a distinctly pungent aroma.

African marigolds. Forming the tallest group, the parent species of these cultivars reaches 3 feet (91 cm), with blooms up to 8 inches (20 cm) across in the wild. Leaves are divided into many long, dark green leaflets. A number of seed series with large double blooms like huge pompons have been developed from this species. The 'Inca' series is highly recommended for 3½-inch (9-cm) blooms on 12-inch (30-cm) plants. Colors include orange, yellow or gold. They are not bothered by rainy or hot weather and bloom right up to the frost.

The 'Galore' series has won AAS and Fleuroselect awards. Blooms are sponge-like, to 4 inches (10 cm) across, and old blooms disappear under new ones, so little deadheading is required. 'Moonshot' is another semi-dwarf African marigold which is still popular, reaching 14 inches (36 cm).

'Toreador', an AAS winner, grows to 30 inches (76 cm) and has rich orange blooms. The tall cultivars 'Doubloon' (yellow) and 'Double Eagle' (orange) are often available in 4-inch (10-cm) pots in shops in the spring.

The African marigolds are daylength-sensitive. For this reason, it is best to sow seeds during the middle of March. If sown later, seedlings must be restricted to only 8 hours of light each day for two weeks during the seedling stage. This means covering the flats with black plastic or moving the flats into a dark closet after 8 hours. Otherwise, blooming will begin later and last for a shorter period. Cover seeds with 1/4 inch (.6 cm) of potting mix. Germination, at 70°F (21°C) soil temperature, takes about 7 days. Set hardened-off plants out in late May, spaced 12 inches (30 cm) apart.

French marigolds. *Tagetes patula* is the parent of the French marigolds. It grows only 6–18 inches (15–46 cm) tall in the wild and has smaller flowers than *T. erecta*. Leaflets are small, giving a more delicate effect than the foliage of the African marigolds. Cultivars with single flowers have one row of petals around the central disk. They are appealing for their freshness and simplicity. The 'Belle' series is triploid and consequently does not set seed. In terms of plant performance, that translates into nonstop bloom in all kinds of weather. Although a lower percentage of seeds germinates, plants bloom approximately 40 days after sowing, a good 23 weeks earlier than similar cultivars which are not triploid. For yellow blooms, try 'Susie Wong', sometimes available in shops. 'Little Nell' is gold with a red stain at the base of each petal.

Most dwarf French marigolds do not have single flowers. They fall into two categories. The crested types have a pouf of petals at the center (the crest), set off by one or more rows of petals around the edge. The broad-petalled types have larger petals, evenly spaced over the flower. Outstanding crested types include the 'Boy' series, which is available in orange, yellow, gold, yellow/maroon bicolor, orange/mahogany bicolor and a mixture of all six. Plants reach 8–10 inches (20–25 cm) in height. The 'Sophia' series is excellent in the broad-petalled class. Separate colors include 'Scarlet Sophia', 'Queen Sophia' (red with a gold margin on each petal), as well as yellow, orange and mixed seed strains. Plants grow to 10–12 inches (25–30 cm). Both the 'Boy' and 'Sophia' series are available in most seed catalogues and some of the colors are usually available in shops as young plants. Another excellent, widely grown, dwarf French marigold is 'Lemon Drop', which reaches 8 inches (20 cm) and is covered with small yellow pompons.

French marigolds are not daylength-sensitive so they are very easy to grow from seed at home. Sow seeds and cover with 1/4 inch (.6 cm) potting soil in mid-March. Germination, at 60–70°F (15–21°C), takes 7 days. Set hardened-off plants out in late May, spacing them 8–12 inches (20–30 cm) apart, depending on the cultivar.

Afro-French marigolds. A new class of marigolds combining the dwarfness of the French with the doubleness of bloom of the Africans was created by crossing both. They are called Afro-French marigolds and reach 12–16 inches (30–41 cm) in height. The offspring are triploid and therefore, like the 'Belle' series, the rate of germination is low. Because the flowers cannot set seed, plants put all their vigor into blooming, becoming very free-flowering. Stokes sell seed for 'Saffron' (yellow), 'Ginger' (gold) and 'Spice' (orange), all of which are recommended. Sow seeds in late March, just covering with 1/4 inch (.6 cm) of vermiculite. Germination, at 70°F (21°C) soil temperature, takes about 14 days. Restrict light to nine hours each day for two weeks after seedlings are up. When transplanting into larger pots, watch for "mule" seedlings; they are unusually large and should be removed. Grow on at 55–60°F (10–15°C). Young plants can start out with single or reddish blooms due to low light and cool temperatures, but will become double when the weather warms. Set hardened-off plants out in late May, spacing them 12 inches (30 cm) apart.

Specialty cultivars. *Tagetes tenuifolia* is the parent of several very dwarf marigolds with dime-sized single or tufted blooms, fine ferny foliage and a mounding habit of growth. They are sometimes referred to as signet marigolds, rock garden marigolds or as tagetes. The outer petals have distinct notches. Cultivars include 'Golden Gem' and 'Lemon Gem', which grow to 6 inches (15 cm) and 9 inches (23 cm) respectively. 'Tangerine Gem' reaches 12 inches (30 cm) and is interesting in small flower arrangements. Stokes and Thompson and Morgan both sell the seed. Follow seeding directions for French marigolds. Set hardened-off plants out in late May, spacing them 8 inches (20 cm) apart.

Tagetes filifolia, Irish lace, is grown for its ferny foliage rather than its tiny white flowers, which appear late in the summer. It makes a bright green mound of edging in bedding-out schemes.

There are many cultivars offered by seed companies and they are always trying new ones. Don't be afraid to try something different. In fact, from time to time Thompson and Morgan offer a collection of new cultivars, which are not yet on the market, for home gardeners to grow

and evaluate.
Bloomtime: May or June to frost.
Height: 6–30 inches (15–76 cm), depending on the cultivar.
Light and soil: Prefer full sun and a moderately rich, well-drained soil. They will tolerate poor, dry soils.
How to grow: Young plants are readily available from shops in spring, or they can be started from seed. See specific instructions above.
Pests and diseases: If planted too early, they may collapse due to foot ROT. SLUGS also eat the leaves of marigolds, and EARWIGS can cause a lot of damage.
Uses: African marigolds are suitable for the middle of the flower border and the taller types are good cut flowers. French marigolds and Afro-French are useful for edging and lovely in containers. Signet marigolds are attractive in rock gardens and containers. Irish lace is an unusual edging plant, suitable also for pattern plantings, as are the dwarf French marigolds.

"Tasselflower" see *Amaranthus*

Thunbergia alata "black-eyed-susan vine" ACANTHACEAE
(Figure 6-11)
   A perennial vine in tropical Africa, black-eyed-susan vine is grown as an annual that can be wintered indoors. It has 3-inch (7.5-cm), arrow-head-shaped leaves along stems that twine counter-clockwise. The flowers have five petals that open up from a narrow, dark purple tube. This gives the effect of a dark hole at the center of the flower and is quite striking. Flowers are most often orange, but mixed seed with cream and yellow flowers is available.
Bloomtime: May to frost.
Height: Climbs to at least 3 feet (1.2 m). If well-fertilized, many shoots develop from the base, making a dense tangle of growth.
Light and soil: Full sun or part shade, and a well-drained soil. In the garden, plants do not seem to mind a bit of bark mulch around their roots to keep them cool and moist.
How to grow: Young plants are sometimes available from shops in spring, or they can be started from seed. Sow and cover lightly. Germination, at 60–70°F (15–21°C) soil temperature, takes about 14 days. Grow seedlings on at 60°F (15°C). Set hardened- off plants out in late May,

spacing them 12 inches (30 cm) apart in the garden.

Pests and diseases: Can suffer badly from SPIDER MITES.

Uses: Black-eyed-susan vine can be grown up a trellis or into a shrub in the garden. Grow also in hanging baskets, either alone or with other plants. It tends to climb up the wires of the basket rather than trail down.

"Tickseed" see *Coreopsis*

Torenia fournieri "wishbone flower" SCROPHULARIACEAE
(Figure 2-11)

Wishbone flower is so named because the small stamens resemble a wishbone. The flowers look like small snapdragons, to which the plants are related. They are a rich, velvety violet with lighter blue and yellow markings. They are produced in abundance in June and continue over a long period if kept cool, shaded and moist. The pale green leaves are narrow, pointed and toothed. A half-hardy annual, *Torenia* is native to Vietnam. Clown mix is a 1989 AAS winner that includes flowers of white, light blue, dark blue and carmine red.

Bloomtime: June onwards, depending on the season.

Height: Up to 12 inches (30 cm).

Light and soil: Part shade and rich moist soil.

How to grow: Although young plants are not generally available from shops, they can be grown from seed. Sow seeds indoors in March but do not cover, as light is required for germination. Germination, at 70°F (21°C) soil temperature, takes about 14 days. Set hardened-off plants out in late May, spacing them 8 inches (20 cm) apart. Support lightly with twiggy branches.

Pests and diseases: Generally trouble-free.

Uses: Try it as an unusual addition to a shady container or bed.

Tradescantia see *Setcreasea*
"Tuberous begonia" see *Begonia*

Tropaeolum majus "nasturtium" TROPAEOLACEAE
(Figures 1-11, 6-3 and 8-6)

When first introduced to Europe from Peru in the 1600s, this popular plant was known as Indian cress, because the Peruvian Indians used the pungent leaves in food. Hence, the original botanical name was *Nasturtium indicum*. (Watercress is *Nasturtium officinale*.) Later, Linnaeus, the Swedish botanist who reorganized botanical nomenclature, changed the name to *Tropaeolum majus*. The generic name refers to the Greek word *tropaion* meaning trophy. In ancient Greece, this was a tree on which victors hung the shields and helmets of those they had conquered in battle. Linnaeus must have seen in the round leaves and pointed flowers the shields and helmets of perished Greek warriors.

Although perennial in the highlands of Mexico and South America, nasturtiums do not like even a hint of frost. All parts of nasturtium have a peppery taste due to an oil they contain; flower buds and young leaves are used in salads and the fresh green seeds can be pickled in the same manner as capers. Of course, do not eat plant parts if any harmful pesticides have been used. The petioles (stalks which attach the leaves to the stems) are able to coil, thus allowing the plants to climb.

The most widely available cultivar in shops in spring is the 'Jewel Mixed', which includes semi-double flowers of cream, orange, yellow, red, pink and bicolors. The 'Whirlibird' series features flowers which sit facing up on the vine and are more visible. Separate colors include gold, scarlet, tangerine, mahogany, tangerine, orange, and cherry. 'Alaska Mixed', a Stokes introduction, has very attractive variegated foliage and is an excellent addition to hanging baskets and other containers (shown in Figure 6-3). 'Empress of India' is a cultivar of the species *Tropaeolum minus*, which is similar to the common nasturtium, but is smaller.

Bloomtime: June to September.

Height: 12 inches (30 cm), or more trailing or climbing.

Light and soil: Prefers full sun, but tolerates light shade. Any well-drained, preferably sandy (even dry) soil. Do not use a fertilizer high in nitrogen or the plant will produce huge, deep green leaves and no bloom.

How to grow: Young plants are generally available from shops in spring, or they can be started from seed. Seeds can be sown directly in the garden, especially in a warm, dry spring. If the weather is very cool and wet, it is best to sow indoors in individual 3-inch (7.5-cm) pots so seeds will not rot. Germination, at 60–70°F (15–21°C) soil temperature, takes about 14 days. Seedlings grow quickly; they can be seeded in April and set out in late May, 8–12 inches (20–30 cm) apart, depending on the cultivar.

Pests and diseases: APHIDS are a serious problem with nasturtiums; they appear so predictably and in such great numbers that it is impossible to ignore them. Insecticidal soap will burn nasturtium foliage and should not be used. Organic gardeners use nasturtiums as companion plants near crops which are susceptible to aphid infestations hoping all the aphids will be attracted to the nasturtiums instead. FLEA BEETLES can defoliate and kill plants in a matter of days.

Uses: Train up trellises; allow to trail from containers and hanging baskets. They can also be grown in the garden as ground cover, trailing over walls or scrambling into deciduous shrubs. Because seeds are large and germinate readily, children enjoy starting nasturtiums.

Verbena × *hybrida* "garden verbena"
Verbena peruviana "Peruvian verbena"
Verbena rigida (V. *venosa*) "vervain"
Verbena canadensis (V. *aubletia*) "trailing verbena" VERBENACEAE
(Figures 4-10 and 8-11)

Garden verbena is an easily obtainable summer bedding plant. The flowers are very bright and fresh, but it is not as free-blooming as some bedding plants and is very susceptible to mildew. Gray-green leaves are triangular in outline with regularly spaced teeth along the leaf margin. Stems and leaves are covered with fine hairs. Flowers appear in a cluster at the end of stalks: each has 5 petals opening from a 1-inch (2.5-cm) tube. Colors typically include scarlet, white and purple, often with a white eye. The habit of some cultivars is somewhat floppy and open. These hybrids are derived mainly from V. *peruviana* and other species from South America, which are all perennials there. 'Trinidad' is an AAS winner with rose blooms and a compact upright habit.

Peruvian verbena has brilliant red flowers with a white eye. It also has a trailing habit and is a welcome addition to a rock garden or hanging basket. It will sometimes survive a winter if given some protection.

Vervain is an upright grower with long, narrow, toothed leaves and lilac or white flowers. It is attractive planted with zonal geraniums.

Trailing verbena has stems which have about 2 inches (5 cm) between each set of leaves. This open rambling habit makes it perfect for growing from containers and hanging baskets. The leaves are darker green than those of the garden verbena, and the indentations into the leaves are deeper and less regular. Flowers also cluster at the end of long flower stalks. Colors include vivid purple, red, pink and white.

Bloomtime: June to frost.

Height: 6–18 inches (15–46 cm), depending on the cultivar.

Light and soil: Prefers full sun and any well-drained soil to which some organic matter has been added.

How to grow: Young plants are generally available from shops in spring, the easiest way to acquire them, as seeds are tricky to germinate. If you are interested in trying it, first chill seeds in the refrigerator for 7 days in March. Sow seeds, cover with 1/8 inch (.3 cm) soil and place flats or pots in the dark. Soil temperature should be 70°F (21°C) in the day and 60°F (15°C) at night. Avoid excessive moisture. Germination is erratic and takes up to three weeks. A good germination rate is 50 to 65 percent. Set hardened-off plants out in late May, spacing them 8 inches (20 cm) apart. Pinch the growing tip to encourage bushiness. If they stop blooming, cut them back by one-third.

Pests and diseases: Verbenas are very prone to POWDERY MILDEW, especially the garden verbena. SLUGS like verbena.

Uses: Garden verbena and vervain as bedding plants; trailing verbena is outstanding for sunny containers and hanging baskets and as a ground cover; V. *peruviana* gives a nice splash of color in a rock garden.

"Vervain" see *Verbena*

Viola cornuta "viola" "tufted pansy"
Viola tricolor "johnny-jump-up"
Viola × wittrockiana (V. *hortensis*) "pansy" VIOLACEAE
(Figure 3-10)

Pansies are some of the most heart-warming flowers to grace our gardens in spring and fall. Their velvety overlapping petals in a rich tapestry of colors and their happy "faces" make the decision of which ones to buy a pleasurable dilemma. Pansies thrive in cool weather and for that reason they are at their best in spring and fall. New heat-tolerant varieties will keep flowering all summer, but with smaller flowers.

Viola cornuta, a native of Spain, is the parent of many cultivars of violas. It resembles the well-known pansy, but the flowers are smaller, 11 inches (2.5–4 cm), and without "faces," and it continues blooming for a longer period in the summer. Seed can be purchased for separate colors including wine-red, blue, apricot, yellow, dark blue, white and a mixture. The 'Crystal Bowl' series are hybrids of *Viola cornuta* developed in Japan, with flowers up to 2½ inches (6 cm) across and clear bright colors. Violas reach about 8 inches (20 cm) in height.

Johnny-jump-ups have very small flowers, ¾ inch (2 cm) across, which have three colors: purple, yellow and white, hence the specific name *tricolor*. They grow to 6 inches (15 cm) high, with spreading stems and are excellent for planting with tulips and daffodils for a spring show. They are native to Europe. The common name refers to the fact that the self-sown seedlings "jump up" everywhere.

Pansies have been developed from three species, *Viola tricolor*, *V. lutea* and *V. altaica*. Although johnny-jump-ups have been well known and commonly grown in European gardens since about 1625, little was done in the way of hybridizing until the early 1800s, when selections were done by a pansy enthusiast in England. By the middle of that century, the British, French and Germans began developing different strains in earnest. Today there are pansies in almost every color imaginable. Some types have rich colors, some have bright colors, many have faces and some do not. Recently, the 'Imperial' series introduced delicate pastel shades; the flowers are very pretty but the plants do not bloom as much as those of the 'Universal' series, which are planted in the thousands in city parks. The 'Universal' series includes 12 different color shades and a mix. They bloom very early and plants remain compact even in some summer heat.

Bloomtime: Violas: June and July. Johnny-jump-ups: May to September. Pansies from a spring planting: March to July, depending on the cultivar and the season. Pansies from a fall planting: September until frost, then during mild spells in winter and again in early spring. Keeping plants well watered and removing old flowers helps extend the flowering period.

Height: 6–12 inches (15–30 cm), depending on the cultivar.

Light and soil: Part shade and a moist but well-drained soil to which some organic matter has been added.

How to grow: Young plants of pansies and johnny-jump-ups are generally available from shops from late February on, but violas are not as common. In addition to being sold in small pots or packs, fall pansies are also field grown. They are grown outdoors in open ground (rather than in a greenhouse), dug and placed in cardboard baskets similar to those in which strawberries are sold. If you have a choice, field-grown pansies are usually the best plants to buy. Nothing can compare with growing in sun and real soil for producing compact healthy pansies.

Pansies can be grown from seed. The easiest way is to sow seeds in June in a nursery bed. An ideal spot is a row in the vegetable garden after the peas, for example, have come out. Let them grow there until you have taken out your bedding plants in the fall and then move the pansies to where you want them to bloom.

Pests and diseases: Generally trouble-free.

Uses: Flower beds and front of mixed borders, containers and informal woodland gardens.

"Viscaria" see *Lychnis*
"Wallflower, English and Siberian" see *Cheiranthus*
"Wandering Jew" see *Setcreasea*
"Wax begonia" see *Begonia*
"Wishbone flower" see *Torenia*

Xeranthemum annuum "common immortelle" ASTERACEAE
(Figure 3-11)

The common immortelle is native to Southern Europe and the Middle East and is one of the oldest known (and still one of the best) of the everlasting flowers. Papery petals of white, pink, purple or lilac keep their color well when dry.

Bloomtime: July to September.

Height: 24 inches (61 cm).

Light and soil: Prefers full sun and any well-drained soil.

How to grow: Although young plants are not generally available from shops, they are easily grown from seed. Sow in the garden in March. Thin to stand 18 inches (46 cm) apart and support stems with thin stakes.

Pests and diseases: Generally trouble-free.

Uses: For soft color in the mixed borders and for cut flowers, fresh and dried. To dry, cut flowers when they are fully open and hang them upside-down in bunches in a cool, airy place until dry.

Zebrina see *Setcreasea*
"Zinnia, creeping" see *Sanvitalia*

Zinnia elegans and *Zinnia haageana* "zinnia" ASTERACEAE
(Figure 4-11)

Much selecting has been done with these two species from Mexico and there is a multitude of heights and flower shapes from which to choose. Zinnias revel in hot, sunny weather and will tolerate dry soil—making them an excellent choice for a planter on a south-facing patio. Most flower colors are bright and festive and are beautifully set off by a large terra cotta pot. Leaves are triangular in outline, to 4 inches (10 cm) long, rough with prominent veins. Don't set zinnias out too early; they are best for late summer bloom, perhaps to follow schizanthus and nemesia, which fade in hot weather.

The large-flowered zinnias make splendid cut flowers, but they may need staking. Cultivars of *Zinnia elegans* are the most widely grown. The 'Peter Pan' series, (an AAS winner), comes in mixed and separate colors of flame, orange, pink, gold, white and scarlet. Plants grow to 12–14 inches (30–36 cm) tall and bear 3-inch (7.5-cm) blooms that are fully double. The 'Ruffles' series are also AAS winners. Free-flowering, they reach 28 inches (71 cm) with 3-inch (7.5-cm) double blooms. These two series are both referred to as "cut-and-come-again" zinnias; the more flowers you cut, the more are produced.

The AAS winner, 'Border Beauty', grows to 20 inches (51 cm) with 3-inch (7.5-cm) double blooms of pink with a touch of salmon, excellent for cutting or a border. For a shorter height, try the 'Dasher' series; in separate colors of scarlet, cherry and orange, or a mix which includes yellow, pink and white, it grows to 10 inches (25 cm) with 3-inch (7.5-cm) blooms. It is especially recommended for wet, cool maritime climates.

Cultivars of *Zinnia haageana* have narrower leaves than *Zinnia elegans* and usually have two-toned flowers. Examples are 'Persian Carpet', 'Old Mexico' (an AAS winner), 'Sombrero' and 'Chippendale'. They are sometimes referred to as old-fashioned Mexican zinnias in catalogues. All reach 15 inches (38 cm), except 'Chippendale' which grows to 24 inches (61 cm).

Bloomtime: June or July to frost.

Height: 6–36 inches (15–91 cm), depending on the cultivar.

Light and soil: Prefer full sun and any well-drained soil. They will do better in a richer soil to which some organic matter has been added.

How to grow: Young plants are generally available from shops in spring,

or they can be started from seed, taking advantage of cultivars not available in the trade. Sow in late March in individual 3-inch (7.5-cm) pots. Germination, at 60–70°F (15–21°C) soil temperature, takes about 5 days. Do not water with cold water or leave plants in drafts. Seedlings are susceptible to damping-off; use a fungicide drench. Set hardened-off plants out in early June, spacing them 8–12 inches (20–30 cm) apart, depending on the cultivar. Seeds can easily be sown directly in the garden in June. Seeds are large and easy to handle.

Pests and diseases: Although zinnias are generally trouble-free, a few VIRUS diseases may infect plants, causing yellow rings on the leaves. If soil is too cold and wet, seedlings may DAMP OFF or die from root ROT. In wet weather, large flowers may get GRAY MOLD and stems of very tall plants may collapse due to stem ROT. LEAFHOPPERS may feed on the new buds and will stop the plants from flowering.

Uses: Good for edging (blooming later than some other edging choices) and for the front of a mixed border for a festive effect. If you find zinnias too bright for your color scheme, plant them in containers on their own or in the vegetable garden for cut flowers.

QUICK REFERENCE CHART	easy to grow	blooms June–Sept.	LIGHT			tolerates dry soil	HEIGHT			USES									plants readily available
			full sun	part shade	shade		under 1 foot (30 cm)	1–3 feet (.3–.9 m)	over 3 feet (.9 m)	use for edging	good cut flowers	suitable for drying	good in containers	massed plantings	cottage garden style	dot plant	hanging baskets	moss baskets	
Abutilon flowering maple		•	•	•				•	•				•				•	•	
Ageratum houstonianum flossflower	•	•	•	•			*	*		•	*		•	•				•	•
Amaranthus caudatus love-lies-bleeding	•		•						•		•	•	•						
Antirrhinum majus snapdragons	•	•	•	•				•			•	•	•	•	•	*			•
Avena and other annual grasses	•							•			•	•	•	•	•				
Begonia semp.-cultorum fibrous begonias	•	•	•	•	•	•	•			•			•	•				•	•
Begonia × tuberhybrida tuberous begonias	•	•		•	•		*	*					•	•	•		•	•	•
Brachycome iberidifolia Swan River daisy	•	•	•				•	•					•		•				
Brassica oleracea ornamental cabbage & kale	•		•					•					•	•					
Browallia browallia	•	•	•	•	•	•	•						•	•			•	•	•
Calceolaria 'Sunshine' pocketbook flower	•	•	•	•			•						•	•			•	•	
Calendula officinalis pot marigolds	•		•			•	•			•	•		•	•	•				•
Callistephus chinensis China asters			•				*	*			•		•	•	•				
Canna × generalis canna lily	•	•	•					*	*				•			•			
Catharanthus roseus Madagascar periwinkle	•	•	•			•	•			•	•		•						
Celosia cristata cockscomb		•	•			•	*	*		•	•	•	•	•					•
Centaurea cyanus cornflower	•		•			•	•	•			•			•					
Cheiranthus & *Erysimum* wallflowers	•		•	•			*	*		•	•		•	•	•				
Chrysanthemum carinatum annual chrysanthemum	•		•					•			•			•					
Chrysanthemum frutescens marguerite daisies	•	•	•					•			•		•	•	•				
Chrysanthemum parthenium matricaria	•	*	•				*	*			•		•		•				
Clarkia amoena godetia	•		•					•			•				•				
Cleome hasslerana spider flower	*		•						•		•			•	•				
Cleretum bellidiformis Livingstone daisy	•	•		•		•	•			•					•			•	

*depending on species or cultivar

146

QUICK REFERENCE CHART

			LIGHT				HEIGHT			USES									
	easy to grow	blooms June–Sept.	full sun	part shade	shade	tolerates dry soil	under 1 foot (30 cm)	1–3 feet (.3–.9 m)	over 3 feet (.9 m)	use for edging	good cut flowers	suitable for drying	good in containers	massed plantings	cottage garden style	dot plant	hanging baskets	moss baskets	plants readily available
Coleus × hybridus coleus	•			•	•		*	*		•			•	•			•	•	•
Cordyline australis dracaena palm	•		•		•			•	•				•			•			•
Coreopsis tinctoria calliopsis	•		•					•			•		•	•	•				
Cosmos cosmos	•		•	•			*	*			•		•	•	•				•
Cuphea ignea cigar flower	•	•	•	•	•		•				•		•				•		
Dahlia hybrids dahlia	•	•	•					•			•		•						•
Dianthus barbatus sweet william	•		•				•				•	•	•	•	•			*	•
Dianthus caryophyllus carnation	•	•	•				•				•		•		•			•	
Dianthus chinensis Indian pink	•		•				•			•	•		•	•	•			•	
Dimorphotheca hybrids African daisy	•	•	•			•	•			•	•		•	•					
Felicia amelloides blue marguerite	•	•	•				•			•	•		•	•	•		•		
Fuchsia × hybrida fuchsia	•	•	*	•	•		•				•		•				•	•	•
Gazania × hybrida gazania	•	•	•			•	•			•			•	•			•	•	•
Glechoma hederacea 'Var.' trailing nepeta	•		•	•			•	•					•				•	•	
Gomphrena globosa globe amaranth	•	•	•				*	*		•	•	•	•	•			•		
Hedera helix English ivy	•		•			•	•	•					•				•	•	•
Helianthus annuus sunflower	•		•				*	*						•		•			
Helichrysum bracteatum strawflowers	•	•	•				*	*	•	•	•	•		•					
Heliotropium arborescens heliotrope	•	•	•	•				•			•		•	•	•		•		
Hypoestes phyllostachya polka dot plant	•		•	•				•			•		•	•					•
Iberis candytuft	•		•			•	*	*		•	*		•		•				
Impatiens hybrids New Guinea impatiens	•		•	•	•			•			•		•	•					•
Impatiens wallerana impatiens	•	•	*	•	•		•				•		•	•			•	•	•
Kochia scoparia summer cypress	•		•					•					•						

*depending on species or cultivar

QUICK REFERENCE CHART

Plant	easy to grow	blooms June–Sept.	full sun	part shade	shade	tolerates dry soil	under 1 foot (30 cm)	1–3 feet (.3–.9 m)	over 3 feet (.9 m)	use for edging	good cut flowers	suitable for drying	good in containers	massed plantings	cottage garden style	dot plant	hanging baskets	moss baskets	plants readily available
Lamiastrum galeobdolon 'Var.' silver nettle vine	•		•	•	•		•		•				•				•	•	
Lampranthus multiradiatus ice plant	•	•	•			•	•				•			•			•		
Lantana camara lantana		•	•				*	*	*		•		•		•	•			
Lathyrus odoratus sweet pea	•	•	•				*	*		•	•		•		•				
Lavatera trimestris mallow	•	•	•				*	*		•	•			•	•				
Limonium & *Psylliostachys* statice	•	•	•					•			•	•			•				
Lobelia erinus edging lobelia	•	•		•	•		•			•			•	•			•	•	•
Lobularia maritima sweet alyssum	•	•	•	•		•	•			•			•	•			•		•
Lotus berthelotii lotus vine			•					•					•				•		
Lychnis coeli-rosea viscaria	•		•				*	*			•		•		•				
Matthiola incana stock	•		•	•				•			•	•	•		•				
Matthiola l. ssp. bicornis evening scented stock	•		•	•				•					•		•				
Mimulus hybrids monkey flower	•	•		•	•	•	•						•	•			•	•	
Mirabilis jalapa four-o'clocks	•		•	•				•					•		•				
Molucella laevis bells of Ireland	•	•	•					•			•	•			•				
Myosotis sylvatica forget-me-not	•		•	•	•		•			•			•	•					•
Nemesia strumosa nemesia	•		•	•			•			•			•	•			•		
Nemophila menziesii baby blue eyes	•	•	•	•			•						•	•					
Nicotiana alata flowering tobacco	•	•	•	•			*	*			•		•	•	•				•
Nierembergia hipp. var. *vio.* cupflower	•	•	•				•			•			•	•			•		
Nigella damascena love-in-a-mist	•		•					•			•	•		•	•				
Osteospermum ecklonis African daisy	•	•	•			•		•			•		•	•	•				
Papaver nudicaule Iceland poppy	•		•			•	*	*			•	•	•		•				
Papaver rhoeas Shirley poppy	•		•			•		•			•			•	•				•

*depending on species or cultivar

148

QUICK REFERENCE CHART

	easy to grow	blooms June–Sept.	full sun	part shade	shade	tolerates dry soil	under 1 foot (30 cm)	1–3 feet (.3–.9 m)	over 3 feet (.9 m)	use for edging	good cut flowers	suitable for drying	good in containers	massed plantings	cottage garden style	dot plant	hanging baskets	moss baskets	plants readily available
Pelargonium × domesticum — regal pelargonium	•			•	•			•					•						•
Pelargonium × hortorum — zonal geranium	•	•	•			•		•		•			•	•			•	•	•
Pelargonium peltatum — ivy geranium	•	•		•	•			•					•				•	•	•
Petunia × hybrida — petunia	•	•	•			•		•		•			•	•			•		•
Phlox drummondii — annual phlox	•		•				*	*		•	•		•	•	•			•	•
Portulaca grandiflora — moss rose	•	•	•			•	•			•			•	•					•
Primula × polyantha — polyanthus	•			•	•		•			•			•	•					•
Rudbeckia hirta — black-eyed susan	•		•					•			•		•	•	•				
Salpiglossis sinuata — salpiglossis	•	•	•					•			•		•	•					
Salvia farinacea — blue salvia	•	•	•					•			•	•	•	•	•				
Salvia splendens — red salvia	•	•	•	•			*	*		•			•	•		*			•
Sanvitalia procumbens — creeping zinnia	•	•	•	•		•	•			•			•	•			•	•	
Schizanthus hybrids — butterfly flower	•		•	•			*	*		•			•	•	•		•	•	
Senecio cineraria and Chrys. ptarmiciflorum — dusty miller	•	•	•			•		•		•	•	•	•	•					•
Setcreasea et al — wandering Jew	•			•	•			•					•				•	•	•
Tagetes — marigolds	•	•	•			•	*	*		•	•		•	•			*	*	•
Thunbergia alata — black-eyed-susan vine	•	•	•	•				•	•				•				•	•	•
Torenia fournieri — wishbone flower	•			•	•		•			•			•				•	•	
Tropaeolum majus — nasturtium		•	•	•		•		•	•				•	•	•		•	•	•
Verbena — garden verbena		•	•			•	•			•			•	•					•
Verbena — trailing verbena	•	•	•	•		•		•					•	•			•	•	•
Viola — pansy and violas	•	*	•	•	•		•			•			•	•					•
Xeranthemum annuum — common immortelle	•	•	•					•			•	•	•	•	•				
Zinnia	•	•	•			•	*	*	*	*	•		•	•		•			

*depending on species or cultivar

Bibliography
and
Sources

Annuals. James Underwood Crockett and the Editors of Time-Life Books. New York: Time-Life Books, 1971.

Ball Red Book: Greenhouse Growing, 14th Edition. Edited by Dick Ball. Virginia: Reston Publishing Co., 1985.

Clark, Lewis J. *Wild Flowers of British Columbia*. Sidney: Gray's Publishing Ltd., 1973.

Crockett, James Underwood. *Crockett's Flower Garden*. Boston: Little Brown and Company, 1981.

Donahue, Roy; Schickluna, John; and Robertson, Lynn. *Soils: An Introduction to Soils and Plant Growth*. New Jersey: Prentice-Hall, Inc., 1971.

The Encyclopedia of Herbs and Herbalism. Edited by Malcolm Stuart. New York: Crescent Books, 1979.

Fell, Derek. *Annuals, How to Select, Grow and Enjoy*. Tucson: HPBooks, 1983.

Hortus Third. Edited by the staff of the Liberty Hyde Bailey Hortorium. New York: Macmillan Publishing Company, 1976.

Hunt, C. *Natural Regions of the US and Canada*. San Francisco: W.H.

Freeman, 1974.

Insect and Disease Control in the Home Garden. Ministry of Agriculture and Food, Province of Ontario, updated annually.

Ontario Soils. Publication 492. Ministry of Agriculture and Food, Province of Ontario.

The Ortho Problem Solver. Edited by Michael D. Smith. San Francisco: Ortho Information Services, 1984.

Pirone, Pascal. *Diseases and Pests of Ornamental Plants, 5th Ed*. New York: John Wiley and Sons, 1978.

Pizzetti, Ippolito; and Cocker, Henry. *Flowers: A Guide for Your Garden*, Volumes I and II. New York: Harry N. Abrams Inc., 1975.

Proudley, B. and V. *Fuchsias in Color*. England: Blandford Press Ltd., 1975.

Readers Digest Encyclopaedia of Garden Plants and Flowers. Edited, designed and published by The Reader's Digest Association. London: 1985.

The Rodale Herb Book. Edited by William H. Hylton. Emmaus: Rodale Press Book Division, 1974.

Practical Gardening Magazine. EMAP National Publications Ltd. Peterborough, PE2 0UW, England, various issues.

Commercial grower catalogue. Ball Seed Company, Missigauga, Ontario, 1987.

Commercial grower catalogue. Northrup-King Co., Minneapolis, Minnesota, 198788.

Commercial grower catalogue. Skagit Gardens, Mt. Vernon, Washington, 1988.

Personal communication, Robert J. Armstrong, Research Horticulturist, Longwood Gardens, Pennsylvania, USA, 1988.

Personal communication, Clive Innes, Holly Gate International, Sussex, England, 1988.

Sources

Seeds, books and accessories

Robert Bolton & Son, The Sweet Pea Specialists, Birdbrook, nr. Halstead, Essex, Great Britain, CO9 4BQ.

Dominion Seed House, Georgetown, Ontario, L7G 4A2.

Park Seed Company, Cokesbury Road, Greenwood, South Carolina,

USA, 29647-0001, (bulbs listed also but they can not be shipped into Canada).

Stokes Seed Company, 39 James St., Box 10, St. Catharines, Ontario, L2R 6R6.

Thompson and Morgan Seed Catalogue, P.O. Box 1308, Jackson, New Jersey, 08527, USA, ship to Canada also.

Unwins Seeds, Histon, Cambridge, Great Britain, CB4 4LE.

Plants, bulbs and accessories (by mail order)

C.A. Cruickshank, 1015 Mount Pleasant Road, Toronto, Ontario, M4P 2M1.

Gardenimport, Inc., P.O. Box 760, Thornhill, Ontario, L3T 4A5.

Plants

Please ask the staff member in charge of buying at your favorite garden center for unusual bedding plants; they may be able to locate them for you. If not, the following nursery, in addition to selling popular bedding plants, specializes in growing unusual annuals.

Pineridge Garden Gallery, Box 222, Brock Road North, Pickering, Ontario, L1V 2R4.

Plant societies specializing in plants covered in this book
(write for current fees and more information)

American Begonia Society (publishes the *Begonian*), John Ingles, Jr., 8922 Conway Drive, Riverside, California, 92503, USA.

American Fuchsia Society (publishes a monthly bulletin), Hall of Flowers, Golden Gate Park, San Francisco, California, 94122, USA.

Canadian Chrysanthemum and Dahlia Society, R.L. Fox, 133 Lee Road, Toronto, Ontario, M4E 2P2.

Canadian Geranium and Pelargonium Society, James Douglas, 3331 Dumfries Avenue, Vancouver, BC, V5C 3S4, Canada.

The Civic Garden Center (publishes *Trellis*), Edwards Greens, 777 Lawrence Avenue East, Don Mills, Ontario, M3C 1P2.

Geranium and Pelargonium Society of Ontario, D. Konradis, 6 Daleside Crescent, Toronto, Ontario, M4A 2H6.

National Fuchsia Society, P.O. Box 4687, Downey, California, 92041, USA.

Index

Pages given in boldface indicate encyclopedia entries.

Carolyn Jones graduated from Simon Fraser University in 1974 with a bachelor's degree in biological sciences. Since then, she has enjoyed her own garden and worked in several areas of the nursery trades—in a wholesale nursery, in garden centers and as a landscape designer. She managed Massot Nurseries Garden Center, Richmond, for two and a half years and was a regular columnist for *Gardens West*. She holds a B.C. Pesticide Dispenser Certificate and is a member of the Vancouver Rose Society, the Alpine Garden Club of B.C. and the Royal Horticultural Society (Great Britain).